ANOKA COUNTY LIBRARY
707 COUNTY ROAD 10 N.E.
BLAINE, MN 55434-2398

P9-DMY-215

Iraq Confidential

Iraq Confidential

The Untold Story of the Intelligence Conspiracy to Undermine the UN and Overthrow Saddam Hussein

Scott Ritter

Foreword by

Seymour Hersh

NATION
BOOKS

IRAQ CONFIDENTIAL
*THE UNTOLD STORY OF THE INTELLIGENCE CONSPIRACY TO UNDERMINE THE UN AND
OVERTHROW SADDAM HUSSEIN*

Published by
Nation Books
An Imprint of Avalon Publishing Group Inc.
245 West 17th St., 11th Floor
New York, NY 10011

AVALON
publishing group incorporated

Copyright © 2005 by W. Scott Ritter

First published by I.B. Tauris & Co Ltd in the United Kingdom
First Nation Books edition October 2005

Nation Books is a co-publishing venture of the Nation Institute and Avalon
Publishing Group Incorporated.

All rights reserved. No part of this publication may be reproduced or
transmitted in any form or by any means, electronic or mechanical, including
photocopy, recording, or any information storage and retrieval system now
known or to be invented, without permission in writing from the publisher,
except by a reviewer who wishes to quote brief passages in connection with a
review written for inclusion in a magazine, newspaper, or broadcast.

Library of Congress Cataloging-in-Publication Data is available.

ISBN: 1-56025-852-7
ISBN 13: 978-1-56025-852-0

9 8 7 6 5 4 3 2

Typeset in Palatino Linotype by Steve Tribe, Andover
Printed in the United States of America
Distributed by Publishers Group West

Contents

Foreword

This book shows just how petty and shortsighted bureaucrats can be when vital questions of war and peace are at stake. It is a book about the unwillingness of the American Central Intelligence Agency and the president's National Security Council to permit an arm of the United Nations, led by an American Marine major, to carry out successful investigations into what weapons capacity Saddam Hussein actually had. Ritter was tipped off about the American double cross by some of his old friends in the British intelligence community. *Iraq Confidential* is a book to make you, like Ritter, angry.

It also helps explain why America's warning agencies, with their thousands of FBI agents at home and thousands of CIA operatives abroad, failed to provide advance information on al-Qaeda's planning for the September 11 bombings. At crucial moments, the FBI would not share its information with the CIA and the CIA, at almost all times, refused to share its files with the FBI.

Ritter was in the middle of such madness as he tried, throughout the 1990s, to sort out what Iraq had, or did not have. Ironically the chaos surrounding UNSCOM was counterbalanced by the remarkable unity and team-spiritedness of its culturally diverse members. Ritter's story sometimes reads like a thriller, as UN inspectors chase and are chased by

Saddam Hussein's henchmen. There is slapstick, as inspections go awry for the most mundane of reasons, and as Washington repeatedly fails to understand the consequence of its actions. And then, finally, there is fear and foreboding in learning how capriciously the most important efforts towards peace and disarmament can be undermined, even when they are led by Americans.

The most important thing to know about Scott Ritter, the man, is that he was right. He told us again and again in 2002 and early 2003 as President George Bush and Prime Minister Tony Blair prepared for war in Iraq that there were no weapons there. The Iraqi WMDs, the main sales tool for the war, did not exist.

With each such statement, Ritter became more and more unpopular – with the politicos in the White House, the neoconservatives in Washington, the war planners in the Pentagon and the American press corps (which was, with a few exceptions, panting for the war). Ritter was in their face, and stayed so – even after the shock and awe began in Baghdad. As the American bombs fell, and embedded journalists filed dramatic stories about young GIs in the battlefield, wearing their overheated chemical warfare suits, Ritter was telling all who would listen that there could be no usable chemical warheads in Iraq, simply because there was no evidence of any chemical warfare production facilities in Iraq. No commander would go to war with chemical weapons left over from the 1991 Gulf War, he insisted – even if such weapons did exist. (Unlikely). He was right about that, too.

I've known Scott as a journalist, and later, as a friend, since the late 1990s and I *think* I understand somewhat, just a little, what makes him tick. He is a purist, an uncompromising believer in empiricism who has never been afraid to tell the truth to superiors. Somehow, he never perceived, or wanted to perceive, that magic formula for bureaucratic success in Washington – never be the bearer of unpleasant facts. He is a Thomas à Becket in a world full of Bush administration yes-men.

His finest, and most controversial, moment came in the fall of 2002, with the war machinery in place. Scott flew to Iraq (against the advice of many of his friends), to speak to the Parliament in Baghdad and try to convince Saddam Hussein to allow the United Nations weapons inspectors to return to Iraq, thus removing the core public justification for the war. Five days after he left, Saddam publicly announced that the inspectors would be allowed back, without any preconditions. It was, so it seemed, an extraordinary personal triumph. Nonetheless, Ritter was widely criticized by his government and by the American media for his effort to stop a war that was based, as Scott knew, on faulty intelligence.

Since March of 2003, Ritter has continued to criticize the Iraqi war, in his speeches and newspaper articles, and he continues to be right. It is not a 'winnable' war, by any means that provide succor to the long-suffering Iraqi people. In this book, Ritter digs deeper into his deep pocket of secrets and tells far more than he has in the past about the inability of the White House – be it Bill Clinton's or George Bush's – and the intelligence bureaucrats to listen to real-time information suggesting that Saddam's WMD arsenal was empty.

Denials will come when this book is published, but I can vouch for Scott's amazing recall and his extensive knowledge of the Iraqi disarmament game. That Scott continues to do what he does says something about his determination, his self-confidence, and his Americanism. He is still gung ho about his country, as a good Marine should be, and he believes that it can be – must be – changed for the better. All I can add is hurry up, Scott – at the time of writing, George Bush has more than thirteen hundred days left in office, and that is a long, long time.

Seymour Hersh
Washington, D.C.
20 June 2005

Preface

In August 1998, I walked away from the best job I ever had, and probably would ever have, in my life. For nearly seven years I had served as a UN weapons inspector who, like hundreds of others of my colleagues, had been mandated by the United Nations Security Council to oversee the disarmament of Iraq's weapons of mass destruction programs as part of the United Nations Special Commission, or UNSCOM. In my role as an UNSCOM inspector, I was provided with an opportunity that was unique – I was able not only to plan and implement inspections, but also to have control of the direction, collection and assessment of the intelligence information used in every phase of these operations.

As a senior member of the UNSCOM staff, I was also privy to the high-level political intrigue that surrounded the work of the inspectors. I was responsible for some of the most sensitive operations, and most delicate liaison activities, that UNSCOM was involved in.

These circumstances placed me in the position of being able to tell the complete story of UNSCOM's secret intelligence operations inside Iraq. Until now, this history has gone unwritten, and the CIA's version of events has been paramount.

While UNSCOM inspections provide the framework around which this story is told, no one should mistake this book as the definitive story of

UNSCOM and the effort to disarm Iraq. This book only includes details relevant to the secret intelligence war that took place inside Iraq and around the world, pitting inspector against Iraqi, and inspector against the CIA. The book describes a dozen or so inspections – overall, UNSCOM carried out nearly 300 discrete inspection missions, and thousands of monitoring inspections. My narrative jumps from inspection to inspection in seamless fashion. The reader needs to understand that my story unfolded while UNSCOM was engaged in a tremendous amount of other work, which took on the form of the intervening inspections missing from the sequence presented here. I place a heavy emphasis on the inspections I was involved with, because I saw them with my own eyes. However, this does not in any way imply a denigration of the tremendous, and critically important, work of the hundreds of others inspectors not mentioned in this book. Without their hard work, dedication and sacrifice, Iraq could not have been disarmed to the extent it had been. I salute these fellow inspectors.

On the sources of information used for this book, I have wherever possible provided an appropriate citation of any document used. The primary source of documents is derived from my personal files accumulated over my nearly seven years of work with UNSCOM. I have also, during my time as an inspector, and afterwards, had the opportunity to speak with important figures who figure prominently in this book.

Where possible, I have identified these individuals, and the date of the interview. Others, by necessity, must remain nameless. Those American officials who have spoken to me about the activities and events cited in this book have done so in confidence. The same is true of the Iraqi sources I have drawn upon. Given the ongoing situation inside Iraq, naming these sources would only put them at risk from the Iraqi insurgency, the Iraqi government or the American military. Some of my Iraqi sources were interviewed before the war, and are currently imprisoned without any criminal charges being made against them. I chose not to identify these Iraqis as well, since to do so might prejudice their treatment in jail. Likewise, I have sought to use the actual names of as many people as possible who appear in this story. However, many of the characters I discuss were, and possibly are, serving officers in their respective intelligence services, and in those cases I have used a pseudonym in order to protect their true identity. Also, given the controversial nature of the subject matter contained in this book, I have used pseudonyms for junior officials whose privacy should be respected.

I am solely responsible for the opinions and facts expressed in this book. I stand by everything I have written, and any errors or omission of fact are mine alone.

I would not have been able to tell this story without the vision and support of Iradj Bagherzade, my editor and the publisher at I.B.Tauris. I am thankful for his faith in my story, and my ability to tell it. I am also grateful for the kind editorial advice and assistance of Abigail Fielding-Smith, another one of the incredibly professional staff at I.B.Tauris who helped make this book a reality.

I am also thankful for steadfastness of good friends who have stuck with me over time and through various trials and tribulations – Chris Cobb-Smith, Roger Hill, Norbert Reinecke and Didier Louis, my former colleagues from UNSCOM, and Bob and Amy Murphy (and their new son, Ryan), Mike and Becky Steiner, Frank and Annie Mellet, and Mark Gibson, who comprised my local support network here in Albany, NY. I am also grateful for the support and friendship of all my fellow firefighters in the Delmar Fire Department who volunteer their time in the service of their community.

I would like to extend a special thanks to Seymour Hersh, an unparalleled journalist and even better friend. Alone in the American media, Sy Hersh listened to what I had to say, and then took the time to do the research necessary to determine that I spoke the truth. America, and the world, owes Sy Hersh a debt of gratitude for his integrity and tenacity in writing the truth, and I for one am proud and honored to call him my good friend.

And finally, I would like to thank my mother and father, Pat and Bill Ritter, and my three sisters, Shirley, Suzanne and Amy, their respective families, and my father-in-law, Bidzina, for all of their continuous and unwavering support. But I especially want to express my appreciation for the love of my wife, Marina, and our two wonderful daughters, Patricia and Victoria. I hope that this book helps explain the many months I was away from home during my time as an inspector, and puts in better perspective who I am and what I stand for.

Delmar, New York
June 2005

Glossary

Ababil-100	An Iraqi short-range missile
ACIS	Arms Control Intelligence Staff, the CIA organization responsible for overseeing intelligence support to UNSCOM in 1991–1992
Air Bag	The SIS covert operation in support of UNSCOM to disrupt Iraqi missile procurement efforts in Romania
Al-Hussein	Iraqi modified SCUD missile capable of ranges of over 500 miles
Al-Nida	Iraqi indigenously produced mobile missile launcher, used with the Al-Hussein missile; required a separate fueling/launch control vehicle to operate
Aman	The Israeli Directorate of Military Intelligence
Amn al-Amm	The Iraqi Directorate for General Security, or DGS, responsible for political security in Iraq
ASARS	Advanced Synthetic Aperture Radar System, a special imaging device that was used on the U-2 aircraft in support of some Olive Branch missions. Can detect moving targets, and distinguish some camouflaged items, can be used at night
C-130	Aircraft designation for a four-engine transport aircraft manufactured by Lockheed, and used by civilian contractors to transport UNSCOM into and out of Iraq from 1997–1999
C-160	Aircraft designation for a two-engine transport aircraft manufactured by a European consortium, and used by the German air force to transport UNSCOM into and out of Iraq from 1991 to 1997

Cabbage Patch Code name for the UNSCOM 61 inspection mission in Iraq, conducted in September–October 1993, which used airborne ground-penetrating radar to detect buried Iraqi missiles

CCT Combat Control Team, US Air Force personnel specially trained in controlling air traffic inside enemy territory

CIA Central Intelligence Agency, the agency within the US Government responsible for overseeing foreign intelligence collection and analysis

CSCI Capable Sites/Concealment Investigations Team, established by order of Executive Chairman Richard Butler on 4 August, 1997, this specialized unit within UNSCOM coordinated the most sensitive intelligence and special inspection operations in Iraq

CSPSU Capable Sites Planning Support Unit, the successor unit to the CSCI team, established in June 1998

DAT Digital audio tape, used by the SCE to record Iraqi communications signals

Delta Force The US Army's elite counter-terrorist unit, formally known as Special Operations Forces Detachment-Delta

DIA Defense Intelligence Agency, the agency within the Department of Defense responsible for overseeing military intelligence collection and analysis

DIS Defense Intelligence Service, the British Ministry of Defense agency responsible for military intelligence matters

DGS See Amn al-Amm

DMI Directorate of Military Intelligence, the Israeli Defense Force's intelligence arm

DNA Defense Nuclear Agency, a Department of Defense agency responsible for overseeing nuclear weapons activities, as well as associated arms control projects

DO Directorate of Operations, the CIA's covert operations directorate

DO/NE Directorate of Operations, Near East Division, the organization inside the Directorate for Operations responsible for the Middle East, including Iraq

DOD Department of Defense

EOD Explosive Ordnance Disposal, special units trained and equipped to make safe unexploded military munitions

FBI Federal Bureau of Investigation, the Department of Justice agency responsible for domestic law enforcement issues, including counter terrorism and counter espionage

FCO Foreign and Commonwealth Office, the British equivalent of the United States State Department

Glossary

Final Curtain	The code name for the CIA/NSA program providing support to the UNSCOM SIGINT activities in Iraq
FIS	Foreign Intelligence Service, the post-Soviet successor to the KGB, responsible for foreign intelligence
FLIR	Forward Looking Infra-Red, a night vision system mounted on helicopters and used by UNSCOM to support night inspection operations
FTG	Foreign Training Group, a unit within the CIA's Special Activities Staff responsible for coordinating training with UNSCOM
Gateway	The name of the CIA's analytical and operational planning support center in Bahrain, used in support of UNSCOM operations
GCHQ	The British code breaking service, equivalent to the US Government's NSA
GPR	Ground-penetrating radar, special devices designed to look underground for buried material. UNSCOM used two types of GPR – airborne and hand held
IAD	International Activities Division, the unit within the CIA's Directorate for Operations responsible for overseeing international operations, and in which resided the Special Activities Staff paramilitary unit
IAU	Information Assessment Unit, the organization within UNSCOM which oversaw intelligence liaison and information analysis
IAEA	International Atomic Energy Agency. The organization responsible for carrying out the nuclear aspects of implementation of Security Council resolution 687 (1991)
IDF	Israeli Defense Force
INA	The Iraqi National Accord, a joint CIA-SIS sponsored Iraqi opposition group
INC	The Iraqi National Congress, a CIA sponsored Iraqi opposition group
IOG	The Iraq Operations Group, a secret unit inside the CIA tasked with overthrowing Saddam Hussein
ISMTF	Iraq Sanctions Monitoring Task Force, the CIA unit set up to coordinate intelligence support to UNSCOM from 1991 until early 1992
JCS	Joint Chiefs of Staff, the US military joint command structure
JRC	Joint Reconnaissance Center, the US military branch responsible for tasking national imagery collection assets
Mass Appeal	Also known as Operation Mass Appeal, the British MI-6 covert operation designed to influence public opinion on issues pertaining to Iraq and WMD
MI6	The British Secret Intelligence Service (SIS)

MIC	Military Industrial Commission, the Iraqi Ministry responsible for overseeing conventional weapons programs, as well as weapons of mass destruction
MOD	Ministry of Defence, usually in reference to the British organization
Mukhabarat	Iraqi Intelligence Service
NIS	Notification of Inspection Site, the document presented by weapons inspectors to the Iraqi authorities which authorized the inspection of a site designated by geographic coordinates contained in the document
NMD	National Monitoring Directorate, the Iraqi organization responsible for overseeing compliance by Iraqi industry with Security Council provisions regarding disarmament
NPC	Non-Proliferation Center, the CIA organization responsible for coordinating intelligence support to UNSCOM from 1992 until 1999
NSA	National Security Agency, the US Government agency responsible for overseeing all communications and signals intercept operations worldwide
Olive Branch	The code name for the U-2 surveillance program provided by the US Government to UNSCOM
OMI	Office of Military Industry, an early name for the Iraqi Military Industrial Commission
OPC	Operations Planning Cell, the secret planning organization within the CIA that fused military and CIA special operations support
OSIA	On-Site Inspection Agency, the Department of Defense agency responsible for coordinating US Military support to UNSCOM
PI	Photographic interpreter, a specialist in analyzing overhead imagery taken from U-2 aircraft, satellites, and other resources
Project 144	The Iraqi missile conversion program which oversaw the lengthening of SCUD missiles into Al Hussein missiles
Resolution 687	Passed in April 1991, the original disarmament resolution of the Security Council regarding Iraq, authorizing the creation of UNSCOM
Resolution 707	Passed in July 1991, in response to Iraqi obstruction of the work of UNSCOM
Resolution 715	Passed in October 1991, mandates long-term monitoring and inspection operations in Iraq
Resolution 1115	Passed in June 1997, condemned Iraqi non-cooperation and established automatic travel sanctions on Iraqi officials should further acts of non-compliance be reported

Glossary

Rockingham	Also known as Operation Rockingham, or OP Rockingham, the DIS unit responsible for coordinating intelligence with UNSCOM
SAS (1)	Special Activities Staff, the CIA paramilitary operations unit, responsible for covert operations involving regime change, insurrection, counter-insurgency, etc
SAS (2)	Special Air Service, British or Australian Commando forces, similar to the US Army's Delta Force
SCE	Special Collection Element, the unit within UNSCOM responsible for carrying out sensitive intercept operations against the communications of Iraqi leadership, intelligence and security targets
SCSO	Special Commission Support Office, a Department of State organization responsible for coordinating interagency support within the US Government for UNSCOM
SCUD	NATO designator for the SS-1/R-17 missile, a short-range missile system originally designed for a range of 300 miles, but modified by Iraq, as the 'Al Hussein', for ranges in excess of 500 miles
SIE	Romanian intelligence service
SIGINT	Signals Intelligence, the collection of electronic data/communications, usually covertly, for intelligence purposes
SRC	Space Research Center, an organization within the Scientific Research Council responsible for designing satellites and rocket launch vehicles for Iraqi space programs
SRG	The Special Republican Guard, the military force responsible for the protection of Saddam Hussein
SSO	Special Security Organization, also known as the 'Amn al-Khass', this was the senior most security organization in Iraq, responsible for the security of Iraqi President Saddam Hussein
U-2	A high-altitude surveillance aircraft made available by the US Government for use on behalf of UNSCOM
UN	United Nations
Unit 8200	The Israeli Military Intelligence Unit responsible for signals intelligence operations. UNSCOM coordinated with Unit 8200 from 1996 until 1998
UNSCOM	United Nations Special Commission, the organization created by Security Council resolution 687 (1991) to oversee weapons inspections in Iraq
WMD	Weapons of Mass Destruction, as used here, Iraq's chemical, biological, nuclear and long-range (over 150 kilometers) missile programs

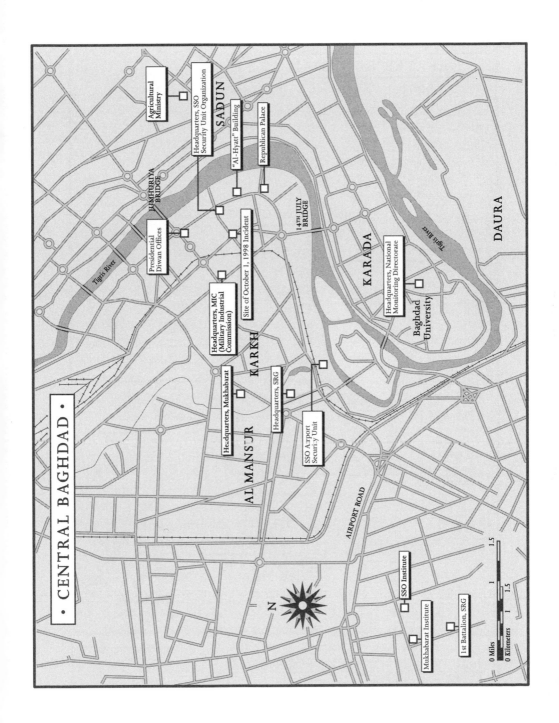

CENTRAL BAGHDAD

Agricultural Ministry

Headquarters, SSO Security Unit Organization

SADUN

"Al-Hyatt" Building

Republican Palace

JUMHURIYA BRIDGE

Presidential Diwan Offices

Tigris River

Site of October 1, 1998 Incident

14TH JULY BRIDGE

KARADA

Headquarters, National Monitoring Directorate

Headquarters, MIC (Military Industrial Commission)

Baghdad University

Tigris River

DAURA

Headquarters, Mukhabarat

KARKH

Headquarters, SRG

AL MANSUR

SSO Airport Security Unit

AIRPORT ROAD

N

Mukhabarat Institute

SSO Institute

1st Battalion, SRG

0 Miles   1   1.5
0 Kilometers   1   1.5

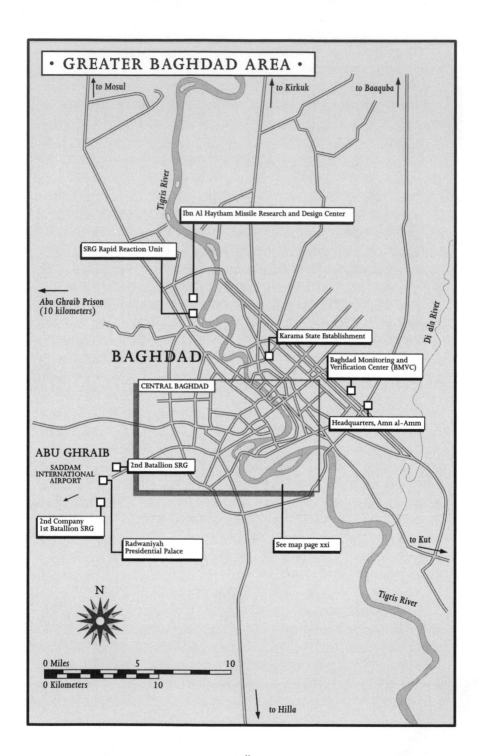

• GREATER BAGHDAD AREA •

to Mosul

to Kirkuk

to Baaquba

Tigris River

Ibn Al Haytham Missile Research and Design Center

SRG Rapid Reaction Unit

Abu Ghraib Prison
(10 kilometers)

Karama State Establishment

BAGHDAD

Baghdad Monitoring and
Verification Center (BMVC)

CENTRAL BAGHDAD

Di ala River

Headquarters, Amn al-Amm

ABU GHRAIB

SADDAM
INTERNATIONAL
AIRPORT

2nd Batallion SRG

2nd Company
1st Batallion SRG

Radwaniyah
Presidential Palace

See map page xxi

to Kut

Tigris River

N

0 Miles   5   10
0 Kilometers   10

to Hilla

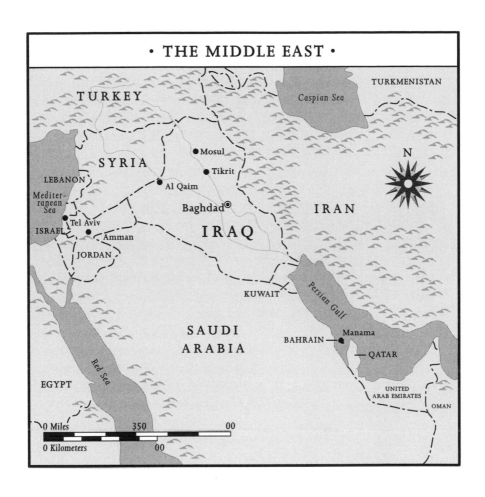

· THE MIDDLE EAST ·

TURKEY

TURKMENISTAN

Caspian Sea

SYRIA

Mosul

Tikrit

LEBANON

Al Qaim

Mediter-
ranean
Sea

IRAN

Baghdad

Tel Aviv

IRAQ

ISRAEL

Amman

JORDAN

KUWAIT

Persian Gulf

SAUDI
ARABIA

BAHRAIN

Manama

QATAR

Red Sea

EGYPT

UNITED
ARAB EMIRATES

OMAN

0 Miles   350   00

0 Kilometers   00

In the Eye of the Storm

Baghdad, 8 March 1998

The long convoy of white Nissan Patrol vehicles snaked its way along the Baghdad thoroughfare towards the Iraqi Ministry of Defense. Inside these vehicles were sitting dozens of grim, stony-faced men. They were experts from the United Nations Special Commission, or UNSCOM: weapons inspectors mandated by the Security Council to disarm Iraq. As chief inspector of this particular mission, I sat in the lead vehicle. We were in no hurry, being more concerned with keeping the convoy together than with speed. Our target wasn't going anywhere, so I was content to crawl along in the slow lane, letting the bustling traffic of a Baghdad rush hour stream on by. By this time, UN inspectors had been in Iraq for almost seven years, and our white vehicles, emblazoned with large black 'UN' letters, were an all-too-familiar sight to the citizens of Baghdad, who signaled to us in a variety of ways as they drove past. Most simply honked their horns and waved, but there were more than a few who shook their fists and cursed us in God's name for the economic ruin brought on their country. Iraq was reeling after more than a decade of UN-sponsored sanctions.

As we neared the Ministry of Defense complex, a shadow convoy of vehicles from the Iraqi National Monitoring Directorate, or NMD (the official government 'minders' who accompanied us on all inspections) appeared out of the blue. Several of these accelerated past mine, taking up blocking positions in front of me. Others hemmed in our convoy from the left-hand lane, trying to squeeze into any gaps that presented themselves. Fortunately we had been prepared for these tactics before arriving in Iraq and the convoy held together, our vehicles driving bumper to bumper to prevent them from splitting us up.

Iraqi police vehicles by this point had commandeered the entire thoroughfare, effectively halting the flow of traffic on one of Baghdad's busiest streets. To my right, the turn-off into the Defense Ministry approached, and without any prompting my driver, a tall former British Royal Marine named Chris Cobb-Smith, veered off towards the main gate.

My heart pounded as the Nissan turned off the thoroughfare. This particular moment, whenever the inspection team unequivocally committed itself to a specific site, had become a tense one for Cobb-Smith and me. It was hard not to think of our previous run-ins with the site guards. During an attempt to inspect the headquarters of the Iraqi Special Security Organization the previous fall, Cobb-Smith and I had come face to face with Iraqi soldiers and security officers who were taken by surprise at our arrival. I ended up with a pistol pointed at my head, and Cobb-Smith was looking down the barrel of a fully loaded machine gun. Only the quick actions of one of the Iraqi 'minders', who literally threw himself between us and the Iraqi soldiers, prevented a disaster from occurring.

I tried not to dwell on such experiences as we approached the gate of the Ministry of Defense. When we were nearer, I noticed that the soldiers manning the gate and perimeter of the complex, elite paratroopers sporting red berets, were springing into action. I was reassured to see that Brigadier Sadiq, one of the most level-headed and quick-thinking of the minders, was riding in the lead 'minder' vehicle. But this time intervention wasn't required. The Iraqi soldiers simply closed the gate and pulled a lever, which exposed a set of spikes known as 'dragon's teeth', designed to puncture the tires of any vehicle attempting to cross over. An Iraqi officer approached, and identified himself as the officer of the guard. He asked what our purpose was arriving at the Ministry of Defense. Through Sadiq, I explained that we were UN weapons inspectors who had come to inspect the site. Without blinking, the officer of the guard noted that he had no authorization to permit our entry. He had to report our arrival to his chain of command.

It was unlikely to be favorably received. A few months earlier, Iraq's deputy prime minister and chief negotiator on WMD issues, Tariq Aziz, had sat down with the UNSCOM chairman Richard Butler and gone through a list of sites UNSCOM wanted to inspect. When the Ministry of Defense came up Aziz had interrupted Butler. 'Don't even think about it,' he said. 'Any attempt to inspect the Ministry of Defense would mean war.'

And here we were. I turned to Brigadier Sadiq, and requested again that the inspection team be given immediate access to the Ministry of Defense. 'I will relay your request, Mr. Ritter,' the Brigadier responded. 'But you know that His Excellency, Tariq Aziz, has said that to inspect this place means war, and as such will never be allowed.' With this, we both retreated to our respective vehicles, to put in place a chain of events that could lead to imminent military action. I picked up my radio, and placed a call to the UNSCOM offices in Baghdad.

My radio call set in motion a number of events. First, Richard Butler, sitting in his office on the thirtieth floor of the UN building in New York, was notified that the team had been denied entry. Butler in turn notified his deputy, Charles Duelfer, an employee of the US State Department, and Bill Richardson, the US Ambassador to the United Nations. Charles Duelfer served as Butler's principal liaison with the national security bureaucracy of the US government, and in this role he placed calls to the staff of the US National Security Council (NSC). Before the inspection began, the NSC had called together representatives from all of the major agencies in Washington involved with issues relating to Iraq. Once Duelfer's confirmation that we had been denied access was received, National Security Advisor Sandy Berger and the NSC went into overdrive: calls were placed to the Pentagon, State Department and CIA. The military and diplomatic machinery necessary for any military action was being set in motion.

Bill Richardson also made some phone calls of his own. First he called a special secure line, reaching a State Department communications officer traveling with the Secretary of State, Madeleine Albright, who was at that time preparing for a formal state dinner with her French counterpart in Paris. Richardson then called the secretary-general of the United Nations, Kofi Annan, letting him know that there was a crisis underway in Baghdad that could test the resolve of the United Nations. Annan had received a similar call from Richard Butler, and was standing by in his office, surrounded by his closest advisors, waiting to see how events would unfold.

I could almost feel the eyes of every inspector on my team boring into me as I put down the radio. The sweat trickled down my neck. The

3

only way for the inspectors to be safe, and for Iraq to be disarmed, was if UNSCOM was seen as a neutral organization. But by this stage I was starting to have serious doubts myself on that score. I was concerned at the growing divergence between the people who were serious about disarming Iraq and the people who wanted to support US foreign policy, and I wasn't sure which camp the UNSCOM chairman sat in.

UNSCOM had been surrounded by such ambiguities since it came into being in 1991. It was created to implement UN resolution 687. This resolution's ostensible purpose was to rid the world of Iraq's weapons of mass destruction (WMD). The reality of resolution 687 was different. Having led an international coalition to drive Iraq out of occupied Kuwait in 1991, while promising to extract a 'Nuremburg-like retribution' for Iraq's actions,[1] George H. W. Bush's government was confronted with the reality that Saddam Hussein, even after a crushing military defeat, still remained in power. Bush needed to get rid of him – for domestic political reasons if nothing else. The CIA believed that any credible effort designed to disarm Iraq of its WMD would not only rid the world of a legitimate proliferation problem, but would also undercut Saddam's standing and jolt the rest of the Iraqi leadership into the realization that their country's interests would best be served if the Iraqi president were removed from power.

As they crafted Security Council resolution 687, American diplomats had destabilizing and undermining Saddam Hussein at the front of their minds rather than the complex business of disarmament. Disarmament was merely a vehicle for achieving the larger US objective of regime change. In order to achieve their ultimate objective of undermining Saddam's power base, the USA pushed for the disarmament mandate to be severe, and the price of non-cooperation to be high. For this reason, under resolution 687, the stringent economic sanctions imposed on Iraq following its invasion of Kuwait were extended until Iraq was found to be in complete compliance with its disarmament mandate. Many members of the Security Council – including Russia and China – deemed this to be too harsh. In order to bring them on board, the USA crafted language which, included as paragraph 14, sought to portray the disarmament of Iraq as a step 'towards the goal of establishing in the Middle East a zone free from weapons of mass destruction and all missiles for their delivery'. However, as the drafters of this language have privately stated to me, paragraph 14 was always intended to be a 'throwaway' element designed to induce faltering Security Council members into presenting a solid front against

Saddam Hussein. There was never any intention on the part of the USA to pursue paragraph 14.

In fact, one might almost say that the entire resolution was a throwaway statement. It was crafted for the purpose of 'putting Saddam in a cage', to quote former US Secretary of State James Baker. The Bush administration had already stated as official policy that economic sanctions against Iraq would not be lifted, regardless of Iraq's compliance with its disarmament obligation, a policy which was in direct opposition to the letter and intent of resolution 687.[2] So weapons inspections were created at the United Nations in an atmosphere of duplicity.

The Iraqis for their part didn't want to be disarmed. Saddam understood that he had to be seen as cooperating with the UN inspectors; his defeat in Kuwait left no room for doubt in that regard. But he couldn't allow his inner circle to perceive him as weak. According to senior Iraqis with firsthand knowledge of events, shortly after the Security Council passed resolution 687, Saddam ordered the creation of a high-level committee which, at the same time as Iraq was submitting a declaration to the UN inspectors detailing its holdings of WMD, was to orchestrate a massive concealment campaign.

The Iraqi 'concealment committee' got straight to work, taking physical control of weapons, production equipment and documents relating to WMD. Documents were moved to secluded holding areas, while weapons and production equipment were placed on vehicles and moved around in smaller convoys in order to escape detection. Cover stories were concocted for facilities engaged in WMD-related activity, and factory workers were coached through the deception by special teams of fake inspectors, who simulated the kind of questions anticipated to be asked when the real inspectors finally showed up. Some facilities were physically altered to hide their true purpose. Saddam's past experience was with International Atomic Energy Agency (IAEA) inspectors (whom Iraq deceived for a decade while secretly pursuing a nuclear weapons program), and he had little regard for either the competence or the tenacity of the UN weapons inspectors. He felt that he could ride out the inspection period for long enough to rally world support around the lifting of economic sanctions.

For both the US government and Saddam, the UNSCOM inspections were viewed as nothing more than a vehicle for their respective races against time. In 1991, the Bush administration was betting that inspections could outlast Saddam by putting just enough pressure on the regime to cause it to collapse from within. Saddam was betting that the world would tire of fruitless and unproductive inspections that simply sustained damaging economic sanctions, and that soon the world's appetite for oil would take over, bringing an end to the debilitating trade embargo. Both sides were looking to wrap up their objectives by the end of the year, and both sides were disappointed. Unfortunately for both of them, some members of the international community actually took the issue of disarmament very seriously.

In 1991, specialists from across the world had been gathered in New York to discuss how to implement the new mandate. Headed by Ambassador Rolf Ekéus, a Swedish career diplomat with extensive experience in arms control, the UNSCOM staff set about the monumental task of organizing, training and dispatching credible teams of inspectors into Iraq. This was an enormous challenge from a diplomatic, operational and logistical standpoint but, by the end of May 1991, the first team had been sent to Iraq – a nuclear survey team to assess the declared Iraqi facilities. In June this mission was followed by several more nuclear teams, and by July inspectors from the fields of ballistic missiles, chemical weapons and biological weapons had joined their nuclear colleagues in the field. The UN had seemingly accomplished the impossible, placing credible disarmament teams in Iraq on short notice. Regardless of what the unstated intent of resolution 687 was, the stated objective of disarmament was being accomplished. As the years unfolded, however, UNSCOM became more and more bogged down in the morass of political agendas. By the time we knocked on the door of the Ministry of Defense on that warm March day in 1998, UNSCOM was operating in very murky waters indeed.

The story of how I got to be at the center of this political game is also the story of how the UN weapons inspection regime came to be consumed by opposing political agendas. It is a story of determination and steadfastness, and of lies and betrayal. I have tried to tell an honest story about the events leading up to the war, which, for the first time, exposes the truth about the UN weapons inspections in Iraq. It reveals the role played by the USA in manipulating, suppressing and fatally undermining the inspections process in support of a different agenda – regime change. Many American and many, many more Iraqi lives have since been lost in support of this agenda. The world may yet pay the price for the CIA's decision to use disarmament as its smokescreen.

PART ONE
BAPTISM

Chapter 1

A Delicate Balancing Act
September–December 1991

I arrived in New York on Sunday 22 September 1991. A veteran Marine Corps intelligence officer who had left active duty in June 1991 with the rank of captain, I had served tours of duty in the former Soviet Union as a weapons inspector and in the Middle East, for Operation Desert Storm, as a ballistic-missile specialist. It was this résumé that brought me to the doors of the United Nations headquarters in midtown Manhattan. I had been summoned by the newly formed United Nations Special Commission, or UNSCOM, a group of international arms control specialists gathered by the Security Council to oversee the disarmament of Iraq's weapons of mass destruction in the aftermath of Saddam Hussein's defeat in March 1991 at the hands of a US-led coalition. I was in New York to help disarm Iraq and, as someone who had been instrumental in carrying out weapons inspections in the former Soviet Union, I knew a thing or two about arms control. However, on my arrival at UNSCOM what I found was more spy story than arms control.

It was a journey that had started quite unexpectedly, with a phone call in August 1991 from an old friend, Douglas Englund. Doug was a colonel in the US Army. I had previously worked for him as a weapons inspector when I had been stationed in the former Soviet Union as part of the Intermediate Nuclear Forces (INF) Treaty. We were both assigned to the On-Site Inspection Agency (OSIA), a Department of Defense activity created for the purpose of overseeing the implementation of that treaty. Doug went on to become the chief of staff for OSIA and, in April 1991, was assigned temporary duty in New York City as the director of operations for a new entity, UNSCOM.

Doug Englund was a huge bear of a man. His large, round face was topped with a shag of black hair turned silver on the edges. Doug was not a stereotypical spit-and-polish soldier. He had a disheveled air about him and, even when wearing a uniform, had a way of looking as if he had just thrown it on. With his trademark toothpick lodged in his mouth, Doug's face was constantly furrowed in thought or wrinkled in laughter, for Doug's intellect was evenly matched by his engaging sense of humor. I was pleased that he counted me as a friend.

I met with Doug in the comfortable home in suburban Fairfax which he shared with his wife, Anne. After catching up on old times, Doug pulled me aside. 'The US has provided UNSCOM with a U-2 aircraft to help support our efforts in Iraq,' he stated.[1] 'We will need help in assembling all of the data we are collecting and organizing it in a useful manner.' Doug then asked the fateful question: 'Would you be interested in coming to New York and helping set up a small team for this purpose?' I tried to mask my enthusiasm as I answered in the affirmative.

My arrival in New York coincided with the start of a very dramatic inspection that was taking place in Baghdad – UNSCOM 16.[2] A joint inspection between UNSCOM and the International Atomic Energy Agency (IAEA, the Vienna-based nuclear watchdog agency which oversaw the nuclear aspects of Iraq's disarmament), UNSCOM 16 would forever be remembered by most people as 'the parking lot' inspection. But, for me, UNSCOM 16 served as a wake-up call about the real nature of the work I was about to become involved in. I had been a weapons inspector in support of the INF Treaty, and I knew what arms control was. I had also worked with covert intelligence agents from the CIA and US Special Forces when I was a marine. I had thought that arms control and intelligence were two distinct spheres. UNSCOM 16 was to show me just how wrong I was.

Like any story of intelligence and intrigue, the UNSCOM 16 inspection had a clear beginning. In May 1991, a senior scientist in the Iraqi nuclear weapons program defected to the West, through northern Iraq. The CIA had a massive effort underway in northern Iraq to seek out such defectors, operating under the cover of the humanitarian relief program 'Provide Comfort'. The agency quickly swept up the scientist, who became known simply as 'defector source DS-385'.[3]

There was some hesitation on the CIA's part over how best to proceed with this new information, which provided a heretofore unseen look into the dark secrets of the Iraqi nuclear weapons program. DS-385 was providing information that had a direct bearing on the work of the fledgling UNSCOM inspections, but the CIA was constrained by US law from sharing such sensitive information, drawn from highly classified sources, with a non-US government body.

This shortcoming was soon exposed in early June when Bob Gallucci, a charismatic senior State Department official who served as deputy to the UNSCOM chairman, Rolf Ekéus, requested from the US government a listing of priority sites in Iraq for inspection by UNSCOM. The CIA office responsible for Iraq published a list of suspect weapons sites which was forwarded to UNSCOM on 10 June 1991. The restrictions of US law, however, meant that the CIA's list failed to incorporate any meaningful intelligence, let alone the gold nuggets DS-385 was providing about the facilities and personnel involved in Iraq's nuclear program and, as such, the sites provided were non-specific, had no supporting data and were practically useless to us.

Bob Gallucci protested when he saw the list. Gallucci didn't know about the existence of DS-385, he just knew that the information being provided by the CIA was totally inadequate. The CIA realized that the only way to give UNSCOM what it was asking for was to provide information that would expose the fact that the USA was controlling a defector. DS-385 was about to be revealed. The CIA prepared a new paper, this one detailing not only the existence of DS-385, but also what he was telling them, which included data about an archive of hidden documents related to the Iraqi nuclear weapons program. To get around the US legal restrictions, the paper was restricted for use by only US personnel on UNSCOM's staff. The UN weapons inspectors were able to start planning the UNSCOM 16 inspection using this information.

UNSCOM would not be preparing for this inspection alone. Prior to UNSCOM 16, the CIA and other US intelligence agencies had all channeled their support and recommendations concerning UNSCOM through the State Department, but the strategic planning of operations was left to UNSCOM, and specifically Doug Englund.

This approach changed dramatically in the summer of 1991. In June, IAEA inspectors had tried to intercept Iraqi vehicles carrying nuclear-related equipment, and the Iraqis had fired warning shots. If the world's only superpower were not going to be made a fool of, weapons inspectors would have to get some serious help. The issue of uncovering incriminating documentation suddenly took on a higher priority, and the CIA, supported by activist elements within the Department of State, pushed for more direct involvement in the operations of UNSCOM and the IAEA. For the first time, the darkest warriors in the CIA's covert army, the Operations Planning Cell (OPC), were getting actively involved in preparing intelligence for UNSCOM's use.[4]

The secret warriors of the CIA were accustomed to plying their trade in the shadows, far away from prying eyes. UNSCOM inspections, however, were carried out in full view of the Iraqi government, representing the antithesis of covert action. The existence of the OPC, as with any CIA affiliation with UNSCOM, was a carefully guarded secret. Officially, therefore, all OPC personnel were presented to UNSCOM as State Department 'experts'. With the exception of a few 'trusted agents' inside UNSCOM, such as Bob Gallucci, Doug Englund and a few other US military officers, nobody in UNSCOM knew the true identity or affiliation of these seconded personnel.

According to the thinking of the OPC planners, UNSCOM needed the ability to strike hard and fast at targets identified by the CIA. To provide this needed muscle, the OPC turned to their brethren in covert warfare, the secret commandos from the 1st Special Forces Operational Detachment-Delta – Delta Force – based out of Fort Bragg, North Carolina. Delta Force were experts at rapid planning and the tactical 'taking down' of a building. The operational factors that went into planning and executing a document search and seizure inspection – such as UNSCOM 16 – were very much the same as carrying out a hostage rescue mission. Delta was the world's best at this sort of operation, and despite their subordinate role in the OPC, the commandos quickly began to dominate the character of the new organization.

Delta brought their hard-charging, hyper-positive 'can do' attitude to the job. During the Gulf War, Delta had been heavily engaged in counter-SCUD operations in western Iraq (the so-called 'Great SCUD Hunt').[5] Their task had been the interception of Iraqi missile attacks against Israel and, despite several high-profile claims concerning destroyed Iraqi launchers, the fact that Iraq was able to strike Israel throughout the war represented a serious blow to the honor and prestige of a unit unaccustomed to failure. It came as no surprise that completing that mission became a dominant underlying theme for the Delta operators assigned to the OPC. The tactics and methodologies had changed, but Delta, through the UNSCOM inspection process, was back in the SCUD-busting business. First though they had to help find the nuclear document archive.

The UNSCOM 16 inspection team was headed jointly by Bob Gallucci and David Kay, the aggressive inspector from the IAEA. The joint UNSCOM/IAEA team had deployed to Baghdad and was due to begin operations a little before midnight New York time on Sunday 22 September 1991, which, given the time difference, was the same day I arrived in New York to start my new life as a UN weapons inspector.

In addition to building an intelligence unit from the ground up, as an UNSCOM staff officer I was required to pull my fair share of 'watch duty'. Given the eight-hour time difference between New York and Baghdad, when inspections having the potential for confrontation took place, we would keep the offices in New York manned twenty-four hours a day, so that the inspectors in Iraq would have a point of contact in case the situation started to deteriorate. I may have been the new kid on the block, but I was required to pull 'night watch' just like everyone else.

Around two in the morning New York time on Monday 23 September 1991, the UNSCOM 16 inspection team had discovered four boxes of classified documents in a building in Baghdad known as the Nuclear Design Center. After nearly six hours of examining the documents, the two team heads, Gallucci and Kay, attempted to leave with the documents and were stopped by Iraqi authorities. As I arrived at the UNSCOM offices for my shift, the inspection team and Iraqi authorities were still deadlocked in a struggle over control of the documents, which by some estimates numbered in the hundreds of thousands. I had to wake Rolf Ekéus and notify him of the standoff, then call other senior staff, who started to arrive at UN HQ, bleary-eyed from lack of sleep.

The head of the Iraqi nuclear program, Dr. Jaffar Dhia al-Jaffar, arrived at the inspection site, demanding that the inspectors cease their work, turn over all documents seized so far and vacate the site immediately. Dr. Jaffar also demanded the film from the inspectors' cameras. The Iraqis had been carefully observing the activities of the inspectors, which included putting the captured documents through a kind of 'triage', sorting out those believed to be of the highest importance, and then photographing those pages in case the Iraqis chose to take the documents back by force. The last thing Dr. Jaffar wanted was for this information to leave Baghdad.[6]

I went to my hotel to get some sleep for a few hours. When I went back on duty, I read the logbooks. In Baghdad, the drama was continuing to play itself out under the hot middle eastern sun. The inspection team had refused to leave the parking lot of the Ministry of Agriculture building without the documents, and made preparations to spend the night. Within hours, the UNSCOM 16 mission had become a media event, with David Kay and Bob Gallucci conducting constant interviews with CNN and other TV and radio outlets about their predicament in the Ministry of Agriculture parking lot. The plot, as depicted by Kay and Gallucci, was a simple one: the good guys (UNSCOM) were being held up by the bad guys (Iraq). The political complexity of the inspections process did not have to be explained to an audience caught up in the soap opera that played itself out live on their television screens.

While the world was transfixed on the Kay-Gallucci show in center ring, two sub-themes were playing themselves out in UN Headquarters in New York, one good, the other not so. On the positive side, there were persistent rumors going around in the corridors of UNSCOM that Kay's team had found a 'smoking gun' document that confirmed the existence of an Iraqi nuclear weapon design, something the Iraqis had vehemently denied ever having (it was, after all, a peaceful civilian nuclear program). On the negative side, Ambassador Ekéus was very disturbed to learn that his deputy, Bob Gallucci, was in direct contact with US officials in Washington, passing on details of the inspection standoff and discussing options on how best to respond. The Iraqi intelligence service had intercepted these transmissions, and a potential problem was brewing. Ekéus was particularly incensed by the fact that he was finding out details of the inspection *after* Washington; indeed, US government personnel were often briefing Ekéus on events in the parking lot *before* he had been informed by the team in Baghdad.

Rolf Ekéus, outwardly a kindly gentleman with a shock of unruly white hair, had an inner core of steel, and was not someone to be crossed lightly. The unauthorized communications between Gallucci and the US government had Ekéus incandescent, and he called the head of the State Department's Political-Military Affairs Bureau, Richard Clarke, to protest. In a sharply worded exchange, Ekéus reminded the pugnacious Clarke of the absolute requirement that he, the executive chairman, be in charge. Clarke countered that the USA had every right to stay in contact with its officials on matters in which it played an important role. Ekéus's reply was icy. He was in charge, and that was how it was going to be. Clarke had no choice but to back down.[7]

After four days of brinksmanship, the Iraqis eventually relented. Four days after locking themselves in the parking lot of the PC-3 complex, braving Iraqi security forces, inhospitable weather and hordes of Iraqi demonstrators, the UNSCOM 16 inspection team was released, with the documents. One of the inspectors had even managed to smuggle out the 'smoking gun' document under his clothes, and although it couldn't be used as evidence of Iraqi non-compliance because it had been illicitly procured, it served as a valuable starting point for intelligence and analysis over the coming years. The relief amongst UN staff in New York was palpable as we all trooped out for beer and pizza to celebrate the end of the standoff.

The UNSCOM 16 inspection cast a spotlight on the curious nature of the UNSCOM-US intelligence relationship. Officially, and for obvious political reasons, it didn't exist, and I was certainly never briefed about it when I joined UNSCOM. However some things were just too obvious about the realities of this relationship for me to ignore. CIA personnel, whom I knew from my past experience in Russia and during the Gulf War, kept showing up to brief Rolf Ekéus, claiming to be 'State Department'. My curiosity was further piqued by Ekéus's outburst over the Gallucci-State Department communication escapade. One of the missions given to me by Doug Englund on my arrival in New York was to create an independent intelligence cell that could receive and organize data independent of outside interference. The feeling amongst UNSCOM's senior staff after UNSCOM 16 was that the scale of US intelligence involvement with UNSCOM was in fact monumental, a reality which needed to be addressed or else UNSCOM would run the risk of losing its credibility as an independent implementer of its Security Council mandate.

The irony was that the biggest defenders of UNSCOM's independence were Americans serving in it, including myself and Doug Englund. On earlier UNSCOM inspections, when presented with intelligence information about aspects of Iraqi non-compliance, Doug had cooperated fully and without hesitation with his assigned CIA briefers. However, a crisis of confidence began to brew out of the 'secret squirrel' methodology pursued by the USA in distributing intelligence information to the Special Commission. In New York, the USA would dispatch secretive teams to its mission at the United Nations for 'US-only' briefings, segregating the American staffers on the Commission from their UN colleagues. Under normal conditions, such compartmentalization would only be logical, given the need to safeguard sensitive intelligence information and sources. But in a multilateral effort headed by the United Nations, this blatant US bias was provocative to many non-US staff, dispatched by their respective governments to support what they thought was a UN effort, but which took on the appearance of a US-run event heavily influenced by the CIA. Doug and I tried to explain to the CIA that they should be more sensitive to the multilateral climate of UNSCOM.

We achieved modest results by doing this. In the old US Embassy complex in Manama, Bahrain, where the inspection teams assembled and prepared prior to going into Iraq, the USA had assembled an organization called 'Gateway'. Gateway consisted of a team of analysts, logisticians and administrators who were tasked with disseminating US intelligence information to UNSCOM inspection teams.[8] In response to complaints about unilateralism, the CIA invited intelligence representatives from the UK, Australia and Canada in order to 'internationalize' the effort.

However, looks can be deceiving, and Gateway was no exception. No information was supposed to be provided to any team member who lacked an appropriate security clearance, which was inevitably tied up with nationality. Awkward situations continued to develop as teams were brought together under the UN flag, only to have a select few taken away for these special briefings.[9] It was even more problematic when the list of those inspectors left behind included a non-American chief inspector who was, in theory at least, running the operation.

Though worried by this practice, Doug Englund, acting in his capacity as a UN official, went along with it without complaint in the hopes that something useful might come out of the process. However, it soon became clear that the political cost of supporting the US-only intelligence effort wasn't worth the gains. The behavior of US inspectors during these inspections, who frequently carried out unsanctioned information collection on behalf of the USA, looking for buildings and material that went beyond the Chief Inspector's brief, was apparent to all, non-US inspector and Iraqi alike. Upon returning to Bahrain these same US inspectors were then hustled away in US Embassy vehicles to the Gateway facility for separate debriefings. The CIA's heavy-handed 'US-only' approach brought into question the integrity of UNSCOM, something that was reported back to their home countries by every non-American inspector who witnessed this process.

I took advantage of the temporary lull in the action at UNSCOM Headquarters in New York in October 1991 to schedule a visit to the Department of State. I felt that there was a need to firmly establish what the US government thought my role should be in the new intelligence unit we were trying to create. Through the Information Assessment Unit (IAU), as it was known, UNSCOM was trying to break the CIA's monopoly on the flow of sensitive information to the weapons inspectors. As the UNSCOM inspection process had transformed itself from being a simple verification unit, designed to certify the accuracy of an Iraqi declaration, to a more robust no-notice inspection team organized to find hidden weapons capability, intelligence was vital.

I was greeted at the State Department entrance by an Air Force Colonel, Sam Perry (pseudonym), whose name I had been given as my point of contact. Tall, slim and gray-haired, Sam Perry had the air of a distinguished southern gentleman. His manner put one immediately at ease.

Sam took me up to the offices of the Political-Military Affairs Bureau and into a conference room where around a dozen people were seated, some like Sam in military uniform, and others in civilian suits. At the head of the table sat a tall, slim man with intense eyes and a hatchet face – Jerry Murphy (pseudonym), the chief of the Special Commission Support Office. Jerry offered me a seat, and made the introductions. It was a blur of names and faces, representatives from the Secretary of Defense, the Joint Chiefs of Staff, the Department of Energy, the CIA and others.

Colonel Perry was effusive about the importance of the newly created Information Assessment Unit in the future of UNSCOM, and the need to do the job right. Jerry Murphy spoke up: 'Scott, I want to emphasize that you work for UNSCOM, plain and simple. While we appreciate a good working relationship with you and others at UNSCOM, you should suffer under no illusion that we are trying to direct your work. The US government wants you to work for Rolf Ekéus. It is in our best interests that you do so. You do your job as best you see fit, and let Sam and I worry about backing you up.'

We finished the meeting with Sam emphasizing his view of what was taking place. 'We are making history. The United Nations is getting serious about international peace and security, and UNSCOM represents a clear test of its mettle. What UNSCOM is setting out to do can change the course of how the world solves its problems. We need to make sure we do everything we can to make their work a success.' I certainly appreciated this sentiment, and had no reason to doubt the sincerity of those delivering it. Unfortunately, it soon became apparent that others in Washington didn't share Jerry and Sam's stated point of view. One of those was John Bird, a veteran intelligence officer who headed the CIA team responsible for coordinating intelligence issues with UNSCOM.

The US intelligence community lived by the old maxim that 'information is power', and they sought leverage over UNSCOM by controlling the information that it had access to. To their thinking, the IAU represented a direct threat to this effort. In order to assert their dominance of the information flow to UNSCOM, the CIA provided periodic sensitive intelligence briefings on inspection proposals. The next such briefing took place on 27 November in New York, at the US Mission across the street from the UN Headquarters. The subject was a proposal by John Bird.

The briefer was a DIA analyst named Larry Smothers (pseudonym), a name I knew well from my past. During Desert Storm, Smothers had published numerous papers concerning the Iraqi SCUD missile capability, and almost all of his assessments had turned out to be wrong. And now, in a secure conference room of the US Mission, he was getting ready to propagate another myth – the missing Iraqi SCUD Brigade.

Larry was postulating the existence of a covert force of Iraqi mobile launchers, some twenty-four of them, which he believed were still unaccounted for. He talked of the continued existence of a first brigade, composed of Soviet-supplied launchers, using as evidence photographs of 'undeclared launcher modifications'. One glance at the images he used to illustrate his point quickly shot down his theory in my view: the picture showed Iraqi decoy launchers of the same sort I had seen footage of taken from a helicopter during SCUD raids in Operation Desert Storm. If Larry was building his case using pictures of fake launchers, which in any case had been destroyed in the war, then we had a problem.

I wasn't skeptical about the idea of a covert SCUD force per se, indeed I had just authored a report for the executive chairman in which I concluded that the Iraqis were probably hiding a force of around a hundred missiles, together with half a dozen or so mobile launchers.[10] Larry continued to flip through his slides, making his case for the existence of a second missing brigade of SCUD launchers. But I needed more convincing evidence for it than this. It was at this point that Larry Smothers' presentation caught my attention: he noted that the Iraqis had declared only four indigenous launchers, known as the *Al-Nida*,[11] and then proceeded to present a satellite photograph taken in March 1991, showing six Al-Nida launchers clustered together at the Taji Military Camp north of Baghdad. This was the first time the USA had presented hard evidence to sustain any notion of a retained Iraqi capability proscribed by Security Council resolution, and I for one sat up and listened.

At this juncture in the briefing, John Bird took over. I had not seen Bird since May 1990, when I had visited CIA Headquarters to help the Arms Control Intelligence Staff he headed on some analytical matters pertaining to my work in the Soviet Union from 1988 to 1990. He was a former military man, in his early sixties, with a thin, pinched face and short gray hair. With a propensity to dress in plain gray suits that matched his hair color, he would accentuate his talks with fluid movements of his hands. Before Smothers' briefing got under way, Bird had come over to where I was sitting and offered his hand. 'It is good to see you again,' he said, but the look in his eyes and the forced nature of his smile suggested the opposite.

Now John Bird was standing before me and the assembled UNSCOM officials, discussing the recommended inspection sites for a renewed 'SCUD Hunt' in western Iraq and Baghdad. The primary site in question was a place called the 'Karama Barracks'. Bird said that there was good reason to believe that transport vehicles used in moving missiles around Baghdad were parked, intermittently, at this site. He thought that a no-notice inspection, including a detailed document search for logbooks that might contain information pertaining to the movement of missiles, stood a chance of discovering evidence of retained Iraqi SCUD missiles. The CIA felt that this was a high-priority target, and Bird was confident that the recently observed activity at the barracks justified their interest. Since Smothers had provided no imagery of this 'activity', we were left assuming that what Bird was referencing was some sort of intercepted Iraqi conversation. The remainder of the sites presented as candidates for inspection consisted of ammunition storage areas or suspected locations scattered throughout western Iraq, where the USA believed the Iraqis might be hiding some material or equipment.

'We know time is very short,' John Bird said. 'We have some operational types down in Washington who are very familiar with the inspection sites we have proposed. Would you,' he concluded, 'like them to come up, perhaps as soon as tomorrow, and assist you?'

Doug Englund, sensing a clear power play on the part of Bird, took strong exception. 'John,' he said, '*we* plan the inspection, not the Americans. If *you* would like to send us up people who can brief us on the sites, that would be of use. But leave the planning to UNSCOM.'

Bird nodded in agreement, but something in his manner indicated that the battle was far from over.

The next day two very fit men, Randall Lee and Gordon Cooper (both pseudonyms), arrived in New York from Washington. Lee and Cooper had both introduced themselves as 'experts from the State Department', although they certainly didn't look like diplomats. Lee was an officer in SEAL Team Six, the elite US Navy commando unit. Cooper was a senior non-commissioned officer with the US Army's Delta Force. Both were veterans of combat operations in Iraq (I recognized Cooper as one of the Delta commandos from the SCUD hunt in Desert Storm.) The two had been assigned to the CIA's Operations Planning Cell unit. Together with Doug Englund, myself and a new inspector named Roger Hill, we sequestered ourselves in UNSCOM's 'bunker', finalizing the plan for the upcoming inspection, which was designated as UNSCOM 24.

Roger Hill was an Australian intelligence officer with service in the elite Australian Special Air Service, who had joined UNSCOM in mid-November to serve as the IAU's chemical/biological weapons specialist. He was a unique character. Of medium height, with short, curly dark hair, and a well-trimmed mustache, Hill on first appearance looked more like a prim British businessman than a rugged Australian commando officer. There was no denying his physical fitness, but he carried himself with such a refined air of dignity that one had some trouble projecting him into the role of a 'snake eater' (a term often used to describe US special forces types). In barely a month of working together, however, Roger's professionalism and dedication to his job shone through in everything he did. Because of his special forces background, Doug had selected Roger Hill to lead one of two inspection elements planned for the operation. My role in the inspection was clearly defined: I would participate in the inspection as the ballistic missile specialist. I would also serve as a sub-team leader, responsible for supervising a team of three inspectors.

The UNSCOM 24 inspection represented a delicate balancing between UNSCOM's drive for independence and the CIA's need to be in control of an operation it viewed as useful to the unilateral policy objectives of the USA. On the surface, these agendas seemed irreconcilable. But we in UNSCOM operated in the realm of political realities, and such differences had to be smoothed over so that we could go forward with our mission. UNSCOM 24 represented such a 'smoothing' action. Its success or failure would determine the nature of UNSCOM's future operations inside Iraq, as well as our relationship with the CIA and the USA.

Chapter 2
The Bumpy Road to Independence
December 1991—February 1992

With the unusual intelligence alliance of UNSCOM and the CIA in place, Roger Hill and I landed in Bahrain to oversee its implementation. In contrast to the winter air of both New York and London, Bahrain greeted us with a blast of heat and humidity. We were met by officials from the UNSCOM field office, who processed us through Bahraini immigration and customs, and put us on buses to the Holiday Inn Hotel in Manama, Bahrain's capital city. In the Middle Eastern heat, the Holiday Inn felt like an oasis with its wonderfully air-conditioned lobby, comfortable rooms and ample bar. The bar's customers were entertained by a live Filipino band that performed remarkable renditions of the most recent Top Forty songs. Whether due to the music or the free-flowing drinks, the bar seemed to call to most of the team members when they arrived. Roger and I checked into our rooms, and headed downstairs to meet and mingle with the team.

Putting an UNSCOM inspection team together was pretty much a gamble. Back in New York, we had listed the various job skills we anticipated we would require, together with the numbers of each. We then tried to spread these requirements out among as many different nations as possible, to give an international, rather than Anglo-Saxon, flavor to the team. We had no control over the actual person who would be sent to fill the job;

it was very much the luck of the draw. But once Hill and I had become acquainted with the diverse mix of characters who were assembling in the noisy, smoke-filled, dimly lit bar at the Holiday Inn, it appeared that fate had treated us kindly. We had the makings of a good team.

With the strains of 'Walk Like an Egyptian' drowning out all conversation but the shouted word, Hill and I introduced ourselves. We had Canadian military explosive ordnance disposal experts, men who made their livelihoods by defusing unexploded bombs and mines. A crazy, good-natured lot they were. The pair on my team quickly got the nickname 'Laurel and Hardy', because of their contrasting body types. There was a German rocket scientist, Dr. Marcus Kreutz (psuedonym), a very able technical expert and veteran of several past inspections. We had two Russians, one a colonel who was an expert in SCUD operations, and the other his translator from the Ministry of Foreign Affairs. There was a large British contingent, a mixed lot of linguists, technical experts and military officers. We also had UN communications specialists and UN linguists, and a pair of UN photographers. There was a pair of New Zealand army medics, a gregarious lot who, like the Canadians, were given to consuming massive quantities of beer. And, joining in the cheer, were Randall Lee, Gordon Cooper and five other physically fit Americans from the CIA's Operations Planning Cell team.

Roger Hill and I had two days to transform the gaggle of individuals who had gathered at the Holiday Inn bar that night into a team of inspectors who could take the Iraqis head-on. The training was intense. We assembled the team in a crowded, poorly ventilated conference room inside a converted aircraft hangar that served as UNSCOM's field office in Bahrain. UNSCOM had made arrangements with the Bahraini Defense Force to allow the weapons inspectors to make use of this hangar, which was located inside a secure Bahraini Air Force facility on the edge of Manama airport. The room had a series of coffee tables placed together to form one large, rectangular table surface. Gray metal folding chairs were placed around the table. At the front of the conference room was a podium, and a portable screen for projecting slides. A pale blue UN flag hung in the background, together with the red and white banner of the State of Bahrain. An air-conditioning unit was mounted in the wall, but made so much noise that it had to be turned off whenever a presentation was being made. In the confined spaces of the conference room, filled with over thirty people, the heat soon built up to uncomfortable levels.

23

The glazed eyes of many of the inspectors indicated that they were either still suffering from jet lag or, more probably, had had one too many at the bar the night before. The heat did not help their predicament, but there was to be no mercy. We had a job to do. The team was subjected to a series of briefings from a half dozen American intelligence specialists from Gateway, who provided the team with U-2 photographs, US military maps and to-scale line drawings of each site to be inspected. The maps and line drawings we were allowed to keep; the U-2 photographs were for reference use only. The CIA weren't taking any chances on these falling into the wrong hands.

Each site had been broken down into sectors, and each sector assigned to a specific sub-team. As a sub-team leader myself, I had to take detailed notes about what my team's responsibilities were. I also had to be sure I understood what was required at other locations, in case the plan were to change with my group called on to do something else. We plotted our routes on maps and carefully studied the aerial photographs, making sure we had located every major landmark and feature.

After a break for lunch, 'Laurel and Hardy' had recovered enough from the previous night's excesses to deliver a frightening lecture on the dangers posed by unexploded ordnance left over from Operation Desert Storm. The two Canadians seemed to relish their job, showing us photographs and drawings of what the munitions looked like, and how easily they could be inadvertently set off. They had big smiles on their faces as they described what these munitions could do to you. In spite of their humorous approach to instruction, 'Laurel and Hardy' made an impression on the team. This was a serious undertaking we were engaged in, one that could mean life or death if we didn't keep our focus.

UNSCOM 24's mission was centered on ballistic missiles, so it was somewhat surprising that most of the inspectors were not missile experts, but operational types. The exceptions to this were myself, Marcus Kreutz and the Russian colonel. The latter had played an important role in deploying SCUD missiles into Afghanistan in the 1980s, and their subsequent use against Mujahideen positions. He had trained the Afghan Army on their use, and helped turn over thousands of SCUDs to the Afghans prior to the Soviet Army's withdrawal in 1989. After the fall of the Berlin Wall, he had supervised the removal from East Germany all of the Soviet Army's short-range ballistic missiles, including SCUDs. There was no doubting that he knew first hand the business of Soviet ballistic missiles.

The final day of training drove home the seriousness of the mission we were about to undertake. The morning started off with a lecture from Randall and Gordon, as the CIA's OPC representatives, on how best to carry out a search of a building or site. Emphasis was placed on establishing a search pattern, and sticking to it. We were taught how to look for hiding places where information could be stored, such as under desk blotters and in roof panels. Gordon emphasized the need for discipline when carrying out a search. 'Secure the area to be investigated, and then pick a point to start your search. Be methodical and thorough. Don't rush. Make sure you cover the entire area before moving on.'[1]

We were introduced to two other Americans, 'Franky the Felon' and 'Lenny the Locksmith', two OPC operators who were experts at picking locks. They were there to keep the Iraqis honest. If a door was locked, then the Iraqis had an option: find the key, or let Franky or Lenny do their business. Another American, 'Bob', lectured us on the intricacies of processing any documentation that we might discover during the course of our inspection. Bob taught us about making a proper record of any documents that we might find, and getting them into the hands of linguists and the technical experts, who could rapidly evaluate them for their relevance to our job.

Just when we thought we could absorb no more, we were taken outside and given a class on convoy driving procedures. Our American instructors stressed the importance of maintaining strict discipline while driving so that the Iraqis could not split up the convoy and divide the team while en route to a site. By the end of the second day we were actually acting like an inspection team. Regardless of whatever comments one had concerning the level of US influence on the inspection process, there was no doubting that these OPC guys were good.

We flew out early the next morning, aboard a German Air Force C-160 Transall twin-engine transport, painted all white with large black UN markings on the wing and fuselage. The aircraft was fully loaded, with two pallets of inspection equipment and the twenty-eight members of UNSCOM 24. We squeezed onboard, sitting on the red web seats that lined the interior of the aircraft. The C-160 taxied out onto the runway, revved up both engines and took off into the clear blue sky over Manama. Below us stretched the pristine waters of the Persian Gulf. Ahead lay Kuwait and, farther north, Iraq. The flight was a little over two hours in duration. There was some excitement once we crossed into Iraqi airspace when a pair of US Navy F-14 fighters came up alongside us. Charged with enforcing the so-called 'no-fly zone' over southern Iraq (established in March of 1991 to keep Iraqi helicopters and aircraft from bombing and strafing a rebellious Shi'ite population), the F-14s provided us with a brief escort before wagging their wings, hitting their afterburners and zooming off into the southern Iraqi sky. Most of the team members slept in their seats, while a few, especially those who smoked, got up and wandered to the back of the plane to light up.

There were several porthole-type windows in the rear, and we were able to look out at the terrain we were flying over. We were flying a line which roughly paralleled the Tigris river, a brown meandering ribbon of water below us. On either side of the river were large green swathes of the palm groves. We saw irrigation canals emanating from the river, creating a bolt of green fields to stab their way into the tans and browns of the desert, and gray highways, heading north towards Baghdad. There was a lot of nervous energy among those of us who were not sleeping; we were heading into an unknown situation armed only with our wits and the skills we had developed as a team in the previous forty-eight hours. We hoped that would be enough.

We touched down at Habbaniyah Airfield, a giant military facility that had formerly been home to various Iraqi Air Force squadrons, but now lay derelict and bombed out, the shattered carcasses of burned-out fighters scattered around their hardened shelters, each one with a hole carved through its reinforced concrete top where a US laser-guided bomb found its mark. We were greeted on landing by an old green and white Iraqi Airlines bus which drove us to a command post recently converted to receive the only foreign guests to pass through this once top secret facility – UN weapons inspectors.

Each inspector had been issued a blue United Nations laissez-passer, and these were collected by the Iraqi authorities for processing. The Iraqis photocopied each pass, then affixed a square piece of paper emblazoned with the seal of Iraq, an entry visa, inside it. While this went on, the inspection team waited in what had once been a briefing room for Iraqi pilots, and now served as a makeshift reception area for UN inspectors. A large black and white photograph of Saddam Hussein hung on the wall and, together with several nervous Iraqi officials, many wearing the black leather coats we associated with their secret police, maintained a continuous watch over us while we waited.

Our visas finally processed, we were ushered back onto the Iraqi Airways bus for the two-hour drive into Baghdad. We passed through villages untouched by modern conveniences, but populated by a vibrant people who waved at us while carrying out their various daily chores. The closer we got to Baghdad, the more the countryside took on the look of an armed camp, with anti-aircraft guns situated on every hill top, and walled-in barracks housing a variety of military units. For all of this military presence outside the city, however, Baghdad was relatively free of soldiers. Traffic police were stationed throughout the city at key intersections, but for the most part Baghdad seemed no different from any other major Middle Eastern city. That is, until you reached the city center. Suddenly, we would confront a massive building, seemingly picked at random out of the numerous other structures occupying the city block, collapsed in on itself as if it had imploded. Block after block, these destroyed buildings presented themselves, reminders of the precision bombing campaign waged against Baghdad during the Gulf War. A few of the buildings had cranes positioned around them, an obvious sign that some reconstruction was taking place. But the majority of the destroyed buildings remained as they had been in the moments after they had been shattered by the air-delivered high explosive.

We were staying at the Palestine Meridian hotel, right across the street from the Baghdad Sheraton hotel (the seventeenth floor of which served as UNSCOM's Baghdad office). These two hotels were, along with the Al Rasheed hotel, the crown jewels of Baghdad's accommodation. Located directly across the Tigris river from the Republican presidential palace, home to Saddam Hussein and his inner circle, the Palestine Meridian was convenient for inspectors and Iraqis alike. Shadowy Iraqi intelligence and security personnel followed our every move from the moment we disembarked from our bus until we checked into our rooms. It became clear that we were operating in the heart of a foreign power that did not necessarily welcome what we needed to do.

UNSCOM 24 got straight to task, setting out early in the morning of 10 December to inspect our primary target of interest: the Karama Barracks. Our vehicles were marshaled from the parking lot of the Palestinian Meridian hotel, and lined up on the main street in front of the hotel, where our Iraqi counterparts were waiting for us. The Iraqis were not too pleased with the size and makeup of our team, and from the start the UNSCOM 24 convoy was confounded by the relentless attempts of the Iraqis to maneuver their vehicles in between ours. Our pre-inspection convoy training held, and we drove through the streets of Baghdad, a wild ballet of swerving vehicles careening forward at high speed, with only a couple of feet separating us.

Furthering our troubles was the foggy weather and the fact that, despite all of our study and examination of photographs and maps during our planning in Bahrain, one of the main roads we had planned to drive on, and which had been clearly marked on the map as running in both directions, turned out to be a one-way street, with us trying to head down the wrong way. The team took all this in its stride, with the navigation vehicle diverting the convoy along a detour in an effort to get us back in the direction we originally wanted to go.

Any concerns we might have had that the Iraqis were aware of our interest in the Karama Barracks were put to rest by the sight of a drowsy guard quickly trying to shut the gates to the facility, which had been left wide open. Iraqi security vehicles had accelerated ahead of the lead UNSCOM vehicle, blocking its way forward in the driveway, but not before our vehicle, a Nissan Patrol, was able to jam its nose forward far enough to block the gate from being shut.

My sub-team looked eagerly at the cluster of buildings known to us as the 'Karama Barracks Annex'. Our intelligence briefing back in Bahrain listed these buildings as an adjunct to the main barracks, with which it shared a wall. We picked up our inspection equipment, comprising mainly of cameras, flashlights and notepads, and made our way to the annex entrance. I looked at my fellow teammates as the stench of the facility became apparent. It smelled suspiciously like a sewage treatment plant. We continued, certain that there had to be a solid reason for having us inspect this site.

With great precision, we fell into our pre-planned inspection drill, just as we had practiced in Bahrain. Despite the noxious odor that permeated the site, we scoured the facility, combing its entire width and breadth for evidence of weapons of mass destruction.

'Scott, over here.' It was Kevin, a communicator from New Zealand. I made my way over to where he stood. He had opened up a large closet, and my flashlight revealed the presence of five large water pumps leading into an underground basement. 'May be a secret underground chamber,' Kevin said. We followed the pipes underground, two stories down, leading us to a raw sewage reservoir. Despite the foul smell, which left us retching, we probed the reservoir with a pole to make sure nothing had been hidden there. Only then did we climb up to the surface, gasping, trying to fill our lungs with fresh air. As we stood there, crouched over, fighting nausea, all four of us had a hearty laugh at our own expense. 'Well, gentlemen,' I sputtered, 'we definitely got the crappiest job of the inspection.' I turned to my much-amused minder, declared the annex free of weapons of mass destruction, and departed to join the main body of inspectors, who were busy at the main site.[2]

For all of the anticipated drama surrounding the inspection of the Karama Barracks, it turned out to be a bust. Randall Lee came closest to finding something of significance when, going through the desk of the unit security officer, he discovered a general communiqué to all military and police units announcing the anticipated arrival of our inspection team in Iraq, and instructing them to 'take the appropriate measures'. The Iraqis claimed that this meant nothing more than making sure everyone was ready to cooperate with the inspectors, and while we suspected otherwise, there was nothing we could do. Other than that scrap of paper, the facility was empty of anything of significance.

We made our way back to our parked Nissan Patrols, enduring the smiles and laughter of the Iraqi minders, who were clearly having a good time at our expense. My sub-team took a particularly pointed ribbing given our actions at the sewage plant. While outside I did my best to retain my composure, inside I boiled over with anger and frustration. 'John Bird,' I thought to myself, 'is this the best you can come up with?'

The next morning the team headed out west in a large convoy, bedding down for the night outside the town of Al Qaim in trailers once used by Polish construction workers while they built a giant phosphate plant located nearby. We were in the heart of SCUD country. During Desert Storm, the Iraqi missile force had operated with relative impunity from the Al Qaim area throughout the conflict. UNSCOM 24 spent two days sweeping the area around Al Qaim for any trace of a SCUD force. We found none.

John Bird's track record only got worse. After Al Qaim, we shifted our attention to the Shab al-Agharri wadi complex, where Larry Smothers had declared, with great confidence, the existence of hidden SCUD bunkers. I knew from my Gulf War experience that the notion of SCUDs operating in this region of western Iraq was illusory. We looked for SCUD bunkers in vain. John Bird's version of the Great SCUD Hunt had fizzled out.[3]

The inspection was over. It was clear that we had to change how inspections were being conceived and planned. We couldn't simply base our inspections on what the CIA had briefed us to inspect. The information provided by John Bird was uniformly poor in quality, which then begged the question: why was the CIA pushing for this particular inspection at this particular time? UNSCOM knew that the CIA had written a paper after the Gulf War giving Saddam Hussein less than six months to survive the fallout from military defeat and economic ruin. Some commentators had said that the inspection regime was designed more to put pressure on Iraq in order to hasten the departure of Saddam than it was to actually find weapons of mass destruction. From what we had observed during UNSCOM 24, this was no longer such a far-fetched concept. The dominance of the CIA in the UNSCOM 24 process, where the inspection had pretty much been planned by the CIA before John Bird briefed the targets to us in New York, was unacceptable to an organization like UNSCOM, charged with implementing Security Council resolutions with integrity and independence.

I returned from Iraq in time to join my family for the Christmas holiday. On my return to UNSCOM after the New Year, it didn't take long for the issue of UNSCOM-CIA relations to resurface, again through the person of John Bird. Under a new Security Council resolution, which had been passed in October 1991, Iraq was obliged to declare its weapons facilities so that they could be monitored. The Iraqis were given a thirty-day deadline to declare their facilites. That date – 11 November – came and went with nothing from the Iraqis.

Iraq's rejection of Security Council resolution 715 presented Rolf Ekéus with a vexing problem. By the first week of the New Year, there was already pressure from certain members of the Security Council, in particular the USA, to push forward with monitoring of Iraq despite the fact that Iraq had not accepted the monitoring plan as set forth in the resolution. In early January 1992 John Bird flew to New York to brief Rolf Ekéus, Bob Gallucci and Doug Englund on how he thought UNSCOM should proceed.

The plan he proposed was in fact one he had tried to pitch a few weeks earlier while Roger and I were away in Iraq. In December 1991, he had advocated an inspection of the massive military complex at Taji, located around twenty kilometers north of Baghdad. Bird's proposal called for a sweep of the entire complex, ostensibly for the purpose of looking for SCUD missiles, SCUD related equipment, and SCUD command and control documentation which might assist UNSCOM in pinpointing the locations of SCUD units and equipment. In reality the plan seemed to be more about gathering information on the regime than finding SCUDs.

What Bird was proposing amounted to a huge cordon and search operation. Given the vast amounts of sensitive information having absolutely no bearing on the disarmament mandate of the inspectors that would be uncovered through such a process, the Special Commission would have a hard time defending itself in the Security Council against accusations of indiscriminate intelligence gathering, something Doug Englund had pointed out repeatedly to Rolf Ekéus. In December 1991, they didn't move on the proposal.

John Bird obviously thought that Iraq's non-compliance with resolution 715 represented an opportunity to press again for the SCUD search plan. He was rejected yet again in a diplomatic fashion by Rolf Ekéus, who designated it 'premature'. Ekéus, however, realized that he needed to be seen as moving the issue of monitoring inspections forward constructively, or else risk the ire of his number one backer in the Security Council – the USA. By the end of the first week of January, it was becoming clear to Rolf Ekéus that UNSCOM would have to dispatch a delegation to Iraq, known as the 'Special Mission', to discuss Iraq's need to accept monitoring inspections. Ekéus hoped to be seen to be doing something about resolution 715 without compromising UNSCOM's integrity.

Despite all of our efforts to support the Special Mission with quality intelligence, it was an abject failure. The Iraqis pushed aside any argument regarding retained weapons as being 'technical', and instead focused more on the 'political' nature of Special Mission's primary task – to compel Iraq to accept long-term monitoring inspections. The Iraqis refused to acknowledge the legitimacy of Security Council resolution 715, and would not submit a declaration of their weapons programs, saying that such a declaration had already been submitted back in May 1991. This appeared to represent a major setback for the inspectors.[4]

Unfortunately for Iraq, Rolf Ekéus was a diplomatic chess master.[5] He took advantage of a summit of heads of state at the Security Council at the end of January, convened to discuss the 'New World Order' and the role the Security Council would play. Resolution 687 was a critical piece of the foundation of credibility and fortitude required of the Security Council if it were to take on this new role as guarantor of international peace and security, and Rolf Ekéus knew that Iraq's refusal to cooperate could not,

31

and indeed would not, go unchallenged. He lobbied the various members of the Security Council hard, briefing them on the details of the Special Mission and the harsh realities of the Iraqi response, and was rewarded for his labors with a clear statement from the Security Council condemning Iraq's refusal to comply with its obligations.

Ekéus moved quickly to take advantage of this backing. He wanted total Iraqi acceptance of Security Council resolutions 707 (the provision of a full, final and complete declaration of all prohibited programs) and 715 (long-term monitoring). Recognizing that he still held some potent political ammunition in the form of the US satellite photographs of the undeclared Iraqi Al-Nida missile launchers, Rolf Ekéus built his main attack around the issue of ballistic missiles.

The Security Council issued a presidential statement which dispatched Ekéus to Baghdad to 'discuss with the highest levels of the Iraqi government for the purpose of securing the unconditional agreement by Iraq to implement all its relevant obligations under resolutions 687, 707 and 715.' The kicker was in the statement's ominous conclusion: 'The mission should stress the serious consequences if such agreement to implement is not forthcoming.' Ekéus now had what he wanted: the full weight of the Security Council behind him.

His visit, however, did not go as planned. The Iraqis were showing themselves to be shrewd diplomatic players as well. Following an exchange of introductory statements, Ekéus made good on his mission to point out to the senior Iraqi official present, Deputy Prime Minister Tariq Aziz, the serious consequences of Iraq's current position. Tariq Aziz was unapologetic, responding to Ekéus that 'the Security Council also had obligations' – the lifting of sanctions.[6]

Tariq Aziz went on the attack. 'The United States,' he noted, 'has said it would not lift sanctions until the Iraqi regime was changed. If this was the case, why should Iraq cooperate with the Special Commission?' He then pounded home Iraq's main point: 'If the Council resolutions were implemented in a fair manner and sanctions eased, Iraq would cooperate. If Iraq got nothing for cooperation, no purpose would be served. There must be reciprocity.'

The inherent inconsistency of the US position on Iraq, which held that economic sanctions would not be lifted until Saddam Hussein was removed from power, with the letter of Security Council resolutions calling for the lifting of sanctions once disarmament had been achieved, was deftly pointed out by the Iraqis. Up against this logic, Rolf Ekéus could get nowhere, and after three days of fruitless talks, he departed Iraq empty handed.

Sensing weakness in the departure of Rolf Ekéus, the Iraqis decided to dispatch Tariq Aziz to New York to deal directly with the Security Council on this matter.[7] This, of course, was for UNSCOM the worst possible outcome, and not at all what Ekéus had intended. The implications of the failure of the Ekéus mission were ominous, and none knew this better than Ekéus himself. The senior political advisor to the secretary-general noted that this was an election year in the USA, and that a military option was still politically possible. 'Does the US have the means to do this?' he asked. 'Yes,' Ekéus replied soberly, adding that he had just met with the commander of US military forces in Bahrain, who had told the executive chairman that 'a surgical strike could be mounted if Iraq did not comply.'[8]

Having turned back the executive chairman, the Iraqis switched their attention to the UNSCOM 28 inspection. UNSCOM 28 was to have begun supervising the destruction of the dual-use items listed in Ekéus's letter. Now, however, the Iraqis were balking. The team was instructed by Ekéus to give the Iraqis a forty-eight-hour window to reconsider their position. The deadline came and went with no change in the Iraqi stance.

Back in New York, Rolf Ekéus weighed his options carefully. Thinking back on John Bird's proposal on a large missile-oriented inspection, Rolf decided that perhaps that concept was, in fact, no longer 'premature'. Now, faced with Iraqi intransigence, John Bird's new 'SCUD Hunt' offered an opportunity for Ekéus to play the one remaining card he still had close to his chest: the photographs of Iraq's undeclared Al-Nida launchers. He had to seize the initiative away from the Iraqis somehow. The scene was being set for a showdown of potentially mammoth proportions.

Doug and I were worried that John Bird might be directing UNSCOM on yet another wild goose chase. We were mollified somewhat by the realization that it was Rolf Ekéus, and not John Bird, who was making the decisions about both the timing and the political context of the inspection. Even so, the road to independence from the CIA was proving to be full of false turns, potholes and roadblocks.

Chapter 3

Showdown in Baghdad

I was put to work on compiling a list of targets for the UNSCOM 31 inspection, which the new John Bird 'SCUD Hunt' had been named. The 'Bird plan' was to serve as the basis for this inspection, with some twists: the USA was pushing hard for the inclusion of the Iraqi Ministry of Defense and the Military Industrialization Commission (MIC) Headquarters, both of which Rolf Ekéus approved on the grounds that since Iraq had submitted a false declaration about weapons related to both of these ministries, UNSCOM had every right to inspect them in fulfilling its disarmament mandate.

Randall Lee and the CIA's Operations Planning Cell support team had flown up to New York, and were preparing to continue with the planning process for UNSCOM 31. I was assigned as the mission planner for UNSCOM. I was assisted in this preparation by Mark Silver, an Air Force Lieutenant Colonel. Randall Lee and the OPC planners had brought with them large photographic prints of the Taji military complex, from which we were going to plan the detailed inspection of that facility. I was in the process of helping Randall affix these to the walls of the 'bunker' when a stranger in a white shirt and tie entered the room. I looked over at the man, trying to figure out who was barging in on our meeting. He was of medium height, had curly black hair with traces of gray sprinkled in, a round face and a slight paunch. His trousers were held up by suspenders, which when combined with his overall appearance gave him the air more of a college professor than spy.

He introduced himself to me as Stu Cohen, who had just taken over from John Bird as the CIA's new arms control chief. Whereas John Bird had been leading an arms control unit left over from the cold war, Cohen was heading up a brand new unit for the new international environment, the Non-Proliferation Center (NPC). Cohen's approach to working with UNSCOM was much more cooperative and genial than that of his predecessor. At the same time, he was CIA, and there was a limit to how open he could be with me. We were to develop a close if complex working relationship over the years.

From an operational perspective, we were ready to go forward with the UNSCOM 31 inspection whenever ordered. However, Rolf Ekéus was concerned about issues of timing. Ekéus felt that UNSCOM could not be seen as deliberately precipitating a crisis through the conduct of a provocative inspection. As such, UNSCOM 31 was going to have to wait until Tariq Aziz's presentation to the Security Council, which was scheduled for mid-March. This way, it would be seen as a response to that presentation. However, the fact that UNSCOM was planning a massive inspection was not kept secret.

For the first few days after his arrival in New York, Tariq Aziz made a point of ignoring Rolf Ekéus, driving home Iraq's point that it should deal with the Security Council directly rather than work through UNSCOM, an organ of the Council. Surprisingly, the Security Council seemed to be playing right into Iraqi hands, giving Tariq Aziz an unprecedented chance to deliver Iraq's case before the Council. If Tariq Aziz were able to make his points eloquently and persuasively, Rolf Ekéus and UNSCOM would find themselves on the defensive.

Instead, Tariq Aziz berated the Council, calling its resolutions on Iraq unfair and unjust. He then went on to say that Iraq was free of weapons of mass destruction, not even attempting to answer the concerns of the Council, either in his presentation, or in response to questions afterwards. His performance united the Council in a way nothing else could and, on 12 March, the president of the Security Council issued a statement that condemned Iraq's stance and reaffirmed UNSCOM as the final arbiter on all technical matters regarding implementation of relevant Security Council resolutions.

Having been rebuked at the Security Council, Tariq Aziz and his deputy for disarmament issues, Lieutenant General Amer Rashid, awaited the inevitable response from UNSCOM. With the reinvigorated support of the Security Council, Rolf Ekéus felt he had achieved a solid political victory, and sought to get on with his disarmament tasks from this new position of strength. With the Security Council behind him, Ekéus felt confident that he could persuade Iraq to accept long-term monitoring. But we were now left with the planned inspection, which Ekéus had only accepted as a way of breaking through the diplomatic stalemate. In the new political context, UNSCOM 31 was simply too aggressive: in its intended form, it might precipitate armed conflict between the USA and Iraq, at which point UNSCOM would be in danger of becoming redundant. As if to underscore this point, US military forces, including a fresh carrier task force, were streaming into the Persian Gulf by 14 March 1992. The Bush administration seemed intent on taking advantage of any opening to place Iraq under pressure it hoped would result in internal unrest that destabilized and hopefully evicted the regime of Saddam Hussein. The drums of war were beating ever louder, and Rolf desperately wanted to silence them, if for no other reason than to give his new lease of diplomatic life a chance to succeed.

Rolf Ekéus needed the Iraqis to make a bold move to dissipate the tension, but he also knew he couldn't wait for them to act on their own volition. Ekéus decided to give them a little nudge. In a private discussion with Tariq Aziz, he disclosed UNSCOM's biggest secret: UNSCOM had photographic evidence that it was prepared to show to the Security Council that proved Iraq had lied about the numbers of missiles and missile launchers in its inventory.[1]

Tariq Aziz demanded to see this evidence, a request Ekéus refused, but the point had been made. The Iraqis had known an inspection was imminent. Now they knew what the inspection would be focusing on, and could prepare for it. Ekéus just hoped they would make the right choices during this preparation, which would be to pre-empt the UNSCOM 31 mission by coming clean on the issue of retained ballistic missiles and other proscribed weapons.

Back in Baghdad, I later found out, Tariq Aziz made a full presentation to Saddam Hussein and the Iraqi Council of Ministers on the results of his visit to New York. An avid consumer of western news reports, Saddam Hussein was aware of the growing US military buildup around his borders. But he did nothing. Unbeknownst to us, Saddam Hussein had in fact unilaterally destroyed stockpiles of WMD in 1991. What he didn't want to do was admit that there had been anything to destroy – which was why Iraq's declaration to UNSCOM had been so evasive.

Like a drug dealer deciding to come clean by flushing his stash down the toilet all the while claiming to the police that he'd never had any drugs, Iraq came clean by disarming itself, without admitting its past guilt. As the US military continued to deploy around Iraq's borders, Saddam and his inner council debated what to do. Amer Rashid pointed out to the assembled ministers that the inspectors were well organized and well informed. If Iraq tried to maintain the fiction that its initial declaration given to the inspectors was correct, there was a good chance the UN inspectors would be able to expose this as a fallacy, with devastating consequences.

Both Tariq Aziz and Amer Rashid had sensed Rolf Ekéus's desire to avoid conflict. The UNSCOM executive chairman was dispatching an inspection team to Iraq, and the expectations were that this would be another highly confrontational mission. Amer Rashid proposed that Iraq pre-empt the inspection by admitting that its initial declarations had been a mistake. Iraq should admit what it had done in the summer of 1991 in the way of unilateral destruction, and cooperate with the inspectors on any effort to investigate and verify the new Iraqi claims.

Amer Rashid's strategy was simple, yet straightforward: admit the past deceit, and agree to submit a new declaration which detailed the unilateral destruction. Iraq should also submit to the inevitability of the destruction of the 'dual-use' equipment. By making these concessions, Iraq would defuse a potentially explosive situation, and buy political capital it would need for its campaign to get economic sanctions lifted. Everyone in the Council of Ministers agreed that Iraq could not accept Security Council resolution 715, and with it the notion of long-term monitoring inspections, until sanctions were lifted.

There were only two objections. Hussein Kamal, Saddam's son-in-law and director of Iraq's Military Industrialization Corporation, argued that Iraq could not admit any aspect of its biological warfare program. 'The world would not understand,' he said, 'and condemn us even though it has been destroyed.' Qusay, the younger son of Saddam who headed the Special Security Organization responsible for presidential security, insisted that, in the declarations to be made, the role of Special Security in the events of the summer of 1991 was never to be disclosed. 'Tell the truth as much as possible, but do not provide any excuse for the inspectors to ask about the president.'

Qusay had another reason as well. Under his direction, the Special Security Organization was holding onto a secret archive of documents pertaining to Iraq's missile, chemical, biological and nuclear weapons programs, documents which provided the 'seed stock' for any future resurrection of Iraq's weapons of mass destruction programs. His motivations for keeping the inspectors from investigating the Special Security Organization went beyond simply trying to protect Saddam Hussein. He was protecting Iraq's continued effort to conceal WMD capability, albeit of a future and hypothetical nature, from the UNSCOM inspectors.

Saddam directed that the Special Committee on Concealment activities prepare a plan for the declaration of unilateral destruction. The Concealment Committee did so, appointing Amer Rashid as the person responsible for its implementation.[2]

In Bahrain, tensions were running high. We inspectors knew nothing of the events transpiring in Baghdad. All one had to do was turn on a television set and listen to the reports of US troop movements on the BBC and CNN to know that events were rapidly spiraling into crisis mode. And now UNSCOM was assembling an inspection team that would not only operate in the midst of this crisis, but might also serve as a trigger for military action.

On 19 March 1992, the Iraqis, having discerned international opinion about their obstinacy and having learned from Rolf Ekéus that there was incontrovertible evidence of their cheating, finally provided their response. In a stunning admission, the Iraqis acknowledged that their earlier declarations had been incomplete, and that in the field of ballistic missiles they had failed to declare some eighty-nine operational missiles and eight mobile launchers. There it was: Iraq's covert ballistic missile force, almost exactly as I had concluded in my analysis of November 1991. In that paper, I had assessed a retained force of a dozen launchers and up to a hundred missiles.

The Iraqis had thrown in a fascinating twist, however. All of the retained material had been unilaterally destroyed by Iraq back in July 1991. There were no missiles or missile-related equipment remaining in Iraq, only destroyed debris. Within the course of a few minutes, UNSCOM 31's mission had been changed from one of confrontational searches for hidden weapons to a more conventional verification and destruction inspection. The Iraqis had played their hand masterfully, cutting the legs out from under the military buildup then taking place, nullifying the secret intelligence that Rolf Ekéus had been holding back, and transferring the onus of verification onto the shoulders of UNSCOM. Verification of material unilaterally destroyed would prove to be a difficult task.

We arrived in Iraq on 19 March, in almost an exact repeat of our experience during UNSCOM 24. Once again the Palestine Meridian Hotel was to be our home while in Baghdad. It had been only three months since I had last been in Iraq, but the change was clearly noticeable. The country was reconstructing itself as best as it could. Bridges and buildings were being rebuilt. Baghdad still bore the wounds of the pounding it had taken during Operation Desert Storm, but these wounds now had scabs on them in the form of scaffolding, bricks and mortar. That Iraq had been expecting even more bombing was evidenced by the proliferation of anti-aircraft artillery around greater Baghdad. It didn't matter that it was early spring, a time of rebirth and regeneration. Despite its efforts at reconstruction, Iraq was a country still very much under the cloud of war and strife.

We held a short meeting with our Iraqi counterparts in the evening, after we had checked the team into the hotel and sorted out our equipment. The Iraqis, led by an Iraqi colonel named Hossam Amin, informed us that everything would be made clear in the morning, and that they proposed that the team wait to ask any questions until after the Iraqi presentation on the new declaration was made.

The following day, our first destination was the Daura refinery, located on the southwestern corner of the Baghdad metropolitan area. At the site, Colonel Hossam Amin introduced two other Iraqi officers who would be helping him. Both officers, Hossam Amin informed us, had been involved in the destruction of the missiles during the summer of 1991 and would be able to answer our questions.

Hossam Amin, a short man of medium build with an aquiline nose, sporting the thick black Saddam Hussein-style mustache which seemed more or less compulsory amongst Iraqi men, was an engineer by training. He had worked in various technical and managerial positions within the Iraqi Military Industrial Commission (MIC) during his career. His last job, before Desert Storm, had been as the head of the office of the deputy director for MIC, Lieutenant General Amer al-Sa'adi. In this position Hossam Amin had become intimately familiar with every aspect of Iraq's weapons of mass destruction programs and the related industrial and military organizations. He was a natural to head the new office in MIC responsible for coordination with the UNSCOM inspectors. Only forty-two years of age in 1992, with his close-cropped hair and black mustache just barely touched by gray, Hossam Amin was a hard worker who had risen to his position by force of merit, above and beyond the fact that his family was from Tikrit, and he himself was a distant cousin of Saddam Hussein.

The UNSCOM inspectors worked off a list of questions prepared in Bahrain immediately after the details of the 19 March Iraqi declaration became known. 'How did the eighty-nine missiles declared by Iraq as having been unilaterally destroyed fit into the accounting for the 819 missiles already declared?' This was an important point that needed to be established right up front. Were the Iraqis declaring an additional eighty-nine missiles, above and beyond the 819 they had declared to have received from the former Soviet Union, or were these newly declared missiles part of the force which the original declaration claimed had been fired?

Hossam Amin read Iraq's answer with little emotion: 'The eighty-nine missiles represented in the recent declaration are included in the 819 missiles originally declared by Iraq. Iraq will provide a full, accurate and complete accounting of how the 819 missiles were disposed of.'

This caught my attention. The Iraqis had been cheating in their original declaration. According to the 1991 declaration, all 819 missiles had been carefully accounted for. We now knew that the Iraqis had padded their original declaration to hide the continued existence of at least eighty-nine missiles. We had suspected as much, which is why I had assessed that Iraq had been hiding up to a hundred missiles. We now knew this to be the case. UNSCOM was going to have to crunch the numbers all over again, and insist on a high standard of verification if this new Iraqi declaration was going to hold water.

The big question came next: 'If these eighty-nine newly declared missiles were destroyed last summer, why is their destruction being declared only now?'

Hossam Amin again read from his carefully prepared answers: 'Iraq was concerned that the political situation that existed in the summer of 1991 – the threat of renewed bombing of Iraq by the United States – would lead to a misunderstanding of Iraq's possession of weapons in excess of the numbers presented in the original declaration.' This raised the question of why Iraq had submitted a false declaration to begin with, something I jotted down in the margin of my notes.

We asked when the missiles had been destroyed, to which Hossam Amin responded, 'Between 15 and 20 July 1991.' As to how they were destroyed, the answer was with explosives. And to our questions about notes, pictures, video or any other documentation to back up Iraq's claim of destruction, Hossam Amin provided the same stock answer: 'No such records were kept of the destruction, as the entire operation was secret and conducted in a manner not conducive to record keeping.'[3]

Writing down Hossam Amin's answers, I was growing more and more concerned that something did not ring true in what we were being told.

The inspection of the destruction sites was anti-climactic. We were shown pits, where the Iraqis claimed to have blown up warheads, and other burial areas, where the Iraqis had disposed of missile components and guidance and control devices. This was a verification nightmare, more an exercise in forensic archeology than arms control. But through it all the technical experts remained focused, trying to accumulate the details that would enable us to assemble as complete a picture as possible about what had happened to those eighty-nine missiles. Each missile destroyed contained parts, such as the engine and missile frame components, which were unique to a given missile. We collected the serial numbers from each of the missile parts we discovered, which enabled us to determine if we had enough parts to verify with certainty that a missile had in fact been destroyed. By the end of our stay, we were able to verify eighty-seven of the eighty-nine destroyed missiles as being accounted for using this methodology. UNSCOM 31 was over, out with a whimper instead of the anticipated bang.[4]

By April 1992, Doug Englund's time with UNSCOM was up. The constant battles with Washington had taken their toll, and Doug was ready to hang up his spurs and retire after a long and distinguished Army career which had seen service from the jungles of Vietnam to the snow of Russia and the sands of the Middle East. In the years ahead, Doug was replaced as UNSCOM's director of operations by a successive string of US military officers, none of whom was able to truly lead UNSCOM in the manner that Doug had.

Spring came, and UNSCOM found itself struggling to redefine its work. We were still trying to come to grips with the 19 March Iraqi declaration on unilateral destruction. Prior to that date, all eyes in the Security Council had been focused on Iraq and the issue of Iraqi non-compliance. Now, with the declaration of unilateral destruction, the focus of attention was on UNSCOM. Was the Iraqi declaration sufficient? Were they now in compliance? Iraq certainly seemed to think so, and was starting a charm offensive within the Security Council, France and Russia in the forefront, that the time was ripe for the lifting of sanctions. The Iraqi government made much of the plight of the Iraqi people, suffering under the burden of economic sanctions. An effort by the Security Council to divert funds raised through the sale of Iraqi oil for the purchase of humanitarian goods, resolution 706 – the so-called 'oil-for-food' agreement – had lapsed on 18 March, and Iraq did not seem inclined to take the world's charity. Saddam Hussein wanted the total lifting of economic sanctions, nothing less.

The UNSCOM mission was becoming complicated. I was busy trying to help put together an inspection that could adequately challenge the Iraqis in the field of ballistic missiles. Everyone was still stinging from what had transpired after UNSCOM 31, when Tariq Aziz had gone over Rolf Ekéus's head and started dealing with the Security Council directly. There was a general consensus that UNSCOM needed to do something in response in order to assert its status as an inspection authority. Dramatic as the 19 March declaration had been, there were still many aspects of the Iraqi ballistic missile program, not to mention the rest of Iraq's weapons of mass destruction programs, that were unverified or unknown.

Throughout the verification process that had emerged since 19 March, UNSCOM had been requesting from the Iraqis documents or any other form of physical evidence that would sustain the substance of their declaration. This was especially vital given the fact that the process of unilateral destruction had, in and of itself, destroyed enough material that a final accounting based on complete verification of the physical evidence was impossible. There would always be gaps in the physical material balance. UNSCOM needed to fill in these gaps with documents that showed what Iraq had, and what the final disposition of this material was. The Iraqi authorities contended that there was no such documentary record, and UNSCOM would have to make do with what Iraq had already provided in the form of the 19 March declaration, and the subsequent inspections.

Deep inside the shadowy realm of the CIA, new inspection ideas were being hatched to address the issue of the missing documents. The general concept for these inspections involved a document search of facilities in and around Baghdad believed to contain archives related to Iraq's prohibited programs. There was a growing concern among UNSCOM's supporters in the Security Council, America and the United Kingdom in particular, that Iraq, having made its 19 March declaration, was gaining the political initiative, and could seize it outright if it submitted a remotely credible declaration concerning its weapons holdings. UNSCOM would then be in a position where it would either have to produce evidence of Iraqi non-compliance, or pass judgment on Iraq's disarmament. The latter, of course, was the last thing the USA wanted to happen given its policy of maintaining economic sanctions until Saddam was removed, and Ekéus was being pressured by Washington to carry out an aggressive program of searches that would either find evidence of Iraqi non-compliance, or at least help maintain the notion that Iraq was non-compliant. Lacking any new intelligence material of our own concerning documents, we had no choice but to turn to Stu Cohen and the CIA for help.

By early June 1992, the CIA's Operations Planning Cell team had put together a shopping list of sites relating to Iraq's chemical, biological and ballistic missile weapons programs, and had assembled a team of document search experts, including Randall Lee and Gordon Cooper, to assist in the inspection of these sites. UNSCOM was organizing several teams, which would go into Iraq in sequence to carry out these searches. I was put in charge of coordinating the ballistic missile effort, which was scheduled to take place in mid-July. By the last week of June, the inspection plan for the missile investigation had been finalized with the exception of one site, which in typical fashion happened to be the most critical of all.

For weeks, rumors had been circulating inside UNSCOM's inner circle about 'Saddam's secret archive', a treasure trove of documents concerning Iraq's prohibited weapons. The source of the information was an Iraqi defector who had ended up in Germany and was in the process of being debriefed by a joint German-British intelligence team. The USA got wind of this information and slipped a target, the 'Office of Military Industrialization archives' (OMI), into the list of sites to be inspected, with a promise that more information would be forthcoming. However, the USA wasn't in control of the defector who was providing the information, and days passed without any new facts, let alone a location. This site was the cornerstone of the UNSCOM 40 inspection, and here we were, a few weeks away from the start of the inspection, and we had nothing.

I took the opportunity during the visit of a senior British intelligence official to UNSCOM to request that a special effort be made to get the required information to UNSCOM as soon as possible. 'It is from a discreet source that the Germans very much want to protect.'

I surmised from this that the British intelligence official was speaking indirectly about a human source, generally considered to be the most sensitive in the intelligence business. I said I understood. 'But,' I added, 'without more information, we may have to scrub the entire inspection. What good is "discreet" information if we can't use it?'

The British official agreed to try. 'If I'm able to get you something, it will need to be strictly compartmented,' the official said, meaning that I would have to limit the number of people aware of the information to as few as possible, on a strict need-to-know basis. I nodded yes. 'Give me a day,' the official said, and left.

The next morning, 26 June, a plain manila envelope arrived by courier from the UK Mission to the UN, addressed to me. Inside was a sheaf of classified papers providing details on the location of the OMI archive, as well as two other sites of interest in Baghdad and one near Mosul. The British had come through.

Using the British information, combined with detailed examination of U-2 imagery of the area, I was able to pinpoint the location of the suspected archive. I finished by double-checking the geographic coordinates so I could type them up in the Notification of Inspection Site (NIS) document required for the inspection. The NIS was UNSCOM's version of a search warrant, and the executive chairman's signature on one meant that Iraq had to grant the inspection team wielding the document immediate and unrestricted access to the designated site. The NIS was among the most important and, because it identified the area of inspection interest, most sensitive of all the documents produced by UNSCOM.

Around 10 a.m. on 1 July, I put together two folders, one containing the UNSCOM 40 paperwork and the other containing U-2 flight notification letters for the Iraqis (the Information Assessment Unit was responsible for submitting this paperwork on time), and I headed toward the Executive Offices. Olivia, Rolf Ekéus's executive secretary, was on leave, so the desk was being filled by Patricia (pseudonym), a UN staff member from Disarmament Affairs. I put the two folders in the chairman's 'In' basket. 'For the boss's signature,' I said. 'Call me when he has signed them, so I can come pick them up.'

Around 2 p.m., after lunch, I started getting concerned about the UNSCOM 40 paperwork. With a big three-day holiday approaching, I was nervous that people, including the chairman, might start trickling out early, leaving the documents unsigned. I headed up to the thirty-first floor, and stopped in front of Patricia. 'Has the boss signed the documents yet?' I asked.

Patricia looked up from where she was working. 'Oh, yes… The courier came an hour ago to take them to the Iraqi Mission.'

My heart dropped to my stomach. In as calm a voice as I could manage, I leaned over the desk, looking at Patricia.

'You mean that the courier picked up the U-2 notifications… What about the NIS documents?'

Patricia got a confused look in her eyes. 'Weren't they all U-2 notifications?'

All she saw was my back as I sprinted out of the Executive Suite, down the stairs, and into Mark Silver's cubicle. 'We have a problem,' I told a stunned Mark.

The next day Mark and I were winging our way across the Atlantic in a last-ditch attempt to jump-start the inspection before the Iraqis realized the gift that had been given them in the form of the NIS documents. If the Iraqis were able to respond before we could act, then any chance we had of finding the secret document archive was lost. We arrived in Baghdad on 4 July, and joined forces with a chemical inspection team already in the country, headed by Karen Jansen, a major in the US Army whom I knew from the Gulf War, when we had both served on the staff of General Schwartzkopf. The coming day, 5 July, would be our date with destiny.

We had arrived at our prime suspect site just before 10 a.m. I noted that its location and layout fitted exactly with the description given by British intelligence. My suspicion that we had indeed hit on the right target was confirmed when the Iraqis promptly blocked our entry, prompting the team to surround the facility in order to prevent anyone from leaving the site without our knowledge.

I was sitting in my vehicle, controlling the positioning of the team over the Motorola radio. Many of the Iraqi minders were congregating in a nearby park under the shade of a huge tree, out of the direct sunlight which was starting to bake Baghdad. My vehicle was standing just in front of a large cement pedestal containing a mural of Saddam Hussein, on horseback, leading a charge of Arab horsemen.

Sitting next to me was the senior UNSCOM linguist, Sami Abu Faris, a Syrian-born United Nations translator who served as the interpreter for the Chief Inspector. 'What's going on?' I asked him, gesturing towards the building to my right. Sami shook his head, almost sadly. 'The Iraqis are objecting to our presence here. They say the building is a ministry, and that it is off limits to inspectors.'

I was surprised to hear this. 'A ministry?', I asked. 'How can we be sure they are not just making that up?' Sami laughed, and grabbed me by the arm. We walked a few steps, until we were face to face with a bronze plaque that clearly had been here for some time. Sami read the Arabic inscription: 'Ministry of Agriculture'.

Karen notified Rolf Ekéus of the situation by satellite telephone. It was Sunday, the third day of a three-day holiday, and Ekéus was having trouble tracking down the president of the Security Council, let alone any of the Permanent Members. At the very moment when UNSCOM needed a swift, decisive action from the Security Council, the Security Council was unreachable.

Three o'clock approached, and still no word from the chairman. It was quitting time at the Ministry, but the workers were locked inside, prohibited from leaving. Employees, mainly women, were gathering in the windows and chanting slogans at the inspectors surrounding the building.

I remained in my vehicle, monitoring the radio. I stared for a while at the mural of Saddam Hussein. 'What is the meaning of this painting, Sami?' I asked the elderly interpreter. He looked at it for a moment, then replied, 'It is the battle of Qadissiyah, the great victory of Sa'd bin Abi Waqqas over the Persians, in the seventh century… Saddam called the Iran-Iraq War the new Qadissiyah… he is depicting himself as a great warrior in the mould of the old myths.'

I looked at the mural again. Originally, I had thought the concept of Saddam and the Iraqis being on the offensive humorous, especially given the recent history of the Gulf War. Now, sitting in my vehicle, watching the event play out around me, I wondered if in fact Saddam wasn't taking the offensive again, in an effort to drive out this new scourge of invaders who called themselves UN inspectors.

By evening in Baghdad, Rolf Ekéus had managed to get hold of the president of the Security Council, which at the time was the Ambassador from Cape Verde, and had briefed him on the situation. However, the Council president wasn't going to convene a meeting to discuss this issue until Monday, meaning we had at least another twenty-four hours before any guidance came forth from New York other than wait and hold.

We had a crisis brewing inside the ministry building that had to be addressed. Around 3 p.m. the Iraqis had started exiting the building, trying to go home at the end of the working day. When the inspectors at the gate insisted on physically inspecting every Iraqi leaving for documents, including women, the Iraqi officials protested, and ordered all Iraqis to return to the building. By 5 p.m. a crowd was gathered at the steps of the ministry building, angry workers who wanted to go home. Glances from the Iraqis to the inspectors became harder, gestures more threatening, and anti-American chants were starting to be called out. If the situation wasn't resolved soon, we were going to have a riot on our hands. I intervened with the senior Iraqi minder, telling him that he was responsible for maintaining order. 'Mr. Scott,' he said, shrugging his shoulders, 'it is you who have created this situation. You seek to insult our women by frisking them. There is nothing we can do.' I went to Karen Jansen and told her something needed to be done. 'Frisk the men, and let the women go with a cursory examination of their purses,' I suggested. Karen agreed. We told the Iraqis what our conditions were, and soon Iraqis were streaming out of the gates, where they were searched by team members in accordance to our agreed procedures. I watched as Iraqi women in voluminous black dresses and robes came out, showed the inspectors the contents of their purses, and left. We really didn't have a choice.

We broke the team up into shifts to better maintain a twenty-four-hour watch on the surrounded ministry. The next morning Karen called New York for an update. Rolf Ekéus had held meetings with all the members of the Security Council, and a draft statement promising 'the severest consequences' if Iraq did not comply with our desire to inspect the ministry was being prepared. However, the good news went sour later in the evening, when Karen reported that the Security Council, in an emergency session, had dropped the reference to 'severe consequences' from the language of the presidential statement. Even worse, the alterations were made at the insistence of the new American ambassador, William Perkins, who had just taken over from the veteran Thomas Pickering.

As opposed to their 'forward-leaning' stance in March, when military forces had sallied forth in an effort to put pressure on Iraq during the UNSCOM 31 inspection, the White House had determined that Saddam's regime, far from being unstable, had actually gained strength from these confrontations, and a decision was made at the National Security Council to avoid confrontation with Iraq until after the presidential election in November. After that election, the Bush administration planned to develop a new policy to undermine and overthrow Saddam Hussein. In the meantime, inconclusive inspections at least kept sanctions up. They saw no need to push the Iraqis particularly hard for access to the Ministry of Agriculture. We were expected to just go through the motions.

What the Americans weren't expecting was for us to unexpectedly hit the jackpot. They didn't know about the British intelligence on the Office of Military Industrialization archive. To the surprise of just about everyone, it turned out to be accurate. White House policy and inspection objectives were not meshing. At the point in time when UNSCOM most needed a resolute America ready to back up our actions at any cost, we instead got a confused and impotent America, unsure of what to do in the face of a growing crisis.

The leadership in Iraq all tuned into CNN for their information, and were well aware of the breaking news from New York. Galvanized by the weak American response, the next morning the Iraqis brought in busloads of demonstrators for protests in front of the Ministry of Agriculture. It was almost comical to see the forty to fifty people mull about, almost as if they were on holiday, then watch the agitators arrive, distribute the banners and placards, and then lead the group down Al Mawsil street to the Ministry of Agriculture building. The media was on hand, and filmed the demonstrators in a manner in which the crowd seemed larger than it actually was. While on camera the crowd put on a dramatic face, but when off camera everything was fun and games. Later, before boarding their buses back to wherever they had come from, Iraqi government officials handed out food parcels to the participants. For them, it had been a good day. For the inspectors manning the perimeter, the demonstrations provided a break from the monotony of standing watch.

Each passing day saw the crowds of demonstrators get larger. By day three there must have been close to 200 people, claiming to be family members of the ministry employees, carrying signs demanding that UNSCOM not be allowed to gather the personnel files of their relatives and turn them over to the Israeli Mossad. Mothers and children paraded down the street with these crudely lettered banners. But the carnival atmosphere gave way to concern as effigies of Rolf Ekéus and President Bush were brought out and hung, and an American flag was burnt in front of my car.

Afterwards, I sat on the hood of my Nissan Patrol, together with Sami Abu Faris and Mike, a burly Canadian explosives specialist, staring at the ashes of the burned flag. After several days of being in the constant presence of one another, a certain bond was forming between the inspectors and the minders. The minders avoided any political discussions, and instead talked about their families and how difficult life was in post-war Iraq. We differentiated these scientists and engineers from the Iraqi security types, for whom we formulated nicknames. There was the one man, blessed with a shock of fire-red hair, whom we named 'carrot-top'. Another man acquired the moniker 'no-neck', for obvious reasons. The minders, all professional engineers, treated these security men with respect, and they were not afraid of them. But the minders didn't have the same nonchalance about a second group of security types who had taken up positions around the ministry in the past day, quiet men in dark trousers and white shirts from the *Amn al-Amm*, Saddam's secret police. We were starting to attract some interesting company.

The UNSCOM 40 inspection, which had begun with a great sense of purpose, started to sputter to a close. As inspectors, we had done what we could to succeed, and we had nothing to be ashamed of. There was now little to do other than keep the rotation at the ministry running smoothly, and administer to the various needs of the team members, who themselves were struggling with the age-old enemy of static operations – boredom. For every inspector who spent hours at a time staring at the brick wall surrounding the Ministry of Agriculture, the thoughts of home and the loved ones were their only solace.

On Friday 10 July, the Iraqis hit the inspectors with the biggest, and most confrontational, demonstration to date. Thousands of people, encouraged by Iraqi government agitators, swarmed around the inspectors' vehicles, shouting slogans and pelting the inspectors with fruit, vegetables and raw eggs. Afterwards, when the protestors had gone, we got out and surveyed the damage. The area around our vehicles looked like a hurricane had just swept through an open-air food market, with apples, oranges, cabbage and broken eggs scattered all around. Our vehicles were likewise a mess, the egg yolk quickly hardening under the Baghdad sun. I notified Karen about the turn of events. 'The Iraqis have been escalating their demonstrations every day,' I said, 'and this was pretty bad. I'm worried about what will happen during the next demonstration, or the one after that.'

Then, in a surprising turn of events, Karen and I were summoned back to New York by Rolf Ekéus for 'discussions'. In New York, teams of experts were gathering to review a new declaration recently submitted by Iraq, the so-called 'full, final and complete declaration' promised by Iraq in the aftermath of the 19 March declaration. In accordance with the executive chairman's instructions, Mark Silver, who had accompanied me to Iraq, was appointed to replace Karen Jansen as chief inspector of UNSCOM 40. Karen and I protested vigorously, noting that our rightful place was here, in Baghdad, with our team, finishing the job we had started. But our protests were to no avail. Rolf Ekéus was digging in for a siege outside the Ministry of Agriculture, and wanted his experts gathered around him in New York as he weathered the storm.

Karen and I arrived in Bahrain to dramatic news from Baghdad: during the daily demonstration, an Iraqi had set himself on fire in front of the ministry, burning himself badly. The scene was broadcast around the world on every television network. The standoff in front of the Ministry of Agriculture was very much on the front page of international news, and it felt odd watching it from a distance.[5]

The demonstrations in front of the Ministry building increased in frequency and intensity. Physical assaults against inspectors in their off-duty hours increased. Roger Hill narrowly escaped being run over by a car as he crossed between the Palestine Hotel to the Sheraton Hotel. Rocks and bottles were thrown at inspectors, and death threats were made via phone and letter. The link between Security Council inaction and the increase in violence against inspectors seemed clear. Unable to come up with anything on their own, the Security Council instructed Rolf Ekéus to fly yet again to Baghdad in order to break the impasse. However, this time Ekéus lacked the kind of strong statement of support from the Council that he had had back in February.

From the moment of his arrival in Iraq on 16 July, Rolf Ekéus was treated with contempt. Playing off the silence of the Security Council, Iraq refused to consider an inspection of the ministry by UNSCOM inspectors. Ekéus offered to do a pre-survey of the site using an experienced inspector, who would determine if a full-scale inspection would be required. Tariq Aziz brusquely rejected this. Ekéus then tried to modify the Iraqi stance, saying that non-UNSCOM inspectors might be acceptable, if they were selected and trained by UNSCOM beforehand. Again, Tariq Aziz waved off even this compromise. The Iraqis knew they had Ekéus cornered. They were moving in for the kill. Rolf Ekéus had no choice but to leave.

The White House, originally trying to avoid a confrontation with Iraq during the height of the presidential political season, started to wake up to the fact that the situation with Iraq was spinning out of control. Soon

American officials finally started to talk of war if Iraq did not cooperate. The Russians warned the Iraqis to back off or pay the consequences, and the president of the Security Council issued a statement rejecting Tariq Aziz's demands.

But the Iraqis were not finished. On 22 July, an Iraqi male approached the inspectors parked in front of the ministry. He was not viewed suspiciously, as he had been mingling with the Iraqi minders for about an hour. Without warning, the man lunged through the window of one of the parked cars and tried to stab the driver, a British linguist named Steve, with a skewer. Steve was able to block the attack, and together with the passenger (one of the OPC operators), subdued the attacker until the Iraqi minders came and took him into custody. But rather than apprehend the attacker, the Iraqi minders passed him off to Iraqi security personnel, who shook the man's hands and allowed him to leave the site. For Mark Silver, this was the final straw. The situation had already deteriorated beyond any acceptable standard, and now the lives of his inspectors were being placed at risk. Mark Silver called New York, and informed the chairman that he was withdrawing the team.

Eighteen days after it had started, the siege of the Agriculture Ministry was over. No longer would I laugh at the thought of Saddam as Sa'd bin Abi Waqqas, leading the attack at Qadissiyah.

The Iraqis had won.

Chapter 4

Counterattack
August–October 1992

The retreat of UNSCOM 40 from Baghdad had been a crushing blow. UNSCOM had, as an organization, been humiliated in the eyes of the world. A compromise was eventually reached, a pseudo-inspection was allowed to take place six days after the withdrawal of Mark Silver's team. In the interim the Iraqis evacuated the archive and, by the time the new inspection had arrived on scene, the Ministry of Agriculture had been emptied.[1] Nothing was found, yielding the Iraqis yet another political victory. There was a lot of anger and frustration in UNSCOM – many hardliners believed the team should never have abandoned the site, even under attack. The more reasonable staff believed that, once abandoned, the site should never have been inspected, since it had clearly been compromised. But the fact is, once we started this process, there had to be closure, and the inspection, as frustrating as it was, represented just that.

I strongly believed that it was critical for UNSCOM to immediately challenge Iraq on the issue of inspection access. But we needed to fight smart. One of the lessons of the UNSCOM 40 fiasco was that UNSCOM could no longer take for granted the automatic support of the USA, or even what form that support would take if any was forthcoming. Having experienced the fallout of an inspection conducted without full US backing, the reality was that UNSCOM planners would have to sell all future inspections not only to the executive chairman, but also to the US government.

I started to look at ways of challenging Iraqi non-cooperation. I needed to look no further than the recently submitted Iraqi ballistic missile declaration for a technical justification for inspection. Based upon my review of past inspection missions in Iraq, I quickly saw that the Iraqi document was full of half-truths and numerous inconsistencies. I leafed through the Iraqi declaration, and began jotting down the potential inspection targets that sprung up from the Iraqi lies. Soon I had ten which could be easily justified on technical grounds.

I walked upstairs to the office of Nikita Smidovich, the Russian arms control specialist. Nikita occupied an office cubicle on the thirtieth floor of the UN Secretariat building, not far from where I sat. When I knocked on his door, he was crouched behind his desk, papers splayed out across it, and a lit cigarette in his fingers. One look at the ash tray on his desk provided proof positive that Nikita and cigarettes were inseparable. The confined space of his cubicle was filled with a blueish haze, and the smell of tobacco smoke permeated the air.

Smidovich was a close confidant of Rolf Ekéus, having worked with him in the past when the two were assigned to their respective missions in Geneva, Switzerland. He was a brilliant man and, when Ekéus was appointed chairman of UNSCOM, one of his first actions was to request that Nikita Smidovich be assigned to his staff. A large man with brooding eyes, Smidovich had a sweeping walrus mustache which, when combined with his thick brow and shock of unruly hair, gave him the look of a wild Cossack straight off the steppes of Russia, even when dressed in his diplomat's gray suit.

Smidovich, like myself, had been offered a permanent staff position with UNSCOM, which he accepted. Rolf Ekéus offered Smidovich the job of deputy director for operations, although the Russian had no military or operational experience whatsoever, knowing that his brilliance and calm demeanor would more than compensate for any deficiency in his operation's résumé. Ekéus was right, and Smidovich was performing his new job in a brilliant fashion. I slid my proposal across his desk, sat down, and awaited his response.

Rolf Ekéus was in Baghdad, chaperoning the face-saving pseudo-inspection following the Ministry of Agriculture standoff. From Baghdad, he was planning to proceed to Vienna, where he maintained a residence. August was the classic vacation month for Europeans and, after the summer he had just experienced, Ekéus was determined to spend some quiet time with his family. If we waited for him to get back, it would be the end of August before any new inspection mission could be launched. I wanted to have an inspection team on the ground by mid-August, helping UNSCOM regain any initiative that might have been lost given the events surrounding the Ministry of Agriculture inspection. This meant forwarding the plan to Ekéus while he was on vacation. Smidovich read over the pages I had handed him, and nodded. 'It's worth a try.'

My proposal was simple: select a few technically supported sites based on high-quality intelligence and subject them to an excruciating level of inspection, leaving nothing unexamined. Simultaneously, the Iraqi leadership at each site would be subject to a detailed interrogation about the nature of the facility. I was starting to envision the proposed inspection as an ambush of sorts, an intellectual trap where the only ammunition that counted was fact. The goal would be to catch the Iraqis in an inconsistency, a contradiction of fact. If enough inconsistencies were uncovered, this would provide the justification required to go after the big sites, such as the Ministry of Defense and MIC Headquarters. Inspections of such high-profile targets would not only have a legitimate arms-control purpose, but would also allow UNSCOM to regain the credibility it had lost during the Agricultural ministry standoff. Smidovich forwarded the plan to Rolf Ekéus in Vienna for his approval, as well as to the US State Department and the CIA for their review.

Rolf Ekéus, having read the inspection proposal, was enthusiastic but a bit hesitant about the inspection, and wanted Smidovich and me to fly through Vienna on our way to Bahrain to brief him in more detail before he would give his approval. We met in his house, and were treated to an outstanding meal by his wife. Afterwards, sitting in a loose circle in the sitting room, Rolf was leant back in his seat, holding a briefing book containing maps, diagrams and analysis of each of the proposed sites while I finished up my briefing. He was relaxed, but clearly engaged.

'This team is designed', I explained, 'to dominate a site, physically and intellectually. Every room, every document and every computer will be searched. Every official will be interviewed. And the operation will be conducted on our terms, on our schedule. When we finish our mission, there will be no doubt in the minds of the Iraqis as to who is in charge.'

Rolf studied his briefing documents some more, underscoring key passages with his pen. 'Precisely,' he said, nodding his head. He looked up from his papers. 'We shall proceed as planned, in that case.' Smidovich and I then traveled from Vienna to Bahrain, where we got straight to work putting together and training a team who would be capable of pulling such an inspection off.

One night, in the bar of the Holiday Inn, I was approached by one of the Americans on the inspection team, Moe Dobbs (pseudonym). A short, wiry yet muscular man with salt-and-pepper hair, Moe was one of the more senior people in the CIA's Operations Planning Cell. Brought up in the culture of the Green Berets, Dobbs had, while enlisted in the Army, been assigned to the CIA to support their covert war in Laos, and never left. He was a senior officer in the CIA's super-secret Special Activities Staff (SAS). In the years since Laos, he had soldiered on in the various secret wars of the CIA, serving in El Salvador, Honduras and Nicaragua. More recently, during Operation Desert Storm, he had led a team of SAS paramilitary operatives on a secret mission to Syria, where they were able to infiltrate approximately one hundred Arab agents into western Iraq prior to the start of the war to assist in the escape and evasion of coalition pilots expected to be shot down in that area. Later, he helped run a secret CIA recruitment and intelligence collection effort among the Kurds of northern Iraq. He was a very experienced covert operator, and someone to whom one would do well to listen.

'Things could get pretty ugly in Iraq,' he told me. The inspection we were preparing to carry out was a step into the unknown. After the fiasco of UNSCOM 40, no one knew how the Iraqis would respond to such an aggressive approach on the part of UNSCOM. We were certain that the Iraqis could sense the change in the policy of America and Great Britain. Ideally, Iraq would have gotten the message that further obstruction of UNSCOM's work would no longer be tolerated, and that our team should be permitted to carry out its mission without hindrance. But there was a real possibility that the Iraqis might choose to meet aggression with aggression, and take the inspection team hostage as a shield against any renewed bombing by the US-led coalition. 'I just want you to know that certain precautions have been taken to deal with any situation that might occur. Peter and Rocky [pseudonyms for two Delta Force troopers assigned to the team] know the plan and, if the need arises, I will come to you. What I need you to do is make sure Nikita doesn't try to stop us from doing what we have to do. If the Iraqis try to detain the team, I am supposed to bring out the entire team, but if there is any hesitation, I will leave with just the Americans.'

I understood where Dobbs was coming from. In addition to himself, Peter and Rocky, there were five other members of the US intelligence community on the team, mainly technical experts and analysts. This would be quite a haul if Iraq were to try to seize them as hostages.

By the time UNSCOM 42 arrived in Baghdad on 6 August 1992, the Iraqis had become used to the sight of a large inspection team disembarking at Habbaniyah airfield. The staff at the Palestine Meridian hotel, too, had streamlined their check-in procedures, so that our team literally flowed from the bus, through the lobby and up to their rooms. Always present, hovering in the background, were the dark figures of the Iraqi secret police, monitoring our every move. Our inspection plans were sealed up in envelopes and kept in a container located in Moe Dobbs's room. At least two of his people were with that container at all times.

The next morning, 7 August, while the main element of the UNSCOM 42 team was getting sorted out, Nikita and I met with Hossam Amin and the senior Iraqi minders in order to coordinate our efforts. Hossam Amin assured us that the Iraqi side would do everything to make this inspection a smooth and successful one.

One of our first targets was the Space Research Center, located next to the campus of Baghdad University. During an intrusive document sweep in the offices of a deputy director, the team uncovered a thick document dealing with the *Ababil*-100 missile, previously declared to UNSCOM as a solid-fuel artillery rocket. This new document showed that the Iraqis were conducting a complete redesign, with the new *Ababil*-100 reconfigured as a guided liquid-fuel missile, in effect a mini-SCUD.

None of this had been previously declared by Iraq to the Special Commission, and it was of no small concern. We seized the document, which brought Hossam Amin to an angry outburst. 'You have no right!' he complained. 'This has nothing to do with your mandate!' Nikita Smidovich patiently explained that missiles *were* our mandate, and that we would make a determination as to the relevance of this document only after we had had ample opportunity to study it in more serene surroundings. Despite Hossam Amin's repeated protestations, Smidovich held firm, and eventually the Iraqis relented, allowing UNSCOM to make a complete copy of the document.

Technically speaking, this was a big find, directly contradicting existing Iraqi declarations, which failed to list the Space Research Center as a ballistic-missile research and development facility. Here we were, at the end of our second day of inspections, and we had already uncovered serious inadequacies in the Iraqi missile declaration, just as I had predicted we would. Had our inspection stopped then and there, it would have succeeded on a scale greater than any other inspection so far that year.

Next, we headed north, onto the main Baghdad-Mosul Highway. Our objective was the Sa'ad 13 factory, a French-built electronics plant specializing in radar, electronics and, as we believed (and the Iraqis denied), ballistic-missile guidance and control. Like Rabiya and the SRC before it, Sa'ad 13 was given the new UNSCOM 42 inspection 'treatment'. While Nikita and I were interviewing Hossam Amin and the director-general of the facility, an inspection team carried out a search of the director's suite. Standing there, watching the inspectors at work, I was deeply impressed with their efficiency and professionalism. Every technique that had been taught was now employed: drawers were skillfully searched; desk blotters were picked up, looking for any documents that might have been hidden underneath; overhead, the roof panels were lifted and an inspector hoisted up to make sure no documents had been stashed away.

We sat down in the reception room of the director's suite, and started our interview. Nikita Smidovich ran down the list of questions, eliciting the same standard answers that we had grown accustomed to hearing. I then took over, asking supplementary questions about documents that seemed to be missing from the factory. I focused on personnel files, which should have existed. 'How do you keep track of your employees?' I asked. 'They are here, at work, but you lack any file management system to track who is here, who is sick, who gets paid, who doesn't.'

The director became confused. 'Of course we have such documentation,' he said. I jumped right in. 'Where is it?' The director looked at Hossam Amin. 'We were ordered to remove all documents from the site.' With that response, Hossam Amin jumped to his feet, and started shouting in Arabic at the director, who rose from his chair and shouted back. Things were very intense, and the two Iraqi officials moved into the director's office, where they shut the door.

We could still make out the raised voices, and had our interpreter fill us in on the details. 'Hossam is telling the director that he had no right to tell the inspection team about the documents. The director is telling Hossam that this stupid ploy has been seen through, and it is making him and his factory look guilty when they are not.' It was a fascinating clash unfolding right in front of us. Within a few minutes, the door to the office opened up, and Hossam Amin and the director emerged, both clearly angry. Hossam spoke up. 'There are no documents,' he said. The director was silent, fuming.

Back in Baghdad, a communication awaited us from Rolf Ekéus. Impressed with the progress made by the team, he had approved the inspection of the Military Industrial Committee headquarters. After talking with Nikita Smidovich, I went to Moe Dobbs, who had been maintaining a fairly low profile. He called over Peter and Rocky, and the four of us went to the roof of the Sheraton Hotel. I laid out what was about to happen, and the likely consequences. Dobbs was prepared. 'Is there any way you can reduce the number of inspectors in the country?' he asked. I thought about it, and said that it was possible. He recommended that we go forward with as small a team as possible, in case we had to make a run for it.

I asked him about US contingencies. 'For downtown Baghdad, there aren't any quick fixes,' he said. 'Peter, Rocky and I are carrying micro-transmitters, which can be used to guide a rescue force to our location. I recommend that we be split up in a way that ensures that if we are snatched, one of us is with each element.'

Somewhere south of us, armed men dressed in black Nomex suits were standing by their helicopters, waiting for the word to move. Combat aircraft, loaded with high explosives, standing by on runways and aircraft carriers, waiting for our team of unarmed inspectors to make a move on the MIC Headquarters building, a target we were now cleared to inspect thanks to the performance of Hossam Amin.

We made preparations that night for our anticipated confrontation outside MIC Headquarters. Some inspectors, selected to leave Iraq before the inspection, were being briefed on evacuation plans. Other inspectors were being formed into smaller groups, with an OPC operator assigned to each in case we were rounded up by the Iraqis. In the middle of our work, we were interrupted by one of our communications staff, who was looking for Nikita Smidovich. I asked what was going on.

'There is a reporter on the phone from Bahrain who says it is urgent that she speak with Nikita. She said it is about tomorrow's inspection of MIC Headquarters.'

I was stunned but, without giving anything away, I went over to Smidovich and relayed the message. I held the team in check for about five minutes while he went downstairs. When he returned, he was shaking his head. 'Tell the team they are dismissed.'

Once the last inspector had gone, I turned to Smidovich. 'What happened?'

He handed me a two-page fax from the reporter. It was the text of an article written for the *New York Times* headed 'Bush Approves Convention-Week Showdown with Iraq'. At the heart of the article was the killer paragraph:

President Bush and National Security Advisor Brent Scowcroft on Thursday approved a plan calling for demanding [sic] access to Iraq's Ministry of Military Industrialization [i.e., MIC Headquarters] ... If Iraqi officials barred access to the building, as they have already threatened to do, unidentified American officials say that American-based aircraft would swiftly bomb the ministry.

There was much more, but this said enough. The site had been compromised, both operationally and politically. There was no way we could proceed with the inspection given this story. If we had this story, we had to assume that the Iraqis did as well. If there was anything of value stored inside the MIC Headquarters building, we could be certain that by the time our team arrived there the next day it would be gone. The Iraqis could make a big show of allowing the team access and then play up the fact that we had found nothing. The political damage caused by this high-profile action would undo everything the UNSCOM 42 inspection team had gained over the course of the inspection.

I had barely taken in this new information when the phone rang again. It was Hossam Amin, looking for Smidovich, who took the receiver, and listened. He spoke softly, answering 'yes' several times before hanging up with a final 'Okay, thank you.' He looked at me. 'General Amer Rashid has invited us to his office tonight to talk. It looks like we are going to get into MIC Headquarters, after all.' We had last seen General Amer Rashid in New York in February, when he had accompanied Tariq Aziz to his meeting with the Security Council. None of us had one-on-one experience with this man, so we knew little about what we could expect from this meeting.

Within an hour of receiving the phone call from Hossam Amin, two black Mercedes Sedans pulled up at the Sheraton Hotel. Two Iraqis in civilian clothes were seated in the front of each car. We were driven through downtown Baghdad, past the Republican Palace, before coming to a halt at a gate. A cluster of soldiers wearing the red beret of airborne commandos, their AK-47 rifles prominently displayed, manned the barrier. They recognized the driver and front passenger of each vehicle on sight, and swung the gates open, snapping to attention and saluting as we entered.

We were ushered into the MIC Headquarters, through a low-lit grand entry way with marble floors, and up three floors in an elevator. I looked to my left as we exited the elevator. Three uniformed guards, wearing brown boots and sporting automatic pistols, were standing, eyeing us carefully. A man approached us from our right. 'This way, please,' he said, leading us away from the entrance to the office of the director, Hussein Kamal, Saddam's son-in-law.

Amer Rashid greeted us politely, speaking English in a gravelly, almost hoarse, voice. 'Thank you for having this conversation with me,' he said, a smile on his face. 'It is useful to have a dialogue for better understanding, and to promote good relations between the United Nations and the Iraqi government.'

There was no doubt that we were in the presence of a really significant figure. Amer Mohammed Rashid al-Ubeidi was a living legend, a man of considerable accomplishments whose reputation extended beyond Iraq. Educated in England, Amer Rashid was an engineer who made his reputation early as an exacting perfectionist possessing broad vision and a penchant for innovation. In the crucible of the Iran-Iraq War he had served as director of the Iraqi Ministry of Defense's Military Research and Development Center (MRDC), where he was responsible for transforming Iraq's air force from a third-rate power into a modern force to be reckoned with. Since 1989, when Hussein Kamal oversaw the absorption of the MRDC into MIC, Amer Rashid had been serving as one of two deputy directors for MIC (the other was the mysterious Amer al-Sa'adi, whom no inspector had yet met).

Dressed in the green fatigue uniform of the Iraqi military, Amer Rashid wore the rank of an air force lieutenant-general. He was tall, standing close to six feet, and had the trim build and upright bearing of a military man. Despite being in his sixties, Amer Rashid's black hair was thick, lightly streaked with gray. His face was narrow and well defined, with high cheekbones and a long, thin eagle-like nose. Amer Rashid sported a mustache, but kept his trimmed more than Saddam Hussein, on whom most Iraqi men modeled themselves. But the most striking physical characteristic about Amer Rashid was his eyes: when Amer Rashid fixed you with his stare, it was if he were looking right through you. His eyes could sparkle with mirth or burn with anger and, as I was about to discover, it didn't take this man much time to shift between the two emotions.

'We just received a phone call from our Mission in New York. Ambassador Ekéus just contacted them from Sweden, and told them not to worry too much, to only depend on what has been stated by UNSCOM.' Amer paused for a second, looking us over. 'This is good,' he continued. 'To cool down. I find that this is positive and useful.'

That was Amer Rashid being gracious. Within an instant, we witnessed Amer Rashid on the attack. His entire demeanor changed. When he spoke, his eyes narrowed, and his voice took on a completely different tenor. 'I want to tell you that I have issued strict instructions to our operational and technical staff to fully cooperate with 687 and others. We now have *nothing* left remaining under 687,' he said, his voice raising dramatically on nothing. 'We have destroyed *all* under 687. We have answered or given you information on *all* our programs.' Amer Rashid was trying to bully us into submission. 'We think we have done *everything*,' he concluded. 'However, what is hurting us is that in the Security Council there is *no* change of heart or attitude. UNSCOM has *not* informed the Council that Iraq has met its obligations, and the execution of inspections are intrusive and based on mistrust.'

'We are not against professionalism,' he continued. 'You have been *very* professional. But you are *too* aggressive. Helicopter operations, you look under carpets, open drawers, behind ceilings. This is beyond Mr. Ekéus's statements.' He leaned towards us, his voice taking on a more gentle tone. 'You have to understand us better,' he said. 'This is annoying our people a lot.'

Amer Rashid looked at me. 'There will always be doubts. We will always have enemies. Information will always be sent to UNSCOM. My intelligence people have told me that the people in the north have just sent a letter to the CIA. They say Iraqi authorities are hiding weapons in hotels, factories, schools, farms, Ba'ath party headquarters in city centers, everywhere. They also report that documentation on chemical, biological, nuclear and ballistic missiles are hidden in trains or in containers on trucks which are always in movement between cities.' Amer Rashid was laughing, as if this were a joke. 'The CIA will flood you with this information.'

He shifted his gaze back to Nikita Smidovich. 'I have a special information unit. I could set you up, easily mislead you. You would think you had concrete information. I could mislead the Special Commission with no problem, and so could the enemies of Iraq. They want to corrupt the relationship between the United Nations and Iraq. Who is the loser? The United Nations? No!' he said, slamming his open palm on the chair with a loud slap. 'Iraq! The Iraqi people! We do not contest that governments want to overthrow us. But your actions are against the innocent Iraqi people, who have *nothing* to do with MIC or the Iraqi leadership. It is the Iraqi people who deal with the results!' Amer Rashid was now yelling at us.

Almost as if he were exhausted, he sank into his chair. 'You have done all, there is nothing left. Yes, we have ambiguities, I admit this. We have given you ninety-eight per cent, but you have given us nothing. This is a crime... there should be an end.' He took a breath, and continued his soliloquy. 'Everything has been destroyed. You can inspect every single inch of Iraq, and you will find nothing. Until when will the Iraqi people suffer? We admit that Iraq made mistakes. We have a resolution. We don't like it, but we will implement it.'[2]

The meeting with Amer Rashid produced instant results. The next day, when we convened a seminar with the Iraqis, Hossam Amin starting talking. Nikita Smidovich and I were seated in a room in the Sheraton Hotel listening to information that Iraq had, until that moment, been trying to hide from the inspectors. Hossam Amin discussed his past visits to Russia and China to purchase missiles and missile-related technology. He told us how the Libyan government had sought to ship its own SCUD missiles to Iraq so that they might be converted to *Al-Hussein* long-range missiles, and how the onset of the Gulf War had stopped this, even as the Libyan missiles were arriving at Benghazi Airport. A similar deal with North Korea never got off the starting block, although Hossam showed us the North Korean visa in his passport, applied for but never used.

On the issue of documentation, Hossam Amin was blunt. 'It is a question of national security,' he said. 'I tell you now, there is nothing related to resolution 687 left – no equipment, no documents. But classified material is protected. When we saw how you were searching for documents, and when we consider how many Americans and British you have on your team, we had no choice but to order that documents sensitive to national security be removed from all sites.'

'The question is how will you treat what I have told you?' he went on. 'We are not as well organized as we should be. You are better organized. You caught us off-guard with the intrusiveness of your inspection, and the directness of your questions. We only have our memory, and it can be faulty at times.'

Hossam Amin's faulty memory was not the only problem we had to face as Nikita and I set about organizing the massive amount of data collected during UNSCOM 42. Already, the technical findings of the inspection were being questioned by the USA, with many of the inspectors who had participated in the UNSCOM 42 inspection leading the charge. No sooner had we touched down in Bahrain than the US experts ran off to Gateway and started filing reports back to their offices about the 'duplicity' of the Iraqis.

Although the US inspectors had been seconded to UNSCOM for the duration of the inspection, and despite the assurances given by the US government that the inspectors provided would do only the bidding of UNSCOM as set forth by the chief inspector, the reality was quite different. Each US inspector worked for his or her own office back in Washington, which could be readily accessed through secure phones and computers located in the 'US-only' sanctum at Gateway. UNSCOM had no control over these proceedings whatsoever. The US experts at Gateway claimed to be privy to 'secret' information about Iraq's programs that they could not share with UNSCOM. This information, they claimed, proved Iraq was not telling the truth.

I couldn't believe it. We had succeeded in pressuring the Iraqis into being more forthcoming, and here were the US inspectors, failing to capitalize on the moment. To the US inspectors and their bosses, the findings of UNSCOM 42 were not something to be embraced, but rather denigrated and rejected. General Amer's accusations concerning the duplicity of the CIA were still fresh in my mind.

Despite the rumbles of unrest from the US intelligence community, I was fairly confident that we had learned enough about the Iraqi missile program that we would soon be able to declare Iraq disarmed, at least in that category, and start focusing on longer-term monitoring issues. While there was a host of minor technical issues left, in my opinion there remained only two outstanding matters of importance: definitively accounting for Iraq's SCUD missile inventory and establishing a similar inventory of missile fuels. If this could be done – and I was under no illusions that this would be an easy task – then I felt that Nikita Smidovich and I would be able to inform Rolf Ekéus that the missile file was closed as far as Security Council resolution 687 was concerned.

We needed an immediate follow-up inspection to UNSCOM 42. Putting an inspection plan together was not a problem. Getting the USA to embrace this inspection was more difficult. I approached Rolf Ekéus about my concerns over the USA withholding information, and how this could impede the progress of our efforts in the ballistic missile field. Ekéus shared my concern, and asked me to draft a list of questions I wanted answered by the Americans. He was going to Washington where he would meet with, among others, National Security Advisor Brent Scowcroft. Rolf promised me that my questions would be handed over during that meeting, and that he would press for a response. Within two weeks he had received a detailed reply, nearly twenty pages of classified information that had been cleared for release to Ekéus and those persons he designated. It was a goldmine of information, which outlined the remaining US concerns about Iraq's missile programs.[3]

For this inspection, I was also proposing a thorough inspection of Iraq's ability to produce missile fuel. Ekéus wanted to know more about this concept. 'There are two angles to a fuel-based inspection,' I responded. 'First, my calculations show that there is a significant amount of fuel and oxidizer unaccounted for. So, on the one hand, we need to carry out a search for hidden fuel stockpiles. Second, we know that the Iraqis had an indigenous effort underway to make their own fuel and oxidizer. So we need to conduct a survey of Iraq's petroleum-refining and chemical-industry capability to look for any evidence of such production.'

Rolf Ekéus took this in. 'Iraq is one of the largest oil-producing countries in the world. This would be a huge task.'

I nodded. 'I know. But it needs to be done, not just for the purposes of searching for hidden capability, but also as a baseline for any future monitoring agreement. Our biggest problem isn't going to be the inspection, but rather putting together the requisite expertise.'

The Americans had reservations about any inspection designed to 'close the file' on missile disarmament issues, and many in Washington doubted UNSCOM's ability to effectively carry out such a technically demanding inspection. However, once they were convinced of our seriousness about moving forward on this inspection, help was forthcoming. By the end of September the Americans had provided us with a leading petroleum-refining expert and five other fuel experts who would go on the inspection.

Fuels were not our only problem, however. It was clear, in going through the Scowcroft paper, that the USA still entertained the belief that

Iraq possessed a significant covert force of missiles. They believed that Iraq must be concealing launchers because they had claimed to have only ever had sixteen, yet the USA believed it had destroyed several during the Gulf War, in which case there must have been more than sixteen to begin with. I wasn't so sure. I had been a participant in the counter-SCUD campaign during Desert Storm, and was intimately familiar with every bomb strike and commando report alleging to have resulted in a destroyed SCUD launcher. In my opinion, none of these claims held any water. I decided to confront this issue head-on. In addition to carrying out the fuels' inspection, we would investigate all of the so-called 'engagement events' where coalition forces claimed to have destroyed SCUD launchers. I approached both the USA and the UK on this matter.

Putting together an inspection of this scope and complexity was a huge task. Team size for what was now named UNSCOM 45 had swelled to over fifty inspectors. As momentum grew for the inspection, the level of enthusiasm for the mission in Washington likewise increased. However, in Baghdad, word of the impending inspection was greeted icily.

On 7 October, as UNSCOM 45 started to assemble in Bahrain for training, the Iraqi foreign minister sent a letter to Rolf Ekéus requesting that the inspection be put off until after the US presidential elections. After the UNSCOM 42 'crisis' with MIC Headquarters, the Iraqis were understandably nervous about any possible linkage between an UNSCOM inspection and the looming ballot. The Iraqis were concerned about UNSCOM being used as a vehicle to trigger a military action designed to bolster the position of President George Bush, who was faltering in the polls in the face of a strong challenge by Arkansas Governor Bill Clinton. Rolf Ekéus responded that UNSCOM's work was determined by the Security Council's mandate, and that UNSCOM could not take into account events outside of that mandate. The Iraqis did not like this response, and Ekéus soon received a phone call from Amer Rashid, again imploring that the inspection be stopped. Once again, Ekéus refused.

In Iraq, a propaganda offensive was mounted against UNSCOM. Saddam Hussein, in a nationally televised speech, referred to the inspectors as 'Stray dogs tearing at the flesh of Iraq'. Such statements from the president of Iraq were very disturbing, and Rolf Ekéus was called in to brief the UN secretary-general, Boutros Boutros-Ghali.

Rolf Ekéus told the secretary-general that he was impressed with the positive results of UNSCOM 42, and believed that if the Iraqis cooperated with UNSCOM 45 in a similar fashion, he might be able to 'go to Baghdad and press the Iraqi leadership for missing information. If this is forthcoming, this will be reported to the Security Council and the oil embargo could be lifted.'

Ekéus also warned the secretary-general of the damage US policy was doing to UNSCOM's mission. 'The US position is that the embargo will not be lifted as long as Saddam is in power. There is no incentive for Iraq to cooperate.'

'What would happen,' Boutros Boutros-Ghali asked, 'if the new team is blocked?'

'I have just talked with the US National Security Advisor, Brent Scowcroft,' Ekéus replied. 'He has assured me that if the Iraqis were to block the team, the reaction would be swift, regardless of US domestic politics.'

Boutros Boutros-Ghali pondered that point. 'It is important that you be assured of US backing.'

Ekéus agreed. 'Iraq is clearly concerned at the prospect of a US reaction.'

Once again, Nikita Smidovich and I found ourselves in a highly volatile situation. In the rollercoaster ride that had become UNSCOM, we were headed back to Iraq not as the practitioners of cutting-edge disarmament work that we had imagined. In the complicated, politically charged environment that surrounded Iraq, we had become something far different. We were now the tip of the spear.

UNSCOM's inspection-based counterattack, designed to restore to the inspectors the dignity and sense of purpose lost during the fiasco surrounding the Ministry of Agriculture inspection, now looked as if it was itself being swallowed up in a wider geopolitical struggle.

Up until now, the White House had kept a low profile regarding the work of UNSCOM, choosing to influence the inspections by proxy, using officials in the CIA, the Pentagon and the State Department to serve as the face of the US government. Now, since the breakthrough of UNSCOM 42, the face of the US government was, more often than not, represented by the national security advisor to the president, Brent Scowcroft. What to do about Iraq had become a key issue of the election campaign, and we were powerless as UNSCOM's work became ever more entangled in the web of US domestic politics.

Chapter 5

Assassinating the Truth
October 1992–January 1993

In Bahrain, the largest inspection team UNSCOM had assembled to date started its training. While the team prepared for its mission, I pressed hard for the provision of data from the US and UK on launcher 'engagement events'. Peter and Rocky, the two Delta Force troopers who had been on the UNSCOM 42 inspection, were back, along with a whole slew of other Delta commandos, part of our 'security' in case the team were taken hostage. All had played a role in hunting down SCUDs during Operation Desert Storm, and in addition to their security responsibilities, were to assist in evaluating launcher destruction locations in western Iraq. Peter was authorized to officially discuss with me the Delta Force 'SCUD Hunt', detailing all of the claimed SCUD engagements and sightings, and the British government had produced an eight-page report detailing what they termed as 'Special Forces SCUD sightings and engagements'.

Sequestering me in a side office at the UNSCOM training facility in Bahrain, Peter grabbed a map and pen, and started to tell me stories about the secret SCUD hunt in western Iraq during Desert Storm. Many of the details I was familiar with from my war experience, but some of what he had to say was new to me. I listened to Peter with undivided attention. Here was a man who had been on the ground, in western Iraq, hunting

SCUDs. While I still believed that the reports of SCUD kills during Desert Storm were questionable, I was bound and determined to make sure that every lead was followed up aggressively, especially one provided by such a brave fighter as Peter.

Once in Baghdad, the inspection unfolded like clockwork. The UNSCOM offices had been moved out of the Sheraton Hotel and into the UN compound located at the old Canal Hotel, on the south-eastern edge of the Iraqi capital. Our inspection team took over most of the ground floor of the Canal Hotel, setting up a giant logistics base as well as the Russian field fuel-testing laboratory. Every morning, we gathered the team and I briefed them on the day's activities. In addition to inspecting over thirty suspected SCUD 'engagement' locations, the team was scheduled to inspect several oil refineries, sending the samples collected in this process back to Bahrain on the UNSCOM C-160 aircraft, where two of our fuel experts analyzed them. We sent teams throughout Iraq, inspecting various sites associated with liquid-fuel and oxidizer storage, where they took samples for testing and evaluation in the Russian field laboratory. It was demanding work, conducted in austere locations, but our training paid off and the team accomplished its mission without a single accident or injury.

In addition to the searches and sampling missions, UNSCOM 45 carried out a robust schedule of interviews with Iraqi experts and officials. One of the highlights of the inspection was a six-hour interview with Lieutenant General Hazem Ayubi, a hero of Iraq, twice awarded the Order of *Rafidain* ('Two Rivers', one of the highest honors in Iraq), held at the MIC Headquarters in downtown Baghdad on the evening of 22 October. Present at the meeting with Nikita Smidovich and me were US defense intelligence specialists, air force targeting experts and Delta Force commandos, all of whom had played a significant role in trying to hunt down Iraq's missile force during the war. They believed they knew everything there was to know about Iraq's use of missiles during that war. Within minutes of the meeting, however, it became clear that they, and the rest of the team, still had a lot to learn, with General Ayubi taking on the role of a stern professor.

General Ayubi walked us through his plan of action, telling us how he split his forces and decentralized his logistics, and how, despite everything the coalition threw at him, he was able to shift his forces from the western front, facing Israel, to the southern front, facing Saudi Arabia – a distance of several hundred miles – at will, massing his small force of launchers to maximize his strike potential, and making the coalition believe that Iraq had a larger missile force than existed in actuality. And how, through it all, *not a single missile launcher was lost to enemy action.*

The American SCUD hunters, Peter first and foremost among them, appeared confused by General Ayubi's presentation. Professional reputations were at stake, as was American national security policy. The US intelligence community had briefed the White House that Iraq had an operational missile capability, and the director of the CIA had gone on record saying that this capability could be quantified in terms of more than 200 missiles. Military medals were issued on the basis of SCUDs having been destroyed in combat, creating a military lore that took on the aura of mythology. General Ayubi's presentation met fierce resistance from those listening to it.

On 27 October, we dispatched two teams via helicopter for fuel sampling missions in western and northern Iraq. It was inconceivable that Iraq would choose to manufacture hundreds, maybe thousands of missiles, and not have a dedicated supply of fuel. Our question was simple: where was the fuel?

The Iraqis brought forward Dr. Taha Al-Jabouri, a fuel expert. Dr. Al-Jabouri admitted that they had imported SCUD fuel from Germany, but the program he described fell far short of the amounts of fuel and oxidizer needed to service the *Al-Hussein* missile force. Despite the forthrightness of Dr. Al-Jabouri, we still had a problem.

'We feel that Iraq must have a hidden capability for SCUD fuel and oxidizer that has not been declared,' I said to Hossam Amin once Dr. Al-Jabouri had finished. 'And the only reason we can come up with why you haven't declared this capability is that Iraq still maintains a covert force of ballistic missiles.'

Hossam Amin had a hurt look in his eyes. 'Mr. Scott... even after your meeting with General Ayubi, you still believe this?'

'There is no other possible explanation available to us,' I replied.

Hossam got up from his seat, and left the room. Within minutes he returned. Hossam looked at Nikita Smidovich. 'General Amer would like to speak to you and Mr. Scott.'

Unlike our last meeting with General Amer Rashid, back in UNSCOM 42, this time there was no pretense at formalities. We met in a conference room adjacent to General Amer's office. The general was waiting, and motioned for us to have a seat.

'What are you up to?' he asked, his eyes narrowed, his teeth clenched.

'We are simply presenting to your experts our calculations -'

I didn't get a chance to finish. General Amer brought his hand down on the table with a loud *SMACK*!

'Calculations!' he bellowed. '*CALCULATIONS?!*' His face was red, and spittle formed at the side of his mouth. 'YOUR CALCULATIONS ARE KILLING IRAQI CHILDREN! You and your calculations can go to hell!' General Amer was really worked up. 'We have cooperated fully with your inspection team, and this is what we get? Calculations?'

Smidovich tried to calm the enraged Amer Rashid. 'General, there is no need to raise your voice. We are simply -'

Nikita, too, was cut off. 'Simply what, my dear Mr. Smidovich? Simply confusing the issue? Simply dragging this charade on and on, to no end? Simply what!' I had never seen Amer Rashid so worked up.

'Shall we leave?' said Smidovich. 'If we cannot discuss with you in a calm manner the issues at stake here, I see no reason for us to be here.'

Amer Rashid sat back. He had made his point, but perhaps sensed in the Russian sitting before him that there was no backing down. 'Stay... stay. But you are making me lose my patience... making all of Iraq lose its patience. We need this to come to an end.'

Smidovich didn't blink. 'Scott has evaluated the data provided by the Iraqi side concerning fuel expenditures, and has discovered some important discrepancies. All we are trying to do is clear these discrepancies up. If the Iraqi side can cooperate on this issue in the same spirit that General Ayubi showed, I see no reason why this cannot be settled quickly.'

Amer slumped in his chair. He motioned to me with his hand. 'Go ahead. Tell me what the great Scott Ritter has calculated about the fate of Iraq.'

So I went through my presentation. General Amer took notes, carefully annotating what I had to say. When I finished, he put his pen down.

'My dear, I can see how this might be of concern to you. By these calculations, you have a point. This must be addressed. I will see to it that you get all the information you need.'

Smidovich and I left General Amer's office shaking our heads in wonder. It was a welcome relief to leave the general and get back to the business of inspections.

The next three days proved to be the most hectic I had ever experienced while serving in UNSCOM. We deployed teams into western, southern and central Iraq in an effort to investigate every site related to SCUD operational activity during Desert Storm – twenty-eight sites in three days. At one point, feeling that the Iraqis were not telling the truth on how they shuttled SCUD launchers between the western and southern front, we sent an urgent request back to Stu Cohen at CIA Headquarters to provide us with data on bridges destroyed during the war. We got a five-page fax detailing every bombing mission, and their results. When we compared this to what the Iraqis were saying, it appeared that the routes they described were feasible after all. And when it was done, we had found no evidence of SCUD launcher destruction.

But the lack of evidence uncovered during our inspection of the SCUD engagement sites did not alter the American position that SCUD launchers had in fact been destroyed during the war. On the evening of 29 October, the Iraqis brought General Ayubi back to speak with the inspection team, and to confront the doubts of the inspectors. In a tour-de-force presentation that lasted many hours, General Ayubi laid all of the American concerns to rest. Even Peter and Rocky, the Delta Force troopers who had participated in several of the alleged 'SCUD kills', now doubted their own assertions, admitting that what they had destroyed might not have been a SCUD after all, but rather a mobile surface-to-air missile launcher (which was very similar in appearance to the SCUD launcher), as claimed by the Iraqis.[1]

After our meeting with General Ayubi we went on for our final meeting with the Iraqi missile technicians. General Amer had been as good as his word, and the Iraqis finally opened up about the whole truth about a number of critical issues, including the discrepancies in fuels.

Within the hour, the Iraqi fuel experts had cleared up all remaining issues regarding their fuel programs. The Iraqis confirmed the basic gist of my calculations, and then described how they planned to build factories dedicated to the manufacture of main fuel and oxidizer. Contracts had been signed with several European companies, and initial deliveries were to have been made in August 1990. The invasion of Kuwait put a halt to this program. 'The only other efforts we had underway were those carried out by Dr. Al-Jabouri which you already know about,' Hossam Amin said.

One of the Iraqi colonels reinforced this point. 'Look, at the end of the war we had 138 missiles left. Logic would have dictated that we would have fired as many as possible at the end of the forty-day bombing campaign – at the peak of the aggression. But instead, we fired gradually fewer numbers towards the end of the war. That's because we were beginning to worry about fuel and oxidizer supplies. We didn't know when the war would end, and we wanted to be able to fire at critical moments if we had to.'

There were more, many more, detailed discussions about the organization of Iraq's missile manufacturing program, relations with other nations concerning ballistic missiles, chemical and nuclear payloads, and a myriad of technical issues. The Iraqis were forthcoming about them all. The data we had collected during the course of our inspections supported most of the claims being made by the Iraqis.

The next day, 30 October, UNSCOM 45 left Iraq, after thirteen days of the most intensive inspection ever undertaken by UNSCOM: thirteen days; seventy-five inspection sites; three major seminars; dozens of informal side meetings; hundreds of pages of notes containing new information garnered about Iraq's ballistic missile program. UNSCOM 45 was over, and it had been broadly successful. We had gathered a great deal of new information, and were able to make a proper assessment: Iraq had been disarmed of ballistic missiles.

On my return to New York following the end of the inspection, the Americans requested a special briefing on the results of the UNSCOM 45 effort. I flew down to Washington where, in a State Department conference room, I met with some thirty missile experts drawn from the entire US intelligence community. They listened in icy silence as I briefed them on the findings. One by one, I refuted or contradicted all of the concerns set out in the so-called 'Scowcroft Paper', provided to UNSCOM by Bob Gallucci in September. Point by point, I tore down the US government's carefully constructed theory of a covert SCUD force. Larry Smothers, the author of that idea, was in the audience. He had been a member of UNSCOM 45, knew the evidence I spoke of, and had nothing to say to refute it. When I finished, I asked for questions. There were none. Some shifted uncomfortably in their seats. None thanked me for my work. But, as I was leaving, I was warned by a sympathetic CIA staff member that the UNSCOM 45 findings were not popular reading in Washington, and to be prepared for some sort of a response.

Within a week that response came. It was in the form of a four-page document entitled 'A Critique of Iraqi SCUD-Related Assertions Made During UNSCOM 45'. Paragraph 2 of the paper pretty much summed up the entire US analytical effort:

The US continues to assess that SCUD-type missiles, launchers, and support equipment, sufficient to provide a covert operational capability, remain hidden in Iraq. We believe that the carefully contrived story presented to UNSCOM 45 is a continuation of the well-established pattern of Iraqi falsehoods designed to deceive UNSCOM and to permit retention of an operational missile capability.

Nikita Smidovich and I had struggled against numerous difficulties to pull off two effective sets of inspections. From the nadir of the Ministry of Agriculture debacle, these inspections had reasserted UNSCOM as a viable arms control agency. We had squeezed the Iraqis hard, and the end result were new disclosures about their ballistic-missile programs that had cleared up every major concern we had listed in our files.

But this wasn't good enough for the Americans. The US intelligence community, when it came to Iraq, seemed interested only in maintaining the perception that the Iraqis were not telling the truth, regardless of what the facts showed. The director of the CIA later testified before the US Senate that Iraq had some 200 SCUD missiles left in its inventory, something that was, simply put, impossible. But facts no longer mattered. Nikita Smidovich and I, together with our fellow inspectors, had uncovered the truth, and now the Americans were assassinating it.

However, despite the negativity of the US response, Smidovich and I decided that our best course of action would be to keep working on how best to move the issue of disarming Iraq's ballistic missile capability forward. I decided that we would need to work on a dual track, one which sought to address the US concerns, the other which built on the considerable progress made with the Iraqis.

I had on file notes from a briefing provided by the US in November 1991 on airborne ground-penetrating radar (GPR). I had an idea: what if UNSCOM flew radar missions over western Iraq, looking for buried missiles? The Americans said the Iraqis had these missiles, and that they were probably buried. Why not try and find them? I sketched out a plan and presented it to Smidovich, who discussed it with Rolf Ekéus. Within days we were given the green light to go forward with the concept.

Smidovich and I juggled the requirements of trying to put together a new missile hunt that would satisfy the CIA. As with earlier inspection efforts, we did our best to co-opt the USA by getting the CIA to invest intellectual and financial capital into the inspection concept. In the case of the hidden

missiles, this meant not only securing US agreement to fund the fielding of
a radar system, but also provide intelligence information which supported
the American claims that the Iraqis were still hiding missiles. Smidovich
and I laughed at how we were stealing a page from the old Mafia adage
about 'keeping your friends close, and your enemies closer'.

Stu Cohen surprised us by inviting Smidovich and me down to
Washington, where we were brought into the work spaces of the Non-
Proliferation Center Headquarters in Rosslyn, Virginia, for meetings with
the CIA. While old hat for me, this was a unique experience for the former
Russian diplomat.

We got off our Delta Shuttle flight, and took the metro to the Rosslyn
station. There, we walked the few short blocks to the unmarked office
building which housed the Non-Proliferation Center. From the outside,
the building was the same as all the others clustered in the neighborhood.
However, once you entered the one-way glass doors of the ground floor
entrance, it became obvious that this was no ordinary office complex.
Armed uniformed CIA security guards stood watch behind desks,
checking the identification cards of all those entering and exiting the
premises. The Russian and I went through, and then were taken upstairs
to Cohen's office.

Stu Cohen briefed us on a number of sites in Iraq where missiles,
warheads, and chemical and biological agent were believed to be
buried. All of this played into the concept of a ground-penetrating
radar inspection, which Stu supported wholeheartedly. These sites were
considered very sensitive, the source of the information being an Iraqi
colonel who had recently defected, and whose reporting in the past had
proven to be accurate. The 'Big Three' sites put forward by the US were a
missile burial site at a Special Republican Guard training camp south of
Lake Habbaniyah, a chemical weapons burial site located on the premises
of the Rashadiya Republican Guard Barracks, and a biological warhead
burial site in some abandoned railroad tunnels just south of Kirkuk.

It was clear that the USA was trying to put some meat on its blanket
rejection of the UNSCOM 45 findings. While I couldn't vouch for the
quality of the CIA source, these sites were being taken seriously inside the
US government, and UNSCOM would therefore need to do something to
address American concerns. However, in the back of my mind I couldn't
help but feel frustrated at the fact that while UNSCOM had assembled a
rock-solid case on Iraqi compliance with its ballistic missile disarmament

obligations, the CIA was able to dismiss this case with little more than secondhand speculation and rumor. I had worked with the CIA on numerous occasions during the late 1980s and early 1990s, producing assessments about Soviet missile-production capabilities that had a direct impact on the national security of the USA. The Agency of that era would never have condoned the CIA approach now being taken. One simply did not weigh in on issues of the magnitude associated with Iraqi weapons of mass destruction with intelligence of such shaky quality, especially when it flew in the face of a veritable mountain of evidence to the contrary.

There were political reasons for maintaining the myth of a secret SCUD force. The policy objective of regime change in Iraq had been passed on unchanged from George H. W. Bush to the new President, Bill Clinton. UNSCOM's efforts to verify the real situation interfered with that objective. Stu Cohen's charm offensive, and the willingness of the USA to provide UNSCOM with personnel and material support, was making me feel as if Stu Cohen and the CIA likewise were employing tactics based upon the 'keep your friends close, and your enemies closer' line of thinking. More and more, I was seeing the hard work and concrete technical results obtained by UNSCOM pushed into the margin by the dramatic, yet inconclusive, intelligence information provided by the USA and the United Kingdom.

But the issue was much more complex than that. Developing new inspection concepts presented no problem. Getting the USA to accept the results of such an inspection was a completely different matter. The longer UNSCOM waited to endorse the findings of the UNSCOM 45 inspection, the more difficult that proposition was becoming. I needed some way to make sure that whatever course of action UNSCOM undertook in the field of ballistic missiles in the future, the findings of that inspection would be treated as final. There could be no room for second guessing.

I was becoming fed up with the whole UNSCOM scene. We seemed to be stuck in a rut, going nowhere. Worse, many of the criticisms leveled by senior Iraqi officials during my recent trips to Iraq about the CIA's role in the affairs of UNSCOM had hit too close to home. Despite all of my efforts to build within UNSCOM an independent intelligence capability, the bottom line was that, in many ways, UNSCOM was now more dependent on US support than ever before.

In order for UNSCOM to succeed in implementing its mandate in Iraq, it would require a change of attitude not only from Saddam Hussein's regime, but also on the part of the USA. Weapons inspections could not simply go on forever. There had to be an end. While I couldn't reach any definitive conclusions about the level of Iraqi compliance in regards to chemical, biological or nuclear activities, I was fairly certain that in the field of ballistic missiles, Nikita Smidovich and I and our teams had accomplished a great deal towards establishing the fact that Iraq had basically complied with Security Council requirements to disarm. With the interim monitoring inspections underway at the various missile sites in Iraq, we had demonstrated just how effective long-term monitoring could be. We simply needed to be allowed to do our job, and Washington seemed intent on not allowing this to happen. The reality was that there were many in the US government who simply did not want UNSCOM to succeed. In this perverse formulation, a failed UNSCOM would forever justify the continuation of economic sanctions against Iraq. If this was true, then everything I had been working for was in fact all for nothing.

If my work with UNSCOM was to have any meaning, then we had to be able to say that the Iraqis were complying when they were. This meant a war on two fronts: on the one hand, fighting to get the Iraqis to tell the truth and, on the other, trying to compel the Americans to accept the truth once it had been uncovered. I don't think I could possibly have realized at the time just how difficult this task would prove to be.

Chapter 6

Shifting the Goalposts
February 1993—March 1994

I was getting impatient with the political games going on in Washington, and I was keen to get started on some actual inspection work. After several months of promising something, the CIA had finally come through with a design for the Ground-Penetrating Radar (GPR). If the Americans wanted to play hardball, so be it. Now that the CIA had committed such significant resources into the development of the GPR sensor, I felt that the inspection was a fait accompli, and as such wanted to make sure that it unfolded on terms favorable to UNSCOM. I was determined to get them to back down from their ludicrous claim that the Iraqis continued to possess a force of some 200 SCUD-type missiles, and drafted a detailed concept of operations plan which focused on just that issue.

I used the US-provided figure of 200 missiles in my opening paragraphs, making it clear that the main purpose of the GPR inspection was to find evidence of the existence of such a force. But I had to maintain my integrity on this issue. My position was clearly reflected in the analysis of the situation. 'There is no hard evidence,' I wrote, 'of a covert force of missiles or missile-related equipment proscribed by resolution 687 being retained by Iraq.'

It was also critical that I did not discredit the findings of the UNSCOM 45 inspection. I put forward an assessment which gave Iraq the potential of still having a force of six *Al-Nida* launchers, similar to those they had tried to hide from UNSCOM in 1991–1992, and up to twenty SCUD-type missiles, which the Iraqis retained by 'cooking' their numbers regarding past missile launches (i.e. by declaring a missile launch when none occurred, thereby being able to keep a missile 'off the books'). I proposed that this unit had been kept in strategic reserve during the Gulf War, and was still operating under presidential control. 'In this way,' I wrote, 'most of the operational data provided by the Iraqi side in UNSCOM 45 could be accurate and still hide [the fact of] the covert strategic reserve.'

I closed my analysis by noting, 'It must be stressed that this assessment is based on analysis that is in no means supported by hard fact. It is based upon assumptions of possible Iraqi capability derived from unsubstantiated data.'[1]

I took the better part of two months to bring all the pieces of this inspection together. It was a massive air-ground operation spanning twenty-one days and involving nearly a hundred personnel. But finally, by early September 1993, we were ready to deploy.

Our training was intense. In addition to the inherent problems of getting a team this size, composed of disparate foreigners, to meld as a unit, we faced additional obstacles because we were throwing into the mix a new technology – ground-penetrating radar – and intensive air-ground operations on a scale never before attempted by UNSCOM.

We were well into the halfway-mark of the training when I was approached in the lobby of the hotel we were staying in by Moe Dobbs and two Delta Force commandos, Paul Mallard and Gregg Raptor (both pseudonyms). The three had been assigned by the OPC to support the UNSCOM 63 inspection, and I had been meeting with them on and off for nearly five months.

'We need to have a word with you,' Dobbs said, motioning me to join them at the bar. 'We have some additional targets we think would be ideal for this inspection,' he said. 'They involve facilities in northern Iraq which we are certain have a relation to Iraqi missile projects.'

Dobbs nodded to Mallard and Raptor, who took over the brief. 'Based upon very reliable sources, we feel that Iraq has maintained a secret hideout in caves located inside the Sinjar mountain range,' Mallard said, referring to a remote region due west of Mosul. 'We know that Iraq had carried out long-range missile tests near Sinjar, and planned on installing the large "Super-Gun" in the Sinjar mountains,' Raptor added.

Dobbs jumped in. 'During the war, in the later stages, my team operated an observation post just over the border, in Syria. We were able to track a large number of Iraqi military vehicles approaching the Sinjar mountain range from the south, where they turned and disappeared into drive-in caves in the side of the mountain.'

'We had contacts with Kurdish groups in the area, who reported that entire villages were evacuated and Iraqi security cordoned off the entire mountain range to prevent any outsiders from getting near,' said Mallard. Raptor nodded knowingly. 'We almost launched an attack on the area near the end of the war. Our unit was to be flown in on C-130 aircraft to launch a raid, but the war ended just days before we were to go forward.'

'We've been following this area very closely since the war ended,' Dobbs said. 'The local Kurds report that the security cordons are still in place. Even more interesting, the Brits and our boys have been flying infra-red photo missions as part of the no-fly zone enforcement, and we've detected some "hot spots" in the mountains that we think could be the entrances to the caves where the Iraqis are hiding the equipment.'

I sat there in silence, taking all of this in. I had been meeting with Dobbs, Mallard and Raptor consistently now for several months, and here we were, halfway through a training program that had been finely tuned for our mission, and the CIA was throwing me a curve ball. 'What do you want me to do?' I asked. 'We're knee deep into this mission. I can't shut the operation down, which by the way the CIA and National Security Council say is based upon the most credible intelligence the US has, and suddenly shift gears to do a wild goose chase in the Sinjar mountains, no matter how enticing your stories are.'

'Look, Scott, I'm just being honest here, but the intelligence behind the GPR mission is crap.' I could feel my stomach churning. 'The analysts at the Non-Proliferation Center haven't a clue what they are doing. To be honest, this stuff about buried missiles is pure guesswork, based on second-rate defector information.'

Mallard took over the conversation. 'We've been trying to get the Non-Proliferation Center to include the Sinjar targets on the GPR inspection since day one, but they don't like it because they didn't come up with it.'

I put down my beer. 'What do you want from me?' I asked.

'Well, you're the guy in charge of this effort.' I interrupted Paul at that point. 'I'm not in charge, Nikita is, and the chairman above him.'

Dobbs broke in. 'Don't play word games here, Scott. This is your plan, your operation. We know that the Sinjar operation will never stand a chance unless you go along with it, so that's why we're coming to you. We think that you've put together a team capable of doing justice to the Sinjar targets, and we'd like you to get these targets on the inspection. We're not sure the US government is going to have the stomach to continue these kinds of inspections after the GPR mission is finished, especially if you don't find anything.'

Raptor spoke up. 'And you damn sure won't find anything if you limit the inspection to the targets the Non-Proliferation Center has put together… there simply isn't anything there.' It was now Paul's turn. 'Sinjar is the key. We are convinced there is something hidden of value at Sinjar, and that your inspection is the only way we are ever going to find it.'

What Dobbs, Mallard and Raptor were saying was outrageous. The concept of the US government spending millions of dollars on an inspection concept designed to uncover hidden missiles, and then to provide us with intelligence they knew to be inferior, if valid at all? It was a set-up for defeat. 'Why wouldn't Stu Cohen pass these targets to me?' I asked. 'He has been a straight shooter on this from day one. I can't accept that he would deliberately withhold information pertinent to this inspection, unless of course he doesn't know anything about this.'

Dobbs laughed. 'Why do you think we're even talking to you? Stu knows about this, but has had his hands tied by the analysts and the bureaucrats. The targets we're talking about have been developed by the operators, not the analysts. The analysts won't back them, because they didn't develop them. Stu has asked us to come to you directly because he wants these targets to be inspected.'

I was stuck in the middle of an internal CIA conflict. I needed advice, and there was only one person I felt I could go to at this point: my old friend from the UNSCOM support office in the State Department, Colonel Sam Perry. I said as much.

Dobbs nodded his head. 'We thought you would say this. Just so you know, Colonel Perry has full knowledge of these targets, and supports our effort. Stu has spoken to him about this.' He then took a more hushed tone. 'Scott, there is more here than meets the eye. Sinjar is just the tip of the spear. We have outstanding information – and it doesn't come from defectors – that the Iraqis are engaged in a systematic effort to pull the wool over UNSCOM's eyes. There is a committee that meets once a week to discuss UNSCOM, and we know where they meet, when they meet, and who is in attendance. It's all the big players. They get together every Thursday night at six. We're trying to get permission to share this with you officially, and then use the GPR team to pounce on them.'

Mallard and Raptor listened in silence. 'Then what?' I asked. 'If we surround the building, do you think they will let us in?'

Dobbs thought before answering. 'Probably not. But they would have to go past you in order to leave the building, and then you could ask to inspect any documents they carry with them.'

I laughed. 'There isn't a chance in hell they'd let us humiliate their senior officials like that. We'd be pushed aside long before they let that happen.' Memories of the Ministry of Agriculture and the throngs of demonstrators filled my mind.

The three men sat there, grim faced. 'Well, then we'd just have to blow them away, wouldn't we?', Dobbs said.

This conversation had progressed about as far as I was prepared to go, at least at that moment. I excused myself, took an early dinner, and went back to my room to think matters over.

The next morning I found Sam Perry at breakfast. 'We need to talk,' I said. 'Moe Dobbs came to me last night with some crazy talk about new inspection sites in northern Iraq near...' Perry cut me off with a wave of his hand. 'Not here. We'll talk more about it when we get to a secure site.' Perry had just answered my question about whether or not he knew about the concept.

We had a number of senior 'observers' from the US government with us at Edwards Air Force Base, including Sam Perry. Perry brought us all together into a conference room, where we were joined by Moe Dobbs, Paul Mallard and Gregg Raptor.

One of the first things I learned was that the Sinjar operation had a name, 'Roller Blade'. The second thing I learned was that Roller Blade had significant support on the operational side of US intelligence/special operations circles. And the final thing I learned was that Roller Blade was dead in the water unless I did something to revive it – right now. I stood up. 'If we are going to prevail in terms of getting Roller Blade activated, we will need to get the chairman's blessing. And the only way Ekéus is going to bless this plan is if Nikita is behind it. Excuse me while I go find the Chief Inspector... unless anyone has an objection?' Only Moe Dobbs spoke up. 'No problem, Scott. Just keep in mind, though, that all we can talk about right now is Roller Blade. Nikita is to know nothing about the Iraqi Committee meeting. In fact, you're not supposed to know anything about the Committee. Not yet.' I nodded, and went in search of my Russian friend.

Nikita Smidovich calmly took in what I relayed to him of the Roller Blade concept and how it had come to my attention. He accompanied me back to the conference room, and listened in silence as Sam Perry and Moe Dobbs made their case. When they were finished, Smidovich chewed on the ends of his mustache while he contemplated what he had just heard. 'We have the perfect team for such a mission,' he finally said. 'Scott and I can write a paper to the chairman recommending Roller Blade, but someone from Washington will need to go to New York and show the chairman the targets, and the intelligence supporting these targets. Without this, we have no inspection.'

In short order it was agreed that Smidovich and I would draft a memorandum for the executive chairman, making the case for the Roller Blade inspection. Stu Cohen would travel to New York and present the targets to Rolf Ekéus. And then we would wait and see.

I thought the Roller Blade issue was resolved once I handed the memorandum to Sam Perry, who would transmit it using US classified communications systems to the US Mission in New York, where it would be hand-delivered to Rolf Ekéus. I didn't take into account the reality that once the memo entered the US system, everyone with security access would be able to read it. As such, I was somewhat surprised when, in the afternoon of the same day the memorandum was transmitted to New York, I was approached by Rick Grotte (pseudonym) and two other CIA analysts assigned to the inspection team. 'Scott,' Rick said, grimly, 'we need to talk.' I ushered the three CIA personnel into a side meeting room, where we sat down around a formica-covered table.

Rick Grotte was a heavy-set man of about thirty. He sported a bushy black mustache and had a fairly good sense of humor, although wrapped in an overly nervous disposition. Grotte had worked closely with the Israelis during Desert Storm, so I knew him to be both a good photographic interpreter and someone capable of pushing a political agenda. 'Roller Blade is crap,' he said. 'I don't know what kind of tale you were told by the Operations Planning Cell, but those targets just don't add up.'

I cut him off at that point. 'Look, the OPC said the same thing about your targets. What the hell is going on here? Is this bureaucratic in-fighting, or is there something else going on here that I'm not aware of?' I was venting my accumulated frustration at the entire US intelligence community, which seemed content with publicizing assessments that had Iraq in possession of 200 SCUD missiles, but proved unable to tell me how they arrived at that number, or where these missiles were. And now, at a critical point in UNSCOM's efforts to attempt to account for these missiles, the US intelligence community seemed to be at war with itself, contradicting and denigrating its own product in the worst, and most unprofessional, manner.

Grotte didn't blink. 'Scott, you know as well as I do that there is an approved way to process raw information into intelligence. Further, there is an approved way for intelligence to be shared with UNSCOM. This isn't simply bureaucracy at play, but a systematic methodology designed to ensure that the information passed to UNSCOM is sound, and takes into account US national security concerns regarding the dissemination of classified information.'

I nodded. 'I understand this, Rick. But understand that, from my standpoint, I received information that came through authorized US channels, and I took action on it. Are you telling me that there has been an unauthorized release of information? Or that the information released is worthless?'

Grotte had a pained expression on his face. 'Both,' he said. 'The OPC is not authorized to make assessments and pass them on to customers, whether in UNSCOM or in the US government. In the case of Iraq and UNSCOM, this is the role that the Non-Proliferation Center plays. Furthermore, the data OPC used to form its conclusions are drawn from raw sources of information, and have not been vetted by analysts for accuracy and veracity.'

'What do you want me to do?' I asked.

'Stop Roller Blade. Don't let it go forward. It is a big mistake. You and UNSCOM should not have been made aware of this information to begin with.'

'Is that because it is inaccurate, or because it is too highly classified?' I said to Rick.

'A little of both,' he answered. 'But mainly the former. We just don't think it is credible information.'

UNSCOM was being squeezed. I honestly did not understand the motive for this conflict, but I knew I wasn't going to get stuck in the middle. I looked Rick straight in the eye. 'All we've done is pass a recommendation by the US government concerning inspection sites to the chairman for consideration. My understanding is that a US team will be traveling to New York to brief the chairman. If this is truly the Operation

Planning Center's final position, I would imagine that the US government briefing team would inform the chairman as much, and the sites would be withdrawn from consideration. However, since this inspection is designed by intent to be the final word on the issue of retained Iraqi SCUD missiles, I would not want to pull from the target list sites for inspection that will only be resubmitted at some later date. If these sites are withdrawn by the US, it must be because they lack any credibility whatsoever.'

Grotte got red in the face. 'If you put it that way, then you'd have to inspect thousands of sites before you'd satisfy the US government.' He knew as soon as he spoke, he had made a mistake.

'What do you mean by that?' I asked. 'The GPR inspection was supposed to have had access to the totality of credible information in the possession of the US government about Iraqi missiles. Are you telling me that there is more information out there that hasn't been made available to UNSCOM?'

Grotte stood up, signaling that the meeting was over. 'I didn't say that. I'm simply saying that this isn't a problem that will be solved by a single inspection, and that the OPC interference isn't helping UNSCOM or the issue of Iraq's disarmament.'

After Rick Grotte and his two colleagues had left, I pondered just what had transpired. *Not a problem that would be solved by a single inspection.* The lines drawn in the sand by the Security Council back in April 1991 were becoming increasingly difficult to discern. What were we trying to accomplish in Iraq? Disarmament? That's what I thought the mission was, and that's what I strove to achieve in everything I did regarding my work with UNSCOM. But the sand storm of controversy, animosity and mis-information all combined to blur the original intent of the Council, until in the end we seemed stuck on a path to nowhere, all reference points and directions obscured into nothingness. Did the USA really want Iraq disarmed? Would Washington ever acknowledge Iraq's disarmament once achieved? These were questions I simply could not answer, and the recent blow-up between two CIA organizations, the Non-Proliferation Center and Operations Planning Cell, made arriving at an answer that much more difficult. All UNSCOM could do at this juncture was keep moving forward, while trying to implement the inspection as professionally as possible.

The Roller Blade targets were briefed to Rolf Ekéus, who approved them immediately. The UNSCOM 63 inspection deployed to Baghdad with tension running high, in part created by the sheer size of the team, the complexity of its mission and the high expectations associated with its targets. After making so much about the potential of this mission, everyone expected something big to happen.

But there would be no such drama. Unimpeded by the Iraqi government, UNSCOM 63 combed the skies and ground of Iraq, searching for any sign of buried SCUD missiles. We broke the entire western desert of Iraq up into large 'search areas' and spent days conducting extensive 'grid' searches. Nothing was found.[2] UNSCOM 63 took months to plan, cost the US government over $12 million to support, and took weeks to execute. The only conclusion that could be reached from its result was that the CIA's estimate on an Iraqi covert SCUD missile force, including the Sinjar targets, was completely without foundation in fact.

Upon my return to New York, Rolf Ekéus informed me that I was to accompany him to Washington on Monday 8 November, to brief senior National Security Council (NSC) staff on the results of the inspection. The post-UNSCOM 63 briefing was held on the third floor of the Old Executive Office Building, in Suite 345. The sign on the door read 'Director, Central Intelligence'. Inside his office, behind a closed door, sat James Woolsey, the new head of the CIA, who was scheduled to meet with Rolf Ekéus after I finished my briefing to the National Security Council staff. There was still a question as to whether or not I would also be asked to brief Woolsey, but this decision would be held off on until after my NSC briefing.

The senior American present was Martin Indyk, the NSC staffer responsible for the Middle East. In addition to Indyk, Bruce Reidel, the Pentagon's Middle East expert, a CIA analyst from Stu Cohen's office, and Jerry Murphy, from the State Department, were in attendance. The chairman and a contingent from UNSCOM were present as well, including his new deputy, Charles Duelfer, a career State Department official. We were sitting around a heavy wooden coffee table, in chairs dragged out from the various rooms and offices that connected to the lobby.

I began the briefing. It was a cut and dry presentation of the facts surrounding UNSCOM's accounting of Iraq's proscribed missiles: nineteen inspections since the summer of 1991, including UNSCOM 63, making full use of intrusive and innovative inspection techniques and methodologies. I emphasized the close working relationship UNSCOM had with the US intelligence community, and that the most recent inspection had made use of the very best information the CIA had on the issue of retained Iraqi missiles. I also discussed the close working relationship UNSCOM had with the British, as well as the important role played by Russia and France in supporting the UNSCOM program of inspections. I went through the detailed accounting of Iraq's SCUD missiles before concluding: Iraq received 819 SCUD-B missiles from the Soviet Union, and all 819 SCUD-B missiles had been plausibly accounted for.

I knew that closing the chapter on Iraq's prohibited missile programs was only the first step in what would undoubtedly be a long and difficult struggle to account for Baghdad's other weapons – nuclear, chemical and the still undeclared biological programs. But this was an important, even critical, first step. By closing the file on Iraq's missile programs, UNSCOM would demonstrate to Iraq and the world the seriousness with which it carried out its task and, ultimately, its capacity for fair, objective and balanced analysis even under the most strenuous and confrontational circumstances. It would provide the proverbial 'light at the end of the tunnel' for Iraq, an important psychological boost that could lead to even greater cooperation with the disarmament process.

I had expected some questions from the attendees, but there were none. The CIA analyst had left the group and crossed over to the other side of the lobby, where the door to Woolsey's office remained shut. I watched as he knocked on the door, opened it and spoke in quiet tones to someone inside. He looked over at Martin Indyk and nodded.

'Well, the director is ready to meet you, Mr. Chairman,' Indyk said, gesturing with his hand for the chairman's group to proceed to Woolsey's office. Indyk looked at me. 'Thank you again for the briefing, Scott. We won't be needing for you to give it again. Bruce and I will be able to relay the gist to the director.' I was left standing alone. Charles Duelfer came up to me before joining the chairman. 'Good job,' he said. 'I just don't think it was the message they wanted to hear.'

Duelfer called me to his office the next day. 'Well,' he said, 'they didn't buy your presentation. The CIA director believes that the negative result achieved by your inspection does not prove a thing. The CIA accepts that perhaps the number of missiles retained by Iraq may be less than the 200 they assessed earlier this year.'

'How many do they think exist?' I asked. Duelfer shuffled in his seat. 'Between twelve and twenty,' he said. 'How did they justify that figure?' I asked. Duelfer shrugged. 'They didn't. Woolsey expressed great admiration for the work of UNSCOM, and the efforts of the inspectors, but in the end he said that the CIA feels that the Iraqis retain too much control over the work of the inspectors to allow any findings to be credible.'

I was appalled. 'They don't want the truth,' I told Duelfer. 'And I don't know that we can do anymore than what has already been done to convince them we are doing a good, credible job.'

Working for UNSCOM no longer had the appeal for me it once had. Sifting through my mail, I found an announcement from Headquarters Marine Corps about the possibility of returning to active duty as part of the Active Reserve force. I filled out the application and mailed it in, figuring I had nothing to lose by trying. The week before Christmas 1993, I received a response from Headquarters Marine Corps. I had been accepted back on active duty, with a report date of 1 March 1994. I would return at my rank of captain. I had until the end of January to accept or decline the offer. Given everything that had transpired over the previous two years, I didn't hesitate to accept their offer. I left UNSCOM at the end of February 1993 for New Orleans, Louisiana, where I would begin my new job as an intelligence officer with the US Marines.

PART TWO
CRUSADE

Chapter 7

New Friends
March–November 1994

Back in the Marine Corps, life proved uneventful and UNSCOM seemed like a dream. Despite the bitterness that had existed at the time of my departure, I had to admit to some nostalgia. The mundane task of coordinating Marine reserve training was a world away from the hustle and bustle of inspections.

Since arriving in New Orleans, I had been getting phone calls from Nikita Smidovich asking where this or that piece of paper or snippet of information could be found. Always guarded, Smidovich held back from divulging any information that could be considered sensitive or proprietary, given my newfound status as a 'US government official'. I detected nothing in his voice hinting that anything was amiss with the inspections.

I called Mark Silver, just to say hello. Like Smidovich, he betrayed no gloom or doom about UNSCOM, but rather the exact opposite. He shocked me with one dramatic revelation. 'We have some new friends,' he said. For some reason, in April 1994, Israel had approached UNSCOM, offering to help.

Israel! This was exciting news indeed. Mark wouldn't reveal any details, but clearly things seemed to be heading in a positive direction for UNSCOM. It certainly didn't sound as if Ekéus were simply spinning his wheels.

It therefore took me somewhat by surprise when, in early July 1994, my phone rang again. It was Marcus Kreutz, my old German friend from UNSCOM 24. 'Scott,' said Kreutz, his heavily accented voice serious, 'we need your help.'

'Anything,' I answered, curious as to what the problem could be. 'Come back to UNSCOM,' Kreutz said. 'We need you back here.' It seemed UNSCOM was stuck in a rut, and were looking for new and innovative ways to get weapons inspections back up and running.

I didn't know where to go with the conversation. 'Well, I'm sort of stuck in this new job here, Kreutz. What exactly is the problem, and I'll see if I can do anything?' He couldn't, or wouldn't, provide any specifics beyond what had already been said. However, he and Smidovich did set in motion a chain of events that had me on an airplane in early September 1994, bound for New York City. Captain Scott Ritter, United States Marine Corps, had been detailed to UNSCOM, at the request of the United States Department of State, for a period of two months, ostensibly to research and write a comprehensive history of the Iraqi ballistic missile program, but essentially to see what, if anything, could be done to kick-start UNSCOM into doing effective inspections.

One of the first things I had to grapple with was the Israel issue. It turned out that the new Israeli cooperation, which Mark Silver had alluded to in our telephone conversation the previous spring, was the most widely known 'secret' in UNSCOM. Israel had provided its first briefing to UNSCOM back in April 1994, and it seemed that since that time every senior weapons inspector had had his or her own 'unique' contact with the Israelis, which was kept secret from all others. In the war-ravaged psychological environment of the Middle East, where most governments saw Israel as the enemy, any public disclosure linking Israeli intelligence to the weapons inspectors would lead to an immediate loss of credibility for UNSCOM.

The key to the UNSCOM-Israeli relationship getting off the ground was Brigadier General Ya'acov Ami-Dror, who was in charge of research for Israeli Military Intelligence. Ami-Dror understood the unique role UNSCOM played in disarming Iraq, and how this process could be improved with Israel's help. In April 1994, Ami-Dror led a team of Israeli intelligence analysts to New York, where they met with Rolf Ekéus to discuss future cooperation. Further meetings were held in May and June, resulting in a stream of extremely detailed information about Iraq's past proscribed programs. Nikita Smidovich was a central figure at these meetings, coordinating the UNSCOM briefings and keeping the Israelis informed about what kind of information could best help the inspectors.

When I arrived in New York in September, I approached Smidovich and asked if I could have access to the Israeli reporting. Without hesitation, he handed me a manila folder filled with the various notes of meetings and technical reports left behind by the Israelis. The Israeli reporting turned out to be detailed, providing hard data that appeared to demonstrate that Iraq had failed to declare significant aspects of its past chemical, nuclear, ballistic missile and biological warfare programs.

My orders were to jump-start the UNSCOM inspection process with the goal of finishing the disarmament mission. This meant either finding weapons, or demonstrating they no longer existed. The new Israeli intelligence bonanza offered the best place to start searching for something that might help me in my task. I wasn't searching the Israeli papers for tidbits of information about possible undeclared activities on the part of the Iraqis. In contrast to previous inspections, when I had been looking for evidence of past concealment, this time I was looking for clues on what the Iraqis were up to now.

UNSCOM had been through this drill before. By launching another inspection designed to investigate historical information, we might be able to compel Iraq to disclose a little more data, and perhaps turn over some new documents. However, even if Iraq were to come clean, the fact that we once again had found their declarations to be false and incomplete made it nearly certain that no one, especially the USA, would ever believe anything the Iraqis ever said, even if it turned out to be the truth. UNSCOM had become trapped by Iraq's past deceit, and had become consumed by a never-ending process of trying to 'prove the negative'. The only way for UNSCOM to win (and I judged victory based on the successful completion of UNSCOM's disarmament mandate) would be to catch the Iraqis actually doing something wrong. If I could build an inspection regime capable of accomplishing this task, I was sure we would either find such proscribed activity or demonstrate, to a level unchallengeable even by the USA, that Iraq was disarmed.

The Israeli documents provided us with something tangible to focus on for the first time. Buried inside the Israeli assessment on ballistic missiles were several paragraphs that talked about two trucking companies, under the operational control of an entity called the 'Special Security Office', which were used to move sensitive material and documents in order to prevent them from falling into the hands of UNSCOM inspectors. The trucks were said to be moved every three to four days, and were always moved out of Baghdad when an inspection team arrived. The 'Special Security Office', the Israeli information stated, was located in Baghdad, was affiliated with Iraqi intelligence, and operated under the command of Saddam's younger son, Qusay.

I recommended that UNSCOM dispatch Smidovich, Kreutz and myself to Israel, where we would brief the Israelis on the information they had provided to us regarding ongoing Iraqi efforts to conceal material from the inspectors, and what we in UNSCOM proposed to do about it. I wanted Israel to help UNSCOM train, equip and deploy covert communications intercept teams inside Iraq, operating under the cover of UN weapons inspectors, so that we could listen in on Iraqi conversations and hopefully detect those that dealt with how the Iraqis were hiding proscribed weapons and activities. In short, we would send teams into Iraq to target organizations and facilities believed to be engaged in the business of hiding weapons, and then listen in as the Iraqis discussed how they were actually going about the business of hiding these weapons. Smidovich and Kreutz were both intrigued by the idea, and it didn't take long to get Rolf Ekéus to agree. Soon the three of us were on our way to the Middle East.

I arrived in Tel Aviv on 8 October 1994 aboard a commercial flight out of Cyprus. Kreutz and Smidovich had flown in on separate flights, as we were trying to minimize our 'profile' for security purposes. Not knowing what to expect, I was surprised to be greeted at the airport by a white stretch Mercedes limousine and a man holding a sign with my name on it. I was taken straight to the VIP reception area, where my passport was collected and processed (the Israelis made sure not to leave any identifying marks or stamps in my passport, issuing me a paper visa instead), and my luggage gathered while I sat in a secluded lounge where I was offered sweets, fresh orange juice and coffee.

The formalities completed, I was driven in the limousine to the Holiday Inn hotel in downtown Tel Aviv. Once there, in a quiet lounge, I found Smidovich and Kreutz awaiting my arrival, drinking beer and snacking on peanuts and olives. Smidovich had already made contact with an Israeli official, who informed us that the limousine would pick us up at 9 a.m. the next morning to take us to our initial meeting. Rolf Ekéus had sent a letter to the Israeli Mission in New York, advising them of our arrival and the tentative items on our agenda. According to the Ekéus letter, we were 'experts on mission' who wanted to follow up on earlier discussions about Iraq's proscribed weapons programs. Left unsaid was the real purpose of coming to Israel – the proposal on sensitive intelligence cooperation. This was a message that we were instructed to deliver to the director of military intelligence, General Uri Saguy, in person.

The next day we arrived outside the gates of the Kirya, the headquarters of the Israeli Defense Force, located in downtown Tel Aviv, escorted by an Israeli Lieutenant Colonel, Moshe Ponkovsky (pseudonym). Ponkovsky was a man of about forty, of medium height, fit, with a shock of black hair and thick glasses that made him look more like an accountant than an Israeli intelligence officer. Sentries on duty outside the gate stopped the limo, and checked the identification of both the driver and Ponkovsky. Ponkovsky's ID card apparently granted him escort status, and the guard waved in the limo with only a cursory look in the back where Smidovich, Kreutz and I sat. Special hydraulic steel barriers were lowered by another sentry, allowing us to drive through. Military police stood watch to the side. Everyone carried an automatic weapon of some sort. Our limo proceeded down the main road for about fifty yards, and then turned right into a parking lot in front of a large, multi-story concrete office building.

A duty officer escorted us to the office of the director of the *Aman*. There, seated at his desk, was Major General Uri Saguy. At fifty years, General Saguy was on the far side of what had been, by any standard, one of the more remarkable military careers in Israeli history. Short, with a stooped shoulder, Uri Saguy had short-cropped salt and pepper hair, heavy rings under his eyes, and a surprisingly soft smile for a man with such a fearsome reputation. A former commander of the famous Golani Brigade, General Saguy was a veteran of the Six Day War, Yom Kippur, and the invasion of Lebanon. His left forearm bore the scar of a bone-shattering wound suffered fighting the Syrians.

Seated next to Uri Saguy was Ya'acov Ami-Dror, the brilliant but controversial deputy director for research and analysis. A career intelligence professional, and an orthodox Jew, Ami-Dror wore a full black beard and skull cap. Brigadier Ami-Dror was the main reason why Israel had opened up to UNSCOM earlier in the year. Colonel Eylan and Moshe Ponkovsky rounded out the Israeli side.

We sat down around the director's desk. I was struck by how spartan the room looked. I had been in the offices of many senior American intelligence officials. Those rooms were always spacious, packed with comfortable furniture, and the walls were filled with mementoes gathered during the course of their respective careers. Uri Saguy's office was the exact opposite – small, dark and crowded, its walls filled with shelves packed with files, books and maps. His desk had the look of a place where someone worked, not just sat.

A soldier came in and delivered drinks, ice water and orange juice. Once the soldier had left, the door closed securely behind him, General Saguy got straight to the point. 'I understand you have a message for me, and only me, from Ambassador Ekéus.' His tone was polite, but it also had an edge to it, like someone who was very busy, and not happy with the interruption to his work schedule. The general motioned his hands towards the others in the room. 'I hope it is all right for me to have my principal advisors on your work present with me tonight. I understand you are concerned about who hears this particular message.'

I looked at General Saguy. 'Israel has provided UNSCOM with information in the past months related to Iraq's prohibited weapons programs. In addition to the technical information on what Iraq had acquired and what they might still retain, your government also provided data on certain ongoing concealment activities run by sensitive security organizations in the Iraqi government, in particular the Special Security Organization.'

'According to this information,' I continued, 'the Special Security Organization is responsible for retaining and protecting Iraq's undeclared weapons of mass destruction stockpile. This is a very serious allegation, one that the executive chairman feels must by fully investigated. Ambassador Ekéus is concerned that these issues must be resolved before UNSCOM can address the issue of Iraqi compliance. Because the source of this information was Israeli, the chairman wants to make sure that Israel is available to help UNSCOM exploit any inspections that might arise because of this information.'

I then got right to the point. 'UNSCOM is proposing to dispatch to Iraq a special team of radio intercept operators for the purpose of exploiting Iraqi communications related to the hiding of prohibited material inside Iraq, and in particular the communications of the Special Security Organization. We would provide the intercept operators, but are requesting Israeli help in equipping and training the personnel involved, and exploiting all captured signals.'

One would have to work in the field of intelligence to understand the scale of UNSCOM's request. In the intelligence business, everything is considered sensitive, some things are considered secret, some things top secret and some things are just never discussed. Communications interception, also known as signals intelligence, or SIGINT, is one of the subjects that are simply not discussed. All nations communicate using radio or telephone links. Some of these links are known to be 'unsecure', meaning that whatever is spoken or transmitted can readily be listened to. Some links, however, are considered 'secure', either because the signal being transmitted has been scrambled using some sort of ciphering mechanism, or because the signal is transmitted along a cable that prevents most forms of interception, or both. When people speak on a 'secure' link, they speak without constraint. The best intelligence can be gathered from eavesdropping in on such 'secure' links and nations spend billions of dollars developing the means to penetrate them.

The problem is, the solutions for accessing 'secure' links often only apply to one particular system. If for any reason the people speaking decide to change what they are doing, either by using a new cipher or by changing the means of communication altogether, then the money spent on the 'solution' is wasted. The combination of potential intelligence value, combined with the enormous expenses involved, make communications interception, or SIGINT, among the most sensitive disciplines in the intelligence business.

And UNSCOM had just asked the director of Israel's military intelligence to open the door to Israel's SIGINT world to a trio of foreigners representing the United Nations.

You could hear a pin drop. For a moment Uri Saguy seemed too stunned to speak. 'I now know why you had insisted on the message being delivered directly to me. I never would have believed it otherwise.' He was suddenly all business. 'This is a most unusual request, and will require much thought and consultation. I do not know where Israel will come out on the matter, because national security issues are at stake here. But I do know that this is a brave request sent by a man of courage. We in this room have an obligation to respect such courage, and assist where we can to help it succeed.'

Uri Saguy rose from where he sat, signaling that the meeting was over. 'We have much to think about. Regardless of the decision we take, however, what you have done tonight is to show us that you are serious about your job. This means much to us. We must find a way to help such serious people.'

We were not going to get an answer to our request on this trip, however. Moshe Ponkovsky met with us the next day. 'This is a big problem for us,' he said. 'We have to weigh many issues, including your safety and our national security. But be assured that the highest levels of our government are giving close attention to your proposal, and we will have an answer for you soon. In any case, Israel is committed to helping make your mission in Iraq a successful one.'

It took the Israelis until 20 November to finally respond. I had by this time returned to my Marine Corps posting in Louisiana, since my original secondment was for a period of only two months, and it had expired in mid-November. Rolf Ekéus was able to persuade the State Department to pressure the Marine Corps into releasing me for another tour, with the understanding that I would wrap up my work with UNSCOM once and for all by the end of December.

Back in New York, I went up to Nikita Smidovich's office, where he slid a two-page letter across his desk. It was from Moshe Ponkovsky. 'It is clear,' the letter read, 'that the cooperation that you proposed, and was being examined by us, entails a great investment of resources by both UNSCOM and IDF [Israeli Defense Force]. Our experts believe that even after investing these resources, we would be unable to guarantee the security of your personnel in such an operation. In light of the assessment of our experts regarding the minimal benefit vis-à-vis the high costs and dangers, especially for your men's personal safety, we have decided not to carry out your proposed special project.'

'So the project is dead?' I said. Smidovich nodded his head, taking a drag off his ever-present cigarette. 'So it would seem,' he said, exhaling a cloud of blue smoke. 'Except the Israelis have invited us back for further discussions regarding special cooperation between them and UNSCOM.'

We flew into Tel Aviv on 3 December and were greeted by the same driver and limousine as during our first visit. The side of the limousine bore the symbol of the Israeli Tourist Industry, two men carrying grapes, a reference to the biblical passage where Moses sent scouts out to find the promised land. The scouts returned with grapes and other evidence of abundance. Smidovich joked that these two men carrying the grapes were in fact the first Mossad agents.

Our driver told us that we were on our own for the evening, but that

Ponkovsky would pick us up at 8 a.m. for our meetings. As before, we were met the next morning on schedule, and driven to the Israeli base outside Herzaliya.

Ponkovsky had a proposal. 'We are prepared to open up the archives of Israeli intelligence to support you and your mission. The problem is that we simply cannot haphazardly give you everything, for obvious reasons. There must be a mechanism of cooperation which would govern the release of information, and help guide our work.'

Smidovich came up with the idea: 'What about photographic interpretation?' he asked.

Ponkovsky smiled. 'What do you mean?'

'UNSCOM has at its disposal the U-2 aircraft, which takes pictures of Iraq. We use these pictures to help prepare inspections, but very rarely do we use the film in an imaginative manner. What if UNSCOM and Israel were to enter into an arrangement where your photographic interpreters worked with our specialists in looking at the film? The examination of the film could be helped along by any intelligence you might have, and could be used to further develop information that might not otherwise be understood fully.' Smidovich quickly reigned himself in. 'Such an undertaking would, of course, be extremely sensitive, and would need the full permission of the executive chairman.'

'And the Americans as well, I presume,' Ponkovsky said.

'Yes, and no,' Smidovich replied. 'The Americans would need to agree to the concept, but would have no say on how we conducted the relationship with Israel. This would be an UNSCOM-Israeli initiative, not UNSCOM-Israeli-American.'

'Who in UNSCOM would lead this effort?' Ponkovsky asked, looking at Smidovich, who in turn looked at me. 'These decisions are up to the chairman, but my guess is that he would choose Scott Ritter.'

This exchange took me by surprise, but I fully supported the idea. For some time now, Smidovich had been listening to me gripe about the flaws in the way UNSCOM managed the U-2 program, and we were both very unhappy with the support UNSCOM was being provided by the CIA when it came to photographic interpretation. Often, the CIA analyst was unfamiliar with the site being briefed, mispronounced the geographic locations depicted in the photographs, and could only impart to us the significance of a given image by pointing out an arrow on the image oriented on an object like a crane or truck, with the annotation 'suspicious activity'. The Israelis were proposing a serious intelligence-based relationship, and I think Smidovich was taking advantage of their offer to address some of UNSCOM's deficiencies.

We discussed further the U-2 concept, with Smidovich and I briefing Ponkovsky on how the U-2 was tasked by UNSCOM, the kinds of products produced by the U-2 and the level of support provided by the Americans.

'How much time would be required to exploit [i.e., interpret] the film?' I asked.

'You should plan on spending two weeks here, every other month,' Ponkovsky responded. 'Of course, in the end the amount of time required depends on the amount of film to be exploited.' Smidovich, Kreutz and I promised to do our best to get support for this initiative in both New York and Washington. The United States intelligence community had not, to date, been performing well, and UNSCOM was paying the price. The Israelis were offering a serious intelligence relationship along lines never even considered by the Americans. I believed that cooperation with Israel was a good idea, and I was committed to making it succeed.

As I worked with the Israelis to develop critical investigative tools, the Iraqis were having an investigation of their own into why it was the UN inspectors continued to believe Iraq was hiding weapons of mass destruction. The goal of the Iraqi intelligence service, *Mukhabarat*, regarding UNSCOM was never to deceive the inspectors. The Mukhabarat was not in the business of hiding WMD, or obstructing the work of the inspectors. Their task was national security. Simply put, the Mukhabarat viewed the presence of UN inspectors in Iraq as a security threat, and therefore monitored the work of the inspectors to make sure the inspectors did not do anything that went beyond the scope of their disarmament task. The methodology used by the Mukhabarat was surveillance. A secretive organization, the Mukhabarat at first had no direct dealings with the Iraqi scientists and technicians who interacted with the UN inspectors on a daily basis, and instead relied on their own teams to monitor the work of the foreigners. The tactics used were tried and true. Hotel rooms were bugged and inspectors luggage was rummaged through. Any bag left unattended for any length of time was grabbed and exploited, and the Mukhabarat was able to gain important insight into the workings of the inspectors this way. A mobile radio intercept vehicle, staffed by English-speaking agents, followed the inspectors wherever they went, usually at a discreet distance, listening in on all the inspectors' radio traffic. Agents were recruited throughout the inspection process, penetrating deep into the workings of the inspectors, both in Iraq and in New York. One of these agents was a UN linguist who had been given unprecedented access to the planning and execution of UNSCOM inspections. In fact, he had served as my own personal linguist on several inspections, before suspicions about his relationship with the Iraqi government compelled us to stop working with him.[1]

Since the Mukhabarat viewed the continued presence of inspectors in Iraq as a threat to Iraqi national security, the best way to get rid of the inspectors was to enable them to finish their job. Through its comprehensive monitoring of the work of the inspectors, the Mukhabarat was aware that the questions being asked by the inspectors had a logic that couldn't be denied. The Mukhabarat officials responsible for following the UNSCOM issue believed that the Iraqi officials from the National Monitoring Directorate (NMD) who were responsible for providing the information needed by the inspectors to complete their disarmament task were not, in fact, being forthcoming with the inspectors. If the Monitoring Directorate was not executing its tasks efficiently, or worse, holding back data and material needed by the inspectors, then the inspectors would just keep coming. The head of the UNSCOM section of the Mukhabarat asked his superiors for permission to monitor the National Monitoring Directorate to make sure they weren't holding back anything from the inspectors. The request was taken to the director of the Mukhabarat, who in turn passed it all the way up to Saddam Hussein, who personally authorized it.

As they had suspected, the Mukhabarat discovered that the National Monitoring Directorate was indeed holding back on the information needed by the inspectors. What they knew, which we inspectors didn't at the time, was that there were no actual weapons of mass destruction left in Iraq; these had been destroyed during the period of unilateral destruction that had taken place in the summer of 1991. And there were no dedicated programs related to the manufacture of weapons of mass destruction; these had been dismantled. What the Mukhabarat found was that the National Monitoring Directorate experts were refusing to acknowledge the entire scope of Iraq's WMD programs, in part to save expensive dual-purpose production equipment from being destroyed by the inspectors, and in part as a political tactic on the part of Tariq Aziz, who decided that the final acknowledgment of critical aspects of Iraq's past proscribed programs – destroyed, but not admitted – would be detrimental to the Iraqi strategic objective of getting economic sanctions lifted.

But it wasn't just Tariq Aziz's unwillingness to discuss the totality of Iraq's past proscribed programs with UN inspectors that plagued the efforts of the Mukhabarat. As the Mukhabarat began the delicate task of trying to coax out of the Iraqi deputy prime minister permission for the National Monitoring Directorate to be more open in answering the questions of the UNSCOM inspectors, they ran into a problem for which there was no solution: the role played by the Special Security Organization (SSO), and indeed Saddam Hussein himself, in the early hiding of WMD capability from the inspectors. The Mukhabarat's protestations in favor of a total accounting collided with the SSO's insistence that nothing related to the president or his security could ever be discussed with the UN inspectors, even if it meant lying about critical disarmament issues such as accounting for the final disposition of the WMD. Saddam had survived numerous assassination attempts and the SSO knew there were CIA agents in Iraq actively plotting his overthrow. They just couldn't take the risk.

This development could not have come at a worse time for the Iraqis. At the same time as UNSCOM inspectors were starting to focus their efforts on uncovering the role played by the SSO in hiding WMD, the Iraqis were digging in their heels, determined that this specific information remain secret. Overlooked in all this was the simple fact that Iraq had, to all intents and purposes, been disarmed. The truth was there, but no one on either side of the issue, either Iraq or UNSCOM, was willing to grasp it.[2]

Chapter 8
A Fresh Start
December 1994–July 1995

I returned to the Marine Corps at the end of December 1994. Marcus Kreutz
and Nikita Smidovich kept calling me, asking when I would be coming
back. According to their information, Rolf Ekéus had approached the
State Department about my being sent back to UNSCOM, this time on an
eight-month assignment. The Israelis were pushing to get the intelligence
cooperation started, and Ekéus agreed that I was best suited to carry out
such a task.

In March 1995, while in Washington on Marine Corps business, I
arranged to stop over at the CIA's Non-Proliferation Center (NPC) to find
out what the status of Ekéus's request was. There I met with Stu Cohen's
successor, a long-time intelligence professional I shall refer to as 'the
Counselor'.

I discovered that the CIA hadn't been idle, and the Counselor showed
a great deal of interest in the Israeli initiative. The Counselor introduced
me to another CIA operative, an officer I shall call 'Burt', who had been
brought in from the Directorate of Operations as his deputy.

Neither the Counselor nor Burt seemed surprised when I mentioned the
U-2 joint exploitation concept, or UNSCOM's desire to embark on a program
of communications interception in Iraq. Both understood the need for good
photographic interpretation support and, if the Israelis could provide that

and unlock the door to the treasure trove of intelligence information that UNSCOM needed to fuel this new push against Iraq's weapons programs, then so much for the better. Likewise, the Counselor and Burt recognized the communications intercept proposal as a much-needed initiative for helping UNSCOM break free of the current inspection malaise.

The concept of an eight-month secondment to UNSCOM had become a political hot potato inside Marine Corps Headquarters. So when the Counselor offered to use CIA money to fund a consulting contract with the Pentagon that would send me back to UNSCOM, I took it, even though it meant leaving the Marine Corps once and for all.

I arrived in New York, and was immediately involved in the issue of UNSCOM's cooperation with Israel. Rolf Ekéus wanted it to go forward, and so a meeting was organized between UNSCOM and the CIA to figure out how to make it happen. Rolf Ekéus's American deputy, Charles Duelfer, served as the focal point for the meeting. I had briefly met Duelfer back in November 1993, in the aftermath of the ground-penetrating radar inspection known as UNSCOM 63. Duelfer was a career State Department employee, a national security specialist, not a foreign service officer, which meant that he operated as an outsider, even inside the State Department.

On 7 July 1995, Charles Duelfer arranged for a lunch meeting between UNSCOM and the CIA at the exclusive Princeton Club, away from prying eyes, in downtown Manhattan. In attendance were Nikita Smidovich, Rolf Ekéus, Charles Duelfer and the Counselor. We were here to discuss UNSCOM's developing relationship with Israel, and in particular the proposal to take U-2 film to Israel for joint exploitation with Israeli photographic interpreters. Rolf Ekéus, back in August 1991, had agreed with the USA that if UNSCOM wanted to share U-2 images with anyone other than the USA, we needed to get prior US clearance. Cooperation with Israel was a particularly contentious issue for political reasons, and Ekéus for this reason wanted to make absolutely sure we had the CIA's blessing before proceeding.

We sat down in the upstairs dining room of the club, a large, spacious setting where the business elite of New York came to socialize and grab a bite to eat. A waiter in a white coat took our lunch orders, and walked towards the kitchen, leaving the five of us seated around the table; on the surface, we looked like any other group of alumni from the Ivy League, dressed in suits, clustered around a table enjoying our elite status in one of the most exclusive private clubs in New York. Before we had placed our orders, I had provided the group with a full briefing on what was being proposed, and was waiting for their responses.

The Counselor had only a few questions. 'What procedures for security do you propose for the handling of the film?'

'What would you propose?' I asked.

The Counselor shrugged. 'I'm not proposing anything. This is your show. You tell me what you are going to do.'

'I could take it to the US Embassy and keep it there when not working with it,' I said.

'No Embassy,' the Counselor responded. 'There are to be no American fingerprints on this.'

'It would be easier if you just told us what your requirements for security were,' I said. 'Then we'd put in place procedures that took these into account.'

'No American fingerprints,' the Counselor repeated again. 'No one in my organization wants anything in writing to exist about this activity. We won't stop you from doing this, and many, like myself, think this is a very good idea. But in Washington, there are two kinds of people – those who support Israel, and those who don't trust Israel. The last thing we want to do is give anyone a scrap of paper that they can wave around to the media about this matter.'

After long and careful discussion, a cautious green light was given. I would go to Israel with several rolls of U-2 film, and begin the operation of a secret intelligence-sharing program that would hopefully empower UNSCOM to come to closure on Iraq's weapons of mass destruction.[1] But if this relationship were ever to become public knowledge, it could be the ruin of UNSCOM.

Full of anticipation, I met Moshe Ponkovsky in Tel Aviv in July 1995. He picked me up at the airport and drove me towards the Kirya, the walled-off district of the city that housed the headquarters of the Israeli Defense Force (IDF). Ponkovsky parked the car, and led me into an unmarked building midway down the road. Inside we were greeted by an Israeli soldier standing guard, who handed me a visitor's badge bearing the crest of the unit that occupied this building: A blue circle, bordered by red, in which black, red and white aperture was wrapped in silver wings, a compass mounted on top, and white lenses affixed to the bottom. We were in the home of the IDF's national photographic interpretation unit.

Ponkovsky introduced me to Mushiko (the Israelis were very informal, referring to everyone by their first name), one of the most experienced, and capable, photographic interpreters in the IDF. Mushiko in turn introduced me to Khezi, Maya, Ori and others, all veteran imagery analysts with thousands of hours on a light table. These were the best of the best, the 'Top Guns' of the Israeli photographic interpretation business.

Under the strict supervision of their top photographic interpreter, the IDF imagery analysts proceeded to 'scan' the film, getting a feel for both the product and the area they were looking at. 'Scanning' meant you were not looking for anything in particular, but rather behaving more like a tourist, taking a casual stroll through Iraq from 75,000 feet. Once all the analysts had 'scanned' each spool of film several times came note-taking time. The analysts reviewed each frame, inch by inch, looking for anything of potential interest, jotting down anything that caught their eye. Only then did the analysts go back to their own offices, where they consulted the various databases of intelligence information they maintained on Iraq. I was involved throughout this process, bouncing back and forth between the light tables and conference rooms, where I met with various experts from the Israeli intelligence community to discuss what we were seeing on the film. This process went on for two weeks, at the end of which the Israelis had produced dozens of viable inspection targets. After two weeks of solid work, I left Israel with several notebooks full of data, a folder containing dozens of photographic prints of target sites in Iraq, and eight rolls of U-2 film.

The Israeli cooperation seemed to wake up the CIA to the fact that they had better start putting something credible on the table in terms of intelligence or find themselves pushed aside. Within days of my return to New York, I was invited down to Washington to a meeting at the State Department to discuss future inspection plans.

The UNSCOM-Israeli U-2 cooperation was part of an overall intelligence plan I had prepared to address the issue of what we in UNSCOM were calling the Iraqi 'concealment mechanism'. Using the intelligence provided by Israel, I had isolated the Iraqi Special Security Organization (SSO) as the critical focus for UNSCOM's investigations. If our intelligence was correct, we thought (wrongly as it turned out) that not only was the SSO involved in protecting weapons of mass destruction in 1991, but that this involvement continued through to the present.

Burt, my principal CIA contact, chaired the meeting, and was accompanied by an entourage from the CIA that included Moe Dobbs, Gordon

Cooper (the Delta Force operative who had served on earlier inspections) and several other analysts and operations types. It had been almost two years since I had last seen Dobbs and Cooper, and we gave each other a hearty handshake. Regardless of what I thought of the CIA and US policy towards Iraq, these were two men whom I tremendously respected.

The meeting started off with a briefing I had prepared on a detailed plan of action which had the UNSCOM-Israeli cooperation playing a critical role in gathering the information about the SSO needed for any inspection UNSCOM might undertake. I briefed Burt and his entourage on some of the targets which had been developed with the Israelis. Burt jotted down some notes, and smiled. 'I think we might be able to address some of these issues today,' he said.

I continued. Taking on a sensitive target like the Special Security Organization, I noted, meant that UNSCOM would need to gain access to new means of collecting information in Iraq, as inspections were taking place. If the SSO was in fact involved in hiding material from the UNSCOM inspectors, this meant that it had to adapt to what the inspectors were doing inside Iraq. This required some form of communications, and I believed that UNSCOM should try to listen in on any conversations which involved moving WMD-related material away from the inspectors. Israel had turned down our request for their direct support of such an operation, but this did not mean that the requirement no longer existed. I had mentioned the issue of communications intercept operations to the Counselor at the first Princeton Club meeting, along with the fact that the USA had twice balked at providing UNSCOM with support along those lines. The Counselor was certain that attitudes in Washington had changed towards the notion of UNSCOM-controlled communications intercept teams, and that if a viable plan could be put forward by UNSCOM, support would be forthcoming under conditions that would be acceptable to Rolf Ekéus. I now presented Burt with such a plan, outlining how UNSCOM inspections of the targets provided by the Israelis could trigger an Iraqi response that communications intercept teams would be able to exploit.

I mentioned the possibility of US support for such an effort to Burt, who handed the issue over to Moe Dobbs. 'We're putting a package together for you and Nikita,' he said. 'When we get it together, we'll brief you and provide whatever training is necessary.'

Burt then turned the meeting over to a CIA case officer who worked northern Europe. He had some startling new information about the

Iraqi concealment mechanism, and the role that the security forces of the Military Industrial Commission – the *Amn al Tasnia* – played.

'The source of this information is a defector of proven access and reliability who is being jointly exploited by the CIA and the host government. I just came back from a meeting in Europe,' the CIA officer said, 'where the source was discussed, and the feeling was that, given the nature of your planned inspection, this information would be of some value.'

According to the source, the headquarters of the *Amn al Tasnia* had moved to Palestine Street in downtown Baghdad, a multi-story facility next to the Ministry of Defense. In addition to the various departments one would associate with an industrial security organization of a police state, the source said that the Amn al Tasnia maintained a dedicated operations center solely for the purpose of tracking UNSCOM and servicing a wider concealment effort which shuttled retained material of a proscribed nature from hide site to hide site. The source provided descriptions for a dozen hide sites that he was personally aware of.

I suddenly had a kernel of hard data around which I could more specifically design an inspection, especially when combined with the Israeli information.

'If we go down this path,' Burt asked, 'how long do you think it will take to achieve a meaningful result? When will we find the weapons?'

I estimated the total time needed for the operation, from start to finish, was around six months. 'If this works,' I said, 'there is no reason that we can't close the file on Iraq by Valentine's Day.'

Chapter 9

Adventures in Amman
July–November 1995

In July 1995, after a year-long investigation by the UNSCOM biological weapons team which involved close cooperation with the intelligence services of both Israel and Germany, the Iraqi government had finally admitted having an offensive biological weapons program, and new information regarding that program was forthcoming on almost a weekly basis. Iraq had been denying the existence of its biological warfare program for more than four years, and its absence from the Iraqi declaration had made selling an investigation of any so-called 'concealment mechanism' in Iraq, believed to be hiding weapons programs like the newly declared biological activity, that much easier. However, following its admission, the Iraqi government had taken a hard-line approach, demanding that the Security Council move to lift economic sanctions against Iraq or else Baghdad would sever all ties with UNSCOM. Iraq had set a date of mid-August 1995 as the deadline.

And then came Hussein Kamal's defection to Jordan. The defection of Saddam Hussein's son-in-law to Amman, Jordan on 8 August 1995, took UNSCOM, and the world, by storm. After all, Hussein Kamal was the former head of the Military Industrial Commission, and the one responsible for all of Iraq's WMD programs. Upon arriving in Jordan, Hussein Kamal announced his intention to lead the fight to remove Saddam Hussein from power. Kamal's defection set off a flurry of activity as the international community scrambled to respond to the development, and dealing with Hussein Kamal's defection became UNSCOM's number one priority. The Special Security Organization investigation I was putting together was placed on the back burner, as was the Israeli cooperation.

Rolf Ekéus traveled to Baghdad to meet with the Iraqi government to discuss the defection of Hussein Kamal and the direction Iraqi-UNSCOM relations would take. In an amazing turnaround, Iraq dropped the bellicose nature of its rhetoric against UNSCOM and instead adopted a tone of conciliatory concessions. Now, in the aftermath of the defection, there was no mention of any deadline, or the lifting of sanctions. Iraq appeared to be bending over backwards to be seen as fully cooperating with UNSCOM and its disarmament mandate.

Prior to his departure from Iraq, and on his way to Jordan to meet Hussein Kamal, Rolf Ekéus received a phone call from Amer Rashid, asking him to delay his departure so General Amer could show him something. Ekéus wondered what was in store for him. That 'something' turned out to be a chicken farm that apparently belonged to Hussein Kamal. Ever the diplomat, Ekéus disguised his frustration at this apparently capricious excursion. But on entering the farm he saw before him the holy grail of weapons inspections since 1991. The farm was stuffed with crates and boxes containing hundreds of thousands of pages of documents, on paper and stored as microfiche, dealing with Iraq's weapons of mass destruction programs. It was the elusive Military Industrial Committee archive, the very same one that UNSCOM had been searching for since the confrontation outside the Ministry of Agriculture in the summer of 1992. At long last, we had our hands on the means to ascertain, once and for all, whether or not Iraq was in fact in compliance with its disarmament obligation.

But in Iraq nothing was really as it seemed. Hussein Kamal's defection set off a wave of panic inside Iraq. According to senior Iraqis who were involved in Saddam Hussein's government during this time, Qusay Saddam Hussein, the younger son of Saddam Hussein and the head of the Special Security Organization, realized that Iraq could no longer hold onto the last vestiges of its weapons of mass destruction programs.

Having decided to get rid of its physical stockpiles of WMD, together with the main elements of its WMD manufacturing infrastructure, through unilateral destruction in the summer of 1991, Iraq had hoped to keep alive the dream of WMD reconstitution by maintaining a dual-use manufacturing capability hidden inside its legitimate civilian and military industrial infrastructure that could be re-programmed once inspections were terminated, and sanctions lifted, with the help of the brain trust contained in the document archive.

But the events of the summer of 1993, when Tariq Aziz's misjudged outburst had set the whole Security Council against Iraq and forced it to accept resolution 715 (the long-term monitoring inspection program), meant that Iraq had had to give up on the notion of a covert dual-use production base. It just couldn't keep it secret under that kind of regimen. All that remained of Iraq's WMD dream was the document archive, which had been carefully safeguarded by Qusay and the Special Security Organization.

Hussein Kamal's defection now put this last remaining vestige of Iraq's former WMD programs at risk. Rather than admit the role played by the Special Security Organization in hiding the documents, however, Qusay dispatched his forces to a series of secret locations on the outskirts of Baghdad where the documents were temporarily hidden, and then over a sequence of several nights transported them to Hussein Kamal's chicken farm. The goal was to shift responsibility for keeping the documents secret away from the Special Security Organization and onto Hussein Kamal. Since Hussein Kamal knew nothing of these documents being at his farm, and as such could not declare their existence to the inspectors or foreign intelligence, Qusay figured that the appearance of these documents would raise questions about the credibility of Hussein Kamal, reducing the potential damage he could cause to the regime of Saddam Hussein.[1]

By turning over the documents to Rolf Ekéus, Iraq had given up the last vestiges of its proscribed weapons programs. But by not telling the whole truth about how it had hidden these documents from the inspectors, Iraq had set in motion events that would come to dominate UNSCOM-Iraq relations for years to come.

On 22 August 1995, Rolf Ekéus, accompanied by his trusted friend and advisor, Nikita Smidovich, along with Maurizio Ziferrero, the head of the IAEA Action Team, traveled to Amman, Jordan, where they met with Hussein Kamal in the grounds of King Hussein's royal palace. According to the accounts of those present, Hussein Kamal was as cocky as ever. He laughed with Rolf Ekéus about the last time they had met, in the summer of 1991, when Hussein Kamal had brandished his pistol on his hip in an arrogant effort to intimidate. 'Those were our orders at that time,' he now said. 'I was instructed to behave that way, but I knew that it was counterproductive.' And now all Hussein Kamal wanted to do, he said, was help. Present at the meeting was Colonel Ali Shukri, ostensibly the head of communications for the palace, but in fact the de facto personal intelligence officer to the King of Jordan.

The Hussein Kamal affair was all about politics. The royal household was extremely cooperative, as evidenced by Colonel Shukri's presence. However, the Jordanian governmental bureaucracy was decidedly pro-Iraq, something which posed problems for the King. There were also sensitive side issues with Egypt, Saudi Arabia and Kuwait, all of whom were still bitter over King Hussein's support of Iraq in 1990–1991. The Jordanian monarch saw Hussein Kamal's defection as having the potential to improve relations with those three nations, thus rehabilitating the reputation and standing of Jordan in the region. For that reason, Hussein Kamal was a political asset that was being 'managed' by the Jordanian throne.

Prior to the arrival of Rolf Ekéus in Amman, the Jordanians facilitated a series of interviews between Hussein Kamal and US and UK intelligence services. The CIA had dispatched a large debriefing team, which joined forces with the Arab specialists in the CIA's Amman Station, to speak with Hussein Kamal. By all accounts, the debriefing was a disaster.[2] Rather than treat Hussein Kamal with respect and deference, the CIA team conducted a very hostile interrogation, demanding answers to its questions about Iraq's weapons of mass destruction programs (Hussein Kamal repeatedly told the CIA that there were none left, something no one in the CIA wanted to believe, an assertion that hurt their confidence in the credibility of Hussein Kamal), as well as the political situation surrounding Saddam Hussein. The CIA linguist involved was an Egyptian, and apparently had difficulty understanding Hussein Kamal's heavy Tikrit accent and Iraqi tribal colloquialisms (like Saddam Hussein, Hussein Kamal came from a poor village from the Tikrit area north of Baghdad), leading to even more frustration among everyone present. In the end, the CIA stormed out, leaving Hussein Kamal alone and dejected.

The British MI6 debriefer, whom I knew as 'the Falconer' because of his life-long passion for the sport, took a completely different approach. He entered right after the CIA departed, and immediately offered a cup of coffee to Hussein Kamal. He then entered into a discussion about the origins of coffee in Mesopotamia, and the history of trade and the spread of commodities throughout the Middle East. The MI6 man, a long-time Arabist who spoke Arabic fluently with the ability to lace his conversation with a few choice Tikriti-accented words, completely won over Hussein Kamal. They spent hours discussing Arab culture and Iraqi history, and before long Hussein Kamal was trying to impress his British guest with his own unique role in modern Iraq's history. Hussein Kamal voluntarily walked the Falconer through the birth of Iraq's WMD programs and his role in building Iraq's military industrial base during the Iran-Iraq War, through to the events of the Gulf War and the dismantling of Iraq's WMD programs in response to the UN weapons inspections. In substance, the content of this debriefing was similar to what had been earlier provided to the CIA. But the tenor of the debriefing was cordial, and by the time the Falconer left, with a promise to visit his newfound friend soon, Hussein Kamal's spirits had lifted and his confidence in himself was rejuvenated. This was the situation when Rolf Ekéus and his delegation met Hussein Kamal.

As Hussein Kamal led Rolf and his delegation through the intricacies of the story regarding Iraq's WMD programs, a similar story was being revealed, in parallel, through the ongoing analysis by UNSCOM inspectors of the chicken farm documentation. Baghdad's contention was that Hussein Kamal was the culprit, a power-hungry man who had unilaterally decided to hold on to the prohibited materials despite Iraq's official stance that all such material must be turned over to the weapons inspectors. Hussein Kamal denied this charge. 'What chicken farm are they talking about?' he asked when informed of the document cache. 'This is ridiculous!' But his story matched Baghdad's in one critical aspect: there was nothing left. All proscribed weapons and their programs had been eliminated, and the worst fears of a retained Iraqi capability – a nuclear device, for instance – were without substance. 'All weapons – biological, chemical, missile, nuclear – were destroyed,' he told the stunned inspectors. 'You have an important role in Iraq with this. You should not underestimate yourself. You are very effective in Iraq.'

While questioning Hussein Kamal on the issue of ballistic missiles, however, Nikita Smidovich stumbled on something of great concern to UNSCOM – the Iraqi concealment mechanism. 'There is not a single missile left,' Hussein Kamal said, 'but they kept blueprints and moulds for production. All the missiles were destroyed.'

'What about launchers?' Smidovich asked.

'I don't have precise information,' Hussein Kamal answered, 'but I know that two Russian launchers were hidden by the Special Guards. One was in dismantled status, and the second was complete... these two launchers are with the Special Guard. They are hidden in the same location where computer disks with information on nuclear programs are. If you find one you will find the other. It is difficult to pinpoint a specific location. President Saddam's son, Qusay, knew where they are. Also, General Kamal Mustafa knows. He was with the Special Guards.'

On seeing the interest his words attracted, Hussein Kamal made a prediction. 'I think,' he told the assembled weapons inspectors, 'you will have a new war of searches.'[3]

Rolf Ekéus returned from Jordan newly convinced that the concealment mechanism investigation I had proposed held the key to closing the final chapter on Iraq's weapons programs. The chicken farm documents were still being evaluated, and final judgment had to be withheld, but Hussein Kamal's statements on the disposition of WMD meant that UNSCOM was probably very close to being able to issue Iraq a clean bill of health.

The only problem was the matter of concealment. It was impossible for UNSCOM to ignore the fact that Iraq had, by its own admission, successfully hidden major weapons programs and developments since from the inspectors for more than four years. Even if these were now all declared, no one in the Security Council, especially not the USA, could accept any finding by UNSCOM of Iraqi compliance as long as the mechanism that had succeeded in concealing this retained capability was still intact. UNSCOM would have to identify the scope and nature of the concealment mechanism used by Iraq, including involved personnel and organizations, and then verify that it was no longer in operation. Once that was done, any technical finding of disarmament put out by UNSCOM would carry more weight.

Time was of the essence. Nikita Smidovich and I started preparing for a major inspection targeting the Iraqi concealment mechanism, looking to travel to Iraq sometime in October 1995. However, we had yet to resolve the matter of communications interception, which was the key to the whole inspection concept. UNSCOM's gambit to get Israel involved in the interception of Iraqi communications seemed to spur on the CIA, and it appeared that the US intelligence community was finally ready to provide UNSCOM with the capabilities it was looking for.

My approach was simple: one or two inspectors would be equipped with small radio frequency scanners and tape recorders which could be either carried in a backpack or operated from a hotel room. As the inspection progressed, the scanner would detect and record all radio frequencies that were active during that time. Once the team had left, analysts would go through the intercepted communications and see if there was any connection between them and the activities of the inspectors.

The CIA appeared ready to support this, and Moe Dobbs had been assigned to work with UNSCOM on the development of a specific communications intercept 'package' that could be carried in by the inspectors. My previous experience in this kind of work made me realize that one needed to be intimately familiar with the equipment before going into the field with it, otherwise there was a risk of being caught or of not using it properly. I was hoping the CIA would provide Smidovich and me with access to the equipment, so we could practice using it under various hypothetical scenarios. The Counselor and Burt kept promising me that Moe Dobbs would be ready 'soon', but their promise did not materialize. I was starting to get worried: the entire operation hinged on the intercept equipment.

In the midst of all this, the Israelis had come up with an intriguing piece of intelligence, a tip-off that the Iraqis were shipping in missile guidance and control parts from Russia, through Jordan, in support of a covert missile program run by a certain Dr. Modher al-Timiny. The Israelis had sent this intelligence to me via their mission in New York. The Dr. Modher mentioned in the Israeli report was well known to UNSCOM inspectors as the brains behind Iraq's indigenous missile program. 'Delivery could be made at any time,' the Israelis had warned.

Dr. Modher had been singled out by Hussein Kamal as one of the main figures involved in Iraq's concealment activities. Hussein Kamal told Rolf Ekéus that Dr. Modher was hiding documents and missile components from the inspectors. The Israeli information now had Dr. Modher involved in a covert procurement effort that, if we could prove it existed, could blow the lid off of the entire Iraqi concealment mechanism. The Israelis were inviting me to come to Tel Aviv to discuss this matter in more detail.

I returned to Israel in mid-September, where I met with specialists from the technical intelligence department. It was this department that had purview over Iraqi procurement efforts, and as such was taking the lead over Dr. Modher's Russian guidance and control shipment. The key person here was Captain Roni Ortel (pseudonym), from the Israeli Defense Force (IDF) Technical Intelligence Office. I met him on the second floor of the External Affairs building. A map of the Israeli border with Lebanon decorated the far wall, facing a shelf containing plaques and medallions from various intelligence services around the world that the External Affairs Division had liaised with over the years. Ortel and I mapped out a strategy for trying to intercept the guidance and control shipment before it arrived in Iraq. The key, we agreed, was to get the Jordanian government to cooperate in seizing the shipment when it arrived in Amman. However, we felt we couldn't go to the Jordanians too early, for fear of tipping off the parties involved. We decided to gather more information before we could act.

Cooperation with the Israeli Military Intelligence had become very broad and complex, involving numerous meetings with analysts and experts involved in assessing Iraqi weapons programs, security and intelligence services, and politics, both domestic and foreign. When my meeting with Ortel was over, Ponkovsky would shuttle in a team of experts from another branch or department, all in our mutual effort to understand more about Iraq and its capacity to produce weapons of mass destruction.

Ponkovsky understood better than most what we were trying to accomplish in uncovering the concealment mechanism inside Iraq. 'It is a problem very similar to what we in Israel face from the terrorists operating out of Lebanon,' he said. 'They are very secretive, compartmented, and always on the move. And yet, we in the Israeli intelligence have had great success in penetrating the layers of security used by the terrorists, and we can find them and get them. I think if we used the same analytical approach with Iraq, we can find and get their hidden weapons, as well.'

'If they have any weapons,' I said.

Ponkovsky smiled. 'If they have any weapons,' he agreed.

All the while the U-2 cooperation continued. Through a combination of analytical programs, the Israelis were able to produce excellent target folders for each site, complete with maps and high-resolution photographs. The counter-concealment inspection plan was finally taking shape.

The CIA, meanwhile, had yet to deliver on its promises when it came to communications interception. The Counselor told me that the main roadblock was over the issue of sharing any intelligence that was collected. I recognized the political ramifications of this cooperation, but felt that Nikita Smidovich and I should at least be trained on the equipment so that we could be ready if and when the time came to carry out the inspection. The CIA didn't see it that way, and no training was provided. The planned inspection was soon pushed off until the end of November to buy the USA more time to make a decision about support.

The intelligence tips we were relying on for this inspection were rapidly becoming dated; Hussein Kamal's defection was months old, and the CIA's European information about the role of MIC Security in the concealment of WMD was likewise going stale. I flew back to Israel on 28 October, trying to update our intelligence database.

While I was worried about Iraqi concealment, the Israelis were worried about Iraqi efforts to import missile guidance and control equipment. The Israeli tip on the transit of missile components from Russia to Iraq was getting old. Surprisingly, the Israelis were able to develop new information on the shipment and immediately upon my arrival in Tel Aviv, Moshe Ponkovsky took me to meet Roni Ortel.

Ortel fingered a single sheet of paper, and read: 'A shipment of 20–25 crates, some described as "big", were flown from Moscow to Amman on August 18th via Royal Jordanian flight RJ 178.' He glanced up from his paper. 'We have a high degree of confidence that the shipment contained ballistic missile guidance and control-related material, and that, as of the week of 24 October, the material in question was still in Jordan.' Ortel put the paper back into his folder.

Ponkovsky took over. 'What we have just told you is extremely sensitive. Many in the Israeli intelligence community were against our sharing it with you. However, I was able to convince the director of military intelligence that you and UNSCOM represented our best chance of preventing this material from getting into Iraq. If we approached the Jordanians directly, there is a chance the information would leak out and the material escape. The same is true if we tried to handle this through the Americans. We believe UNSCOM, with its UN mandate, has the authority and credibility to pull this off. I hope that our trust has been well placed.'

I acted quickly, drafting a message to Charles Duelfer in New York, which the Israelis promised to deliver through their Mission. I recommended that Duelfer press the executive chairman to open a line of communication with Colonel Ali Shukri, the Jordanian official who had assisted UNSCOM in the debriefing of Hussein Kamal, to determine the feasibility of cooperation regarding the interception of the Russian missile components.

I spent the remainder of the week working closely with the UNSCOM photo analyst assigned to the Israeli operation, Gerard Martell (pseudonym). He was a short, stocky French paratrooper who understood operations, and how to make photo interpretation support operations. An Anglophile who wrapped himself in British culture, Martell spoke outstanding English and had an amazing sense of humor, which manifested itself in cartoons which he would sketch as the mood struck, usually in restaurants after the beer had flowed and stories were told. Suddenly, he would grab a pen and a paper napkin, and with a few deft strokes create a drawing with a suitable caption that had everyone at the table heartily laughing. Martell and the Israeli photo-interpreters worked hard to develop targets for the UNSCOM 120 inspection, jointly analyzing the U-2 film we had brought with us. The inspection was scheduled to take place in less than a month, and there was still much work to be done.

I was due to leave Israel for New York on 10 November. On the afternoon of 9 November, I was summoned to Ponkovsky's office, where I was handed a phone. Duelfer was on the other end, and he sounded excited. 'The executive chairman has sent a letter to Colonel Shukri requesting an urgent meeting. Colonel Shukri has agreed, and you are to meet with him tomorrow, in Amman, Jordan.'

Early the next morning, I left Tel Aviv for the Israeli-Jordanian border, where I boarded a Jordanian bus for the ride over the Allenby Bridge into Jordan. My fellow passengers were a mix of Palestinians, Jordanians and some western tourists. We all stared in silence as the bus made its way across the heavily fortified border, passing reinforced concrete bunkers that served as Israeli strong points. The Allenby Bridge itself was pretty ordinary, a narrow structure with wooden planks that rattled ominously as the bus crossed over a thin ribbon of reed-lined green water that did not at all resemble what I thought the River Jordan should look like.

On the other side of the bridge, now inside Jordanian territory, the bus was stopped by a blue-uniformed police officer, who boarded the bus and asked to see the passports of all the passengers. Upon examining mine, he looked at me. 'Mr. Scott?' I nodded. 'Please, come with me,' he instructed, and I was led off the bus towards a large white Mercedes Sedan with a sergeant from the Jordanian Army standing next to it. 'This soldier will take you from here,' the policeman stated, and left me standing next to my new caretaker, who spoke no English.

Amman turned out to be a cleaner, better-organized version of Baghdad.

My military driver took me straight to the Inter Continental Hotel, where I was informed by the receptionist that I would be a 'guest of the royal palace'. I was shown to a very nice room, and had barely begun to settle myself in when the phone rang. Colonel Shukri's aide was on the other end. 'A driver will be downstairs in ten minutes to take you to the palace,' the aide informed me.

As promised, ten minutes later a second military driver appeared and wordlessly directed me to another Mercedes Sedan, this one black. We wove through the streets of Amman, before exiting the main road at a turn-off marked by a blue sign that proclaimed 'Royal Palaces' and another sign that warned 'Entry Prohibited'. We drove through military barracks and to a checkpoint, where smartly attired military police checked my passport and verified that I was on the entry list. We entered into the palace grounds, and I was amazed by the brilliant green lawns, wide streets and large, gleaming white buildings. Halfway down the road, the Mercedes made a turn to the left, and parked in front of one of those same white buildings, which turned out to house the Communications Office of the Royal Court and the offices of Colonel Ali Shukri, nominally the director of communications but functionally the chief intelligence officer of the Royal Court of Jordan.

I was ushered into the building by an aide, and led to the private office of Colonel Shukri. It was a plush office, befitting a close aid of the King, with rich silk carpets on the floor and buffed wooden panel walls. Smaller wooden tables were set out around the office, each holding a memento, clock or framed photograph. There were numerous photographs of Ali Shukri and his immediate family, the King of Jordan, and other older Arab gentlemen whom I took to be Ali Shukri's relatives. I was seated in a leather sofa, set out in front of Colonel Shukri's heavy wooden desk. On the desk were several phones, including a pair of US government-issued secure telephones, evidence of the close links the USA maintained with the Hashemite Kingdom of Jordan. After being served fresh orange juice and sweet Turkish coffee by a waiter, Colonel Shukri entered the room, wearing casual civilian clothes topped off with a smart leather jacket.

'Welcome to Jordan,' he exclaimed, extending his hand. A handsome man of medium build and height, Colonel Shukri had dark eyes and hair and a large, warm smile and firm handshake. While friendly, he was also businesslike, noting that it was the weekend, normally not a time for receiving visitors. He added that his 'good friend' Rolf Ekéus had indicated some urgency concerning this visit, and that he was ready to help in any way possible. Colonel Shukri settled back in his chair and invited me to present my case.

I thanked the Colonel for receiving me at such short notice and went straight to the reason for my visit, informing Colonel Shukri of the Israeli intelligence (without naming Israel as the source), and indicating the urgency of the need for action. Colonel Shukri was writing everything down. When I finished, he picked up one of the telephones on his desk. He spoke into the handset directly, without dialing. The conversation was mostly one-way. Ali Shukri had just summoned the deputy director of the General Intelligence Department, General Batikhi. It was Batikhi's people who controlled the airport and the customs storage places, Shukri explained to me after he hung up, so Batikhi needed to get involved.

About an hour after my arrival at the palace, General Batikhi made his appearance. A short, heavy-set man with graying hair, Batikhi was dressed in the uniform of a Jordanian Major General. Despite Batikhi's seniority in rank, it was quite apparent that Colonel Shukri held the upper hand in this relationship. General Batikhi shook my hand, and then took a seat opposite me. Speaking in Arabic, Colonel Shukri briefed General Batikhi on my mission and the information I had shared. Without comment, General Batikhi placed several telephone calls to his officers at the airport. Ali Shukri interpreted for me. 'He is instructing his people to search for the material in question using the loading documentation from Royal Jordanian flight RJ 178 on 18 August 1995, in accordance with your information. We have done all we can do at this point, and now we will begin the waiting game.' He promised to keep me informed as the situation unfolded.

Later that night I got a call at my hotel from Ali Shukri, 'I have great news for you,' he said. 'The items in question have been identified and seized by Batikhi's people. Apparently, a partial shipment had already been sent on to Iraq earlier, but fifteen crates are now under the control of the General Intelligence Department and are in the process of being opened and exploited further by Batikhi's men.'

Ali Shukri paused. 'We have been blessed with good fortune. The seized material had already been issued a pass clearing it from customs, and was most probably scheduled for shipment into Iraq first thing tomorrow morning. Only the timely intercession of your information and our quick actions, together with the fact that it was a Friday and thus a non-working day, enabled the material to be seized.'[4]

I quickly placed a call to New York, where I reported the news of the intercept to Rolf Ekéus. The relief in the chairman's voice was noticeable. I told Ekéus just how much of a close run the mission had been – the slightest hesitation on either side would have resulted in the material making its way to Baghdad. We had reached it just in time. I congratulated him on his decision to approve the mission, and relayed to him how positive and timely Ali Shukri's handling of the matter had been.

The operation was a morale boost for everyone. In the morass of process-driven inspections, we had managed to find a decent lead and act on it. Inevitably though, our self-satisfaction was not allowed to last for long.

Chapter 10
A Breach of Trust
November 1995–January 1996

Still buoyed by the success in Amman, I returned to New York and got right down to planning a new inspection based on communications interception. I felt sure that, with a well-planned operation, we could catch the Iraqis moving material in anticipation of our inspections.

I was getting increasingly worried, however, about the CIA's failure to come through with the intercept equipment. We were running out of time. Letters needed to be sent to governments requesting personnel and coordination issues involving US political and military backup for the inspection had to be resolved. I called up the Counselor and warned him that we might have to cancel the inspection. Within a day Nikita Smidovich and I were told that a solution to the communications intercept question had been found, and that we would receive the equipment and training almost immediately.

The letters requesting personnel from several governments were signed and sent off. UNSCOM 120, as the inspection was now known, represented the largest inspection undertaken by UNSCOM in over two years, and was now was gathering momentum.

On 16 November, Smidovich and I flew down to Washington, at the invitation of Burt, the Counselor's point man for sensitive issues. The location for our meeting, just off Route 7, in Tysons Corner, pointed to the shadowy nature of our task: nestled away in this corner of American suburbia, safe in its disguise as yet another small business trying to make ends meet, was a redbrick apartment fronted by an innocuous sign proclaiming the occupants as 'Overseas Ventures, Incorporated'. Not a total fabrication, since 'Overseas Ventures, Inc.' was a CIA proprietary company fronting for the CIA's paramilitary arm, the Special Activities Staff.

Since Smidovich and I both lacked US security clearance, sensitive meetings were usually held at a conference room at the State Department. But there were some issues that were too sensitive even for the State Department. Communications interception was one such issue, hence the location of our current meeting.

Nikita and I stared at the nameplate, wondering if we had come to the right place. Suddenly the door opened, and we stepped into a foyer. Once inside, we were met by Gordon Cooper, the Delta Force operative who had served with distinction with UNSCOM throughout 1991 and 1992. Cooper was once again serving a rotation with the Operations Planning Cell, helping out with the preparations for the UNSCOM 120 inspection. Behind him was a fit, enthusiastic Delta Force officer we in UNSCOM had nicknamed 'Captain America', because of his aggressive, flamboyant 'can-do' attitude during the several inspections he had been on.

This was a standard small-office complex, consisting of several smaller office rooms, a large conference room, a waiting area, kitchen and bathrooms. In the kitchen, on top of the refrigerator were stacked a number of coffee cups emblazoned with an eagle, wings spread, talons bared, and the words 'Foreign Training Group' written in gold. Black secure telephones were visible throughout the place, reinforcing its status as a classified government location. On the walls were Spanish-language posters exhorting the viewer to struggle against the *Sandinista* oppressors. Other posters provided instruction on firearms and communications equipment, again in Spanish. I remembered Moe Dobbs and his history of involvement in the Contra movement. This particular safe house seemed to have such history.

'Where's Burt?' I asked. Burt had set up the meeting, and I was expecting him to be there.

Cooper was having a hard time looking me in the eyes. 'Burt got caught up, and couldn't make it. We'll take over the meeting,' he said, nodding towards 'Captain America'. They gestured towards the conference room, where in the back I saw a small, black commercial backpack.

Cooper took the lead. 'Before we start with training, Burt asked me to pass on to you some conditions concerning the use of this equipment. The US government stipulates that this equipment cannot be operated by US citizens inside Iraq. Only non-US personnel are authorized to use it.'

'Does the US ban include Americans serving on the UNSCOM staff, like myself?'

Cooper shifted uncomfortably in his chair. 'From what Burt told me, this includes all Americans, even those serving on the UNSCOM staff.'

'Can we at least see the device.'

Now he really became embarrassed. Like an actor given a bad part, he reached into the backpack and took out a small handheld commercial communications scanner, of the sort one would buy in an inexpensive electronics store. Attached to it was a small tape recorder. He started going through the operations of the scanner.

I couldn't believe what I was seeing and hearing. UNSCOM was proposing a bold operation designed to investigate Iraqi communications in Baghdad in order to identify and isolate communications that might reveal important information about any ongoing concealment effort related to weapons of mass destruction. This was a potentially dangerous job, one that needed to be done with the best means available. Instead of top-of-the-line equipment, which had been promised by the Counselor, we were getting an off-the-shelf toy, a toy that required significant physical manipulation by the operator, setting and changing frequencies by hand. There was no capability to pre-set frequencies, and only one frequency could be monitored at a time.

This was a joke. There was absolutely no way even the best professional could operate this device effectively and not get caught. And Smidovich was no professional; for him to try and use this in Iraq would be suicide.

I told Cooper as much. He sat there, awkwardly, holding the device in his hand, not even trying to offer a counterargument.

'Would you use this on a covert operation inside a hostile city?' I asked.

Sheepishly, he shook his head. 'No.'

'Then why would you be proposing that UNSCOM use it?' I asked.

Cooper was clearly embarrassed. 'You need to ask Burt. Look, Scott, we had nothing to do with this. We were given this device this morning, and told to train you and Nikita. I don't know what's going on. You need to talk to Burt.'

Smidovich and I talked the situation over during our drive to the State Department. 'We can't be expected to take that device into Iraq,' I said, and Smidovich agreed. 'Without the communications intercept equipment, there is no reason for this inspection. The targets would be wasted. The whole concept revolved around intercepting communications.'

The planning for this operation was already well advanced. The operational wheels were starting to spin. As we spoke, dozens of personnel from around the world were getting ready to board aircraft for the flight to Bahrain. Smidovich and I had allowed the process to go forward because we had been promised a viable communications interception package. Now we had nothing.

We were scheduled to meet Rolf Ekéus at the State Department, where we were to conduct a final briefing of the inspection concept of operations to him and senior American officials. 'We have to cancel the inspection,' I said finally. 'We have no choice.'

Smidovich chewed on his mustache, contemplating what I had just said. 'Only the chairman can make this decision,' he said, firmly. 'We must brief the chairman, and we can pass on our concerns. Maybe the chairman can get the US to reverse its position.'

When we arrived at the State Department, there was a large crowd already assembled around the conference table. Anticipation filled the air; UNSCOM 120 was a huge operation, designed to be confrontational. Smidovich and I took Ekéus aside, and briefed him on the day's events. 'This is unacceptable,' Ekéus said grimly. 'The Americans clearly understood that this inspection required the use of the communications intercept equipment. And you are telling me we have nothing. I will speak to the director of the CIA,' he continued, 'and see what he proposes. If it is not acceptable, then we cannot go forward with the inspection as planned.'

The briefing was postponed while the State Department arranged for Rolf Ekéus to contact John Deutch, the new director of the CIA who had taken over from Jim Woolsey shortly after the Somalia fiasco in 1993. Ekéus soon returned. 'They have nothing new to offer. This is very disturbing. We have no choice but to cancel the inspection until this matter is resolved.'

The cancellation created an operational security issue. UNSCOM had clearly signaled that something big was in the air, and now nations wanted to know what was going on. We were certain that word of the aborted inspection quickly made its way to Baghdad, where the Iraqis had plenty of time to reflect on what UNSCOM could be up to.

For nearly three weeks neither Burt nor the Counselor made any effort to contact Smidovich or me, a sharp departure from the almost twice-daily conversations we had been having with the CIA up until the cancellation of the inspection. It was as if the CIA had broken off all contact.

And then, suddenly, Charles Duelfer was invited to attend a series of meetings in Washington on 4 December 1995, to discuss not only the communications intercept issue, but also the expanding UNSCOM-Israeli relationship, which was clearly making some in the CIA nervous. Duelfer arrived at CIA Headquarters in Langley, Virginia, and was escorted into a large conference room where a veritable who's who of CIA officials had gathered, including director of operations Dave Cohen.

Charles Duelfer started off the meeting by reminding the attendees of the contents of the Security Council resolutions which governed the activities of UNSCOM, noting that Rolf Ekéus was adamant that UNSCOM had the legal right to carry out activities such as the proposed communications intercept operation as a means of detecting ongoing Iraqi efforts to withhold from UNSCOM proscribed material and activities. This comment set off an explosion of pent-up frustration from within the ranks of the CIA personnel in attendance, especially those who worked in the covert world of the Directorate of Operations. The CIA agents derided UNSCOM's undertaking as amateurish and poorly planned. SIGINT operations were very complex in nature, they explained, with the Iraqis changing frequencies on a regular basis, making detection and categorization difficult. They also added that the signals, even if detected and recorded, would most probably be encrypted. If UNSCOM were to come to the USA for support, there would most likely be a problem in sharing such information, as it would compromise US capabilities in that field.

Duelfer countered by reminding them that this inspection idea had been discussed by UNSCOM and the CIA since 1993, and that the Directorate of Operations had found the idea attractive at the time. It had only been rejected by Rolf Ekéus because of the CIA's insistence that the operation be an all-American affair, not for operational reasons. Frank Anderson, the outgoing CIA Near East Division chief, said that what his office had supported in 1993 was a general survey of Iraqi communications in Baghdad, a much less daunting operation than the one being proposed by UNSCOM now: isolation and interception of radio frequencies directly affiliated with the Iraqi Special Security Organization. This was much more complex and dangerous.

At this point, Dave Cohen interceded. Cohen stated that the CIA wanted to support UNSCOM fully on this problem, but that they did not really understand what the mission objectives of UNSCOM were. What was the reason for using communications interception? What did UNSCOM expect to gain from its use? What was the overall nature of the problem facing UNSCOM? In a back-and-forth exchange with Cohen, Duelfer indicated that this had been spelled out very clearly in the past, but that if it would be of assistance, then he would have a paper prepared which delineated the Commission's mission objectives and the role of any communications intercept operation in achieving these objectives. He emphasized that he would deliver this paper very soon. He requested that the CIA respond to it with equal alacrity. Cohen reemphasized his desire to support UNSCOM as much as possible, and that he looked forward to UNSCOM's paper.

Duelfer was then summoned to the office of the director for central intelligence, John Deutch. In addition to Deutch, Duelfer faced off against George Tenet, the deputy director of the CIA, and Mike O'Neil, a special assistant to Deutch. The primary topic of discussion was the cooperation between UNSCOM and Israel involving CIA-generated U-2 imagery. Deutch was very concerned about this program. The CIA director felt that the Israelis were 'using the Commission to get information about Iraq that was being denied to them by the United States'. His biggest concern was that the Israelis were developing target data that would enable them to 'plan an F-16 strike' into Iraq. He felt that this would not go down well on Capitol Hill, and that he faced a problem with how to brief this to Congress. Mike O'Neil observed that there was a significant difference between providing prints, which the US government had done in the past, and actual film, which was being done by UNSCOM. 'The Israelis are able to make precise measurements from the film that could not be obtained from prints.'

Duelfer was taken aback by the intensity of suspicion regarding the Israelis. He told Deutch that UNSCOM derived a large amount of very useful information from the U-2 cooperation with Israel, and that it should be allowed to go forward. The CIA director and his lieutenants remained silent. 'I don't think we've seen the last of this issue,' Duelfer warned me upon his return to New York.[1]

The meeting Charles Duelfer had attended with the CIA was the manifestation of a dramatic rethinking of America's Iraq policy inside the CIA and the halls of the US national security establishment. While

UNSCOM and the United Nations were focused on disarming Iraq, Washington already had its eyes set on another objective – getting rid of Saddam. President Clinton had inherited from the Bush administration not only a policy of sanctions-based containment, but also a secret 'lethal finding', signed in October 1991, which authorized the CIA to create conditions inside Iraq to facilitate the elimination of Saddam Hussein. To implement this policy, which was often referred to as 'containment-plus', the CIA had formed an operational team within its Directorate of Operations known as the Iraq Operations Group.

The Iraq Operations Group initially limited its activities to simple propaganda-style efforts (such as funding anti-Saddam radio broadcasts) that had no real chance of bringing about regime change in Baghdad. The radio broadcasts were conducted in ostensible support of an Iraqi opposition organization known as the Iraqi National Congress (INC), a loose umbrella group of Iraqi expatriates opposed to Saddam Hussein's regime who came together in late 1991 under the leadership of a controversial former Iraqi banker named Ahmed Chalabi. In 1992, Chalabi and the INC began receiving direct funding support from the Iraq Operations Group and, by 1993, Chalabi had opened offices inside Kurdish safe havens in northern Iraq operating under the protection of American and British air power. But the INC was not able to mount a serious threat to the regime of Saddam Hussein.

In October 1994, the Iraq Operations Group established a full-time clandestine operations station in Salahuddin, an INC-controlled town in northern Iraq. The goal of the Iraq Operations Group was to gradually strengthen the military capabilities of the INC and their erstwhile Kurdish allies, and drive Saddam's forces from northern Iraq altogether. The Iraqi move on Kuwait in October 1994, and the resultant American military buildup in Kuwait, exposed the fragile political realities associated with the American policy of 'containment-plus'. The White House had lost patience for the kind of long-term strategy of attrition being pursued by the CIA in its support of the INC. A new strategy was needed, together with a new cast of characters.

In the aftermath of Charles Duelfer's grilling by the CIA, I prepared the paper he had promised for Dave Cohen. In it I outlined what was, for all practical purposes, a declaration of war between UNSCOM and the Iraqi Special Security Organization. The Special Security Organization, I wrote, was 'actively involved in activities designed not only to keep data, information and material proscribed by Security Council resolution from the Special Commission, but also defeat the monitoring plan of the Special Commission'. I set forth a mission concept which put into context the efforts being undertaken by UNSCOM to improve our intelligence support, including the Israeli U-2 cooperation, and UNSCOM's desire to use communications intercept equipment in Iraq.[2]

My paper answered all of Dave Cohen's questions about the overall objective of UNSCOM's operation against the Special Security Organization, how we planned to integrate communications interception and what we expected to achieve. I delivered it to Charles Duelfer, who forwarded it on to the CIA. 'I would like to suggest that you and your colleagues take a couple of days to review this,' Duelfer wrote in his covering letter. 'We desire an early report on your ability to assist so we can make alternative plans as necessary.' The ball was now in the CIA's court.

In mid-December 1995 the interception of the missile guidance and control material in Amman was made public by the Jordanian government. This move surprised many in UNSCOM, like myself, who were operating under the assumption that this matter would be handled discreetly so as not to put at risk sources of information (although to their credit the Jordanians provided no details regarding the UNSCOM-Israeli connection).

The Iraqi government at first denied everything, saying that the entire episode was a fabrication. However, when the scope of what had occurred in Jordan became clear, the Iraqis soon reversed themselves and started speaking of a 'rogue operation' run by none other than Hussein Kamal. UNSCOM inspectors in Iraq initiated an investigation into what was becoming known as 'the Gharbieh affair', named after Wi'am Gharbieh, the Palestinian businessman who served as the intermediary between Russia and Iraq for the procurement of these and other devices. With the cooperation of the Iraqis, the inspectors were taken to a site on the Tigris river where the guidance and control equipment brought into Iraq by Wi'am Gharbieh had been dumped. Iraqi divers recovered the devices (they were the same as the ones seized in Jordan), and samples were flown to New York, where Rolf Ekéus displayed them during a press conference.

While the 'Gharbieh affair' played out, we were also opening lines of investigation on other procurement activity. The 'chicken farm' documents (see Chapter 9) were revealing a huge number of contracts between Iraq and a variety of countries in the field of ballistic missile-related technology, including Russia, Ukraine and Romania. The Iraqis were claiming that all of these contracts represented the unilateral actions of Hussein Kamal and his clique, and that all had been terminated. I assembled two dossiers, one containing the various contract documents, and the other a listing of Jordanian front companies identified in the chicken farm cache. Trying to capitalize on the momentum achieved by the interdiction, I arranged to travel to Israel and Jordan in an effort to broaden our investigation and develop new leads.

I arrived in Israel on 19 December, and immediately entered into discussions with Moshe Ponkovsky and Roni Ortel about the Gharbieh shipments and what UNSCOM was finding out about the level of Iraq's complicity. Both Ponkovsky and Ortel were thrilled with the November interception. 'UNSCOM has proven itself to be a huge asset to the Israeli political leadership,' Ponkovsky said. 'Your success has opened many doors, and silenced many skeptics.' The Israelis were keen on expanding our cooperation in the arena of counter-proliferation, and were willing to put at UNSCOM's disposal any and all intelligence they might gather relating to similar covert procurement. But Ponkovsky was disturbed by the actions of the CIA while I was in Israel. Stan Moskowitz, the CIA station chief, was asking questions about UNSCOM and the direction Israeli support was going. According to Ponkovsky, Moskowitz was very interested in the Gharbieh affair, and what UNSCOM had told Israel about the intercepted material. Moskowitz had also spoken disparagingly about me, referring to me as a 'known security risk'. 'Be careful, Scott,' Ponkovsky warned. 'You have some powerful enemies.'

Just how powerful became clear when I met with Colonel Shukri in Amman a few days later, when I submitted a request from UNSCOM for more information on Gharbieh. Colonel Shukri expressed some surprise hearing my request. 'But you should have this already,' he said. 'The Americans came to visit me shortly after you departed, and General Batikhi gave them this information, as well as copies of the shipping invoices and manifests related to the seized material. The Americans also took samples of the seized material, and technical photographs, all of which they said they would share with UNSCOM. In fact,' Shukri said, 'the Americans said that they were acting on UNSCOM's behalf.' 'The Americans', it turned out, meant David Manners, the CIA's station chief in Amman, and a team from the CIA, who, in addition to taking control of the seized material, also passed disinformation about me to Ali Shukri, who repeated some of it to me. 'The Americans say that you are in the pocket of the Israelis, and cannot be trusted,' Shukri told me. 'They said that this interdiction was really an Israeli plot to get their hands on sensitive Soviet missile technology.' I assured him that this was absurd, and hoped that he would continue to encourage Jordanian support of UNSCOM's disarmament mandate.

As calm as my response to Ali Shukri was, inside I was steaming mad. The entire trip back to New York I kept thinking about the information I had received in both Israel and Jordan. Try as I might to discern the logic of it all, the fact was that in the end none of this made any sense. I was determined to get to the bottom of what was going on regarding the Gharbieh gyroscopes, the CIA and Jordan. I requested a meeting with the CIA's top guidance and control experts to discuss the technical details surrounding the interdicted equipment and its usefulness regarding any Iraqi missile project. Once the meeting convened, I brought up Ali Shukri's comments. At first the CIA experts, whom I had known for many years, denied everything, including ever visiting Jordan. However, one of the analysts, who had been on the delegation that went to Jordan, finally came clean: 'David Manners wanted to take over the operation, so we were brought in to take control of the seized material in order to keep it out of UNSCOM and Israeli hands.'

It turned out the seized material was from dismantled Soviet submarine-launched missiles, useless for anything the Iraqis might have been planning in the field of ballistic missiles. The CIA's intervention was twofold: maintain the public perception that this interdiction was the tip of the iceberg regarding hidden Iraqi capabilities (it turned out, however, that it was, as the Iraqis said, simply a rogue operation not tied into any official Iraqi missile project),[3] and also, because the intercepted material was of such high technical quality, no one in the US government wanted Israel to get their hands on them, something they feared would happen if UNSCOM were to gain control of the items.

The Iraqis contended that Hussein Kamal, together with Dr. Modher al-Timiny (a protégé of Saddam's son-in-law and one of Iraq's key missile specialists), had embarked on their own initiative (i.e. completely independently of the government) to improve the accuracy of the *Ababil*-100 missile and bring it up to modern standards. The technical specifications which the middleman, Gharbieh, was given were within permitted limits of technological accuracy. However, Gharbieh had verbal instructions from Dr. Modher to get the best equipment possible. Gharbieh, operating on the fringe of legitimacy, and knowing nothing about ballistic missiles, made contact with Russian black marketeers, who sold him the salvaged submarine guidance components, even though they were totally useless for any Iraqi missile design.

We had caught the Iraqis violating sanctions, but it seemed there was no governmental involvement, and it didn't get us very far. Furthermore, the weapons system in question, the *Ababil*-100, was a permitted system, and was being developed under the full monitoring of UNSCOM inspectors. This is one reason why we had wanted to proceed slowly and quietly with the Gharbieh investigation, to make sure we had all of the facts before any conclusions were reached.

The decision by the Jordanian government to go public with the gyroscope interception, done at the behest of the CIA, was designed to publicize the case and prejudge the Iraqis as guilty in the court of public opinion. UNSCOM simply was not operating from the same play book as the CIA was. UNSCOM wanted the facts as they pertained to our disarmament mission. The CIA wanted the perception as it sustained their regime change mission. Facts are a valuable asset, but only when they are accompanied by a perception that recognizes the facts as such. If perceptions are formed void of facts, or in spite of the facts, then the perception becomes the reality, not the facts. UNSCOM had the facts, but the CIA had the means to shape perception. In the case of the Gharbieh affair, the CIA had simply outplayed us.

In early January 1996, Charles Duelfer handed me a paper from the CIA containing a series of questions as to what the operational parameters for any UNSCOM-run communications intercept operation I was envisioning were, I shook my head in wonder. Having just been sandbagged by the CIA in Israel and Jordan, here was the same organization, acting as if they were my closest ally. My first instinct was to send the CIA's request back with a handwritten note telling them where to go. But I was bred in the tradition of service to my country, and against my better judgment I sat down and drafted a response.

And so the cycle began anew.

Chapter 11
The Listening Post
January–March 1996

The new year moved on, and I had to hope (against my better judgment) that the CIA's request for information indicated a new attitude. Maybe they were starting to recognize that they had fumbled badly in November in failing to support UNSCOM 120 and were now making a serious effort to address our requirements and needs. I was half right. Although I didn't know it at the time, Steve Richter, the head of the CIA's Near East Division, had made a decision that, rather than fight UNSCOM and thereby provoke an unwelcome debate within the US government about Iraq policy which could compromise their secret coup plans, the CIA would work more closely with the Counselor and the Non-Proliferation Center to find a way of making UNSCOM useful to them. The CIA therefore would extend a helping hand, as long as they made sure their other hand was pushing UNSCOM into a position of assisting the coup plans.

The first clue that the CIA wasn't being totally sincere about its offer of assistance was a note that came back in response to the paper I had drafted in 1996 answering their questions about the communications intercept plan. The CIA asked yet more questions about what technical configuration I might be looking for, and then, as an aside, noted that while the USA might support an UNSCOM communications intercept initiative, there would be no US personnel involved in any aspect of the operational work.

With Americans unavailable, I needed to find a source of trained manpower. Israel was out of the question. Germany was problematic. UNSCOM would need people proficient in the Arabic language, as well as technically capable in the communications intercept arena. We needed trained professionals. I decided to give the British a try. I went to see Rolf Ekéus. Charles Duelfer and Nikita Smidovich sat in on the meeting. Ekéus agreed to let me approach the British for intercept operators, and the Israelis for exploitation and analysis.

From the very beginning of my involvement with UNSCOM, I had maintained friendly relations with the British. Often, on my return from Iraq, facing an eight-hour layover at Heathrow, I would take the tube into London to pay a quick visit to the analysts at Operation Rockingham, the Defence Intelligence Staff (DIS) unit set up to support UNSCOM with intelligence information. Rockingham provided the British staff for the Bahrain Gateway operation (the CIA-run intelligence support unit in Manama), and while the American staff proved at times to be standoffish, the British could always be counted on for a beer or dinner, or both. The British staff rotated out of Bahrain every few months, so I had become familiar with many of them, and there was always an open invitation to stop by and say 'hello' whenever I was passing through London.

With this in mind, I sent a message to Sarah Parsons (pseudonym), the newly appointed chief of Operation Rockingham, that I was coming bearing a sensitive proposal from the executive chairman. In a routine that was by now all too familiar, I took the tube from Heathrow to Charing Cross Station, walked down the Strand, past Trafalgar Square, and on to the Old War Office, where DIS had their offices off Whitehall. Sarah Parsons greeted me warmly, and listened politely as I spoke.

'The executive chairman has given approval for UNSCOM to dispatch, in a covert fashion, a communications intercept team into Iraq whose mission it will be to help uncover Iraq's methodologies and the organizations used to conceal prohibited material from UNSCOM. We would like British assistance in providing trained personnel with language skills who can intercept and analyze communications which we think relate to this concealment program.'

I further explained UNSCOM's abortive efforts to work the communications intercept issue with the Americans, and the reasons for its collapse. 'The United States is willing to provide the equipment and training required for this mission,' I said, 'but not the personnel. Rolf

Ekéus insists that any communications intercept operation be under the full operational control of UNSCOM. If the UK were to provide personnel to support this mission, they would be seconded to UNSCOM as fully fledged inspectors.' Sarah Parsons took some notes, placed a few phone calls, and then invited me to a meal in a classic English pub around the corner from the DIS building while we awaited a response to my request.

After lunch, we walked back to her office, where we found two British officers waiting for us, Major Clive Provost and Lieutenant Colonel James Swingle (both pseudonyms), from the British Special Projects Activity (SPA), a Ministry of Defence organization that specialized in covert SIGINT activities around the world. I repeated my briefing for the two officers, who took detailed notes as I spoke. Clive Provost spoke up. He said they would have to report this to higher authorities, and seek the proper permission if they were to proceed with UNSCOM. 'But,' he added, 'I can say that this is just the sort of mission we prepare for, and I for one see it as entirely appropriate for us.'

After London I flew back to the Middle East. Stopping for a few days in Iraq to follow up some leads on the Gharbieh affair, I flew on to Tel Aviv, where I met with Gerard Martell, the French photographic interpreter who was helping me manage the Israeli U-2 program. We were looking to restart the aborted UNSCOM 120 inspection sometime in March, and Martell was putting together updated imagery support packages. The analysis of all the sites we wanted to inspect was done in the October 1995 time frame. Martell and the Israeli photographic interpreters were looking through new imagery taken since that time to see if they could detect any meaningful changes in the sites we were interested in.

While in Israel I briefed Moshe Ponkovsky on the developments regarding the communications intercept operation, and passed on the executive chairman's offer to share the 'take' with Israel in exchange for Israeli support in properly exploiting it. This was a new proposition, one that I had got the chairman to agree to in principle on the condition that UNSCOM would be in total control of the SIGINT collection effort. The Americans had proven themselves to be inconsistent allies in this effort, and it only made sense to hedge our bets by building in some duplication of effort. If the Americans cooperated fully, then the Israeli support would be merely supplemental in nature. But if the Americans once again balked at delivering on a promise, then we in UNSCOM would have an effective backup in place.

UNSCOM was no longer asking Israel to help facilitate a communications intercept operation; we were seeking that type of assistance from the British. What I was proposing to the Israelis was expanding our already considerable intelligence relationship. Just as Israel was assisting UNSCOM in effectively exploiting the 'take' from the U-2 overflights, I was now asking for Israel to open up the world of its own secret signals intelligence capabilities. I was gambling on the notion that Israel, even with its considerable intelligence collection capabilities, did not have access to the kind of communications penetration of Iraq that UNSCOM was proposing. I knew how intelligence services worked, regardless of nationality, and when given an opportunity to access what had been deemed an impenetrable target, all intelligence services behaved the same.

Israel proved to be no exception. Once more I found myself sitting in the office of the director for military intelligence. Uri Saguy had retired from the post of DMI in the summer of 1995, and was replaced by Major General Moshe Ya'alon, a former paratrooper and commando officer in the elite *Sayret Matkal*, Israel's equivalent of the US Army's Delta Force. He was joined at the meeting by Brigadier General Ya'acov Ami-Dror, Colonel Eylan, and Moshe Ponkovsky.

I got straight to the point. I was asking Israel to receive tapes of intercepted communications from the anticipated UNSCOM-British operation, process the data so that it was usable (i.e., break any codes or ciphers the Iraqis might be using), translate the conversations that were overheard, and analyze these conversations to determine if anything related to UNSCOM's mandate of disarming Iraq could be discerned. In addition, I asked that if the Israelis were able to pick up any intelligence from their own signals intelligence capabilities, then this information, too, be shared with UNSCOM.

General Ya'alon looked at Ami-Dror and Moshe Ponkovsky. They started speaking in Hebrew. Both Ami-Dror and Ponkovsky answered, and by the smile and nods of Ya'alon, I gathered that the director clearly liked the answers he was getting. Later that evening, after the meeting, Moshe Ponkovsky told me that General Ya'alon had authorized Israel to cooperate with UNSCOM. 'This is big, Scott,' Ponkovsky said. 'We don't share this with anyone.'

While I was in Israel, the British had formally replied to UNSCOM's request for assistance on the communications intercept project, agreeing to support the effort with personnel from the British military with the understanding that while the CIA would provide training and equipment, operational control would be exercised by UNSCOM. Charles Duelfer and Nikita Smidovich flew to London, where they met with Sarah Parsons, Clive Provost and James Swingle. Within hours the deal was sealed. The UK had delivered on its promise. On my return from Israel I immediately informed Burt (the Counselor's deputy and my principal liaison point on sensitive matters) of the British decision. Burt promised to get the CIA to fast-track the acquisition of communications intercept equipment, a trainer and a training facility.

On 4 February 1996, I greeted the British team as they arrived at Washington's Dulles Airport – five intercept operators led by Gary, a short, fit man in his early thirties. Together, these five would become known as the 'Special Collection Element' (SCE). I drove them to a Holiday Inn in Fairfax, Virginia, just outside Washington, which would be their home for the next two weeks. The next morning we met with Burt, the Counselor and a retired CIA communications intercept technician known as 'Mike'.

It was Mike's job to train Gary and his team on the suite of equipment that the CIA was providing for our use, basically high-quality commercially available communications scanners and digital audio tape (DAT) recording devices. For training purposes, 'Mike' had set up an antenna in one of the hotel rooms, which doubled as a training facility. This antenna enabled the SCE team to practice intercepting local frequencies. The Baghdad set-up, however, required an antenna mounted on the roof of the Baghdad Monitoring and Verification Center so that the team could get 360-degree line-of-sight coverage of most of Baghdad. When I asked Burt about this antenna (I wanted to see it so I could start planning for its installation), I was asked to wait. 'We're still procuring it, Scott,' Burt said. 'It will be ready by the time you deploy to Baghdad.'

The Brits proved to be fast learners, and I was back in Northern Virginia by mid-February, checking up on the preparation of the SCE team before escorting them and their equipment to Bahrain and on to Baghdad. Everything seemed in order – except the antenna. I asked Burt about its status. 'Don't worry, Scott,' he said, all smiles. 'The antenna is already installed. We had "the Engineer" take it in and install it as part of his camera support mission. He disguised it as a surveillance camera on top of the building.'

'The Engineer' was an Air Force officer on secondment to the CIA.[1] In 1993, the Engineer had been placed in charge of installing a dozen or so monitoring cameras in Iraq. By 1995 this had grown into a system of over one hundred. Camera monitoring had become its own empire, run by the Engineer without any direction or supervision. Each monitored site had four or more separate cameras. Installation was a huge undertaking, requiring dozens of trips throughout all of Iraq.

The Engineer seemed to be calling the shots on which sites would get cameras. Hundreds of videotapes were made, but no plan had been put in place to evaluate them. Having not been consulted when the cameras had been put in, the monitoring teams had no interest in viewing the tapes. This problem was compounded with every new camera installed. The situation wasn't helped when the Engineer stepped in and volunteered the services of an air force intelligence unit to review the tapes, under his direct supervision. UNSCOM was now involved in a massive data collection scheme that was not only directed by the USA, but also appeared to benefit the American intelligence services alone. And now the Engineer was installing secret SIGINT antennae in Iraq. His involvement had me very concerned.

'For Pete's sake, Burt,' I said, raising my voice, 'we can't go around installing anything without the express permission of the chairman! This is an extremely risky operation, and I promised the chairman that I would keep him in the loop every step of the way. He has not given permission for this team to deploy to Baghdad, let alone for an antenna to be installed. And who gave you permission to tell the Engineer, or anyone else for that matter, about this mission? The chairman controls who gets to know, not you. Dammit, Burt, you've compromised the entire operation. This has to be an UNSCOM effort, not CIA!'

Burt seemed taken aback. Gary and his fellow British soldiers were looking at each other, wondering what in the world just happened. The Counselor interceded. 'Scott, you're right,' he said. 'We didn't think this one through. Of course the chairman is in charge... we just thought we were doing his bidding. We will make sure to respect the chain of command in the future.'

Despite the Counselor's words, I wasn't comfortable with the role the Engineer was playing, and the secretive, backhanded manner in which the CIA had managed it. The Engineer and his mission just didn't fit. Something was amiss, although I couldn't quite put my finger on it at the time.

Gary and the SCE team deployed to Iraq on 20 February 1996. To help facilitate their 'blending in' to the normal daily life of UNSCOM in

Baghdad, I went along as a chaperone. Initially my plan was simple – that the SCE team would go into Iraq under what was known as a 'transparent cover'. This was a kind of double bluff which meant we acknowledged to select UNSCOM staff that Gary and the team had a 'secret' mission. However, we spread the idea around that their mission was to detect bugs in UNSCOM HQ. This alibi would enable the SCE team to explain its abnormal hours and its secretive nature.

We had the SCE set up in a spare room in the rear of the monitoring center. The team strung a curtain behind the door to their room to block the view. There were five intercept stations, each connected to a DAT digital tape recorder. One station was permanently tuned to the radio frequency used by the Iraqi minders while escorting UNSCOM inspectors around Baghdad. Two stations were manned by an SCE specialist in traffic analysis and signal recognition. These stations were used primarily to intercept enciphered traffic. A specialist could identify enciphered traffic by the static-like sound produced by the encryption device. The remaining two stations were used for listening in on actual conversations. The team was trying to establish a baseline of 'normal' communications activity so that they would be able to tell if UNSCOM's actions were provoking increased communications. Despite the secrecy of the Iraqis, the intransigence of the CIA and the cautiousness of the Israelis and the British, UNSCOM now had a covert communications intercept team operating inside Iraq, reporting directly back to UNSCOM.

But I had one more task I wanted to attempt. Hussein Kamal, whose defection last August had created such a storm of controversy, was still in Jordan. Conversations with Ali Shukri, the Jordanian official who was 'managing' Hussein Kamal's stay in Jordan, during my visit to Amman in December had revealed that Hussein Kamal was not fairing well. The CIA and British intelligence had stopped talking to him, as had everyone else. Hussein Kamal's reputation as a brutal authoritarian made it difficult for any anti-Saddam opposition group to rally around him, let alone ask him to join their cause. Hussein Kamal, Ali Shukri told me, was a bitter, angry man teetering on the brink of psychological breakdown.

I believed that his current position might make him more likely to cooperate with UNSCOM in pinpointing targets that had been used in the past by Iraq to hide weapons of mass destruction. The earlier debriefings of Hussein Kamal never got into that much detail. I wanted to bring in maps and photographs, and walk the former head of the Iraqi military industry through a detailed, step by step identification of all sites in Iraq that could be of interest regarding the upcoming concealment mechanism inspection. This was a sensitive proposal, and Rolf Ekéus had asked that I pass my questions for Hussein Kamal through him for his approval prior to UNSCOM requesting that the Jordanians grant us an audience with the senior Iraqi defector.

I drafted the questions, and handed them to Nikita Smidovich for his review and comments. Within an hour I got a call from him. 'Turn on CNN,' he said. Hussein Kamal and his entourage had returned to Baghdad from Jordan. And within days of his return, Hussein Kamal and his brother, Saddam Kamal, were gunned down in the Baghdad villa of an uncle, apparently on the orders of Saddam Hussein himself. I asked Gary and the SCE if they had picked up anything of interest, but they hadn't. Hussein Kamal, the man who had informed UNSCOM and the CIA that all weapons of mass destruction had been destroyed in Iraq, while at the same time revealing the existence of a centralized mechanism of concealment designed to hide weapons of mass destruction from UN inspectors, was dead.

Less than a week later, I was back in Bahrain as part of the UNSCOM 143 inspection team, preparing to target the Iraqi concealment mechanism. The UNSCOM 143 inspection was a revived version of the mission that had been cancelled when US support for a communications intercept capability collapsed, UNSCOM 120.

While there was considerable grumbling at the hectic pace of the training, the team was coming together nicely. The only air of real dissent, surprisingly enough, came from within the American contingent. Given the confrontational nature of the planned inspection, concern over the team being taken hostage by Iraq was real. Whereas in the past we had had a complex rescue mission on standby, there wasn't time to prepare one for this inspection. As Moe Dobbs told me outside the Holiday Inn, 'There is no rescue package. You guys are going in naked.'

Dobbs was concerned about such a high-profile mission as ours going into Iraq without adequate protection. 'You may want to tone down the inspection a bit,' he cautioned. 'Don't get overexposed, because if you do, you're on your own. Me and my team won't be hanging around for too long. We'll take the American personnel and make a run for it.' This was a very abrupt way of telling me that the USA was going to abandon ship at the first sign of trouble.

Mitigating Moe Dobbs's concerns was the fact that my team had a pair of very experienced Delta Force operatives assigned to it. They were bringing along a secure satellite communications radio which they would use to transmit hourly situation reports to the US military command in Bahrain, as well as to receive any breaking intelligence from Gateway. The Delta commandos exhibited a confidence that was addictive. Hostage rescue was their business and if they were comfortable with the plan, then who was I to argue? I wrote off Moe Dobbs's jitters as interagency rivalry, and got on with the mission.

Burt from the CIA's Non-Proliferation Center had deployed to Bahrain with a team of CIA analysts, and was working with Gerard Martell to assess Iraqi reactions to UNSCOM 143 and give us any tip-offs that might be found through the examination of imagery taken several times a day from satellites orbiting high over Iraq. The National Security Agency, America's premier communications intelligence organization, also had a team in Bahrain to review the results of the work being done in Iraq by Gary and his team of communications intercept operators. Despite Moe Dobbs's ominous warning, I deemed the inspection team ready, and on 8 March we moved to Iraq, with Nikita Smidovich serving as the chief inspector.

UNSCOM 143 had flown in to Baghdad with great fanfare, and the Iraqis were on high alert for some sort of activity from the team. They soon found out what we had in mind: that night we surrounded what we believed to be the MIC Security Headquarters, as identified by the CIA. Within minutes of our arrival, however, the Iraqis were claiming that the building we had surrounded was in fact the Ministry of Agriculture (indeed, a freshly painted sign was placed outside, proclaiming it as such). Among veterans of the UNSCOM 40 inspection in the summer of 1992, this familiar 'news' was not well received. Senior Iraqi officials started arriving, and were allowed to go into the site. Among them was Amer al-Sa'adi, a senior advisor to Saddam Hussein and the former head of the Military Industrial Committee.

During the standoff, Nikita Smidovich spent a great deal of time on the phone to Rolf Ekéus, who passed on the changing views of the Security Council on the confrontation as it developed. Unlike the situation we had faced the last time we had surrounded an agriculture ministry in Baghdad, this time UNSCOM definitely had the Security Council's attention. The Iraqis were quick to discern this, and suddenly they were prepared to discuss terms for entry and inspection of the building by the team. After a series of back and forth conversations with the chairman and the Iraqis, Smidovich began the inspection, entering the building with a dozen inspectors. It was a thorough inspection, with everything – all rooms, file cabinets and computers and diskettes in the building – being searched. Thousands of documents were found, but we had to conclude that nothing of interest was present.

Hossam Amin explained that the building had been given to the Ministry of Agriculture in mid-January 1996, and the Ministry, its personnel, documentation and equipment was still in the process of being moved into the building. Prior to January 1996, the building had been home to the MIC-affiliated Al Fao establishment, which was heavily involved in construction work. According to the Iraqis, the Al Fao organization had occupied the building in early 1992. Before that, the building had served as the headquarters for the Military Industrial Commission. Hossam Amin then told us that when the Al Fao establishment occupied the building, an internal security unit of the Military Industrial Commission remained behind. He claimed that this unit had left the building in mid-January 1996, at the same time the building was given to the Ministry of Agriculture. If we had been able to do this inspection when originally planned, in November 1995, we would have found the MIC Security section. But not any more.

Our next inspection target was a Republican Guard Barracks at Kirzah, where intelligence information, again provided by the CIA, indicated that SCUD missile launchers were being hidden in buildings normally used for tank repair workshops. Kirzah was home to the Hammarabi Armour Division of the Republican Guard and, with the assistance of the Israelis, Gerard Martell had been able to pinpoint the location of the tank repair facilities inside the sprawling military compound. The team was considerably delayed in gaining entry to the site (the Iraqis stated that it was a national security site of great sensitivity), but once we did get in we found nothing to confirm the CIA's suspicions.

As sensitive as a Republican Guard base was to the Iraqis, their concerns escalated to another level when we tried to inspect locations belonging to Saddam's personal bodyguard unit, the Special Republican Guard. The CIA had indicated that some Special Republican Guard sites around Saddam International Airport were being used to hide WMDs. After a long standoff we were eventually able to gain access to these sites, but only under the personal escort of the director of the Special Security

Organization, Zuhier Muhammed. In the end we found nothing, although we noted that the size of some of the buildings would make them suitable for hiding WMDs.

We wrapped up our inspection the next day, investigating a complex in north Baghdad that turned out to belong to the Special Republican Guard. Nikita Smidovich and I felt that the Special Republican Guard had played a major role in the concealment strategy of Iraq, and it would make sense for a unit such as this to be involved. We went through the Special Republican Guard emergency operational headquarters with a fine-tooth comb, looking for any clues that might point to its past involvement in hiding proscribed weapons. We found none.

UNSCOM 143 was over. Although delayed out of the starting gate, the mission had accomplished what I had envisaged: UNSCOM had established a listening post inside Iraq, keeping a careful watch out for any signs of an effort by Iraq to conceal weapons of mass destruction activities from the inspectors. UNSCOM 143 wasn't intended as a mission of discovery, where we would actually find the hard evidence of Iraqi non-compliance. It was part of a larger strategy of putting pressure on the Iraqis so that if any so-called concealment mechanism did in fact exist, we would flush it out and find it. We had learned much from this inspection, and I was hoping to learn even more once I could begin the process of evaluating all of the data we had collected during this inspection.

Intelligence analysis is an arcane art where the answer is not always in what is evident, but rather what lurks behind the scenes. However, in order to discern this shadow activity, the analyst must have a grasp of all the different pieces of the puzzle that is being assembled. UNSCOM had pulled together many different pieces of this puzzle, and with the communications intercept data, were in a position not only to gather more pieces, but also to get an idea of the image we were trying to construct. Whether this image pointed in the direction of Iraqi compliance or non-compliance couldn't be determined until the puzzle was completely assembled.

Chapter 12
The Managers
March—May 1996

Within a few days of arriving back in Bahrain for a debriefing, I flew on to Israel, carrying several boxes of digital audio tapes containing the fruit of the SCE team's labor over the past few months. I also had copies of the logbooks, as well as computer disks holding the database of all the radio frequencies used by the Iraqis in the Baghdad area. As usual, Ponkovsky met me directly at the airport. Once I had checked into a hotel and freshened up, Ponkovsky took me out for a bite to eat before taking me to an apartment in an upscale neighborhood of Tel Aviv.

This was the home of a warrior, of that there was no doubt. The map of the Golan Heights depicting the operations of an Israeli armored unit during the 1973 Yom Kippur war only reinforced the impression. It was also the home of a cultivated family, filled with books and paintings. It was the home of Moshe Ponkovsky's parents, and for the moment it served as a safe house of sorts, the location of a clandestine meeting between me and representatives from Israel's ultra-secret Unit 8200, their version of the USA's National Security Agency. Ponkovsky had arranged the meeting at my request. I had brought with me a box containing almost a hundred digital audio tapes, along with two diskettes which held the database of frequency activity in and around Baghdad over the past few months. I had already given this information to the USA to analyze, but I had good reason to believe that Israel might be a better intelligence partner for UNSCOM.

With the permission of Rolf Ekéus, I was going to pass these on to the Israelis in the hope that they would bring their considerable capabilities in this field to help UNSCOM's cause.

The doorbell rang, and Ponkovsky rose to answer. He returned with three young men in civilian clothes. Ponkovsky introduced them to me: 'Scott, meet Lieutenant Dani, the team leader of the unit assigned to evaluate your proposal of cooperation.' The lieutenant was accompanied by two men identified as a sergeant and corporal in his unit. We shook hands.

I briefed the Israelis about the technical details pertaining to the Special Collection Element's work, as well as the nature of the product I was handing over. 'Is there a logbook or anything that would help us make sense of what is on the tapes?' Dani asked. I pulled out a blue binder which contained the detailed intercept logs maintained by Gary and his team, time coded and broken down by individual DAT tape. 'We can do a lot with this,' Dani said.

I had been in the intelligence business for quite long enough to know that one doesn't get something for nothing. Israel was opening the doors to its secret world of intelligence in an unprecedented manner, and UNSCOM was responding by becoming the best source of high-quality intelligence on Iraq that Israel had ever had. This was a mutually beneficial relationship that only worked if both parties were honest about their goals and objectives, and these goals and objectives were the same. UNSCOM's mission was to disarm Iraq. Israel claimed to have approached UNSCOM because it shared this objective. But our relationship was crossing the boundary of simple technical assessment. Iraq had, in the past, lied to UNSCOM and hidden weapons of mass destruction from the inspectors. Now Iraq claimed they were clean, but had failed to produce the evidence necessary to sustain that claim. The job fell by default to UNSCOM. But in order to prove Iraq's innocence or guilt, UNSCOM needed to gain access to an unprecedented amount of information, much of which had nothing to do with our mandate of disarmament. UNSCOM needed to sift through this data, and make sure Iraq wasn't trying to hide any proscribed capability.

Some of this data, however, touched on the most sensitive aspects of Iraq's national security, including the security of Saddam Hussein. This information, in the hands of a party which wanted to do Iraq harm, was priceless. In cooperating with Israel in this manner, I was exposing UNSCOM to charges that we were facilitating the ability of Israel to attack

Iraq, or overthrow Saddam. However, I believed the Israelis recognized the reality that UNSCOM was an effective organization which could succeed in disarming Iraq, and thus eliminate the threat posed to Israel by Saddam Hussein. Israel's best bet was to empower UNSCOM with intelligence, not undermine UNSCOM by misusing data garnered from our cooperation. I also believed that, by becoming so closely entwined with the Israelis, we made any final assessment produced about Iraq, by extension, Israel's assessment, since the intelligence and analysis any such assessment would be based on was one and the same. If UNSCOM were to give Iraq a clean bill of health, then having Israel agree with us was invaluable. That alone justified the risks we were taking.

I flew from Tel Aviv to London, where I met up with Roger Hill, the veteran UNSCOM inspector from Australia. We were in London to participate in a joint debriefing of the SCE operation that had just been completed in conjunction with UNSCOM 143. Expectations were high. A tremendous amount of material had been collected, all of which had been declared 'extremely useful' by the CIA in its frequent mission updates passed to the SCE while in Baghdad. My own limited assessment of the SCE data showed it to be more than 'extremely useful', and I was looking forward with great anticipation to what the Americans were going to tell us.

Roger and I made our way to the Old War Office, where we were met by Sarah Parsons and Clive Provost, who ushered us into a Defence Intelligence Staff conference room. Waiting for us were Gary and the SCE team. We sat, waiting for the Americans to arrive from the US Embassy, where they were supposedly retrieving the report and getting last-minute instructions. After fifteen minutes of small talk between the Brits, Roger and myself, Burt and the Counselor finally breezed in, accompanied by 'Debbie', a senior National Security Agency representative from 'B' Group (responsible for the Middle East) who had debriefed the SCE team in Bahrain when they withdrew at the end of UNSCOM 143, and a second official, also from the NSA, who worked in what the Agency called 'B441', the team responsible for Iraq. There were no introductions or formalities, or apologies for being late. The Americans simply took their seats, pulled out notepads from their bags, and waited.

The seconds clicked by, and an uncomfortable silence fell. I looked at the Americans, who were making no move to start things, and over at Sarah Parsons and Clive Provost, who seemed to be perplexed by the silence. Sarah finally spoke up. 'Well, we are glad that everyone was able to come together for what we believe to be a very important meeting concerning some interesting work undertaken by UNSCOM in the past weeks.' She looked over towards Burt and the Counselor. 'We are anxious to hear what you have to offer in this regard.' Both Burt and the Counselor smiled, and looked towards 'Debbie', who remained impassive. 'We have nothing to report,' she said. 'We were under the impression that this was an UNSCOM meeting, and were expecting to hear from UNSCOM their assessment of how the mission went.'

I looked over at Parson and Provost, who seemed quite taken aback. I gave a small shrug, as if to say 'What now?' Sarah put a forced smile on her face. 'I believe it was the impression of everyone here that since UNSCOM was not in possession of all the relevant data concerning the SCE, our US partners in this effort would provide a report that integrated the SCE effort within the framework of the overall UNSCOM 143 inspection.' 'Debbie' didn't budge. 'We have no report,' she said impassively. 'We are prepared to receive any information UNSCOM might be willing to share at this time.'

I glared at Burt and the Counselor. It seemed clear that the response from 'Debbie' was not what they were expecting, either. I was getting irritated. 'Look,' I said, trying to keep my voice level, 'the deal struck between the United States and the executive chairman prior to the SCE being sent into Iraq was that UNSCOM would provide the raw data collected by the team to the United States, and that the United States would conduct an analysis of this data to determine what, if anything, was pertinent to the mandate of UNSCOM, and what direction, if any, UNSCOM should take with future SCE efforts.'

I looked over at 'Debbie.' 'You were in Bahrain... you took possession of the data... and you know very well what the terms were when you took possession of that data. The tapes, logbooks and computer disks that were turned over to you are the property of UNSCOM. The executive chairman authorized me to release this data to you, but only under the condition that the United States would provide the required reports. I would assume that if you have no report for us, then you will be returning to me all of the data that you took into your possession so I might go elsewhere for support.'

'Debbie' was turning red in her face, clearly embarrassed. Burt finally spoke up. 'I think what "Debbie" is saying, Scott, is that at the moment, there is nothing in the data you provided that merits a report.'

It soon became evident that the meeting was, to all intents and purposes, over. According to Sarah Parsons, the Americans – in particular the two experts from the NSA – had made it perfectly clear that there would be no report forthcoming from the USA. 'Debbie' and her colleague left shortly thereafter, followed closely by Burt and the Counselor. Before leaving, Burt came up to me. 'We'll meet for dinner tonight, Scott. I guess we need to clarify what happened here.'

Once the Americans had left, the British vented their exasperation with what had just transpired. 'We were assured that the Americans would be coming with a report,' Sarah Parsons said. 'We have already received a copy of the report,' Clive Provost added, 'which Gary and his team had reviewed with GCHQ [General Communications Headquarters]. Everyone was quite happy with a sanitized version of that report being released to UNSCOM. Like you said, Scott, the data clearly showed the communications intercept operation to have considerable promise.' The British had no idea why the Americans had backed out at the last moment. We were all in agreement that Burt and the Counselor needed to have a good explanation at dinner that night.

Burt wanted curry, so we dined at an Indian restaurant recommended by the Counselor. The food was good but, despite this, dinner was very tense. I told Burt and the Counselor that what had happened back at DIS headquarters was unacceptable. The Counselor was visibly embarrassed by the whole affair. 'Look, Scott,' he explained, 'we were just as surprised as you were. We expected a report, but when we went to the Embassy, there were instructions not to release anything to UNSCOM.'

'Instructions from who?' I asked. The Counselor and Burt remained silent. 'Let's not forget who is driving this ship,' I said. 'It is *not* NSA.'

Burt started to chime in, but I cut him off. 'Roger and I are here because the chairman thinks you have something for us – for him, really. The Brits signed up believing that they were carrying out an operation in support of UNSCOM. Everything you did today discredited UNSCOM and the operation. If you guys are about killing this effort, you're doing one hell of a job. But if you truly want to see this work, then something had better be done, and done soon, that convinces the chairman that he, and UNSCOM, haven't been taken for a complete ride. And while you're at it, try mending some fences with our British friends.' I was furious at the CIA's cavalier treatment of the British, who had taken a great risk putting their people on the ground in Iraq, where they were exposed to arrest, execution and torture if anything went wrong with the operation. 'It's their asses on the line in Iraq, not yours or anyone's in NSA,' I reminded them.

That exchange pretty much defined the dinner. Roger and I left knowing that the entire counter-concealment effort was at risk should Burt and the Counselor not deliver something of substance soon.

I didn't speak with the Counselor, or Burt, for nearly one month following the fiasco in London. I was assured by both of the CIA officials during our meal that they would produce a report which met the requirements of the executive chairman. Without warning, on 25 April, the Counselor arrived in New York, and was in Ekéus's office, delivering a report which allegedly fulfilled this commitment. In accordance with the rules, the USA, through the Counselor, was delivering a report for Ekéus's eyes only. But everyone knew that the Swedish diplomat was in absolutely no position to ascertain the veracity of what was in the report. There was, in fact, only one person in UNSCOM who could ascertain the report and that was me. And I had been purposefully excluded by the USA from seeing this report. All I could do now was to sit and wait, and see what transpired.

While the Counselor met with Ekéus, I could only sit in my office and wait and wonder how the conversation was going. My phone rang, interrupting my thoughts. It was Olivia, Ekéus's secretary. 'The chairman will see you now,' she said, summoning me upstairs. Ekéus was waiting for me in his office. He beckoned me to enter, and then shut the door. I sat down at the conference table, while he retreated to his desk and pulled out a metal document container, dialed in a combination, and opened it, pulling out a slim report. Without a word, he handed me the document. The paper was marked 'Top Secret/FINAL CURTAIN/Release executive chairman UNSCOM Only' and consisted of four pages.

'Final Curtain' was a codename that the CIA had given to the reporting of information derived from 'certain sensitive intelligence programs, some of which are conducted in cooperation with the Special Commission'. I now knew I was looking at the fruits of the SCE effort. The communications intercept project seemed to be working after all.

But my enthusiasm was quickly dampened as I read on. The paper purported to present information drawn from multiple sources, and related to the events in Iraq surrounding the UNSCOM 143 inspection. It spoke of an effort by Iraq to take missile components and bury them in a garage, covered by cement. But this information was dated to a time prior to the UNSCOM 143 inspection, or the SCE, being in Iraq. It spoke in non-specific ways about the 'high level of interest' by senior Iraqi representatives in the work of UNSCOM 143, but we already knew this. It added 'transcript extracts' from intercepted communications which hinted at the potential compromise of the UNSCOM 143 inspection. But these transcripts were from the clear-voice intercepts that Gary had already shared with me, and which I had already passed on to the chairman. The CIA was sharing nothing from the content of the more sensitive encrypted conversations which comprised the vast majority of the data that had been collected by the SCE. This so-called Top Secret document was a charade, a fraud. UNSCOM had been duped.

I handed the paper back to the chairman. 'What do you think?' he asked me. 'Mr. Chairman, if this is the best the Americans can do, then we are wasting our time. This paper doesn't even begin to reflect the nature of the data collected. Our friends in Washington are either lying to us, or are incompetent, or both. I recommend that you go back to whoever gave you this, and let them know that this is unsatisfactory. If they are unwilling to do what it is we requested, then I am afraid I would have to recommend that we terminate the project, although I have to say that the potential for great success is there, if we simply got the level of help we requested.'

Over the next few days, I reflected on the Final Curtain report. I was reluctant to just give up on the counter-concealment plan. We just had to have the courage to see it through. I drafted a new conceptual outline for a communications intercept operation, and submitted it to the chairman for passing on to the Brits. I was looking at a follow-on mission to UNSCOM 143, starting in early June, and lasting little more than a week. I didn't yet know the exact targets for the inspection, but thought that focusing on the Special Republican Guard and other elements of presidential security inside Iraq would be the best way to stimulate communications traffic.

Hussein Kamal had highlighted the concealment role played by the Special Republican Guard since 1991 during his talk with Rolf Ekéus and Nikita Smidovich following his defection to Jordan in August 1995. And the UNSCOM 143 inspection had shown the potential of the large presidential areas in and around Baghdad to serve as an all too convenient 'out of bounds' sanctuary from the inspectors. While the Iraqis might be able to block UNSCOM from gaining entry to these locations, they couldn't stop the SCE from listening in on Iraqi communications that documented such blockages. Intelligence gathered in this way would be critical if we were going to detect efforts undertaken by the Special Republican Guard to conceal proscribed material from the inspectors.

The UNSCOM 143 inspection had ruffled feathers around the world, but nowhere more so than in Baghdad. The Iraqis were incensed over the mission, and questioned the reasons behind UNSCOM's return to large, intrusive and confrontational inspections after a hiatus of more than a two and a half years. The Iraqis were especially upset that the UNSCOM 143 inspection, and the questions raised by the team, reflected a new position in UNSCOM that seemed to reject the efforts made by Iraq to be more open and forthcoming in the aftermath of the defection of Hussein Kamal and the revelation of the chicken farm documents. Given the aggressiveness of the Iraqi response, both in terms of the tone of the communications between Tariq Aziz and Rolf Ekéus, and the diplomatic offensive undertaken by Iraq to win sympathy in the international community, Rolf Ekéus understood that he needed first to go to Baghdad to smooth relations with the Iraqis, before he could dispatch a new inspection team to Iraq and continue down this new path of confrontation. Upon his arrival in Baghdad, Ekéus came under a blistering attack from Tariq Aziz, who strongly criticized the tactics employed by the UNSCOM 143 inspection. 'The return to these tactics of the past,' Tariq Aziz told him, 'means that UNSCOM has fallen under the influence of those who are afraid of the cooperation we have shown since the events of last August. For you to authorize such missions means that you are doing the bidding of the Americans.'

Tariq Aziz saved his best volley for me. 'Mr. Ritter is an American, a Colonel in the CIA. He is in Iraq only to collect intelligence about the security of our leadership, and to provoke confrontation so as to destroy the cooperation we have built.' The Iraqi deputy prime minister underscored this by referring to the inspections of the Republican Guard and Special Republican Guard units. 'Why does UNSCOM need to inspect these sites?' he asked. 'These are sensitive to the security of Iraq. Why does Mr. Ritter ask questions about the activities of these units? This has nothing to do with weapons of mass destruction, and we see such actions as dangerous to Iraq. We ask you to stop these inspections, and focus on the technical job of disarmament.'[1] Rolf's difficult position was further compounded by the fact that the US Ambassador to the United Nations, Madeleine Albright, in a speech delivered at Georgetown University on 26 March, noted that sanctions against Iraq would not be lifted as long as Saddam Hussein remained in power. This was the kind of rhetoric that allowed the Iraqis to be truculent about the security of Saddam Hussein.

Ekéus's meeting with Tariq Aziz had made clear that the Iraqis were taken aback by the aggressive nature of the UNSCOM 143 inspection, and would react strongly to any further incursions. To avoid a confrontation while sensitivities were still raw, Ekéus asked me to go to Iraq and try to establish a dynamic of cooperation. The Counselor decided to move ahead and offer SCE support to future missions, and I felt that they shared my belief that the SCE effort was working.

I was partly correct in my assessment: the CIA was prepared to work more closely with UNSCOM on the matter of future inspections. But where I saw them assisting UNSCOM in furthering the investigation into the concealment mechanism as a vehicle for disarming Iraq, the CIA saw the inspections as a unique instrument for intelligence gathering that needed to be more carefully managed. The UNSCOM 143 inspection had sent a shockwave through the CIA, especially the offices of Steve Richter, the director of the Near East Division of the Directorate of Operations. Richter had long denigrated the potential effectiveness of UNSCOM as a tool for the collection of intelligence. However, UNSCOM 143's ability to gain access to some of the most sensitive locations in Iraq, including presidential areas, Special Republican Guard command posts, Republican Guard headquarters, and Iraqi intelligence facilities, woke Richter up to the vast intelligence collection potential inherent in UNSCOM's inspections that was going untapped by the CIA.

Richter ordered Moe Dobbs's team in the Special Activities Staff to start coordinating more closely with the CIA's Iraq Operations Group, which was busy plotting a new coup effort against Saddam Hussein. The Iraq Operations Group had built a plan of action around an Iraqi defector, Mohammad Abdullah al-Shawani. Al-Shawani had three brothers who were officers in the Iraqi security services, including one who was in the Special Republican Guard. Al-Shawani had convinced Steve Richter and the CIA that he would be able to recruit a large number of officers and men who would support the overthrow of Saddam Hussein. All al-Shawani needed was the CIA's technical support, in the form of secure communications equipment, and the CIA's assistance in shaping the conditions under which a coup could most effectively be carried out.

Richter was aware of my focus on the Special Republican Guard. He contacted the Counselor, and told him that the Operations Directorate was ready to cooperate with UNSCOM. For months I had been badgering the Counselor and Burt for access to the CIA's best analysts on the Special

Republican Guard and the Special Security Organization – to no avail. Suddenly, out of the blue, I received a phone call from Burt, asking me to come down to Washington for a meeting. There, in the CIA safe house near Tyson's Corner, I was introduced to Dave and Darcy, two analysts who specialized in Iraqi security organizations.

I was planning a comprehensive inspection of Special Republican Guard facilities in the Baghdad region, designed to 'squeeze' any prohibited material into pre-designated safe zones. I believed that if the Special Republican Guard was involved in hiding proscribed material and documents, then it would protect them using the same methodology as was used to protect Saddam Hussein. If material was stored in safe houses around Baghdad and UNSCOM threatened these safe houses, then I believed the Iraqis would evacuate the material into the presidential palace areas around Saddam International Airport. This was the plan they had for the president, and it seemed only logical that they would adapt this plan to protect any hidden weapons of mass destruction capability.

The CIA, drawing on the data that Dave and Darcy had gathered during our meeting, incorporated my Special Republican Guard inspection concept into its Iraqi coup plan. If UNSCOM inspections could somehow be used to trigger a massive military attack against the Special Republican Guard, then Saddam's personal security force could be decapitated and the way cleared for al-Shawani's plotters to make their move. Steve Richter, the man responsible for this plan, just needed to make sure that the CIA could influence the timing and direction of this inspection. The job of doing this, which meant, in effect, managing me, fell to Burt, the Counselor's deputy over at the Non-Proliferation Center.[2] Unlike the Counselor and other analysts who worked at the NPC, Burt was a former covert operator with the Directorate of Operations and, as such, had the trust and confidence of other operators such as Steve Richter and the personnel of the Near East Division. Richter and the others in the Near East Division were not so comfortable with direct liaison with me, but they wanted to know what I was doing so that they could better influence and react to my actions as UN inspector. Burt provided the 'bridge' between Richter and the Near East Division and myself. As such, he would come to play a major role in the work I did.

So while I was preparing an inspection to take advantage of the communications monitoring that was now available to me, the CIA were, unbeknownst to me, taking advantage of my access to the Special

Republican Guard in Baghdad to pursue their coup plan – using my inspection to enable their agents to communicate with potential plotters in the Special Republican Guard.

The Iraqis were meanwhile conducting their own post-mortem of the UNSCOM 143 inspection. The Mukhabarat had, since the fall of 1994, maintained a dedicated unit focused on the work of UNSCOM. After the visits of Nikita Smidovich, Marcus Kreutz and myself in the fall of 1994, when we exposed severe inconsistencies and inaccuracies in the Iraqi declaration on ballistic missiles, the Mukhabarat's counter-UNSCOM unit was instructed by its director to fully integrate itself inside the National Monitoring Directorate, not only to keep a closer eye on the work of the inspectors, but also to find out why the Iraqi technical experts were providing false and misleading information to the inspectors. The Mukhabarat's task was to get sanctions lifted – Iraq's number one national security priority. But sanctions could not be lifted until the UNSCOM inspectors were convinced that Iraq was disarmed. The director of the Mukhabarat had been told by Saddam Hussein himself that Iraq had disarmed, and no longer had any interest in developing or maintaining weapons of mass destruction capability. But sanctions could not be lifted until the UNSCOM inspectors reached that conclusion for themselves. So the Mukhabarat had an interest in getting the National Monitoring Directorate experts to cooperate with the inspectors. However, the NMD experts for their part were petrified of being seen by the Special Security Organization as compromising the regime's security, and as such were loath to discuss any aspect of past proscribed activities without explicit permission from a higher authority. If they were found to have done so, the consequences for the individuals involved would have been brutal.

UNSCOM 143 had been right on target when it had inspected the Special Republican Guard Emergency Operations Headquarters and the associated 'rapid reaction' transport unit on the last day of the inspection. I had thought it part of the Iraqi concealment mechanism, and told Hossam Amin as much. Hossam Amin had denied this, stating that the Special Republican Guard was a sensitive unit which had nothing to do with these matters. However, during the Iraqis' own internal investigation following the UNSCOM 143 inspection, a document was uncovered which showed that the trucks involved in transporting weapons of mass destruction material to destruction sites in July 1991 had come from the very same rapid reaction unit we had inspected during UNSCOM 143, and that these vehicles were operating under the direct orders of the Special Security Organization. This document was taken into custody by the Special Security Organization, and the Iraqi minders were ordered never to discuss its existence, or the role played by the Special Security Organization, with the UNSCOM inspectors.

In the aftermath of UNSCOM 143, Hossam Amin wanted to correct the record with the UNSCOM inspectors, and drafted a letter for this purpose. However, Qusay, Saddam's younger son who ran the Special Security Organization and was responsible for the security of his father, still viewed the Special Security Organization, and by extension the Special Republican Guards, as being off limits for discussion with the inspectors. Even though these organizations were no longer involved in the business of hiding weapons of mass destruction, any admission of their past involvement would only pave the way for an intrusive investigation. Given that these organizations were responsible for protecting the Iraqi president, allowing any investigation of them was an impossibility. Qusay directed that the appropriate cover stories – lies, in effect – be constructed to explain how weapons of mass destruction were hidden, transported, and destroyed. Tell the truth about everything, Qusay said, except the role played by the Special Security Organization. Hossam Amin's letter was never sent.

The fact was that our investigations into the Iraqi concealment mechanism had become a genuine national security risk to Iraq. The Special Security Organization mobilized its resources to counter our efforts. A new program of concealment was developed, not to conceal weapons but rather to hide and deny the involvement of the Special Security Organization in past concealment. This created an absurd situation where the more we dug, the more they resisted investigation into the Special Security Organization, and therefore the more convinced we were that they were hiding something. It was a vicious circle.

Inspections became trapped in a prison of process where the notion of 'truth' had lost its meaning. The Iraqis were convinced that they had told the truth about disarmament, that they no longer had WMD. That indeed was true. But UNSCOM felt that not only had the Special Security Organization been engaged in a massive program of WMD-related concealment in the past, but also that a massive program of Special Security Organization-run concealment continued to the present. That indeed was true, too.

The Mukhabarat counter-UNSCOM unit redoubled its efforts to

penetrate the workings of the inspectors. The Special Security Organization wanted as early a warning as possible of any inspection effort targeting the president or presidential security. Electronic surveillance of UNSCOM computers in Baghdad, Bahrain and New York was established. With the help of the French (whether a rogue element, or with official permission is still unknown), the Iraqis were able to break the code of the encrypted phones used by UNSCOM to communicate securely between Baghdad and New York.[3] Empowered by advance knowledge of UNSCOM's plans (the Iraqi evacuation of the Al Fao building a stark example), the Iraqis were able therefore to pre-empt inspections at will.

UNSCOM and Iraq were condemned to bounce from one crisis to the next, each one ricocheting off the same subject – the Special Security Organization – and each reaching a different conclusion. For UNSCOM, the conclusion was that based on Iraq's demonstrated record of lies and deceit, the continued lies and misrepresentations made by Iraq made us suspicious that Iraq was still hiding aspects of its past proscribed weapons programs. For Iraq, there was a growing perception that UNSCOM would never recognize the reality of Iraq's disarmament, and that the Security Council-mandated disarmament mission had been taken over by those, especially the USA and the UK, who were using it to pursue their own unilateral policy objectives of regime removal. The UNSCOM inspection process had become, in the minds of the Iraqis, a direct threat to the security of Saddam Hussein.

After Rolf Ekéus's visit to Baghdad in early May 1995, the Iraqi leadership knew that it would have to continue allowing UNSCOM inspections to proceed. But Iraq needed to make sure that these inspections were not poised to threaten the security of Saddam Hussein. Tariq Aziz convened a meeting with General Amer Rashid, Amer al-Sa'adi, Hossam Amin, and representatives from the Special Security Organization and Mukhabarat, including the chief of the counter-UNSCOM unit. The consensus was that the individual responsible for getting UNSCOM involved in these inspections was Scott Ritter. Tariq Aziz tried to dismiss me as being nothing more than a CIA agent, whose job it was to disrupt UNSCOM-Iraqi relations and spy on the security of Saddam Hussein. Iraq should put pressure on Ekéus to get rid of Scott Ritter.

The chief of the counter-UNSCOM unit corrected Tariq Aziz; Ritter, he said, was actually correct in his assessments. Every site visited by Ritter's inspection team had a past link with weapons of mass destruction. The problem wasn't Ritter, the Mukhabarat agent said, but rather the Special Security Organization's refusal to allow the truth to be told about what had really happened between the months of April and July of 1991, to which the Special Security Organization representative reminded everyone present that disclosing the role of the Special Security Organization was non-negotiable.

Amer Rashid opined that Scott Ritter was a reasonable person who truly believed in what he was doing. Ritter, he said, had a good record of fair, if unpleasant, investigations, and wasn't afraid to embrace a conclusion that Iraq was disarmed. Iraq needed Scott Ritter to remain in UNSCOM. Iraq just needed to find a way to influence Ritter, to keep track of what he was thinking. Ritter was going to continue to pursue his concealment investigation, Amer Rashid said. Iraq would just have to manage this effort carefully, and find a way to convince Ritter that his investigation had no bearing on Iraq's final disarmed status.

Tariq Aziz turned to the chief of the Mukhabarat's counter-UNSCOM team, ordering him to assign an officer whose job it was to gain the confidence of Scott Ritter, to get to know how Scott Ritter was thinking. This officer would become a confidant of Ritter's, a source of off-the-record information that would help Ritter resolve problems without having to resort to intrusive inspections. The Mukhabarat officer had the ideal candidate: a ballistic missile engineer, known as 'the Serb' (he had been educated in the former Yugoslavia) who had worked closely with UNSCOM, and Ritter, over the years.[4]

I, of course, knew nothing at the time of either the CIA's efforts to manage me via Burt, or the Mukhabarat's efforts to manage me via the Serb. I was too busy trying to manage my own extensive work schedule, which at this point had me deploying back to Baghdad to confront the Iraqis over the issue of concealment.

On 2 May, Rolf Ekéus sent a letter to Amer Rashid, informing him of my mission, which was to 'engage in discussions with Iraq's relevant authorities and personnel who were involved in the collection and protection of materials and documents related to proscribed activities'. According to this letter, I was in Baghdad for the ' purpose of conducting a special interview mission with personnel from [the Special Republican Guard and Special Security Organization] concerning the safeguarding activity of proscribed material and relevant documents'. Ekéus informed the Iraqis that what UNSCOM needed wasn't just access to personnel for interviews, but also any and all supporting documentation that might be assembled which could verify what these persons might say during the course of an interview.[5]

I arrived in Baghdad on the afternoon of 8 May 1996 to begin my task of trying to get the Iraqis to volunteer enough information to avoid another aggressive inspection. I immediately requested a meeting with Amer Rashid. The Iraqis informed me that they had agreed to a meeting, to be held at the Iraqi National Monitoring Directorate headquarters that evening. Upon my arrival, however, I was surprised to find not Amer Rashid, my normal counterpart for high-level discussions, but another General, Amer al-Sa'adi, waiting for me. Like Amer Rashid, Amer al-Sa'adi had been at the forefront of developing Iraq's weapons of mass destruction during the late 1980s.

Lieutenant General Amer al-Sa'adi was a fit man, and soft spoken. Dressed in a fine gray silk suit, with his carefully combed silver hair and trim mustache, he looked more like a businessman than the brains behind Iraq's WMD programs. His importance was underscored not only by his considerable reputation, but also by the hulking bodyguard standing nearby. I had been aware of al-Sa'adi for some time now, though he had been invisible to UNSCOM for a long time. He crossed our radar shortly after the defection of Hussein Kamal, when he served as the focal point on the clarification of Iraq's biological weapons programs. Since then, General al-Sa'adi had been a regular presence in the Iraqi-UNSCOM relationship, but this meeting marked the first time I had met this icon of Iraq in person.

General al-Sa'adi opened the meeting by graciously welcoming me, presumably to put me at my ease. He then gently began to prod: what exactly was the purpose of my mission? Seated to his left and right were Hossam Amin and three other National Monitoring Directorate officials. I was joined by Charles Harper, a British diplomat seconded to UNSCOM as its spokesperson in Iraq (and now assisting me as note taker), and a British interpreter. I reiterated UNSCOM's interest in the mechanism used by Iraq to conceal proscribed material and activities from the inspectors, and noted that the existence of the chicken farm documents only reinforced the legitimacy of our concerns. 'I suggest that it is better, from the perspective of the Iraqi government, to deal with a small group of inspectors meeting around a table with their Iraqi counterparts, than having a fifty-man team conducting on-site inspections of facilities and locations considered by

Iraq as being sensitive to its national security.' I underlined the importance that the executive chairman placed on the need to respect the sensitivities outlined by Tariq Aziz during their April meeting in Baghdad. I also emphasized that my task was to execute my mission in a very thorough manner. 'I promise you that while my investigation will be very intensive,' I concluded, 'I will also be honest and direct. There will be no tricks on my part in pursuing this matter.'

General al-Sa'adi took in what I had to say calmly. 'We welcome your mission,' he said. 'I agree that sitting here is more productive than you coming to Iraq with fifty people.' He then launched into a long explanation regarding the circumstances surrounding the chicken farm documents. Amer al-Sa'adi noted that the process of collecting documents had begun before the Gulf War, in an effort to preserve the 'fruits of the Iraqi science and defense industries', and that after the war this collection continued to prevent such sensitive papers from falling in the hands of Iraq's enemies. After the 'events of September 1991' (i.e. the seizure of the PC-3 archives by the UNSCOM 16 inspection), a decision was made to collect all documents into a single archive. This was done under the supervision of Hussein Kamal, who used Special Republican Guard soldiers assigned to his personal protection detail for this task. Only six Special Republican Guard personnel were involved – two officers and four enlisted. Everything was managed through the private bureau of Hussein Kamal; no one else in Iraq knew anything of this matter. 'This is why we were really surprised when these documents emerged following the defection of the traitor [i.e. Hussein Kamal],' Amer al-Sa'adi said. 'The documents were supposed to have been destroyed, not kept. But we are not afraid of these documents. That is why we gave them to you freely.'[6]

We agreed on a schedule of work for my mission, with interviews of critical personnel to take place over the course of the following two days, and tours of facilities related to the chicken farm documents to be conducted on the third day. Having completed this schedule, I still had not accomplished anything with regards to the investigation of the Special Security Organization. I mentioned this to Amer al-Sa'adi, noting that it was UNSCOM's intention to proceed down this path. 'It would mean war,' he said.[7] Amer al-Sa'adi cancelled our scheduled meeting that night, and the next day Hossam Amin informed me that Iraq would no longer cooperate with my mission, that I was touching on presidential security, and this had nothing to do with WMD.

I was careful in my response. 'I remind you of my statement the other day that it would be better for Iraq to deal with a small team such as mine, than it would to have a fifty- to sixty-person team come to Iraq for the same purpose. Both Tariq Aziz and General al-Sa'adi have said that such an action would lead to confrontation, even to "war", to quote General al-Sa'adi. No one wants such confrontation; such actions are in the interests of nobody. But I must tell you, without these interviews and site visits, my mission will have to be considered a failure, and I would have to report this back to the chairman. I hope you understand the gravity of the situation that might result if I were to leave Iraq without completing my mission.' Hossam nodded.[8]

Amer al-Sa'adi's refusal to discuss anything dealing with the Special Security Organization or Special Republican Guard cemented Rolf Ekéus's decision to send another inspection team to Iraq for the purpose of investigating the concealment issue. Ekéus's choice was made easier when the State Department informed him that the inspection had the full support of the Secretary of State Warren Christopher and the National Security Advisor Tony Lake. When I returned to New York, I was directed by Rolf Ekéus to begin final preparations for a major new inspection to take place in June.

Chapter 13
Blowback
June 1996

The dialogue route had, it seemed, failed. The Iraqis were extremely concerned about their national security, but the only way we could get the answers we needed would be to probe into the Special Security Organization. We were on course for confrontation.

Moe Dobbs and the paramilitary wing of the CIA was taking an extraordinary interest in this upcoming inspection, and Dobbs had assigned three other operatives – 'Jake', 'Paul' and 'Rob' – to coordinate logistics and communications support for the team. I was suspicious, but at the time, just glad to get the help we so badly needed.

As usual, Dobbs was concerned with security issues, and was proposing that we embed a dozen of his paramilitary specialists from the Special Activities Staff throughout the team, under cover as team communicators, but in reality as hostage rescue support. 'If we get grabbed, just hold tight and stay close to my operators,' Dobbs told me.

With the assistance of Dobbs and the SAS operators, Nikita Smidovich and I put together a coordinated inspection plan, which had us 'squeezing' Special Republican Guard facilities in the Baghdad area in the hope that we might flush out some concealed material. With Israeli help, I had found the location of every Special Republican Guard unit around Baghdad, and had factored them all into the inspection plan. Strangely, Moe Dobbs and the SAS objected to one of these targets, a barracks facility belonging to the 3ʳᵈ Battalion of the 1ˢᵗ Brigade. 'There's nothing there,' Dobbs said. 'We've checked it out.' When one of the CIA's top covert operatives says that something has been 'checked out', who could argue? We dropped the battalion from our target list.

For this operation, we were in Basingstoke, an hour's drive from London, rather than in Bahrain. There was concern after UNSCOM 143 that the Iraqis had penetrated the UN bureaucracy, and we wanted to remain unplugged from it for as long as possible.

Unlike UNSCOM 143, where we briefed each target to the team and allowed them to prepare for the inspection with exact knowledge of each site to be inspected, for UNSCOM 150 we took a different approach: no sites whatsoever were briefed. All the team members were told was that we were going to carry out inspections of certain 'types' of facilities – office buildings, military barracks, storage complexes. We trained them on inspection concepts and specific operational methodologies, but not on the targets themselves. This is where 'Rob' and the rest of Moe Dobbs's CIA paramilitary operatives came in handy. They knew the targets, and the techniques needed to inspect them efficiently. The training syllabus they put together focused on the techniques without compromising the targets.

We went to Bahrain via a US Air Force C-141 'Starlifter', and then on to Iraq using the new UNSCOM C-130, operated by a South African company under contract to the UN. The Iraqis were very concerned about this inspection, and tried hard to get Ekéus to postpone it. Tariq Aziz put in a personal call to Ekéus. 'We know you are concerned about hidden missiles,' he said, referring to a speech made by Ekéus in which he had said that there might be between six and sixteen SCUD missiles remaining in Iraq. 'We promise not to fire any of the missing missiles until your inspectors arrive,' the deputy prime minister joked. Ekéus refused to put off the inspection, instead briefing the Security Council that they should be prepared for a crisis. The feeling in New York was that the Iraqis did not want the UNSCOM 150 inspection to disrupt the ongoing oil-for-food negotiations, which were reaching their final stages. However, the truth was the Iraqis were worried about something much more serious.

The CIA had been very busy plotting its coup against Saddam Hussein. The Iraq Operations Group had formed a special team of agents which was dispatched to the CIA's Amman Station to coordinate coup planning with the Iraqi National Accord (INA), a group of Iraqi expatriates led by a former Ba'athist official, Iyad Alawi. Alawi had been responsible for monitoring, on behalf of the Mukhabarat, the activities of Iraqi students studying in London in the late 1970s. However, he had developed a taste for money and the high life of the West, and sometime in 1978 reached out to the British Secret Intelligence Service (MI6) and offered his services as a double agent. Alawi's move was detected by the Mukhabarat, which dispatched a team of thugs to Alawi's London home in an effort to kill him. Alawi survived the attack, which pushed him solidly into the camp of British intelligence. During the Gulf War, Alawi was a founding member of the INA, which was initially a front organization for a Saudi Arabian intelligence anti-Saddam propaganda effort which broadcast radio programs into Iraq from stations in Riyadh.

After the Gulf War, Alawi returned to London, where he continued his contacts with MI6. Sometime in 1994, Alawi told MI6 that he had fantastic contacts inside Iraq that were in a position to remove Saddam Hussein from power, if they could just get some help. MI6 passed this information on to the CIA's London Station, which in turn reported these developments to the Near East Division and Steve Richter. Richter brought Alawi and al-Shawani, the former commander of Iraqi Special Forces who had defected to Amman and was recruited by the CIA, together. The two defectors quickly convinced the CIA that they had the resources in Iraq to pull off a coup.

Steve Richter briefed the White House on what was being called the 'Silver Bullet' coup. The White House was under political pressure to be seen to be doing something about Iraq. Economic sanctions were crumbling, and international support for continuing aggressive weapons inspections was faltering. Instead of being weakened, Saddam Hussein's government was actually gaining strength. When the CIA said they had a plan to get rid of Saddam Hussein, the White House approved it, ordering John Deutch, the CIA director, to move forward. Of course, being the White House, there was a political dimension to this issue: the upcoming presidential elections in November 1996. Tony Lake, the national security advisor to President Clinton, was sensitive to any notion of an 'October Surprise' and, in private discussions with Deutch (denied by both Deutch and Lake, but acknowledged by many CIA insiders), ordered that the coup be wrapped up by early summer at the latest. Deutch passed these instructions on to Steve Richter, who ordered the Iraq Operations Group to execute the coup sometime during the third week in June 1996.[1]

The only problem was that this coup, supposedly planned in great secrecy, was well known to the Iraqi government. Many of the defectors being used by the INA and CIA were actually Mukhabarat double agents and, through a series of tragic mistakes, the Mukhabarat actually took control of one of the CIA's secure satellite communications units used by the INA to communicate with the plotters in Baghdad. In this way, the Mukhabarat learned every detail of the plan, including the fact that the CIA was linking the timing of the coup with an UNSCOM weapons inspection planned to take place in early June 1996. According to the intercepted conversations overheard by the Mukhabarat, the UNSCOM inspection would be used to trigger a crisis with Iraq, and serve as a justification for a military attack by the USA, which would be used as a cover for the plotters to remove Saddam Hussein from power. So when Tariq Aziz asked Rolf Ekéus to delay the UNSCOM 150 inspection, it was with good reason. With the goal of lifting economic sanctions first and foremost in mind, the Iraqis did not want the issue of weapons inspections to become caught up in the political fallout of the impending *coup d'état*.

Rolf Ekéus and the rest of UNSCOM were completely unaware of the CIA's ulterior motive regarding the UNSCOM 150 inspection. As the primary mission planner, I knew who Moe Dobbs was, and who his team of SAS paramilitary operatives worked for. As a student of Iraq policy, I was also aware of the real US objective for Iraq – regime change. I had certainly observed, and been a victim of, the CIA's dishonesty and manipulation of inspections in the past, and I was aware of an undercurrent of intrigue surrounding the Iraqi defectors I had helped debrief in Amman the previous May. But, perhaps because I was so focused on the upcoming inspection and my overall campaign to uncover an Iraqi concealment mechanism, I was oblivious to what was really happening.

UNSCOM 150 arrived in Baghdad on 10 June 1996 to the watchful, if somewhat hostile, stares of our Iraqi minders. There was a certain tension in the air, and the usual friendly banter exchanged between UN inspector and Iraqi minder was missing. Our first day of inspections, 11 June, was an indication of things to come: half of the team was prevented by the Iraqis from inspecting known Special Republican Guard barracks in Abu Ghraib (the same facilities that had been used to hide nuclear material back in June 1991). The other half of the team, led by myself, inspected what we thought would be the headquarters of the MIC Facility Security Organization, only to find that the Iraqis had recently moved that organization, and replaced it with a unit of the Mukhabarat, M-21, that specialized in explosive assassinations, something that while being very interesting and alarming, was outside our mandate to pursue.

Undeterred, we continued with our schedule, dispatching the team to the location of the 1ˢᵗ Brigade, Special Republican Guard on the second day, 12 June. The Iraqis were having none of it, however, and UNSCOM 150 found itself in a standoff with automatic-rifle-wielding Special Republican Guard troopers. The inspection team blocked all entrances to the facility, and established observation points around the perimeter of the barracks to make sure the Iraqis didn't attempt to destroy documents or hide material. The Special Republican Guard soldiers were not amused when we deployed a large night vision scope, allowing us to track their movements once the sun went down. A squad of soldiers was assigned to watch our inspectors, at one point aiming their weapons at the inspectors.

Rather than let the Iraqis control the pace of the inspection, Nikita Smidovich and I decided to split the team further, leaving a detachment at the 1ˢᵗ Brigade, and sending two sub-teams on to the next targets, other Special Republican Guard units located to the north and south of Saddam International Airport. Roger Hill took his team south, to the barracks of the 2ⁿᵈ Mechanized Battalion, 4ᵗʰ Brigade, Special Republican Guard. I led the other team to the north, the location of a Special Republican Guard special forces training camp and logistics headquarters. Hill and I immediately discovered that we were to be given the same treatment as Smidovich – no entry.

Our inspection team was now scattered across central and southern Baghdad. We started sending inspectors back to the hotel for showers and naps, developing a rotating series of shifts that would man the positions we had established around each site on a continuous basis. As the deputy chief inspector, my job was to roam between the three locations, making sure everything was taken care of. It was during one of these trips that I set in motion events that almost turned tragic. I had pulled up to the 1ˢᵗ Brigade site, and was talking with some of the inspectors, when a brand-new, metallic brown Porsche 928 drove up the road at high speed. The Porsche passed where the inspectors were standing, turned left, and circled around the block, making a second high-speed approach. I asked the Iraqi minders to get the car to slow down as it was creating a safety hazard, but none of the Iraqis would even acknowledge the vehicle's presence. I looked at the Special Republican Guard soldiers, they wouldn't even face the vehicle. So as the vehicle screamed past, I stepped out in the road and shouted after it, 'Slow down!'

The Porsche came to a screeching halt, and backed up at high speed to where I stood. The Iraqis were acting as if none of this was happening. The windows on the car were heavily tinted, preventing me from seeing who was inside. But slowly the passenger side window was lowered, and I found myself staring into the face of Saddam Hussein's older son, Uday, who had a much deserved reputation for having an explosive temper. I wasn't about to back down. 'Slow down,' I repeated, looking Uday straight into his designer sunglasses. The window was rolled up, and Uday raced away in a shriek of tires and a cloud of burnt rubber.

I thought that would be the end of the episode. However, once back at his residence, Uday got on his secure radio phone (which Gary and the Special Collection Element were monitoring), and called up two of his friends, who happened to be relatives of Saddam Hussein's *Murafaqin*, or personal companions – the ultimate bodyguards. Uday screamed at them that he wanted the UN inspectors to be taught a lesson. That night Uday's two friends drove up to the front of the 1st Brigade headquarters, and stopped next to a white four-wheel drive Sedan, which they mistook for a UN vehicle. Having duly fortified themselves with alcohol, the two stepped out of their vehicle to confront the inspectors, the one on the passenger's side pulling out a pistol. As he withdrew the pistol, however, he accidentally pulled the trigger, shooting himself in the leg, and fell to the ground, screaming. Panicked, the driver ran over to his friend, and ordered the National Monitoring Directorate minders who had been sitting in their Sedan to get out. The driver dragged his wounded companion into the NMD Sedan, and drove it away – leaving his original vehicle behind. The head of the Special Security Organization's Security Directorate himself was brought in the next day to investigate. The evidence led straight to the culprits, but no one wanted to confront Uday on this issue. Additional guards were assigned from the Special Security Organization to protect the inspectors. Despite these measures, tensions ran high for the remainder of our time in Iraq.[2]

The Security Council finally reacted to Baghdad's non-cooperation on 12 June 1996 by passing a new resolution, 1060, which 'deplored' the denial of access and demanded that Iraq cooperate fully. Two days later, on 14 June, the inspectors were still parked in the sun. The president of the Security Council, at that time chaired by the French Ambassador, issued a statement condemning the failure of Iraq to comply with resolution 1060, noting that the Council considered Iraq's actions a 'clear and flagrant' violation of its resolutions (not, however, a 'material breach', language which would have been used by the USA to legitimize any military strike planned against Iraq). UNSCOM 150 was pulled out of Iraq, and Rolf Ekéus was dispatched by the Security Council to give the Iraqis a 'final chance' to comply with the resolutions of the Council.

The decision to send Rolf Ekéus to Iraq was, on the surface, curious. Clearly, had the USA wanted to bomb Iraq, they would have pushed harder for a finding of 'material breach'. By sending Rolf, the Council was removing any pretext for a military strike against Iraq and the Americans were encouraging this direction.

The sudden US support for diplomacy was driven by the fact that the CIA coup plot was collapsing around them. While UNSCOM 150 was parked out in front of the Special Republican Guard facilities, the CIA Station in Amman was desperately trying to contact the ringleaders of the coup plotters in Baghdad, to get everyone in place for the upcoming military strike. But their entire network in Baghdad was silent. It was as if they had disappeared off the face of the earth. The reality was that the coup plotters were being rounded up by the Mukhabarat. Saddam's intelligence service had so thoroughly infiltrated the coup plot that there wasn't a single CIA-controlled asset left in Iraq that hadn't been arrested by the Mukhabarat. Desperate to regain a semblance of control over what was going on in Iraq, the USA was now looking to Rolf Ekéus to bring order to the chaos the CIA had helped create.

Thanks to the work of the Mukhabarat, Tariq Aziz had a full picture of what was really going on regarding the interplay between weapons inspections and the CIA's thwarted plans for regime change. While the senior Iraqi leadership felt that there was a clear case to be made for terminating all relationships with UNSCOM, the Mukhabarat's UNSCOM cell had convinced Tariq Aziz and others, including Saddam, that UNSCOM was being used and was not a witting player in the coup plotting. The Iraqis knew that economic sanctions could not be lifted without a favorable report on compliance from UNSCOM, so the decision was taken to give Ekéus one more try to realign his inspection efforts away from US policy imperatives, and back on track with the original disarmament mandate.[3]

Tariq Aziz met with Ekéus at the Iraqi Foreign Ministry on the evening of 19 June. Ekéus's opening remarks showed that he was open to compromise, noting that 'our two sides should grasp this new opportunity and move forward soon so that it might lead to a situation where the council could address the lifting of sanctions.'

This was, of course, what Tariq Aziz wanted to hear. But first he had to make a few points. 'There are two governments, the US and UK, which officially or formally say they would like to change the government of Iraq,' he said. 'Iraq cannot take lightly the fact that UNSCOM receives information mainly from these two governments, and then you send teams to the Special Republican Guards.' Tariq Aziz pressed home his point, stating that 'We in Iraq have serious concerns and suspicions. You [Ekéus] sent your team, UNSCOM 150, anticipating a crisis… I am complaining about the timing of the inspections. It might not concern you, but we in Iraq see it differently.'[4]

Ekéus had no real political ammunition. While at the Security Council the US and UK representatives talked of 'material breach', the fact was that with the coup plot foiled, there was no longer a viable military plan in place to strike Iraq. The CIA knew full well the extent to which the Iraqis had penetrated their plot against Saddam, and how this information might be used by Iraq, and its allies in the Council, if the USA were to proceed with a military attack. The unity of the Council needed to maintain economic sanctions could crumble. In an odd coming together of minds, both Iraq and the USA wanted Ekéus to reach a compromise, Iraq to get sanctions lifted, and the USA to keep sanctions in place.

Ekéus engaged in a lengthy one-on-one meeting with Tariq Aziz where the issue of lifting of sanctions was discussed.[5] Ekéus promised to work hard to get sanctions lifted, but needed help in undermining the US policy of sanctions-assisted regime change. Inspections needed to continue, Ekéus said, and they had to incorporate a serious investigation of the concealment mechanism. If Iraq would accept such an investigation, Ekéus would find a way to make sure these inspections could not be used by others to violate Iraq's national security interests. Tariq Aziz summoned Amer Rashid and Amer al-Sa'adi, and over the course of two days an agreement was reached.

On 22 June, Rolf Ekéus and Tariq Aziz signed what became known as the 'Agreement for the Modalities of Sensitive Site Inspections', which governed how UNSCOM would go about inspecting sites deemed sensitive to Iraqi national security – Republican Guard, Special Republican Guard, Special Security Organization, Mukhabarat and other security institutions, including all presidential and ministerial buildings and facilities. There were seven specific modalities cited in the document, but perhaps the most controversial concerned the number of inspectors permitted into a 'sensitive' site:

> The entry into the site will be made by a limited group from the inspection team (the Chief Inspector, one or two inspectors and one or two linguists – a total of four). The entry group will survey the site to determine if a proscribed nature could be associated with items, documents and related activities.[6]

Rolf Ekéus had done his job – averting a war, while keeping weapons inspections on track. But the result, while a short-term fix for the USA, was a strategic disaster for US Iraq policy. The ramifications of the collapsed coup attempt had yet to sink in. Many in the CIA were harboring hopes that the coup plotters would magically reappear, establish contact and indicate their continued readiness to go after Saddam. But any such hope was quickly quashed when, on 26 June, the CIA's Amman Station allegedly received a transmission from one of their secure satellite phones. It was from the Iraqi Mukhabarat, who told the surprised CIA agents that the game was up. Within days the CIA team in Amman vanished. All traces of the CIA's involvement in a coup plot against Saddam were eliminated. The USA had just witnessed a covert action fiasco of a kind not seen since the Bay of Pigs in 1961. Saddam Hussein's security services had rounded up over 800 suspected plotters, most of whom were subsequently tortured and executed. As for the CIA's links with UNSCOM, Moe Dobbs and his SAS team didn't stay around in Bahrain for the post-mission debrief, instead getting on planes for flights back to America. It was the last time I, or anyone in UNSCOM, saw Moe Dobbs or worked with anyone in the SAS.

Chapter 14

The Poison Pill
July—August 1996

The failed coup debacle in Baghdad shredded the credibility of the CIA. Having had no backup plan in place if the coup went awry, the USA was now left trying to revive the old 'sanctions-based containment' plan. But this plan was contingent on UNSCOM maintaining the notion that Iraq was not complying with its obligations to disarm. Now, with the new inspection modalities agreed on by Ekéus, the USA feared that Iraq and UNSCOM might actually reach an understanding regarding disarmament. Washington was swept up in the throes of a policy disaster, and everyone was looking for someone to blame.

The logical choice for the chopping block was Steve Richter, the chief of the CIA's Directorate of Operations' Near East Division. The June coup plot had been his plan. But Richter was a crafty insider experienced in the art of shifting blame. According to the CIA, it was UNSCOM's investigation into the concealment mechanism which tipped off the Iraqis that defectors were cooperating with the West, allowing the Mukhabarat to unravel the coup plot. This logic not only failed the test of credulity, it was also chronologically impossible (the CIA's secure transmitter was had been captured by the Mukhabarat in January 1996, four months before my meetings with the defectors in Amman). As far as the CIA's covert operators were concerned, Richter wasn't to blame; Ritter was. But in the strange world of intelligence-based politics, the CIA did not move to attack me just yet. With the new US priority now being the destruction of the agreement Ekéus had made, I was considered useful as the logical choice to test the modalities of that agreement with a confrontational inspection.

Back in New York, most of the UNSCOM staff viewed the new Ekéus modalities as a decisive defeat for the inspectors. I, however, did not share this opinion. 'The Iraqis have trapped themselves into having to let us into a site,' I said. 'There can no longer be any excuses. If UNSCOM organizes itself like a forensic crime scene investigation team, we should be able to detect evidence of concealment that will be useful in getting the Iraqis to finally confess the truth about concealed weapons.' I was anxious for an opportunity to put the agreement to the test.

On 24 June 1996, I got it, in the form of a CIA-provided photograph that showed a gathering of vehicles on 11 June outside a Special Republican Guard site on the southern tip of Saddam International Airport, which I labeled 'Site 1a'. At first I was skeptical of the U-2 image, since it showed nothing more than a score or so of Sedans, together with a few light trucks, circling around a building inside a walled compound. However, SCE intercepts of Iraqi minder communications showed that, at the time the U-2 photograph was taken, Hossam Amin was demanding to know where every inspector was, and instructing his minders that the movements of every inspector be frozen, around the same time the photograph was taken.[1] Looking over the photograph, I asked myself why that might be. As I scanned the blurry images of vehicles, the answer seemed to be because the Iraqis were preparing to move something they didn't want the inspectors to observe. In this photograph, I believed UNSCOM had evidence of ongoing concealment activity, and as such, a location in Iraq that was an ideal candidate for testing the sensitive site modalities.

Within days of his return to New York, Ekéus was visited by both the US and British ambassadors to the United Nations, and subjected to withering questioning concerning the wisdom of his compromise. Ekéus defended his decision as a perfect example of diplomatic compromise, and told both ambassadors that in his mind inspections had been enhanced, not degraded, by the new agreement. But words alone would not carry the day; Ekéus needed substance, and so instructed Nikita Smidovich and me to return to Iraq to test the new agreement.

We arrived in Baghdad on 15 July, my thirty-fifth birthday. The next morning we got straight to work. It was blistering hot; the wind blowing in from out of the western desert was baking this corner of Iraq with

171

temperatures unseen in years. The medics on the team were saying that it easily exceeded 120 degrees Fahrenheit. And it was only 9 a.m.

I sat in the front seat of my Nissan Patrol, the lead vehicle of a four-vehicle convoy that was approaching our target – a military compound on the southern edge of Saddam International Airport. I was very familiar with this particular checkpoint – our advance had been stymied here twice in the past, during UNSCOM 143 and UNSCOM 150. But this time it was supposed to be different. The sensitive site modalities agreed between Rolf Ekéus and Tariq Aziz in June were designed to prevent similar standoffs from occurring. East of us, another four-vehicle convoy was converging on the target area, as was a third convoy, approaching from the south. If everything went as planned, we would close in on the target along all potential routes of egress, trapping any documents or material that might be located there.

Suddenly our Nissan Patrol was halted at a checkpoint by a Special Republican Guard soldier holding a loaded AK-47 rifle at the ready. I could see his colleagues pulling 'dragon teeth' spikes across the road behind him, designed to blow out the tires of any vehicle trying to cross over them. This most certainly was not unimpeded forward progress. This was a replay of the past, something the modalities were supposed to prevent.

Despite my repeated protests, the Iraqis held us in place for forty-five minutes. Then, suddenly, we were allowed to move ahead, towards Site 1a, where we planned on making contact with the rest of our team. We snaked our way down the western side of Saddam International Airport, passing numerous anti-aircraft artillery and missile batteries, before coming to a second checkpoint. Like the first, this was manned by members of the Special Republican Guard. Expecting to be waved right through, I was stunned when the soldiers leveled their weapons at our convoy and pulled the gates shut.

Careful not to alarm the soldiers, I slowly exited from my vehicle, and approached the gate, all smiles. The senior Iraqi minder was there already, speaking to a plain-clothed security official from the Special Security Organization. He turned to me. 'I'm sorry, Mr. Scott. This is a new Special Republican Guard unit. We had permission only from the other unit. We need new permission to move forward.'

The intense heat combined with the humidity of the streams and ponds that permeated the presidential areas surrounding Saddam International Airport created an oven-like effect, driving everyone into whatever source of shade they could manage. After thirty minutes, the Iraqis came back with their answer: 'I'm sorry, Mr. Scott,' they said. 'You cannot continue down this path. It is strictly forbidden.'

'Strictly forbidden.' These were words we had heard many times before, during UNSCOM 143 and 150. According to the new modalities, these words were supposed to be a thing of the past. But the reality was that, when it came to the security of Saddam Hussein, the only rules that counted were those binding to the twenty-year-old Special Republican Guard soldier aiming his rifle at us.

It didn't matter which direction we tried to approach the inspection site from, the results were the same. Stymied at our current location, we circled south, past massive air defense facilities and the 2nd Mechanized Battalion barracks facility of the Special Republican Guard that had been the scene of the previous month's standoff. We drove down a small, winding road, through a patchwork quilt of irrigation ditches and farmers' fields. Ahead of us, perched on top of a large man-made hill, sat a gleaming structure topped with bright red tiles, one of the many massive villas that dotted the Radwaniyah presidential palace complex. This one was rumored to belong to Uday, Saddam's eldest son.

As we drove through the bucolic countryside, along small dirt paths bordered by fruit orchards and gardens of vegetables and flowers, I noticed that there were many men in the common dress of Arab peasants, but who looked very fit, wore military-style haircuts and carried AK-47 automatic rifles. These fields were cared for by members of the Special Republican Guard, who lived in the surrounding villages with their families when not protecting the presidential palaces. Their hostile stares clearly told us we were not welcome here. Earlier in the day, an UNSCOM vehicle had been ambushed by a pair of the off-duty Special Republican Guard 'farmers' as they crossed one of the little bridges spanning an irrigation ditch. The men had been hidden in the brush alongside the road, and had sprung out at the vehicle, weapons loaded and aimed squarely at the inspectors inside. It took the intervention of the Iraqi minders to calm the situation down, and then only with the arrival of a carload of Special Republican Guard officers, who instructed the 'farmers' to stand down. It appeared that these off-duty soldiers were never, in fact, off duty. Even when working the fields, they served as a barrier between the presidential palaces and any intruders.

The Iraqis had agreed to let UNSCOM inspect a barracks facility adjacent to Site 1a, home to the 2nd Armour Battalion of the Special Republican Guard. However, the situation changed as we tried to move towards our final destination. There was a gate on the southern tip of the 2nd Armour Battalion's perimeter that we needed to pass through to get to Site 1a. If we could get through this gate, then we had a straight shot of about 300 yards to the target. But the gate was locked, and the guards told the minders that under no circumstance was anyone to pass. We returned empty handed to our offices in the Baghdad Monitoring and Verification Center, the UNSCOM wing of the larger UN Headquarters. Behind the scenes, there was a frantic exchange of telephone calls between Rolf Ekéus, Tariq Aziz and Amer Rashid. It appeared that Ekéus was desperately trying to preserve the modalities agreement, even if it meant tolerating what amounted to a flagrant violation on the part of the Iraqis.

Two days later, on 18 July, under instruction from Rolf Ekéus to try and resolve the issue of access, we again tried to inspect Site 1a. Ekéus had been assured by the Iraqis that the events of 16 July were an anomaly, and that this time the inspection would go smoothly. By mid-afternoon, however, the team had advanced its position by only a few yards, still held back at gunpoint by Special Republican Guard guards manning a checkpoint leading towards Site 1a. Within minutes of our being stopped, Nikita Smidovich and I were joined by Amer Rashid, who politely inquired as to where we were trying to inspect. 'You are in a very sensitive area,' he told Smidovich, looking down the road. We were surrounded by AK-47-toting Special Republican Guard soldiers. They eyed us warily, but the presence of a high-ranking minister seemed to calm them. Down the road, near the crossroads, another cluster of soldiers manned a machine-gun nest, the barrel of the weapon aimed directly at all of us, inspector and minister alike. These soldiers worked for the president, something Amer Rashid was trying to point out. 'My dear, you cannot go any further than this. Beyond here it is simply too sensitive. It is presidential, and therefore forbidden.' Smidovich pointed to the gate. 'Can we not just go forward to the crossroads? At that point, our destination will be very clear. I promise you we have no intention of inspecting a presidential palace.' Amer Rashid shook his head. 'The crossroads are a presidential palace,' he said. 'This is impossible.'[2] The team again withdrew to the communications center.

The UNSCOM team cooled its heels for three days before finding out what its next step would be. Rolf Ekéus, confronted with the reality that his 'extraordinary diplomatic achievement' was rapidly collapsing, had struck a deal with Tariq Aziz and Amer Rashid, who 'guaranteed' the safe and immediate passage of the UNSCOM team to the site we wanted to inspect. Rolf had agreed to give the effort one more try, only this time, to ensure success, he agreed that the team would be led to the inspection site by Amer Rashid.

And so, on the morning of 21 July, we formed up outside the Baghdad Monitoring and Verification Center. At the initial Special Republican Guard checkpoint just on the edge of Saddam International Airport, the two convoys – Iraqi and UNSCOM, joined together and proceeded down the road, with Amer Rashid in the lead. We passed through the next two Special Republican Guard checkpoints without problems. But then, as we closed in on Site 1a, we came to a new Special Republican Guard checkpoint, and these soldiers weren't playing around. They had taken up positions in a horseshoe pattern, and were aiming loaded rifles, machine guns and grenade launchers at all vehicles, including Amer Rashid's. Amer Rashid spoke to a Special Republican Guard colonel accompanying our convoy, who approached the soldiers. There was no budging; these soldiers didn't take their orders from this particular colonel. Suddenly a vehicle arrived in front of us, on the other side of the checkpoint. Two officers stepped out, took a quick look at the situation, and barked some orders. They were obviously the proper chain of command, and the gate was opened.

We moved on. To our left was the southern edge of Saddam International Airport, and to our right a fenced-in game park where several different species of gazelle and antelope frolicked in a lush field – Saddam's personal stock for his culinary enjoyment. The road turned south, towards the game park, and suddenly we were at the wall, our forward progress blocked by a gate. To our right and left were enclosed compounds. We had finally reached Site 1a. The Iraqis had had days to sanitize the facility of any incriminating evidence but, having tried so hard to get here, I decided that the least we could do was to give it the 'UNSCOM treatment'.

As soon as the inspection began, I understood why the Iraqis were so nervous about our presence at this facility. The eastern compound was, as we thought, affiliated with the Special Republican Guard. But it wasn't simply any Special Republican Guard unit – it was Saddam Hussein's personal bodyguard unit, the Radwaniyah Platoon, 2nd Company of the 1st Battalion, Special Republican Guard. This unit was equipped with shiny silver Mercedes Sedans, which were parked in a line under a covered lot.

Two of the Sedans had tarpaulins pulled over them, which, when pulled back, showed the effects of an earlier ambush. One had been riddled with machine gun bullets, shattering the bullet-proof windows and penetrating the armored doors of the Sedan. The occupants of the second Sedan had gone through an even more terrifying experience. It had obviously been struck by a rocket-propelled grenade.[3]

A drive around the facility showed that it was a standard military barracks. A search of the files revealed nothing more than administrative orders concerning training, personnel transfers and logistics. Two of these orders caught my attention. One was a recent security memorandum from the Special Republican Guard Command Headquarters, Office of Security, which directed that all personnel assigned to the Special Republican Guard, and their families, were prohibited from any and all contact with non-Iraqi personnel, and that they should immediately report any such contacts by their colleagues and/or family members to the appropriate authorities. The second was an emergency administrative notice, declaring that the 3rd Battalion (Special Forces), Special Republican Guard, was 'liquidated', and all of its members were placed on administrative leave pending further notice. All units were ordered to review their personnel files and report on any 3rd Battalion officers and soldiers who had been assigned to their unit in the past year.

I had a sinking feeling in my stomach when I read about the fate of the 3rd Battalion, remembering that this had been the unit singled out by Moe Dobbs and the CIA as being off limits for inspection during UNSCOM 150. 'There's nothing there,' Dobbs had said. 'We've checked it out.' I now realized what this meant – stay away, those are our guys.

While I investigated the 2nd Company compound, other inspectors were inspecting a guesthouse and kitchen adjacent to the compound, where they were surprised to find an important 'guest' waiting for them – Tariq Aziz, the deputy prime minister. Smoking his trademark Cohiba cigar, Tariq Aziz was none too happy to see – and be seen by – the inspectors. He told the inspectors that he was there 'to help resolve any disputes' that might develop. His presence only reinforced my impression that the Iraqis knew exactly where we were headed, and that nothing of a prohibited nature would be found.[4]

My fellow inspectors, Nikita Smidovich included, felt let down by what had transpired, viewing Ekéus's caving in on the modalities as a decisive blow against UNSCOM and the credibility of inspections. But I saw the situation differently. The Iraqis may have thought they had stymied UNSCOM's investigation of the concealment mechanism. But the reality was that, armed with the information contained in the two documents I had found, we were in a position to expand the investigation. I headed back to New York as resolved as ever to get to the bottom of things.

Transiting through London, I again took advantage of my lengthy layover at Heathrow to pay a visit to my friends at the Defence Intelligence Staff's Rockingham cell. I was dressed very casually, wearing jeans and a polo shirt, with the desert dust of Iraq still stuck in the crevices of my hiking boots. My hair was long, and my face unshaven. I looked very rough, but this was just a social visit, a chance to get a quick bite to eat with friends. Or so I thought.

Sarah Parsons, the chief at Rockingham, was very pleased to see me, and invited me up to her office while she placed a few phone calls. 'You don't have any pressing engagements, do you?' she asked as she replaced the handset from her last call. 'Just a flight to New York in a few hours,' I responded. 'Good. The director [of DIS] would like you to sit in on the meeting he is about to have.' I looked down at my jeans and boots. 'But I'm not dressed for such a meeting.' She laughed as she got up. 'Don't be ridiculous. The director doesn't care how you look. He wants you to see something we think is of importance.'

I was led upstairs to a suite of offices and shown to a receiving area, with hardwood paneling, nice carpets and stuffed leather chairs. A pair of British officers, in civilian clothes, greeted me. One was the personal assistant to the DIS director and the other was a staff officer from the Ministry of Defence. 'Just back in from the wild, are we?' the MOD official said, smiling. I apologized for my appearance. 'Always travel in comfort, that's my motto,' he replied, jauntily.

The door to the director's office opened, and the director himself walked out, a tall man in his early fifties, with a broad smile and firm handshake. He was accompanied by several other men, each holding a variety of papers and folders. 'There you are!' he exclaimed, seeing me. 'I've been reading all about your adventures. You must give us all the gossip when we have more time.' He gestured across the receiving area, towards a conference room. 'Please join us in there, will you. We have something we want you to read and comment on.'

The aide passed around a series of folders, marked 'Top Secret', with a codeword following. I passed the folder back. 'Excuse me, gentlemen, but

I think I need to point out that I am not affiliated with the US government in any way, and I do not possess any form of security clearance. I shouldn't be reading what is in here.' The officer from the Ministry of Defence looked at me, a smile on his face. 'Well, we all know a few people who aren't to be associated with their governments now and then, old chap. But let's not make too much of an issue of it, okay?' I looked over at Sarah Parsons, who was sitting in on the meeting. 'Sarah, you know I don't have the clearances to read this.' She nodded towards the director, who was smiling. 'You're an American, Scott, and this is England. We'll decide who gets to read our stuff. So read on, and don't worry.'

With that I opened the folder. Inside was a lengthy report, again classified 'Top Secret', but this one contained several US codewords I was very familiar with, signifying material of great sensitivity. I looked at the subject line: 'UN COMMUNICATIONS INTERCEPT OPERATION UP AND RUNNING IN BAGHDAD'. I then glanced down at the list of addressees. This document had been sent around the world, to every embassy and military headquarters the USA maintained. I read the report itself, which detailed the mission being carried out, who the personnel involved were, by name, and what their nation of origin was. This was more than just letting people know a SIGINT operation was underway. This was blowing its cover to smithereens. There were even a few sentences about me, noting that while I had helped establish the communications intercept operation, I was not cleared for any of the intelligence being gathered.

I looked at the addressee list again. There were no British organizations listed. I pointed this out to the director, who laughed. 'We have our own spies, you know. Let's just say we got this from a very well-placed liaison.' The Ministry of Defence official spoke up. 'Not that it would take much effort to get a copy of this report, since the Yanks seemed to have sent it everywhere except Tariq Aziz's own office.'

That was the crux of the issue. The British had viewed the Special Collection Element deployment as a covert operation, and worked hard to shield it from unauthorized disclosure. Very few people in London knew about the SCE operation. And now the details of this operation, including the real names of the personnel involved, had been broadcast, literally, around the world. 'This represents an unacceptable breach of protocol and security,' the director said. 'We would like your opinion on this matter.'

I didn't hesitate. 'Clearly we have to take the best interests of the SCE team itself, first and foremost. This report represents a compromise of their security, which is unacceptable. From an UNSCOM point of view, we must cease the SCE operation immediately.'

The director looked at me for a few seconds. 'This is what we were hoping you would say,' he finally replied. 'It demonstrates to us the seriousness which you place on the security of our lads.' Then he looked over at the others seated around the table. 'But we cannot simply let this matter rest here. We need to find out why the Americans behaved in such an atrocious manner, and if this was indeed a simple accident, then what they are going to do to fix it.' He looked at me. 'Of course, those conversations are indeed a matter of confidentiality between the United States and Great Britain, so leave these matters to us. We will contact you when this issue is resolved, but I'm sorry to say we must act as you recommended, by pulling back from the SCE effort until such time as we can be assured that all parties, especially the Americans, are respectful of our security requirements.'

Whether done on purpose or accident, the American transmission of the sensitive details of a covert British intelligence operation, operating under UNSCOM cover, was an incomprehensible act which only underscored the cavalier attitude the US intelligence community had towards matters pertaining to the work of UNSCOM. But this was only the beginning of things to come. On my return to New York, I discovered that the fallout from UNSCOM 155 had been immediate and harsh. Accusations and counteraccusations flew back and forth between Washington and New York.

The ramifications of the failure of the CIA's June coup were starting to be felt by UNSCOM. Since the CIA's bungled effort was not public information (even in the halls of power in Washington, not everyone knew the full story about what had transpired), there was great confusion about what was really going on vis-à-vis UNSCOM and weapons inspections. To many American officials not privy to the CIA plot, it looked as if UNSCOM had been pressuring the USA to back weapons inspections but, when push came to shove, UNSCOM backed down, leaving America holding the bag. This, of course, was not the true situation, but one the CIA and its supporters in the Clinton administration were willing to promote in order to divert attention away from their own failures.

'Concealment' became a term associated with defeatism, a false rallying cry which UNSCOM had used to lure American support. The perception in Washington was that we cried concealment to get US backing and then exploited the complexities of concealment issues to avoid tough action.

But to UNSCOM, concealment was an all too real matter, one which we took very seriously. From our perspective, the concealment investigation had faltered because of the failure of the USA to provide serious intelligence support. I wanted the blame for any failures associated with the concealment investigation to be placed squarely on the shoulders of the CIA. Charles Duelfer, as the senior US government representative assigned to UNSCOM, was caught in the middle, relaying messages back and forth and trying to repair injured egos all around. He was serving two masters, and I felt almost sorry for him as he spent hours trying to put out the political fires that raged in all directions.

I was able to escape the political turmoil raging in New York and Washington for a little while, traveling to Israel as part of UNSCOM's continuing relationship with that country. I dropped off a new package of tapes from Gary and the SCE for Dani and his team to exploit. But my main purpose for being in Israel was to coordinate how to keep the counter-concealment inspection effort moving forward despite the problems that had emerged.

Moshe Ponkovsky and the Israeli photographic interpreters sat down with me to go over the events leading up to the inspection of Site 1a, why UNSCOM had decided to inspect it, and what we had found as a result. Everyone agreed that there was every reason to believe that the site had been involved in moving something in response to the UNSCOM 150 inspection. A big question that remained unresolved was about any material that possibly was still being moved: was it going to another hide site, or coming from a previously established hide site? The Israeli photographic interpreter Mushiko and his analysts were confident that the Israelis would be able to answer that question if UNSCOM could bring to Israel the rolls of U-2 film related to the UNSCOM 150 inspection.

I returned to New York only to find UNSCOM still in turmoil. Charles Duelfer called me up to his office, and informed me that I needed to go down to Washington and help repair relations with the US intelligence community. He warned me that many in the CIA felt that UNSCOM was straying too far from the US government, and that certain relationships – Israel first and foremost – were under particular scrutiny. I told him that the only thing that would make the CIA happy was for UNSCOM to give complete control of the inspection process to the USA. That wasn't going to happen. I reminded him just how valuable the intelligence cooperation with Israel had been. 'If we wrote down the contributions made by Israel to the work of UNSCOM, I could fill a book,' I said. 'I'd have trouble filling a page with the CIA's accomplishments.' I decided that rather than defend UNSCOM's decision to engage with Israel, I would instead challenge the US intelligence community to rise up to the task of providing effective and responsive intelligence support.

On 5 August, Nikita Smidovich and I flew down to Washington, where we met with representatives of the CIA, led by Burt, at the CIA safe house in Northern Virginia, off Tyson's Corner. The offices of 'Overseas Ventures, Inc.' had not changed since the last time I had visited. We were buzzed in by the same CIA security man, and sat in the same conference room, with the same Sandinista posters decorating the walls. Coffee was served in the same 'Foreign Training Group' mugs. The only thing that had changed was the atmosphere. Whereas before, these meetings at least pretended to be friendly, that day there was an air of open hostility.

I tried to warm things up by focusing on the positives. I told them about the progress made under UNSCOM missions 143, 150 and 155, and said that with significant help with our intelligence capabilities we could be close to finally cracking the issue of Iraqi concealment.

Burt and his CIA colleagues remained cold. The UNSCOM proposal was unrealistic. They could consider increasing imagery support, but the idea of UNSCOM photo interpreters working side by side with their CIA counterparts was out of the question. They might allow that kind of arrangement in Israel, remarked one of Burt's colleagues disparagingly, but not in the USA. On the SCE material, Burt said it was out of his hands, but the bottom line was that UNSCOM would not get direct access to any intelligence garnered from this source because of the sensitive nature of the methods involved.

Smidovich and I got up to leave, not even bothering to shake hands. 'You need to understand something,' I said to Burt before leaving. 'UNSCOM is responsible for disarming Iraq, not the USA. We will do it our way. If you want to block us, go ahead. But understand that there are a number of countries out there who want us to succeed, and who are working very hard to help us do just that. We're not going to just roll over and die because the CIA doesn't want to play ball.' We left the meeting further divided than we were when it had started.

The situation continued to escalate. On 20 August, the deputy national security advisor, Sandy Berger, convened a special meeting of the Deputies Committee, one of the highest-level policy-deliberation bodies in the US national security hierarchy, to discuss the matter of UNSCOM and Iraq. The Deputies Committee is where the deputy heads of the major institutions of US foreign policy – Defense, National Security Agency, State, CIA, National Security Council and others – meet to hash out policy. Once they get a policy nailed down, the actual heads of the departments meet to finalize it. The meeting was held at the White House, in the Situation Room located in the basement of the West Wing. Charles Duelfer had not been invited to attend, but was provided with a detailed report by several of the attendees after the meeting concluded.

The CIA was mute on the issue of the failed June coup and its possible ramifications. The focus was on UNSCOM and the new inspection modalities agreed on by Ekéus. Many on the committee felt that Ekéus, in agreeing to these modalities, had fatally undermined UNSCOM's capabilities and credibility to the point that the US government could no longer risk supporting UNSCOM along the lines it had in the past. Some on the committee, including the CIA, felt that UNSCOM had run its course. Economic sanctions would remain in place no matter what, they maintained, and it was time to bring the US-UNSCOM relationship to a close. Others, led by the State Department, argued that such a course of action would only play into the hands of the Iraqis, who had cultivated many friends on the Security Council in the past months. If UNSCOM failed, then the blame for that failure would be placed on the USA for withdrawing its support. Likewise, if the USA pulled back, UNSCOM would only have more reasons to continue to accommodate the Iraqis. In the end, the Deputies Committee decided to continue to support UNSCOM technically and politically.[5]

In reality, however, this vote of support was meaningless. To support UNSCOM 'technically and politically' without agreeing that, if UNSCOM achieved its task of disarming Iraq, economic sanctions would be lifted against Iraq, was tantamount to not supporting UNSCOM. But to reject US support would leave UNSCOM dead in the water, a derelict organization with a mandate that no longer had any meaning. UNSCOM needed to find a way to balance itself between working with the Americans on the one hand and honestly implementing its mandate of disarmament on the other. As the person who was responsible for executing this balancing act as it related to the CIA, I had been given a particularly heavy burden. This seemed like an impossible task, but the only other option was to quit. Having started down this path, quitting wasn't an option.

Chapter 15
The Con Game
August–December 1996

While events were unfolding on the political front with the US government, I returned to Iraq. There, I conducted interviews with Iraqi personnel involved in the security, safeguarding the movement of the documents and material from Hussein Kamal's chicken farm turned over to UNSCOM in August 1995. While the Iraqis, led this time by Amer Rashid, were very forthcoming with the provision of personnel requested for interview, and in securing answers to all of our questions, there were many fundamental problems in the story being presented by the Iraqis, first and foremost the total denial of formal involvement by either the Special Republican Guard or Special Security Organization in the concealment activity.

The interviews were conducted over the course of several days. By this time, UNSCOM inspection teams had stopped staying at the Sheraton and Palestine Meridian Hotels (their management said that having inspectors there hurt their business), and had instead taken up residence at the Bourj al-Hyatt, a hotel first used by the German helicopter crews (who rented an entire floor for their exclusive use), and then gradually by all visiting inspection teams. We got a great rate, good service and guaranteed rooms available at short notice. We also got the special attention of the Mukhabarat, which had its agents placed throughout the hotel staff, and maintained a special room behind the main office where their personnel monitored the phone calls and conversations of inspectors, through the listening devices implanted throughout the hotel. We didn't mind the listening devices, and in fact welcomed them, as we knew our conversations were being listened to and so we were very careful about what we said. We also had a bevy of Mukhabarat agents who took no pains to hide who they were, sitting about on the ground floor and in the restaurant, simply watching everything we inspectors did. Again, far from being intimidated, we became used to their presence and, in a way, welcomed it, since they brought with them a sense of security.

But, because of this Mukhabarat presence, I was somewhat surprised when, at the end of a long day of interviews I was approached by 'the Serb'. He asked me if I could spare a few minutes after dinner, so we could discuss something. I was taken aback. 'You want me to come back to the National Monitoring Directorate?' I asked. No, he said, he would come to the hotel. He asked if I could meet him in the lobby around 7 p.m.

Alarm bells were going off in my head, telling me to be careful. True, this was not the kind of discreet approach one would expect if one was being recruited by an intelligence service. Nevertheless, I had my guard up when I came down to the lobby. The Serb was already there, sitting in a chair, reading a newspaper. He stood as I approached. 'Why don't we get a bit of fresh air,' he said, and we exited the hotel. We walked around the block where the hotel stood, something that took about fifteen minutes to do at a leisurely pace. At first we simply rehashed old inspections, trading war stories and personal observations about people, Iraqi and inspector alike. The Serb was a bright, articulate man who had a good sense of humor.

We finished one lap around the hotel, and he indicated he was ready for at least one more. 'You have got all of Iraq watching what you are doing,' he told me. 'When I say this, I mean all of Iraq's leadership, including the Big Man himself.' I said I was pleased the work of my team was being paid attention to. 'Why do you want to know about the Special Security Organization?' the Serb asked. I pointed out that my position on this matter was quite clear: I believed that the Special Security Organization had been involved in the concealment of weapons of mass destruction in the past, and was concerned that they were involved in similar activities today.

'Your analysis has always been proven right,' he told me, 'and many in Iraq respect you for this. They know you believe in what you are doing. I cannot disagree with your analysis of the past, although you won't find anyone who will say this officially. What I can say is that there are no longer any weapons of mass destruction in Iraq. We think you know this, too. We know we have made mistakes on how we have told this story to you, and between you and me, we continue to make mistakes. Many things you heard today were mistakes, and I know you will soon figure them out. There is a political aspect to what is happening here, and we have to let this happen naturally.' He stopped walking. We were in front of the al-Hyatt hotel. 'Thank you for your time,' he said. 'I hope we can have another walk soon. I've enjoyed your company.'

I didn't know what to make of the Serb's discussion, or his decision to approach me. Clearly, he had had official permission to meet with me, because we had been observed by at least a dozen Mukhabarat personnel as we walked and talked. I found nothing threatening in what he'd had to say, however, and so decided not to make anything more of it.

On the last day of interviews, during a break, I was asked by General Amer Rashid to stay and talk. Amer Rashid pressed me hard for an explanation of why I pursued the issue of concealment so strongly, when all available facts pointed to Iraq no longer having any WMD. I drew a diagram on a piece of paper, showing a box with a series of lines coming in at one end, and a single line coming out of the other.

'The Iraqis admit that there was concealment,' I said, pointing to the numerous lines entering the box. 'Documents, some material, even programs. And yet,' I noted, pointing to the single line on the other end, 'you want us to accept at face value your contention that nothing remains.

'I am not contesting your statements that nothing remains. And you do not contest my statements that there was concealment. All I want to know is what happened inside the box,' I said, tapping the diagram with my finger. 'Once I know that, your statements that no WMD remain in Iraq will be more easily accepted.'

General Amer picked up the paper, stared at it, and then slid it to me. 'I'm afraid your box is in reality a Pandora's Box, and once opened will unleash events we cannot control.'

I wondered about General Amer's words, their meaning, and any relation between his conversation and my walk with the Serb. I felt I was being sent mixed messages from the Iraqis. They wanted me to embrace their contention that there were no WMD left in Iraq. But they also recognized that I had a valid point when it came to the issue of concealment, and seemed ready to help me prove my thesis without telling me what I needed to know. In the end, I decided all I could do was keep pressing forward.

So, in spite of Amer Rashid's warning, I proceeded with a trip to Israel, which I hoped would provide me with the intelligence to find what out what was really going on in the Special Security Organization. I met Gerard Martell, the French photographic interpreter, who was waiting with the rolls of U-2 film from both the UNSCOM 150 and UNSCOM 155 inspections. Once again, the Israelis proved their professionalism. By scanning successive rolls of film, the Israelis had detected that an unusual number of Sedans had been moved on 11 June from a site we were inspecting on the Airport Road to Site 1a. A review of past imagery of the Airport Road site indicated that there had been no similar concentration of vehicles for several months. This indicated that something was being concealed at the Airport Road site. I had the Israelis make prints of the new targets so I could brief the chairman.

While I was in Israel, UNSCOM had dispatched to Iraq a special delegation of technical experts, headed by Nikita Smidovich, in his new role as chief technical advisor, to begin implementing the 'Joint Program of Action' agreed between Tariq Aziz and Rolf Ekéus on 22 June. Tariq Aziz himself greeted the delegation, and immediately set forth the Iraqi case that all of its disarmament obligations had been met. It was a skilful presentation, which incorporated excerpts from UNSCOM's own reporting to the Security Council about the status of disarmament.[1]

The Iraqis were dismissive of any notion of ongoing concealment activities, but did acknowledge that there was a need to clear up misunderstandings about unilateral destruction in the summer of 1991, as well as the issue of supporting documentation. The bottom line was that from a technical standpoint, UNSCOM no longer had a viable case regarding substantive Iraqi non-compliance. The foundation of UNSCOM's current concerns rested on the issue of concealment and the related issue of inspector access. Unless UNSCOM could prove concealment, however, the matter of access was a matter of process, not substance, making it hard to guarantee Security Council's support in the case of future confrontation.

Reflecting this reality, the CIA suddenly reversed course, and requested that UNSCOM again present a paper outlining the basic elements of its strategy for addressing the issue of Iraqi concealment activities, as well as any specific requests for intelligence and technical support from the US government. I prepared this presentation, which reflected UNSCOM's current understanding of how the Iraqi concealment mechanism functioned.[2]

On 17 September, I flew to Washington, where I again met with Burt and other CIA officials in the 'Overseas Ventures, Inc.' safe house, to discuss the UNSCOM proposals. Tensions were running high. I felt personally betrayed by Burt and the CIA, and they were on the defensive, not being able to admit what had really been going on (the failure of the coup plot) while seeking to shift the blame to UNSCOM for everything that had gone wrong. Burt told me we should agree not to discuss the matter of the Special Collection Element and communications intercepts; the USA simply could not meet the UNSCOM requirements of support. I surprised Burt by then demanding that the US government return to UNSCOM over 900 DAT tapes that had been collected by the SCE, and subsequently passed on to the CIA, since it was UNSCOM's property. I also requested all logbooks and other supporting documentation. I told Burt that, regardless of the CIA's failure to support it, UNSCOM would seek to continue the SCE effort, using the British and Israelis as our source of technical and analytical support.

Burt then stunned me by accusing UNSCOM, and by extension me, of understating or misstating both our requirements and objectives, making it very difficult for the CIA to adequately support the work of the Commission. I vehemently disagreed and, in a confrontation that became quite heated, challenged Burt to back up his assertions with documents. I picked up the thick collection of documents I had prepared for this meeting, and flung them across the table. 'Don't call me a liar, Burt, or accuse me of playing games. I've been straightforward with you and the CIA from day one, and these documents prove it. If anyone is lying or playing games here, its you and your partners at the CIA.' I left Burt sitting there, red faced.

Burt tried to smooth things over by having me flown down to Washington and introducing me to Robert McCall, the head of the CIA counterintelligence cell. This time, instead of the usual 'Overseas Ventures, Inc.' location, Burt arranged for our meeting to be held in the conference room of a major Tyson's Corner Hotel. The specific conference room to be used wasn't known until the last minute.

Unlike our meeting in September, this time Burt was all smiles and warmth, as if none of the issues that existed between us mattered any more. The reason for this was simple: Burt, by introducing me to McCall, was trying to shift the focus onto UNSCOM's operational problems, as a way of avoiding discussions about the CIA's. Burt wanted to go over the concerns the CIA had in providing enhanced intelligence support to UNSCOM along the lines I had requested. 'We think there is a security problem inside UNSCOM,' Burt said, 'and we would like you to work with Robert to identify the problems, and come up with solutions.' If this was done, Burt said, then the CIA might be in a better position to provide the kind of support UNSCOM was asking for. I agreed, but reminded Burt that UNSCOM had a job to do, and we could not be held hostage to security concerns, legitimate or otherwise. 'Why don't we agree that UNSCOM is penetrated, and find a new way of doing business in a secure manner,' I said, 'rather than wasting time and effort in chasing down ghosts.' Burt said that the CIA wanted this review, so over the course of several days I spent countless hours scrutinizing the operational methodologies used by UNSCOM, the personnel involved and the record of possible past compromises in order to try and find a pattern that could point out where the inspection system was failing. While we developed many conspiracy theories, nothing ever emerged from our work that had any substance.

One of the areas that Robert McCall and Burt focused on was the ongoing UNSCOM cooperation with Israel. 'This is a serious problem,' Burt told me. 'We are concerned that sensitive information the US government shares with UNSCOM is making its way to the Israelis outside approved channels.' I pointed out that Israel had nothing to do with the notion of Iraqi penetration of UNSCOM. Furthermore, I reminded Burt that every aspect of the Israeli cooperation had been fully shared with the CIA, through my interaction with Burt himself, and that nothing occurred with Israel unless the CIA knew of it, and approved of it, in advance. This was true, whether we were discussing the U-2, where the CIA provided the film we took to Israel, the SCE, where the CIA was fully aware of UNSCOM providing tapes and logs to the Israelis, or special cooperation such as in the Jordanian affair, where Charles Duelfer had passed on the details of my proposal to the CIA before Ekéus had even approved my visit to Amman in November 1995.

Burt replied that no one was accusing me of violating any trust, or worse. 'The problem isn't you, but rather Israel,' he said. 'The Israelis are very clever when it comes to gaining access to the information they need, and many in the CIA are uncomfortable with the fact that you have such a close relationship with the Israelis that is totally outside the control of the United States.' I said that this was to be expected, since we were talking about an UNSCOM operation, not a CIA operation. But I again reiterated that there was nothing going on with Israel that the CIA wasn't already fully aware of.

In late November, I flew to Iraq as the chief inspector of UNSCOM 158. Our mission this time was to continue to pursue the concealment mechanism, and we conducted a series of interviews with senior Iraqis about this subject. We did several site inspections, including one of a building off the Airport Road that the Israelis had identified as possibly being related to the suspicious vehicle movement we had detected around Saddam International Airport in June 1996. The building turned out to belong to the Special Security Organization, and was indeed a document storage site. A senior officer denied that any sensitive documents had been stored there, just administrative files, and claimed that no documents had been removed. Under further questioning he admitted that there may have been an 'inventory' of documents on 11 June 1996, and that several Sedans may well have been parked outside the facility, but he denied that any of the documents were placed in the Sedans. The empty rooms, clean floors and cleared shelf space surrounding him seemed to contradict his assertions.[3] It was hard to escape the impression that we were being deliberately misled. There was nothing we could do immediately, however, and we wrapped up the inspection without further incident.

The end of an inspection was always a time of great relief. The C-130 which would fly us home always radioed in when it had departed Bahrain. That was our signal to load up the UNSCOM bus with our gear, and depart the Canal Hotel for the two-hour drive to Habbaniyah airfield. If everything went smoothly, we would expect to see the C-130 land just about the time we pulled up to the Iraqi 'terminal'.

We arrived at Habbaniyah airfield without incident, and went through the normal drill of turning in our blue UN certificates for the Iraqis to stamp with an exit visa. A cheery UN staffer from New Zealand, nicknamed 'Shorty', responsible for getting inspectors in and out of Iraq, was in charge. Although I was the chief inspector, my mission was over now, and I, like the rest of the team, was looking forward to getting back to Bahrain to unwind.

Shorty soon came back with our certificates, and as he did we could see the lumbering shape of the C-130 'Freedom Bird' as it descended for landing. There were a large number of UNSCOM personnel departing Baghdad that day, not only members of my team, but also a ballistic missile team and several resident monitoring staff who were going to Bahrain for rest and relaxation. Because of this, we made use of an Iraqi bus to transport us to the parking apron where the C-130 was waiting.

As soon as we pulled up to the C-130, I knew something was amiss. Surrounding the aircraft was a contingent of a dozen or so Iraqi Special Forces soldiers, AK-47 assault rifles at the ready. They had formed a loose perimeter, and were facing inwards, toward the airplane. Clustered near the ramp of the C-130 were half a dozen Iraqi plain-clothed security officers, automatic pistols tucked into their waists. Since we had administratively placed ourselves under the care of Shorty, I decided to stay in the background while he sorted out what was going on.

Shorty had a chat with the senior Iraqi security officer, who pointed at the flatbed truck carrying my inspection team's equipment. Shorty came over to where I sat. 'They say the plane can't leave until they inspect the baggage to make sure that no one has tried to smuggle out pieces of Iraqi missiles,' he informed me. I was incensed. That was my team's equipment, and I was chief inspector. I was no longer a passive observer.

I went to Shorty's Nissan Patrol, and made a radio call back to the UN Headquarters in Baghdad, passing on a situation report. I asked that this message be passed on to the director of the Baghdad Monitoring and Verification Center immediately and that, unless otherwise instructed, I would not permit the Iraqis to inspect the baggage.

I walked over to the Iraqis. 'Who is in charge here?' I asked. They all looked at me and remained silent. 'Who is in charge?' I repeated. There was no reaction. I went to one of the older men. 'Are you the boss?' I asked.

He smiled. 'No.'

'Who is your boss?' I fired back.

He continued to smile. 'He is not here.'

I looked at the assembled group of Iraqi security men. 'Look, whoever is senior among you, I want these soldiers removed immediately.' I pointed in the direction of the special forces troops surrounding the aircraft. 'There is no need for these weapons to be here, and I view it as a threat to the security of my inspectors.'

The Iraqi who had spoken to me finally said: 'They are here for your security.'

I looked at the soldiers. They were facing the aircraft. 'Well,' I responded, 'if they are securing me, why aren't they looking the other way. I know of no threat to the security of my inspectors that is in the vicinity of this area. Unless,' I continued, looking at the Iraqi security officer, 'they are protecting us from you.'

He smiled. 'No, they are here for your protection. Maybe to protect you from yourselves.'

'Look,' I explained, 'we are going nowhere, so why don't you pull back away from our airplane. There is no need for you to be here.'

The Iraqi who had spoken to me again replied. 'We are under orders to prevent you from loading your baggage until we have inspected it. We will stay here to make sure you do not load it onto the airplane.'

'Who gave you these orders?' I asked.

'His Excellency, Tariq Aziz,' was the response.

I needed to document this. I called over for an inspector with a video camera. The Iraqi security officer intervened. 'No pictures. Photography is prohibited.'

I was getting fed up with this. 'Listen, you are in violation of Security Council resolution here. Our luggage and equipment is not to be inspected by Iraq. You cannot impede the movement of this aircraft. The presence of these soldiers threatens the security of my inspectors. You are in violation, so I am going to document this on videotape.'

The security officer shook his head. 'No photography. If you do so, we will seize the camera.' He rested his hand on his pistol.

I was furious. 'Okay, then.' I called over John Smith (pseudonym), the chief inspector of the ballistic missile team that was heading back to Bahrain with us. 'John, could you get a tape recorder, please?' He went to the bus, and came back with a tape deck.

John stood next to me as I again asked the Iraqis who was in charge. Seeing the tape recorder, the Iraqi shouted, 'No taping!' and three Iraqis jostled John, bumping and pushing him as they seized the tape recorder and removed the cassette.

This had gone too far. I looked around me. The confrontation had attracted the attention of many of the UNSCOM personnel scheduled to depart on the flight. They were milling about, watching the unfolding events. Given the way John had just been treated, I viewed this as a potential safety hazard. I turned to the inspectors. 'Get everyone on the bus, please,' I said. 'I need everyone away from here right now, and back on the bus.' The inspectors complied.

Once I was convinced that all of the UNSCOM people were out of harm's way, I turned my attention to the Iraqis. 'What the hell do you think you are doing?' I yelled at them. 'How dare you lay a hand on an inspector!' I demanded that the tape cassette be returned immediately. 'That cassette is inspection equipment, and you have no right to take it.'

The Iraqis were ignoring me. 'Damn it, I want to know who is in charge here, and I want to know now!' I went from Iraqi to Iraqi, pointing my finger in their chests. 'Are you in charge? Are you?'

Finally, one of the Iraqis spoke up, a different fellow from the one who had spoken up earlier. Clearly, he was some sort of senior security officer. He sneered at me. 'You UNSCOM people think that you are the law here in Iraq,' he said. 'Well, this is not the case.' He patted the butt of his pistol at his side. 'Here in Iraq, this is the law.'

The Iraqi security officer was issuing a not-so-veiled threat. There was no way I could accept this. In my best Marine Corps drill instructor voice, I bellowed into the Iraqi's face. 'Are you threatening me?' The security officer seemed stunned. 'Well,' I shouted, 'if that is what you are doing, then shoot me. Pull out your pistol and shoot me.'

I was yelling at the Iraqi at the top of my voice. I put my finger to my head, simulating a pistol. 'Pull out your damned pistol and put it to my head! DO IT!' I was wild with anger. 'If you are not going to shoot me, then never threaten me or my inspectors again! Do I make myself clear?' I was nose to nose with the Iraqi security officer, blazing with fury.

The Iraqis were looking at me as if I had gone insane. Perhaps I had. In any event, the security officer and his colleagues backed away from the plane, and formed a huddle away from the ramp. However, I felt that there was no way I could have preserved the integrity of my or other chief inspectors' missions had I allowed myself to be intimidated. I had had to stand up for our rights.

The Iraqis weren't the only ones looking at me as if I had lost my marbles. The UN inspectors were, too. What I had done was not, so to speak, normal diplomatic discourse. But then again, what was happening in Iraq with the work of UNSCOM was not a run-of-the-mill UN operation either. We in UNSCOM were being called upon to carry out stringent disarmament tasks, often in what diplomats would refer to as a 'non-permissive' environment. This, of course, was a polite way of referring to the sort of incident that had just unfolded, where armed Iraqis would bully and threaten the unarmed inspectors as a means of intimidation designed to guide the inspection effort in directions more favorable to Iraq. They knew it was unlikely in the complex and divided international environment that we would get concentrated diplomatic support to punish this kind of behavior. I had been playing the cat and mouse game now for over five years now, and was, frankly, fed up.

I stood vigil at the base of the C-130, interposing myself between the Iraqis and our aircraft. The morning dragged on, with discussions taking place between the executive chairman and Tariq Aziz. Finally, the Iraqi authorities acknowledged that there had been a mistake, and the soldiers and security officers were withdrawn. The inspectors, and their baggage and equipment, were loaded onto the aircraft without further incident, and we finally departed for Bahrain. The other inspectors gave me a wide berth on the plane after my outburst, and I sat alone, glaring out of the window at the retreating landscape.

By mid-December the CIA had yet to respond to any of the requests for support submitted by UNSCOM. I needed a breakthrough to stop UNSCOM stalling. I tried my best to get Burt to lean on the CIA to come through with intelligence, and wrote a paper detailing yet again our intelligence needs.[4]

Within a week, I received a response. The CIA said that the issue of intelligence support was a non-starter without a solid inspection concept of operations in place that detailed the support required. I went to Charles Duelfer, and vented. 'What the hell are they talking about?' I demanded. 'UNSCOM has been on record for the last year and a half with a solid concept of operations.' Duelfer was sympathetic, but passed on that the CIA felt my concealment mechanism concept was 'too nebulous', lacking in substance.

I explained that we needed more intelligence of a specific nature before we could solidify specific plans, and that is why we had the Special Collection Element team in place – to pick up the Iraqi reaction to UNSCOM's actions. The USA had killed the SCE, so now we had nothing specific to go on. We needed specific intelligence, without which weapons inspections were going nowhere. I had tried my best to develop sources of information, but had been stymied by the CIA. 'So either the CIA helps us collect the information we need, or they provide it to us themselves, or we fold up our tents and go home.' Duelfer spoke to Burt, who soon called him back. 'We have hard intelligence, solid stuff, about an Iraqi operational ballistic missile force,' Burt said. 'We need to get this stuff cleared for release to you, but in the meantime why don't you plan an inspection that focuses on finding a ballistic missile force.'

Duelfer called me up to his office on the thirty-first floor of the UN

Secretariat to explain what was going on. I nearly exploded when I heard this. 'A what?' I asked him, incredulous. 'A ballistic missile force. The CIA wants to go on a SCUD hunt,' he said. 'We've been through this before, Charles,' I replied. 'There are no missiles in Iraq.' Duelfer shook his head. 'Look, Scott, first you say the CIA isn't giving you information, and now when they say they have information, you say you don't want it. Make up your mind.' I knew the CIA was taking advantage of this situation to try and revive the myth of an operational SCUD force, and do it in a way that made UNSCOM look as if we believed it. Duelfer, strangely enough, didn't disagree with me. 'Write a plan, Scott, and let's call their bluff. If they have anything good, we'll soon find out. And if it's garbage, then we don't have to do an inspection, do we?'

I did as I was ordered, developing a detailed inspection plan, designed to 'detect and/or compel Iraq to reveal to the Commission a suspected force of retained ballistic missiles'.[5] I was hoping this might help us with the concealment efforts, on the basis that the Special Security Organization probably used the same methods to protect WMD-related material as they did to protect the president.

The CIA promised me that they would deliver inspection sites related to the covert Iraqi missile force. I assumed that the Iraqi Mukhabarat would be good enough to predict the objectives of any UNSCOM inspection sent out against these sites soon after our team arrived in Bahrain for training; what I was hoping for was not to catch the missiles at the sites we expected to receive from the CIA, but rather to flush out the covert missile force from these sites, and detect them while they moved, first to the Special Security Organization 'sanctuary' of the Radwaniyah presidential area, and then, under more UNSCOM pressure, to the area around Tikrit, Saddam's hometown. Although I doubted the existence of any such covert missile force, any insights into how Iraqi concealment worked would be very useful.

Charles Duelfer delivered the concept to the CIA on Christmas Eve. I was told not to expect a response until after the new year.

My proposal caught the attention of a Clinton administration desperate for progress regarding Iraq. Ever since the August 1996 'Deputies Meeting' held in the White House Situation Room, the Clinton national security team had been fearful that UNSCOM was somehow 'slipping away' from a path of accommodation. Like President George H. W. Bush before him, Bill Clinton and his political handlers were sensitive to public perception, especially during the 'funny season' that characterized a presidential election year. The failed June 1996 coup attempt had in large part been influenced by domestic American political considerations, both in terms of the mission (get Saddam) and the timing (early summer, before the Republicans had nailed down their candidate).

Similarly, the CIA's 'go-slow' attitude to UNSCOM after the coup reflected the administration's desire to play down the Iraq issue until the election. Now that Clinton had been reelected by an overwhelming majority, his administration were in the mood for an aggressive breakthrough on the Iraq front. The mild-mannered Secretary of State Warren Christopher was replaced by the US Ambassador to the United Nations, Madeleine Albright. Albright was a tough-talking internationalist who believed in proactive American leadership. Unlike Christopher, Albright wasn't afraid of controversy or confrontation, or so her record of speaking up while UN Ambassador led one to believe.

To suddenly be presented with an inspection concept of operations that not only was aggressive, but spoke of uncovering the Iraqi crown jewels – a covert SCUD missile force – was too good to be true. The only problem was, UNSCOM wasn't promising the crown jewels – the CIA was. UNSCOM didn't even believe that a SCUD missile force existed in Iraq. My fears about UNSCOM being caught up in a classic con game were being realized. But the new Clinton administration was suddenly offering UNSCOM a level of political support that it hadn't seen for a while. It was hard to resist.

Chapter 16

White House Blues

After taking a short holiday, I was told by Charles Duelfer to prepare a briefing that I would deliver, in person, to the National Security Council, at a meeting of the Deputies Committee in the White House Situation Room on 7 January 1997. I protested to Duelfer that this was premature, as we had not yet received the specific intelligence information from the CIA about the existence of a covert ballistic missile force, something the entire plan was predicated on. He told me not to worry, that he was promised this information would be forthcoming, and that UNSCOM should proceed with the briefing as if such a missile force existed. I told him that this was lunacy, but he reminded me that we were 'playing with the grown-ups' now, and I should trust that the CIA wouldn't play confidence games at this level. 'These are serious people, Scott,' he told me. 'So go prepare a serious briefing.'

On the morning of 7 January 1997, Charles Duelfer and I took the Delta Airlines Shuttle into National Airport and then hired a cab which brought us to the gates of the West Wing of the White House. Duelfer had sent a message to the National Security Council earlier, providing all of the details pertaining to our visit. We walked over to the White House security checkpoint, where we were screened, in a process similar to that conducted at most major airports, issued with a 'cleared' visitors badge and told to proceed.

No one was waiting for us, so Duelfer led the way, having been to the White House several times in the past. We walked up to the side entrance, and went through the door. No one stopped us, or questioned our right to be there. Having entered the West Wing, we headed down a hallway and turned right, walking down a staircase that took us to the White House Communications Center. Here, a military staff member in civilian clothes took our names, checked our badges, and then ushered us through a doorway, and into the White House Situation Room.

My first impression was that the room was much smaller than I had expected for the nerve center of the world's only superpower. A large conference table dominated the room, with chairs situated all around. Television screens were mounted on the wall, serving the video conferencing capability of the Situation Room, allowing officials outside the room to see and hear the briefing being given. I was told that the US Mission in New York would be attending today's meeting via this link. My briefing was simple, a handout of eighteen pages, and a series of overhead slides.

After about fifteen minutes, people began showing up – representatives from the State Department, Defense Intelligence Agency, CIA, Joint Chiefs of Staff, experts from the National Security Council, and the acting deputy national security advisor, Jim Steinberg, who was filling in for Sandy Berger. They took their seats around the table, and soon all eyes were on me. I launched straight in to presenting the inspection concept.

I laid out my plan in detail, and reminded the audience that the entire inspection hinged on the CIA's yet-to-be provided 'hard' intelligence on a covert missile force. If the missiles didn't exist, the plan was irrelevant. However, if these missiles existed, then UNSCOM would find them, I believed, as long as the plan was followed exactly as set out.[1]

When I finished, Jim Steinberg turned to the personnel in attendance for comments. The Joint Chiefs of Staff representative said that they would support the plan with additional U-2 resources. The State Department was concerned about defending this inspection at the Security Council. 'It will be a confrontational inspection,' they said.

'It won't matter, if we find the missiles,' I responded. Everyone was happy with that answer, until I continued: 'Of course, to do that we need the intelligence information, which we are still lacking.' The Counselor and Burt were in the room, as was General John Gordon, the deputy director of the CIA. They assured everybody that the intelligence on the hidden Iraqi missiles would be forthcoming, and that the plan I had just presented was sound. Everyone present expressed their confidence in the project, and before long Charles and I were able to return to New York, both content at having secured the full support of the United States government.[2]

The hyped expectations for the new UNSCOM inspection received another high-profile boost when the CIA prepared an item for the presidential daily brief (the top-secret daily intelligence brief the president receives from the CIA every morning) titled 'Scott Ritter's Quest in Iraq', linking me personally to the goals, objectives and expectations of the planned mission. It was the perfect 'cover your ass' document; by bringing the matter up before the president in such a high-level manner, the CIA was advertising its involvement in case things went well. But by placing sole ownership of the ideas and concepts behind the inspection on my shoulders, the CIA was creating the ideal scapegoat in the event of the inspection turning sour.

I flew to Britain to propose to Sarah Parsons and Clive Provost, the British Ministry of Defence communications intercept guru, that they reexamine the question of whether to deploy a Special Collection Element (SCE) team in Iraq. There were still many ruffled feathers about the classified American message that had been dispatched around the world at the end of the UNSCOM 155 inspection, discussing the most sensitive details of the operation. The British were concerned about command and control, and were still very unhappy about the lack of support being provided by the Americans when it came to actually having UNSCOM use the intelligence gathered by the SCE effort. I told Parsons about my confrontation with Burt, and my demand for the USA to return all of the tapes produced by the SCE team back to UNSCOM's control. The CIA had actually done this, and I offered to turn the entire cache over to the British in exchange for their continued support. She called in Provost, who was the military officer responsible for providing the British personnel used by the SCE. He had some concerns about the security of the team, and how we at UNSCOM were going to explain their presence in Baghdad. The bottom line was that Parsons and Provost would have to resell the SCE to their respective bosses. But my offer to provide the 900 intercept tapes, filled with unique data, proved too good of a deal for any intelligence service to refuse. Gary and his communications intercept operators would be back in action.

The Israelis were hard at work supporting this mission as well. The CIA had failed in its gambit to close down the U-2 cooperation. The new director of central intelligence, John Deutch, had pressured Charles Duelfer in December 1996 to pull the plug on my frequent trips to Israel, but Duelfer, somewhat surprisingly, had defended the cooperation. The Israeli success at putting together what had happened on 11 June regarding the movement of Sedans from the Special Security Organization Airport Road facility to the Radwaniyah Presidential Security Unit had impressed Rolf Ekéus, and was a big factor in his allowing the program to continue in the face of US objections. The only change was that the USA now demanded that the CIA-supplied U-2 film be stored at the US Embassy when it wasn't being used by UNSCOM, something I had offered to do from the very start, but which the Counselor had at that time turned down.

Gerard Martell, the intrepid French photographic interpreter, was nearing the end of his assignment with UNSCOM, and was about to be replaced by an Australian named 'Spike'. Martell, Spike and I flew to Tel Aviv, where I met the CIA Station Chief, Stan Moskowitz, and established the film storage and retrieval procedures that UNSCOM would be using. Martell and Spike remained in Tel Aviv after my departure, working with the Israelis on mapping out all the Special Republican Guard and Special Security Organization locations in the Tikrit area where WMD-related material might be evacuated to. It seemed that when we 'squeezed' Baghdad, material was relocated to Tikrit. We therefore had to find out who was receiving the material in Tikrit. We had been waiting in vain for the CIA to give us intelligence on this, so I was pleased that the Israeli photographic interpreters were working so diligently to act on my request to find such a lead.

Meanwhile, the CIA's promise to deliver target information about the covert missile force was not materializing. The machinery of inspections was in motion, with personnel and equipment starting to move into position all over the world. Notifications were sent out to various countries requesting support, and the personnel and equipment scheduled to be used on the inspection were deployed to Bahrain on 22 February. There the inspection team began two weeks of intensive training for its missions ahead.

And, still, no intelligence information on ballistic missiles was provided by the CIA. I had prepared a contingency for this situation, and had the Israelis prepare a backup set of targets where we thought missiles and missile-associated activity might be found. But this was far from the 'solid intelligence' promised by the CIA, which would have served as the intellectual core of our inspection. Then, at the last moment, Burt and the

CIA produced a briefing on four sites in Iraq where 'suspicious activity' had been identified by US imagery analysts. Two of these sites were already included in the Israeli list of targets, and the other two were so unconvincing that everyone in the room simply sat silently when they were being presented. I had a sinking feeling in my stomach. The CIA had failed to deliver on its promise of support, and as such the inspection was doomed from the start. But events had progressed so far, politically and operationally, that there was simply no turning back. UNSCOM was going on a SCUD hunt, but there were no SCUDs to be hunted.

The inspection's real purpose as far as I was concerned was to provoke concealment activity which the SCE could pick up on. We therefore targeted sensitive sites. On 9 March we stepped up the pressure, heading for sites belonging to the Special Security Organization, Mukhabarat and the Special Republican Guard. We didn't expect to find anything more than the odd clue; the entire purpose was to start stressing the system of concealment.

But the act of walking around the corridors of buildings and institutions where the elite of the Iraqi security services were trained seemed surreal. At the Special Security Institute, upon entering the main hall, there was a large marble monument containing a long quotation from the 'director of special security' Qusay Saddam Hussein, extolling prospective agents to be true to the values and principles of the Ba'ath Party, and to be forever true in service to the 'Father of all Iraq', Saddam Hussein. The Institute itself was very similar to a small community college, with classrooms, lecture halls, a library, and a small cafeteria. There were around 300 students in attendance, aged between about twenty and thirty, and everyone looked at us with great curiosity as we roamed the halls and peeked our heads inside their classes.

The inspection of the Mukhabarat Academy was even stranger. We observed classes for high-speed driving and discreet surveillance while operating a vehicle, and language labs for Turkish, Arabic, French and English. There was a class for 'secret communications', and another for 'operating under disguise'. But the most disconcerting was the classroom for 'explosive assassination', complete with a table where all the nefarious devices for this task were laid out – booby-trapped bottles, cans, tires and, most disturbingly, children's toys.

But there was nothing related to weapons of mass destruction. As we returned to our vehicles, I was approached by the director of the Academy. 'What did you think of our facility, Mr. Scott?' he asked. I noted that in many ways it mirrored what one would find in similar American institutions – with the exception of the booby-trapped toys. The director smiled unapologetically. 'Maybe when sanctions are lifted, you can come back as a guest lecturer and talk to us about how you think we should do our business.'

The list of sites rolled on – Mukhabarat vehicle garages, Special Republican Guard barracks, and more – and at each location the result was the same – nothing. If one plotted out the locations we had inspected on a map, it would show an increasing level of pressure being exerted on units and organizations believed to be involved with concealment. This pressure was designed to push the concealment teams, and any material they were protecting, in the direction of Saddam International Airport.

With our inspections coming up empty, and the Iraqis displaying no emotion about what we were doing, I was becoming more and more convinced that the inspection was a giant failure.

During this entire time, Gary and the SCE had detected nothing out of the ordinary in the way of Iraqi communications. There were only the routine communications associated with the minders accompanying the inspection teams. Gary had detected a surge in communications affiliated with presidential security that could have been linked to the inspections of some of the Special Security Organization and Special Republican Guard sites, but overall the Iraqis were staying off the air.

Likewise, we were getting no reports from the imagery analysts in Bahrain. Gerard Martell, assigned to work with the CIA imagery analysts, had been moved from Israel to Bahrain, and was supposed to be assisting the CIA in going over the photographs taken by the U-2 in support of the inspection. However, when I talked to Martell via secure phone, he told me he had been sequestered by Burt and the CIA, and was not allowed to play a major role.

I became very concerned when Martell told me that the Americans were changing the U-2 flight schedules without coordinating with him. This was very disturbing, as I had designed an intelligence collection plan that had the U-2 overflights timed to coincide with inspection activity on the ground. The inspectors were assiduous about being on time, playing their part in what was supposed to be a carefully orchestrated movement. If the U-2 was missing its overflight schedules, then there could be no correlation between what it was taking pictures of and what the inspectors were doing on the ground. In short, the entire U-2 imagery support plan, so carefully interwoven into the fabric of the inspection, had been destroyed by American manipulation. The only way UNSCOM was going to find any WMD material in Tikrit was to stumble upon it. And while the UNSCOM 182 inspection spent two days scouring the area in and around Tikrit, not only did we not stumble upon anything proscribed, but it became painfully obvious to all that there simply wasn't anything there to begin with.

The Serb had been following the events in Tikrit with great interest. Back in Baghdad, after a wrap-up meeting with our Iraqi minders, he took me for a 'long block' walk. 'Someday you will have to explain to me what that was all about,' he said, referring to the inspection mission we had just completed. 'This mission was so unlike you. It lacked focus. And it has caused some in our leadership to wonder who is calling the shots in UNSCOM.'

I had to laugh at that. 'You give me far too much credit. Trust me, the person calling the shots is most definitely not me.'

The Serb didn't like that answer. 'Don't belittle yourself, or what you are doing,' he said, as we brought our walk to an end. 'You have had a huge impact here in Iraq. You've started something that many believe must be finished. But if people start to believe that you cannot finish the task, or are unwilling to finish the task, then the support you enjoy now will vanish.'

The UNSCOM 182 inspection was over. By any measure, it had proven to be a dismal failure. It was a high-profile, very confrontational inspection that simply fizzled – exactly the kind of scenario the USA had said it wanted to avoid because it gave the Iraqis and their allies in the Security Council political ammunition to use against America's policy of sanctions-based containment. What the USA wanted was for UNSCOM to continue with a quiet inspection regime, out of sight of the Security Council, and to continue issuing inconclusive biannual reports, making Security Council movement on sanctions unlikely. What they didn't want was high-profile inspections (except when it suited their purpose, as in the 1996 coup attempt), which produced nothing and would prompt the Security Council to question the purpose of UNSCOM. UNSCOM 182 had been a controversial break from the low-profile approach, one that promised everything, but delivered nothing. Faced with a disaster of this magnitude, clearly heads were going to roll.

As the main supporter of the UNSCOM 182 inspection, Charles Duelfer was concerned that the head that was going to roll was his. While

UNSCOM 182 was settling in Bahrain for the team debrief and initial report writing, Duelfer was back in New York, assembling a 'lessons learned' brief without the benefit of actually knowing what had happened. He had scheduled meetings at the White House Situation Room (for the National Security Council Deputies Group), and the State Department (for the various lower-level inter-agency working groups and support cells), where the UNSCOM 182 inspection leadership, myself included, would explain what had happened, and why . The briefings were scheduled for 26 March – little more than twenty-four hours after the team was due back in New York.

On 26 March, Charles, Roger Hill and I went to the White House, where once again we met in the White House Situation Room with the Deputies Committee of the National Security Council. The room was packed, a new addition being Steve Richter, his deputy, Robert McCall, and a third CIA operative – Tony Bracco (pseudonym), whom I had last seen in Baghdad in March 1996. At that time, Bracco had been responsible for operating the complex camera monitoring system that the US Air Force officer known as the Engineer had installed throughout Iraq. When I had seen him in Baghdad, Bracco had had long hair, was unshaved, and behaved like a California beach bum. Here, in the White House, his hair was closely cropped, his face clean-shaven, and he wore a crisp suit with a conservative tie. He was clearly something more important than the low-level technical engineer he had claimed to be in Baghdad.

As we entered the Situation Room, an aide was busy removing nameplates from around the table which read 'President', 'Vice President', and other titles I couldn't discern. Senior officials from the various US government bureaucracies began to arrive, and took their places around the table. Peter Tarnoff, the Under Secretary of State for Political Affairs, represented the State Department. The CIA was represented by General John Gordon, the deputy director. A Navy Admiral sat in for the Joint Chiefs of Staff, and a brace of Army Generals represented the Department of Defense. Jim Steinberg, the deputy National Security Advisor, chaired the meeting. There was an undercurrent of energy, and soon the room was filled with the buzz of half-whispered conversation, as everyone speculated about what was about to occur.

I was asked to give a presentation on the actual conduct of the inspection, which I did, outlining our course of action and the sites inspected. Afterwards, I was asked by General John Gordon, the CIA's deputy director, to comment on what went wrong with the inspection. Stunned with the audacity of the question, I responded 'Nothing went wrong with the inspection, Sir. We did everything we were required to do. The problem wasn't with the inspectors, but with the intelligence support we received. The collection plan was never in sync with the inspectors, and the target data promised did not live up to its pre-mission hype.'

Peter Tarnoff, the third-ranking official at the Department of State, jumped in. 'Obviously you continue to believe that the Iraqis are hiding something. Where, then, are they hiding it?'

I put up a map of Baghdad and Tikrit on the overhead projector, and pointed to the large expanse of territory which encompassed the presidential palace areas located in each region. 'We have plenty of strong circumstantial evidence that there is concealment going on in Iraq today. Whether this relates to weapons of mass destruction, we don't know. That is the purpose of the investigation in the first place. We just finished a comprehensive inspection of units and facilities we believed were involved in this concealment activity, and for a number of reasons we found nothing whatsoever. Therefore,' I concluded, pointing my finger at the map, 'I believe that the logical location for this material, and any supporting infrastructure, if it exists, is inside these presidential palace areas, which have become sanctuaries off-limits to UNSCOM inspection.'

My response caused a minor uproar. The participants in the meeting were gesturing and talking among themselves. Jim Steinberg tried to bring order to the meeting by asking Steve Richter, the CIA official responsible for Iraq, if he concurred. Richter simply shrugged his shoulders. Steinberg thanked me for my thoughts, and for our work, and declared the meeting over. Steve Richter and his CIA colleagues left without a word. Several of the military officers, from both the Joint Chiefs and the Department of Defense, came up and shook my hand, wishing me well.

Roger Hill and I made our way to the State Department, where we found ourselves seated before a room full of openly hostile officials from all agencies of the US government. The White House meeting had been for the decision-makers. Here, in the State Department, were gathered the 'working class' of the national security establishment, the staff officers and analysts who actually implemented policy. I was supposed to be giving them a chance to ask questions about the inspection.

The leader of the group, a senior civilian from the Joint Reconnaissance Center with the Joint Chiefs of Staff, set the tone by noting that 'when a fiasco of this magnitude occurs, it is normal for those responsible to do the honorable thing and resign.' He was looking at me when he spoke.

I stared back for a moment before responding. I had not expected this sort of hostility. 'If you want to apportion blame, then let us be fair,' I replied. 'You misled us about what you were willing to contribute to this mission. You failed to deliver in terms of U-2 capability. You flew the wrong targets, with the wrong sensors, at the wrong time. You provided worthless information, and in the case of the most important intelligence, the heart of this inspection, you provided no intelligence at all. If I were to evaluate your performance from an outsider's perspective, I would be hard put not to reach the conclusion that you had deliberately sabotaged this inspection from the start.' I looked my accuser straight in the eye. 'While I will take all responsibility regarding the shortcomings of the inspection team, you in turn should take responsibility for your own failings. If there are to be any resignations springing from this debacle, they should all originate from the cast of characters seated on your side of the table, and yours should be first.'[3]

A State Department official quickly intervened, and did his best to get the meeting on track. I let Roger Hill take over, and he did a remarkable job in diplomatically fielding questions from the assembled Americans, all now rather tense. But in the end, the crux of the problem came down to intelligence support. All eyes were once again on me, and I couldn't resist pressing home my point: 'In short, you lied to us. You said you knew something existed, and it turned out you knew no such thing. You sent us on a wild goose chase. And now you belittle us. I can't speak for the executive chairman, or the others seated in this room, but from my perspective,' I paused, looking over at the man who had asked for my resignation, 'and I plan on being around for a long time, so my perspective does count. You have behaved as if you are the enemy of UNSCOM. You have actively conspired to undermine the credibility of UNSCOM and its inspectors. I hope I'm wrong, but if this is indeed the case, then UNSCOM might be better off rethinking who it is willing to do business with.'

Relations between UNSCOM and the US had hit an all-time low. If UNSCOM had any hope of completing its mission in Iraq, these relations would have to be repaired, and UNSCOM put back on track in conducting effective inspections to investigate Iraq's concealment mechanism. This was no small task. In fact, it would prove to be the hardest mission of all.

PART THREE
BETRAYAL

Chapter 17
The Truth Emerges
March–May 1997

UNSCOM 182 had left a bad impression with many, including Rolf Ekéus. We had aimed high, and delivered nothing. My own role in this debacle was being widely discussed in Washington. I did not hold myself above fair criticism, but I felt what was going on represented more of a witch hunt than fact finding. I was summoned to the thirty-first floor of the UN building in New York and asked to give the executive chairman a briefing on the status of the concealment mechanism investigations.

'Good afternoon, Scott,' Ekéus opened up the conversation affably. 'I hope you are rested after your adventures in Iraq.'

I gave the chairman a rundown on my take on what had transpired at the White House, with a special emphasis on Peter Tarnoff's question and my response. 'The bottom line,' I concluded, 'is that for a combination of reasons – US incompetence, bad luck and an effective concealment strategy on the part of Iraq – the inspection failed. I think UNSCOM has gone as far as it can on the direct approach to finding any remaining weapons that might still be in Iraq. The Iraqis seem to have hunkered down inside sensitive areas, making a true no-notice inspection highly unlikely. I recommend that we take a new approach, one that seeks to find evidence of concealment as opposed to the weapons themselves.' This wasn't really a new approach, as it had been my tactic from the very start, before the CIA intervened with the false missile information. But I sensed that after my outbursts in Washington, Ekéus was in no mood to hear another attack on the USA.

'Precisely,' he said. 'The old formula no longer seems effective. And I think it is a good idea for you to turn your efforts towards finding a new formula.' The meeting was over. Unlike Charles Duelfer, Ekéus displayed no outward sign of being irritated by the results of the UNSCOM 182 inspection.

I took the chairman's words about 'finding a new formula' to heart, and on the last day of March 1997 laid out some new thoughts for the chairman in a memorandum titled 'Concealment Mechanism Talking Points'.

'There should be no doubt,' my memo started, 'that there was, and most probably still is, an organized mechanism of concealment orchestrated by senior levels of the Iraqi government for the purpose of safeguarding activities and material proscribed by Security Council resolution.' I noted that Iraq had, from the very beginning, denied the existence of such a mechanism, and had resisted any effort to engage in a discussion about the issue.

To date, I went on, the Iraqis had tried to blame Hussein Kamal for all of the deceit and lies that emanated from Iraq over the years. However, as I explained to the chairman, 'Information available to the Commission indicates that, while Hussein Kamal did indeed play a supporting role, he was not part of the "inner circle" of decision-makers driving the concealment process.'

I reminded Ekéus that any effort by the Iraqis to steer the Commission toward purely technical work (i.e. the issue of establishing a 'material balance' which accounted for one hundred per cent of Iraq's weapons of mass destruction) without a discussion about concealment only guaranteed that a verifiable and accurate 'material balance' would never be attained. The key to this logic was the unilateral destruction carried out by the Iraqis in the summer of 1991. Iraq's whitewashing of these events, and inability to substantiate their often contradictory verbal claims with documents or other supporting evidence, made an accurate assessment of the 'material balance' all but impossible to achieve. To have a material balance would logically seem to be in the best interests of Iraq, since this was the only means by which UNSCOM could issue the finding of compliance that would lead to a lifting of sanctions. The only conclusion I could reach when assessing Iraq's obstinacy concerning the 'material balance' was that Iraq was afraid of what a true assessment of the 'material balance' would show – unaccounted for weapons of mass destruction.

'This,' I noted, 'is part of the strategy of the concealment mechanism. Since the concealment mechanism has succeeded in distorting and misrepresenting this data, there can by extension be no final material balance without a full understanding of the scope and breadth of the concealment mechanism.'

I concluded by reminding the chairman that this investigation was, by its very nature, a very controversial one. The targets of this effort were the most sensitive organizations in Iraq – its intelligence and security services, including those related to the president. I emphasized to Ekéus just how unprecedented our openness about the scope and subject of this investigation had been with the Iraqis: 'The targets of the Commission's investigation have been elaborated to the Iraqis, both through the Commission's reporting to the Security Council, as well as through the inspection teams themselves. The Commission has been as transparent as possible in regards to this sensitive subject.'

Within a day of my submitting the concealment memorandum, I was again summoned to the chairman's office. Ekéus was, as usual, all smiles and courtesy. 'A very important paper you have written,' he said. 'I agree that we need to proceed, but carefully. You should develop a plan of action.'

'I would need to make several trips to coordinate with our supporters,' I said.

'Of course,' the chairman said without hesitation. And, like that, I was back in the concealment business.

Washington wasn't exactly a safe haven for me. The fallout from UNSCOM 182 still affected the intelligence bureaucracy on a daily basis as officials, called to task for an expensive operation (redeploying the second U-2 alone cost millions of dollars) that yielded nothing but political trouble, looked for places, and people, to blame. I decided to start in more friendly environment, and I called Sarah Parsons in London. We scheduled a meeting for 7 April.

It was a glorious day as I flew into London. By now, the drill with the uniformed matrons who watched over the entrance to the Old War Office, as well as the badge switch prior to entering the Defence Intelligence Staff sanctuary, was old hat. Sarah Parsons, ever polite, met me and escorted me through the process and up to the 'Rockingham' office space. Waiting for me were several of Parsons' colleagues, including Clive Provost. We agreed that concealment was the issue in Iraq and that we had to use intercepts rather than search and destroy inspections in order to uncover it. I pressed again for the redeployment of the Special Collection Element (SCE).

A representative from GCHQ, the British code-breaking agency, spoke up. 'There is more to it than that, I'm afraid. Even if we could handle the material, the special relationship between the UK and the Americans prevents us from sharing the take with an outside agency, such as UNSCOM, without the express permission of the Americans. So far, I'm afraid that this permission just isn't being given.'

I was shocked. I had come over to Britain to try and escape from under the shadow of American influence over UNSCOM, only to be confronted with it yet again, this time disguised as the 'special relationship' between the US and UK.

The meeting with the British went on for several hours, and in the end it was decided that UNSCOM would try to arrange a seminar, sometime in May, at which point the UNSCOM position concerning Iraqi concealment would be briefed by UNSCOM to a joint US/UK audience, and operational concepts discussed among the three parties in more detail. I was pleased to have some prospect in sight of reactivating the SCE. However, I didn't want to delay following up on UNSCOM 182. Assuming the concept was authorized at the seminar, I wanted to have a plan in place so we could begin inspecting immediately. To make a plan, I needed more intelligence leads, which meant going to Israel.

I met up with Gerard Martell in Tel Aviv. This was to be his last trip to Israel as an UNSCOM photographic interpreter, as his tour was up and his parent unit wanted him back in France. In Israel, Martell had played a major role in shaping the U-2 cooperation, and whatever successes we enjoyed were directly attributed to his hard work and professionalism. The Israelis and I would miss him very much.

I put Martell and the Israeli photographic interpreter Mushiko straight to work trying to nail down concealment targets in and around Tikrit. I desperately wanted to find the Tikrit equivalent of the Radwaniyah Presidential Security Unit, and it was up to the photographic interpreters to find them. In the meantime, I split my time between meetings with Israeli intelligence officers and writing my concealment mechanism presentation. With the Israelis, I was able to bounce off my theories and opinion, and seek new information to fill in whatever gaps I had. I met with political intelligence officers, including one whose task was to 'get inside' Saddam's head. I spoke with experts on the Mukhabarat, Special Security Organization and Special Republican Guard, as well as those who understood the Iraqi tribal hierarchy and its impact on Saddam's regime. We would meet during the day, and I would write at night.

By the time my visit was finished, Martell and Mushiko had provided me with three solid targets in Tikrit, including one, just outside of Auja, that Mushiko was certain contained the unit I was looking for. I had also finished my paper on the concealment mechanism. It was proving to be a very fruitful trip.

The 'Concealment Seminar' began on 19 May 1997. The political backdrop was propitious: Ekéus had told the Security Council the preceding month that UNSCOM was determined to end Iraqi concealment. The seminar was hosted by the State Department in the main conference room of the Political-Military Affairs Department. In addition to myself and Charles Duelfer, the seminar was well attended by the Americans, with representatives from the State Department, Defense Intelligence Agency, Joint Chiefs of Staff and the National Security Council in attendance, along with the CIA, headed by Burt from the Non-Proliferation Center. I had not talked to Burt since leaving him in Bahrain, right after UNSCOM 182 pulled out of Iraq. I had been angry then, and let Burt know that I held him personally responsible for both the bad information about there being SCUD missiles in Iraq, and the fiasco concerning the lack of U-2 support. Burt didn't seem to be holding a grudge, and greeted me with a sincere smile and handshake.

The State Department had brought up trays of soft drinks and bagels, as well as a cart with two large pots of coffee. We all lounged around the conference room, engaging in small talk, while we waited for the British to arrive.

The British delegation consisted of two people, Sarah Parsons and Clive Provost. They were escorted into the conference room, and joined everyone for refreshments. Charles Duelfer called the meeting to order, and everyone took their places around the table. I was left standing in front of the table, alone. I handed out copies of my just-completed paper, 'The Iraqi Concealment Mechanism: The UNSCOM Model', and proceeded to brief the assembled audience on its contents. After the divisiveness of UNSCOM 182, I fully expected the Americans to come down hard on my findings, since I was still being blamed in many quarters in Washington for providing bad analysis in support of the UNSCOM 182 inspection.

However, I was more than prepared to respond to any such criticism. As I had explained to Charles Duelfer several times in the past, I had made nothing up. Over the years I had accumulated a vast amount of intelligence about Iraq's concealment mechanism, much of it from discussions with the very people seated in the State Department conference room. What I had done with the concealment paper was to tie all of this intelligence into a single, coherent picture of concealment, something that up until this time had not been done by any intelligence service anywhere.

It soon became clear that no one was going to challenge me on any aspect of my paper. Perhaps it was because they recognized so much of their own sensitive intelligence in the body of the paper, or maybe they had done their own independent review and had come to the same conclusions. But the bottom line was that both the Americans and the British agreed that the model of the Iraqi concealment mechanism that I had put together, which spoke of a centrally controlled apparatus run out of the office of Saddam Hussein himself, and using forces associated with presidential security, such as the Special Republican Guard and Special Security Organization, to safeguard retained weapons of mass destruction, was dead right.

In preparing this paper, I also took an extraordinary step, from both an analytical and operational point of view. While I made it clear that UNSCOM had no hard intelligence regarding the continued existence of weapons of mass destruction in Iraq, I decided that, in order to better focus our intelligence support requirements, I would detail what we believed Iraq *might* be holding onto. This section of my paper was by far the most controversial, and yet went completely unchallenged. I had gone to the heads of each inspection discipline in UNSCOM – Missile, Biological, Chemical and Nuclear – and asked them to prepare for me a list of all the weapons and weapons capabilities they believed were unaccounted for, what form these weapons and capabilities could take, what the storage requirements were (controlled temperature, no exposure to direct sunlight, continuous source of power, etc), and how big the containers holding this material would have to be. I did the same regarding any documents that might be retained by the Iraqis – what I termed the 'brain trust' of any future reconstitution of the various programs.

I then made an assessment of how many vehicles, and of what type, would be required to move this material around. Through this work I believed I had put together the basic building blocks of analysis that would serve as a starting point for where to search in Iraq for any missing weapons. However, my analysis was embraced as fact by many of the Americans, so that an unaccounted for VX nerve agent program became an active nerve agent program, and a potential capability to manufacture dry powdered Anthrax became a de facto capability. No matter how many times I qualified the assessments in my report with 'suspected', 'possible' and 'potential,' in the end people took from my paper what they wanted to take, and the postulated existence of WMD became fact. For better or worse, my paper came to represent the definitive model that all parties – UNSCOM, US, UK and Israel – would work from when speaking of Iraq's weapons capability and UNSCOM's inspections.

We also agreed that it would be best if UNSCOM stationed a permanent team in Iraq which could respond quickly to any intelligence information generated by UNSCOM and its supporting nations (the goal was for UNSCOM to have a team deployed to any location inside Iraq within twelve hours of that site being identified by any supporting intelligence service). This team would incorporate SCE-type collection, and would stay in Iraq on a full-time basis.

Lastly, it was agreed that the USA and UK needed to streamline and focus their respective intelligence activities operating in support of UNSCOM, so that 'actionable intelligence' could be provided on a timely basis.[1] I couldn't have asked for anything more.

The seminar finished, I left Charles Duelfer to conduct some 'American-only' business with Burt and the other Americans and headed to a bar near the hotel where Sarah Parsons and Clive Provost were staying. The British had something they wanted to tell me, without Duelfer present.

Once the beers had been ordered, Provost got straight down to business. 'We have some concerns that we need to share with you about the security of the Special Collection Element operation. In processing the signals collected by Gary and his team during UNSCOM 182, we have noticed several unidentified "burst" transmissions emanating from the UN Headquarters building. Gary examined the frequencies, and can find no logical correlation with any of UNSCOM's work.'

'Burst' transmissions involved the compression of data into a tightly-packed digital file, which could then be broadcast in a very short period of time. For instance, instead of taking five minutes to broadcast a five-minute conversation, if the conversation was digitized and compressed, it could be 'burst' transmitted in less than a second. This was a tactic normally employed by intelligence services communicating in a hostile environment, where enemy units could lock in on a lengthy transmission and identify where it was being sent from.

Parsons spoke up. 'We were just going to write this off as one of those things, when we came across an intercept from some of our assets in the Middle East of an Iranian agent in Baghdad communicating to his home station.' She was probably referring to the British communications intercept station in Cyprus, which listened in on radio transmissions throughout the Middle East, but I didn't probe. 'According to this intercept, the Iranian – who was apparently conducting his own signals survey – reported that he had detected evidence of a CIA communications intercept operation underway inside the UN Headquarters in Baghdad. This operation collected data which was then compressed and "burst" transmitted to U-2 aircraft when they overflew Baghdad.' If this were true, then the CIA was operating its own version of the SCE team inside Iraq, using UNSCOM as a cover.

Provost picked up the story. 'We went ahead and tried to correlate the timings of the signals we had intercepted with U-2 overflights, and we found a match. So we went back to the "burst" signal and examined it in greater detail. The signal itself is a compressed data signal containing specific intercepts collected over a significant period of time, well beyond the loiter time of a U-2.' What he was saying was that while the U-2 might be flying over Baghdad for one or two hours, the data transmitted to it was collected for days ahead of time. 'The signal had to be collected by a static, fully automated SIGINT collection system. It appears that it is linked to an automatic transmission system that is triggered remotely by the U-2 when it overflies Baghdad.' In other words, the CIA had a 'black box' operating in Baghdad, which collected communications signals over the course of several days, compressed the data, and then when the U-2 flew over, received a signal from the U-2 to 'burst' the data to a receiver on the U-2.

'If this is what it appears to be, and the Iranians have stumbled on it, then we are very concerned that the Iraqis, with their outstanding counterintelligence capabilities, would also pick up something suspicious. Normally, this would be a CIA security issue, and we wouldn't get involved. But we have a team on the ground. We are actually very concerned that the CIA might be using Gary and the SCE as a cover for their work. And if the Iraqis become suspicious about any mysterious signals activity in the UN Headquarters and decide to aggressively investigate, this would put our team at risk.'

Parsons spoke up. 'We aren't asking you to do anything official, at this point. Our people at GCHQ will make some discreet inquiries, and we will do our best to keep things quiet. We just wanted you to know that this situation existed, and that it could jeopardize our ability to fully support you in the future.'

Provost interjected. 'One more thing. We have been receiving from the NSA reports from the intelligence collected during the UNSCOM 150/155 missions.' UNSCOM 150 had gathered information about the Special Security Organization's involvement in past concealments. UNSCOM 155 had investigated the U-2 imagery of vehicle movements outside Saddam International Airport. 'We had always assumed that this data, which of course we have not been allowed to share with you or UNSCOM, was a result of Gary and his team's work.' I was listening closely. Someone in the USA was getting good communications intercept data as a result of our inspections.

'However, when we began independent processing of the UNSCOM 150/155 tapes, we found that the quality of the signal was extremely poor, making any technical processing too laborious to be of any use. GCHQ questioned Gary and his team about the methodologies taught them by the CIA in Virginia in February last year, and we discovered that these techniques actually were designed to deliberately distort the signal, making the tapes all but useless.' Clive's expression was grim. 'The CIA's methodologies were designed on purpose to make the tapes all but useless.' If what Clive was saying was correct, then the CIA had been sabotaging the UNSCOM SCE effort from day one. Again, this would only make sense if the USA was using the SCE as a cover for one of its own operations.

'We have developed new procedures,' Provost said, 'designed to overcome this problem, so any tapes collected in the future should be of high quality, and quite usable. However, our assessment of this situation is that whatever information was collected by NSA and shared with us, although represented as coming from the SCE product, was in fact coming from another, parallel effort, and that our boys are simply being used as a cover operation for whatever it was the CIA was doing.'

'You see,' Parsons said, 'we believe the CIA is carrying out an operation even the NSA doesn't know about. The NSA officers who spoke with Gary praised him for the high quality of his work and the clarity of the signal, and yet when we examined the same tapes, we found them to be useless.

The turnaround times associated with the recovery of information from these signals is much too fast given the low quality of the tapes. The data had to come from elsewhere. We asked our contacts at NSA about this, and they reluctantly told us that the CIA has installed a black box in the UN Headquarters which burst transmits to U-2 aircraft passing overhead.' In short, the CIA was using UNSCOM as a cover for its own intelligence gathering effort in Iraq.

I took the British warning seriously, and immediately set out to find out if there was any substance to the allegation. I went back to the time of January–June 1996, when Gary and the SCE team were at work, and started taking a closer look at the remote camera monitoring system that was installed by the US Air Force officer I call the Engineer. The first thing I did was backtrack on the Engineer's chain of command. I knew that from 1993 to early 1995 he had been assigned to Wright Patterson Air Force Base, in Dayton, Ohio. This, of course, was in keeping with his status as the commanding officer of the reserve intelligence unit that was supporting UNSCOM by assessing the video tapes produced by the monitoring system. However, in September 1995 the Engineer was transferred to my old organization, the On-Site Inspection Agency (OSIA) in Washington. My conversations with OSIA personnel indicated that this transfer was very unusual, and had in fact been forced on OSIA by the CIA.

As I continued to dig, the case of the Engineer became even murkier. From September 1995 to June 1996, he had undertaken numerous 'maintenance' visits to Iraq which bypassed the normal UNSCOM chain of approval. The UNSCOM communications officer, an experienced Australian major, had raised several questions to Colonel James Moore, the UNSCOM director for operations, about the Engineer's activities, and tried to bring them under tighter UNSCOM control. The Engineer told the Australian major to mind his own business, and in an extraordinary exchange witnessed by several, did the same to Colonel Moore, although Moore outranked the Engineer. In a stunning turn of events, Colonel Moore tried, in late 1995, to file charges of insubordination against the Engineer, only to be rebuked by a senior air force general, who told Colonel Moore that if he continued to obstruct the work of the Engineer it would be he, not the Engineer, who would be facing charges.

This episode had gone by largely unnoticed in 1995, with other issues such as the Jordanian gyro intercept mission taking center-stage. But in retrospect, it made perfect sense. UNSCOM 120, with its communications intercept mission, was proceeding too fast for the CIA's own plans for a communications intercept operation in Iraq, and had to be slowed down. That is why the CIA deliberately downgraded the promised level of support at the last minute, offering us utterly substandard recording devices to take into the field in November 1995.

Steve Richter, we now knew, had been planning a coup against Saddam Hussein. The CIA needed the best possible intelligence about the security of Saddam Hussein, so that the coup plotters would be able to know exactly where to strike and when. The CIA also needed to keep track of the Iraqi military order of battle; that is, where specific military units were, what kind of units they were, what kind of equipment they had, how many men they had, what kind of training they had had, and whether they'd be likely to defect.

Gradually, as my investigation progressed, through a number of different sources, a picture emerged. The information that the CIA needed, and more, could be accessed through an effective communications intercept program. The CIA, and their colleagues at the National Security Agency, had done this sort of work before, usually using US embassy buildings as a base from which to carry out their information collection. But there was no US embassy in Iraq, no place for them to operate from. Moe Dobbs and his CIA paramilitaries had actually carried out a test communications intercept operation in September–October 1993, using the UNSCOM 63 inspection as the cover. The goal was to determine if a sufficient collection operation could be carried out from the hotels where the inspectors stayed. In the end this plan was scrapped as too risky.[2]

The CIA had long been involved in placing a remote camera surveillance system in Iraq, using the Engineer. Back in early 1995, when the discussion of mounting a coup against Saddam Hussein started gaining momentum, someone at the CIA posed the question, 'Why not convert the camera monitoring system into a communications intercept system?'

Steve Richter liked the idea, but wanted to go one step further. Covert operations need to have an aspect of deniability. If things go wrong, or someone gets caught, a good covert operation builds into its plan a way to shift blame away from the true sponsor of the effort. If the CIA was going to use the United Nations weapons inspection process to insert a covert communications intercept operation into Iraq, there was already an element of deniability: if the operation was compromised by the Iraqis, the UN would get the blame. But any such effort, if compromised, would create a huge crisis for the USA with the United Nations, and particularly inside the Security Council. The fallout from such a crisis could put at risk a number of US policy objectives, namely maintaining economic sanctions against Iraq. But if UNSCOM was asking the CIA for communications intercept support, to help operate its own communications intercept operation in Baghdad, then if the CIA's effort was compromised, the CIA could shift responsibility to the United Nations, saying they were only doing what the UN wanted them to do.

It became apparent to me that the CIA's support of the SCE was never intended to provide UNSCOM with intelligence; the CIA would be getting its own intelligence from the Engineer's communications intercept operation. The SCE effort was only supported insofar as it facilitated the operational security of the CIA's activities. In November 1995, the CIA had trashed the SIGINT concept. Now, in early 1996, they were suddenly all in favor of supporting the UNSCOM initiative. They just had to make sure that the UNSCOM communications intercept program never really worked. If UNSCOM gained access to the intelligence the CIA was collecting, it could threaten any covert operations the CIA was planning based on that intelligence. The SCE would be allowed to be deployed; it just wasn't going to be allowed to succeed.

The Engineer needed to get his operation in order first. Again, through my contacts at OSIA, I found out that OSIA was managing a warehouse on behalf of the Engineer and the CIA, used to store the equipment for the remote camera monitoring system. OSIA had no records of what was stored in the warehouse, and anyone who asked for an accounting was rebuked on the grounds of national security. The equipment stored in this warehouse poured into Iraq from September 1995 through June 1996. UNSCOM was never provided with a list of what the Engineer was bringing in, but was rather presented with a fait accompli.

I thought back to the incident involving the installation of the covert antenna for Gary's SCE team back in February 1996. The Engineer had been given that task by Burt without my knowledge or permission, for that matter without the knowledge or permission of anyone at UNSCOM. And he did this work using an antenna *already in place inside Iraq*. To me, this meant the Engineer was already involved in a communications intercept effort, and had his own cache of equipment already in place inside Iraq *before* UNSCOM had formally approved the SCE intercept program.

I dug out the old personnel records of inspectors assigned to support the Engineer's missions. These individuals, known as 'sensor technicians', were responsible for manning the remote camera monitoring system's suite in the Baghdad Monitoring and Verification Center, an 'American-only' area off-limits to everyone but the sensor technicians. Prior to January 1996, these positions had been filled by reservists from the Engineer's air force reserve unit in Ohio. But January 1996 brought about a critical change in the nature of the personnel assigned to this position. Steve Trumbell (pseudonym), a retired Delta Force commando under contract to the CIA, arrived at the BMVC. I knew Trumbell from his time as an inspector during UNSCOM 45. He was a savvy operator with significant covert operations experience, not the sort one would assign to rudimentary electronic babysitting chores.

In March 1996, Steve was replaced by Tony Bracco, the gregarious character who rapidly became known by his radio call-sign, 'Zulu', and whom I later met at the White House during my briefing in the Situation Room following the UNSCOM 182 inspection. Zulu took a special interest in the work of Gary's SCE team, and made a particular effort to bond with the British operators during their off hours. Zulu told Gary and the SCE team that he was a retired combat swimmer from the US Navy on contract with OSIA and, with his long hair, wild walrus mustache and casual beach boy attitude, this cover story was indeed convincing. I, too, had fallen for it, as had the others, until I bumped into him at the White House debriefing. Then, he had a short haircut, clean-shaven face, sunglasses and coat and tie, and was in the company of Robert McCall, a senior operations officer with the CIA's Near East Division. Zulu was CIA paramilitary operations, all the way.

I had seen enough. While I lacked a 'smoking gun' in terms of indisputable proof that the CIA was running a covert operation using UNSCOM as cover, I certainly had enough circumstantial evidence to raise this matter to my chain of command which, given the sensitivity of the matter and the American link, meant Charles Duelfer. I carefully typed up a point paper outlining my concerns and specifying the information I had gathered,[3] and requested a meeting with Duelfer in the UN cafeteria.

I slid the paper across the table to Duelfer, and began my brief. He listened without expressing any emotion, casually reading the paper as I made my case. He sat in silence for some time after I finished, contemplating what I had said. Finally, he looked at me. 'Scott, I can't comment on any of this. All I would say is that you probably would do very well not to ever mention it again.'

'Charles, we work for UNSCOM,' I replied. 'If what I have written here is true, we have the potential for a compromise that not only could end UNSCOM, but perhaps endanger the lives of some of our inspectors. We have to inform the executive chairman of this, and at least launch some sort of inquiry with the United States to find out if there is any validity to this, and if there is, to stop it before it's too late.'

Duelfer looked at me, frustrated. 'Scott, I can't make it any clearer than this. I cannot discuss this. This never happened. And if I were you, I'd drop the matter right now. If you go forward, even to tell Ekéus, you will be opening a huge bag of trouble for you. I would imagine you'd have the FBI come down on you very, very hard, and you don't want that. Take my advice and back off.'

I sat there, letting Duelfer's words sink in. Was he aware of the operation? If so, he didn't seem to have run it by Ekéus. I was in a quandary. I had, since day one, operated under the code that I worked for UNSCOM, and that I did nothing without Ekéus's permission. Now I was sitting on a keg of dynamite that had the potential of blowing up, taking UNSCOM with it. To do nothing was wrong. But to do anything meant bringing disaster down on me and my family.

Finally, I looked up at Duelfer. 'As an American, I won't do anything that would jeopardize the national security of my country. So I won't take this to Ekéus. But as an UNSCOM officer, I have a responsibility to report this to my chain of command. So I'm reporting this to you, officially.' I pointed at the paper he still held in his hand. 'What you have there is evidence of a problem that could ruin UNSCOM. Regardless of what you say about not being able to comment, I am going on the record as reporting this issue to you as the deputy executive chairman of UNSCOM. What you do with it is your business.'

Duelfer didn't say a word, but rather folded up my paper, put it into his coat, got up from the table, and returned to his office, never to mention our conversation again.

I stayed at the table for a few moments after he had left, frustrated with my own indecisiveness. I was being lied to by the CIA, and the man appointed as my supervisor was not backing me. Part of me wanted to get up and walk away from this mess. The deceit of the CIA was a reality I had to live with. But so was the UNSCOM disarmament mission in Iraq. If I walked away from UNSCOM I would undermine its mission, and those in the CIA who had sought to undermine it would have prevailed. If I went public with what I was alleging, the FBI would find a way to silence me. The best way to get back at all those in Washington who were promoting a policy that continued economic sanctions by refusing to permit Iraq to be disarmed was to redouble my efforts to complete the disarmament mission. By pushing Iraq to give up the final vestiges of its weapons of mass destruction programs, or if in fact Iraq was telling the truth, and no such weapons existed, by compelling Iraq to provide UNSCOM with all of the data necessary for UNSCOM to verify the Iraqi claims and sustain a finding of compliance before the Security Council, I would be forcing the USA to admit publicly what everyone knew in private: that the USA had no intention of abiding by the Security Council's promise to lift sanctions once Iraq had been disarmed.

I left the table more determined than ever to get on with my job.

I also left aware about the reality of the role being played by the CIA and Charles Duelfer. I no longer harbored any illusions that they were my friends and colleagues. As far as I was concerned, they were the enemy, and I would have to find a way to neutralize them if I was going to have any chance of success.

Chapter 18
Unraveling Concealment
June 1997

As demoralized as I was about the CIA's covert SIGINT stab in the back, I had to put that behind me and begin to focus on the way forward with the concealment investigation. I drafted a paper for the chairman outlining the results of the concealment seminar we had just finished at the State Department, and attached to it a proposal to aggressively test the Iraqis in June, prior to any new counter-concealment unit being formed. 'UNSCOM 182 was in March,' I said. 'If we wait until August until we launch a new inspection against the concealment mechanism, we will be at a strategic and tactical disadvantage. The Iraqis will have adjusted their concealment tactics, meaning we will need to start from scratch in order to figure out how they are going about concealing their programs from the inspectors. And their allies in the Council will have reason to attack any new aggressive inspections, especially if we don't find anything incriminating.'

Ekéus looked over my proposal. 'This is risky,' he said. 'It is imperative that any inspection you lead achieve a result that is explainable in the Council. If you can't do this, then it is better for us to wait until August before trying.' I knew in my heart that waiting until August would be fatal to the investigation. UNSCOM 182 had knocked the wind out of us, and if we didn't regain our momentum soon, then the whole effort would stall. I also felt that this time, left to my own devices, I could get the goods on the Iraqis, at least enough to convince the Security Council that our inspection goals and methods, when it came to the issue of concealment, were legitimate. After some misgivings, Ekéus agreed we should proceed, and we were back in business.

By now I knew that for any major inspection in Iraq, you had to have the best people possible to back you up. Early on in the UNSCOM experience, we had made use of the CIA's Operations Planning Cell to provide experienced operational specialists to stiffen the technical expertise of the more conventional inspectors – in short, we brought in men who knew how to drive a car, read a map, communicate on a radio, and physically search a building, to assist those who knew only about chemical laboratories, biological experiments, and computer modeling. If you're going to go after weapons of mass destruction, you need to have the scientists and engineers who understand the technical aspect of the work. But you also need the facilitators, the men who make things happen, and who get things done. The CIA's OPC, which brought together Delta Force commandos and CIA paramilitary specialists, had provided such 'facilitators'.

Since the UNSCOM 150/failed CIA coup debacle in June 1996, however, these resources – especially Moe Dobbs and his CIA paramilitaries – were neither offered, nor wanted. UNSCOM needed its own brand of 'operators', and we had them in Roger Hill (the veteran Australian inspector), and a British guy called Chris Cobb-Smith. I first ran across Chris Cobb-Smith's name in the spring of 1995, when his résumé had been passed to me by Operation Rockingham for consideration regarding filling a missile monitoring position. At first I handed the résumé back, asking if this was a joke. 'This guy is a Marine Gunner (artillery), for goodness sakes!' I said. 'What the heck does he know about ballistic missile design and engineering?' The Rockingham staffer who had passed me the résumé noted sheepishly that Cobb-Smith had served in a surface-to-air missile battery, so he had some expertise. I was ready to run the résumé through the shredder when the truth came out. 'Look, Scott,' the staffer said, 'Chris is a good friend who is down on his luck at the moment. He was just given early retirement from the military, and is in between jobs. He's the hardest-working man I know, and as dependable as the day is long.' I threw the résumé on my desk, promising to do my best. As it turned out, they were doing me a favor: Chris Cobb-Smith was hard-working, fiercely loyal and unassuming. He was the kind of man that forms the backbone of any unit.

UNSCOM 194 arrived in Iraq on 2 June 1997, having already generated some controversy before we even got started with our work. On 29 May, Rolf Ekéus had sent a letter to General Amer Rashid, notifying him that the UNSCOM 194 team would shortly be arriving in Iraq, that it would be led by myself, and that its mission was to investigate the concealment mechanism. Ekéus's letter also stated that I would be seeking to interview five Iraqi officers, listed by name, whom we believed to have been involved in past concealment activities. On 30 May, Amer Rashid responded with his own letter, asking that the UNSCOM 194 mission be postponed or cancelled, since the concealment mechanism investigation was invalid and therefore unnecessary. Ekéus replied on 1 June, telling Amer Rashid that the team would proceed as scheduled, and that the concealment investigation represented a required verification exercise that had been agreed to by Tariq Aziz as part of the June 1996 inspection modalities agreement. Ekéus asked that the Iraqis provide my team with their full support.[1]

Given our short preparation time in Bahrain, I wanted to go slowly in terms of operations, so I took a 'crawl, walk, run' approach to the inspection. We would 'crawl and walk' on day one, 3 June. I planned inspections at two sites, a Special Republican Guard Brigade Headquarters and a suspected convoy protection unit in downtown Baghdad. The intelligence on both was very weak, but these inspections would allow inspectors and Iraqi minders alike to get used to working with one another before we got to the heart of the inspection.

After finishing in Baghdad, the team headed north, to Tikrit, where for three days we probed around Saddam Hussein's hometown. My theory regarding ongoing Iraqi concealment assumed there to be a Special Republican Guard unit that was based both in Baghdad and Tikrit, and was used to shuttle sensitive material between the two areas. Back in Tel Aviv, I had asked Mushiko to find such a unit in Tikrit; as usual, the Israeli photographic interpreter had delivered what I had asked for. One of the sites we visited turned out to be the Tikrit Special Security Organization Presidential Security Unit. We quickly ascertained that the duties and responsibilities of this unit were the same as those of its twin in Radwaniyah, making it a suspect for any concealment-related vehicle movement.

But the big coup came at the next site, again selected by Mushiko and his crack team – the Headquarters of the 2nd Company, 1st Battalion detachment known as the Auja Presidential Security Unit. At first the Iraqis tried to deny the unit's existence, claiming they were a special purpose unit tasked with resolving tribal disputes. But when I noticed that all documents were missing, I called General Amer Rashid, who was the senior Iraqi present, aside. 'Look, either the commander of this unit provides some documentation to back up who he says he is, or I am going to turn this place upside down. I know this is a sensitive unit, and want to respect that, but I need some honesty here.' Rashid talked to the commander, who in private confided that this was, indeed, the Auja detachment from the 1st Battalion. His job was presidential convoy security, a very sensitive mission, which is why he lied.

I had just uncovered another important piece in my concealment puzzle. The Iraqis had denied this unit existed. The 2nd Company belonged to the Baghdad-based 1st Battalion. The 2nd Company maintained two facilities, one in Radwaniyah, the other in Auja. We had already established that the 2nd Company had been used to move documents within the Baghdad area in June 1996. We now had this same 2nd Company shuttling back and forth between Baghdad and Tikrit. By discovering this Special Republican Guard unit in Auja, and uncovering the connection with its twin Special Republican Guard unit in Radwaniyah, I was one step closer to proving that Iraq not only used the Special Republican Guard to shuttle prohibited material between Baghdad and Tikrit back in 1991, but that they probably maintained that capability today as part of an ongoing concealment mechanism. I left the facility, and returned to Baghdad with my team, confident that we were that much closer to solving the concealment puzzle.

That evening I got a visit from the Serb. The oil-for-food program was starting to kick in, and Baghdad was a city coming back to life. New cars filled the streets, and shops and restaurants were opening up across the city. Our 'long block' walk took us past a few new restaurants and cafes, and it was good to see Iraqi families out enjoying life for a change. 'You should be pleased with yourself,' the Serb said. I told him I thought the inspection was progressing well. 'You have everyone's attention now,' the Serb noted, 'especially those surrounding the Big Man. Some are asking what it is you really are looking for. Some close to the Big Man think you are getting too close to the Big Man himself.'

I kicked a rock down the road. 'I have no interest whatsoever in the Big Man,' I said, 'unless he is hiding weapons of mass destruction, and in that case, he should plan on a visit in the near future.'

The Serb laughed. 'That would be a sight to see,' he said. 'But it won't happen, at least how you envision, because there are no weapons.'

I stopped walking, and looked the Serb in the eye. 'Your side is lying about concealment. I have the proof. And until you stop lying, I have to assume the lies are about hiding weapons.'

The Serb reflected on what I had said. 'If there are lies being told,' he finally replied, 'then I agree with you; it is because they are protecting something from being discovered by you. You need to determine whether what is being protected relates to your mandate. I am telling you it doesn't. You must be very careful in how you proceed with your investigation from this point on. You are close to learning the truth, but if you push too hard, then there are those who will say for the sake of our security we must stop your investigation.'

'Why can't you just come out and say what you're trying to say?' I asked. 'You want me to know something, so why not just tell me what that is?'

The Serb smiled. 'This is your search, not ours. From our perspective, there is nothing more to say. There are no weapons left in Iraq. You need to decide if, from your perspective, there is anything left for you to learn. Until you decide that, there isn't anything we can say or do that matters.'

I was reminded of Plato, and his allegory of the Cave. In it, prisoners held in a cave got their perceptions of the world only by observing shadows flickering on a wall. I told the Serb that I was beginning to feel this way about our talks. He laughed. 'Then you must be like the prisoner in that story, who freed himself and saw the real world. But beware,' he added, concluding our talk. 'When the prisoner went back to the cave, and tried to explain to his fellow prisoners what he had seen, no one was able to comprehend what he was saying.'

UNSCOM 194 was armed with intelligence leads developed thanks to Israeli cooperation, leads that took us to the Special Security Organization. As we began our investigation the Iraqis balked, and I was summoned to Amer Rashid's office.

I explained the background of the mission, the issue of concealment that he was all too familiar with, and what we hoped to accomplish – a final accounting of Iraq's WMD so that sanctions might be lifted. Amer Rashid challenged me on the logic of my thinking, so I produced a copy of my paper, 'The Iraqi Concealment Mechanism: The UNSCOM Model' – the same one I had provided to the Americans and British during the

May Concealment Conference, and read selected passages to show him that I wasn't just making this up.

Amer Rashid wasn't impressed. 'Please don't use the McCarthy approach,' he barked. I was startled by this apparent reference to US Senator Joe McCarthy and the witch hunt he led in the 1950s to expose communists in America, based on wild unsubstantiated allegations. 'Either you have information or you do not. Which is it?'

It was my turn to get aggressive. 'You challenged me once to go out to the rest of the world with a tender, asking for all of their intelligence about what they believed Iraq to be hiding.'

Amer Rashid agreed he had done this. 'But this should not last forever… this is not an endless game,' he said.

'Hussein Kamal's defection changed everything,' I said. 'You recognize that. Concealment became a serious issue after that.' He said nothing, so I continued. 'Well, we put out a tender, so to speak, and this paper is the result. This is what the world, and UNSCOM, believe Iraq to be hiding.'

I then went through a point by point recitation of what I had written in my paper, based upon the analysis conducted by the experts in UNSCOM about what was still unaccounted for. I told the general that UNSCOM believed Iraq was still hiding chemical weapons, and that Iraq still had the ability to produce chemical weapons, using civilian factories disguised as pesticide plants. I told him UNSCOM believed Iraq had produced VX nerve agent, and that this agent was stored in bombs and artillery shells. I said UNSCOM believed Iraq had mobile biological laboratories, as well as agent production factories, likewise mobile.

Amer Rashid was stunned by this charge. 'So we are hiding a mobile facility?' he asked.

'Yes, we believe you are,' I answered.

Hossam Amin was present, and he was writing down every word I was saying. Amer Rashid, too, was taking notes. I sat in my chair, unsure if I was doing the right thing in discussing this or not. 'And missiles?' he asked. 'Do we still have missiles, too?'

This was a potentially explosive topic, given our past history of volatile discussions during UNSCOM 45 in October 1992. The other problem was I didn't believe any of what I was about to say. This was the CIA assessment, not mine, but if we were talking about hidden weapons, I had to give Amer the whole picture. 'Yes,' I said, 'we believe you are hiding two mobile launchers and up to twenty-five missiles, and that these missiles are tipped with biological and chemical warheads.'

Amer Rashid finished his note taking. He was surprisingly calm. 'Your whole idea is based on two things – hidden items, and hidden capabilities.' He then admitted that there were discrepancies in the Iraqi accounting ('a few missiles, but we are converging… the same with chemical and biological… we are converging'). But, he noted, 'The critical thing here is coming together on the material balance. We believe this can be accomplished. If we can achieve a material balance, then the issue of concealment is moot. What is important is resolution 687. It is the Iraqi dismantling of its weapons, and making sure that Iraq does not reactivate it. All other issues are irrelevant.'

The existence of my concealment paper, while disturbing to Amer Rashid, impressed upon him the seriousness of my mission. He thanked me for coming to see him, and for being so frank. He then left, saying he had to report the results of our meeting directly to Tariq Aziz, who was waiting for him.[2]

It had been an unusual meeting, and had the potential greatly to affect the work UNSCOM was doing. I wasn't sure how Ekéus would respond to the news that I had basically committed UNSCOM to the notion that Iraq was hiding weapons. I was uncomfortable with what I had done, but felt that I had been trapped by General Amer Rashid. If I hadn't answered in the way I did, forcefully and directly, I'm certain he would have stopped the inspection right then and there. At that point UNSCOM would have had to explain to the Security Council why I was traipsing around Iraq, going to sensitive presidential security locations less than a year after the CIA had botched an effort to remove Saddam Hussein, and in the process used an UNSCOM inspection team to facilitate the coup. By putting my cards on the table, so to speak, I had tried to forestall any suspicions that might have been developing about the political motive for our inspections. Even Amer Rashid recognized this. I only hoped Rolf Ekéus saw it that way, as well.

On 12 June, after three days of fruitless inspection, I took the team back to the 1st Battalion of the Special Republican Guard. The Iraqis had told me, back during UNSCOM 182, that the 1st Battalion of the Special Republican Guard had no personnel or units assigned to the Tikrit region, and yet I had just found that the 2nd Company of the 1st Battalion maintained a garrison just outside of Tikrit, in Auja. The 1st Battalion commander took our discovery of the Auja detachments in his stride. When asked why he had denied any connection with Tikrit when I last spoke to him, he shrugged. 'It is a new development since then.' He was lying, and I knew it. I turned to Hossam Amin when we had finished. 'He is not telling the truth, and it is lies like this that make us so suspicious in UNSCOM regarding the issue of concealment.' Hossam did not look very happy as he drove away.

After following up other leads, I was still intent on pursuing the issue of the 2nd Company of the 1st Battalion in Tikrit. The 1st Battalion commander had just told me that the Auja deployment was a new development, and yet when I inspected the Auja barracks, those troops had looked as if they had been there for some time; their vehicles, parked in the garage, all carrying Tikrit license plates. The 2nd Company, we now knew, maintained two detachments – one in Radwaniyah, at what we called Site 1a, and one in Auja, at the barracks we just inspected in Tikrit. UNSCOM had been able to link the Radwaniyah detachment to suspected document evacuation activity involving a Special Security Organization facility off Airport Road. The Radwaniyah detachment was commanded by the 1st Battalion, which we now knew commanded the Auja detachment as well. I had long suspected that the Special Security Organization and Special Republican Guard had transported WMD-related material back and forth between the Baghdad area and Tikrit. Right now, the only Special Republican Guard link we had between those two cities was the 2nd Company, 1st Battalion. I wanted another look at Site 1a.

We left our position on the Airport Road, reversed course through Abu Ghraib, and drove down towards the northern entrance to Saddam International Airport, where we were finally stopped by the Iraqis at the Special Republican Guard checkpoint that had foiled our movements so many times in the past. When I insisted on being allowed to proceed, the Iraqis pulled the plug on cooperation altogether. The head minder came up to me. 'Tariq Aziz has ordered us to stop all cooperation with you, since you are no longer were dealing with WMD, but rather attacking the security of the president of Iraq.' I reported this to Rolf Ekéus, who instructed me to terminate the inspection. Although it had not been our objective, we had just triggered another confrontation with the Security Council.

As I later found out, after he left UNSCOM 194 at the 1st Battalion facility, Hossam Amin had proceeded to the Republican Palace, where Tariq Aziz was in consultations with Amer al-Sa'adi, Amer Rashid, a senior official from the Special Security Organization, and the chief of the Mukhabarat's counter-UNSCOM cell. The Iraqis had believed, following the UNSCOM 182 inspection, that the concealment investigation being conducted by UNSCOM was containable. The inspectors had not dug too deep into issues of presidential security, and Iraq's allies on the Security Council, in particular the French and Russians, had indicated that there would be little tolerance for unnecessarily aggressive inspections by UNSCOM in the future.

However, circumstances had changed. The Iraqis were now analyzing the sites visited by the UNSCOM 194 team, the questions being asked, and the answers being given. Amer Rashid had briefed Tariq Aziz on the nature of the concealment investigation, as I had briefed him in the Oil Ministry, and the Iraqis were starting to worry. The concern wasn't about UNSCOM finding weapons; there were no weapons to find. The concern was about UNSCOM proving that the Iraqis had in fact had an organized concealment mechanism in 1991 that was run by the Special Security Organization. The exposure of the Auja Security Unit, and the inconsistencies in the Iraqi cover story about the past role of the Special Republican Guard and Special Security Organization were apparent to all. They had reached an uncomfortable conclusion: UNSCOM 194 was rapidly unraveling the web of deceit the Iraqis had built to shield the past involvement of the Special Republican Guard and Special Security Organization in concealing WMD.

'Why not just tell the truth?' the Mukhabarat officer asked. He had been receiving reports back from the Serb about my attitude towards concealment, and believed that if the Iraqis told the truth, this issue could be wrapped up quickly. But the Special Security Organization official said that presidential security was off limits to UNSCOM inspections. He noted that UNSCOM had already been used by the CIA to attempt an attack on the president, confirming in their minds the reality that UNSCOM could not be trusted to handle any new revelation about the past role of the Special Security Organization in concealment responsibly. Amer Rashid noted that it was too late, in any case. If the Iraqis now admitted the role of the Special Security Organization, it would simply open up an entire new round of inspections that would only lengthen the time until the lifting of sanctions. Tariq Aziz told everyone that a new line of thinking needed to be developed to deal with UNSCOM's concealment mechanism investigation, but for the moment the Iraqis had to conduct damage control, and this meant stopping the work of Scott Ritter and the UNSCOM 194 inspection.[3]

The Iraqi response to UNSCOM 194 caused an uproar in the Security Council. Without hesitation, the Council passed a new resolution, 1115, condemning the Iraqi actions. But this one had a twist: the Council voted to impose travel restrictions on Iraqis designated by UNSCOM as being involved in WMD activity. These new travel sanctions were suspended, but would automatically be imposed if UNSCOM reported any violation or interference by the Iraqis. For the first time ever, the Council put the power to punish Iraq directly in the hands of the inspectors.

It was an event of major significance, but one that Rolf Ekéus would not be around to appreciate. After six years in office, the Swedish Ambassador was stepping down, with effect from the middle of July 1997. Rolf Ekéus, who had so ably served as UNSCOM's chairman since 1991, was ready to hand the inspection program to Richard Butler, confident that he was leaving his successor a solid team that was clearly in position to accomplish its mission. I wasn't happy about the change in leadership at this critical juncture, but I did have a good feeling that for the first time the pieces of the concealment puzzle were starting to fall into place.

Chapter 19

New Directions
July–October 1997

In the final weeks of Rolf Ekéus's term as executive chairman, the staff of UNSCOM did little but prepare detailed briefings in anticipation of the arrival of our new boss. Ekéus had wanted to personally introduce Richard Butler, the flamboyant former Australian Ambassador to the United Nations, to his new staff, and for that purpose we had all put together presentations designed to acquaint Butler with who we were and also brief him on the status of our investigations to date.

Richard Butler, however, had other plans. He delayed his arrival at UNSCOM, in effect avoiding a Rolf Ekéus-controlled turnover of authority. July came and went, Ekéus departed the scene, and Richard Butler and I had yet to meet. Butler traveled to Baghdad in late July, where he met with Tariq Aziz. Butler told the deputy prime minister that too much time had been wasted without achieving disarmament, and that the sanctions in place were hurting the people of Iraq. 'We are on the last lap,' Butler informed him. Butler rejected what he termed the 'forensic approach' to disarmament, instead noting that 'We [UNSCOM] will work using the tools of science and logic.' The Iraqis were ecstatic. By forensic Butler was referring to the kind of intrusive inspections I had been carrying out. The Iraqis were anxious to bring an end to these inspections, as they touched on national security. By focusing on 'science and logic', Butler had narrowed the discussion to simply the issue of whether or not these weapons still existed, not the issue of past concealment. But not everyone shared the Iraqis' enthusiasm. No sooner had he returned to New York, than Butler found himself on the receiving end of numerous phone calls and visits from concerned US and British officials, who pounded away at the central theme that Iraq could not, under any circumstances, be let off the hook. Duly chastened for too readily embracing the 'science and logic' approach to disarming Iraq, Butler changed course, and finally agreed to a meeting with the most 'forensic' of all his inspectors.

In early July, following my return from Baghdad, I had prepared a concept paper on the establishment of a new unit in the UNSCOM bureaucratic structure that Ekéus had agreed to support, the Capable Site/Concealment Investigation team, or Concealment Investigation (pronounced, tongue in cheek, as 'Sissie'). Up until now, strategic planning and presenting of counter-concealment operations had been done by me, pretty much alone.

Charles Duelfer, Nikita Smidovich and I all agreed that the sooner we got the Concealment Investigation team up and running, the better. Duelfer was cordial, even affable, as though our conversation about CIA meddling in UNSCOM the previous May had never occurred. The new power given to UNSCOM by the Security Council in resolution 1115 needed to be sustained, we thought. We needed inspections to be ongoing, maintaining constant pressure on the Iraqis while the Council still retained its seriousness and focus. The plan was in place. All we needed was a signature on the concept paper authorizing us to go forward. Ekéus was ready to approve the concept in front of Richard Butler, a seal of approval designed to ensure our success. When Ekéus left, however, the proposal was left unsigned, because Ekéus believed that Butler had to approve of the concept, too.

With Richard Butler feeling the heat from the USA about his 'soft' approach toward Iraq, Duelfer decided it was time to make his move. He spoke to Butler about me and the work I had been doing, and set up a briefing so that I could explain all of this to the new chairman. On 4 August 1997, with Charles Duelfer and Rachel Davies, the chief of the UNSCOM Information Assessment Unit (IAU), present, I briefed Richard Butler on the nature of my work for UNSCOM, and my proposal for the creation of a new inspection unit, the Concealment Investigation team. The briefing was held in a secure conference room inside the UN Secretariat which belonged to the British Mission. The British controlled access to the room, and periodically swept the room for listening devices. It was normally used exclusively by British diplomats, but Rachel Davies, the IAU chief, had been an analyst with the British Defence Intelligence Staff, and was able to pull some strings at the UK Mission in New York to have the room made available.

Until now, I had yet to formally meet the new executive chairman. I had seen him in passing, but knew little about who he was as a person. Butler came across as more of a car salesman than a diplomat. He walked into the conference room with a sense of purpose, trying to immediately establish that he was in command. The conference room itself was not very large, so it accentuated Richard's size, making him that much more impressive. He sat down, after introductions, and slapped his hand on the table. 'All right. Let's get things started. I understand you have something you want me to hear.'

I was somewhat surprised when, after listening to my proposals (which were derived directly from the May concealment seminar results), Richard Butler responded by lambasting what he called the Iraqi 'Defeat UNSCOM Industry', and deploring what he viewed was the continued decision by Saddam Hussein to 'maintain the capability to produce weapons of mass destruction'. There had been no discussion whatsoever of the merits of the argument I was putting forward. I believed strongly in what I was saying, and was prepared to defend them aggressively, if need be, but Butler had simply embraced my ideas without question. I was also taken aback by his personal attack against Saddam Hussein. No matter what his personal views on the matter were, Butler was a servant of the Security Council, and an employee of the United Nations. Sweeping statements like the ones he had made, especially so early on in his tenure when he lacked both the experience and depth to make them, spoke more of a hotheaded dilettante than seasoned diplomat.

Richard Butler approved the creation of two new units, the Concealment Investigations Unit in New York, headed by myself, and the establishment of a 'Sissie' team in Baghdad, working directly for the Concealment Investigation team.[1] Butler appointed Charles Duelfer to personally oversee the work of these units, and me.

Approving the creation of these two new units was one thing; implementing that decision was another. By mid-August I was ready with my formal requests for support, which were sent out to the US, British and Australian governments.

The British had been ready since July to deploy a three-person Special Collection Element team to Baghdad as part of the new Concealment Investigation team, together with the mobile communications intercept equipment. This was a big step, as the British had been withholding SCE support until they clarified with the CIA what was going on regarding any covert CIA communications intercept capability operating in Baghdad under UNSCOM cover. The British didn't tell me what, if any, the results of their investigation into that matter were. Obviously it had been resolved to their satisfaction, because they were agreeing to let the SCE deploy. Furthermore, the British were ready to dispatch Gary, the former head of the SCE, to New York to serve on the staff of the new Concealment Investigations Unit as SCE coordinator.

In addition to Chris Cobb-Smith, Gary and the SCE, the Concealment Investigation team was flushed out with two Americans, one serving as the deputy team leader, the other as a communicator, and an Australian medic named Andy Russell.[2] Filling out the new arrivals was Bill Michaels (pseudonym), a former Delta Force master sergeant who helped run the Delta Force intelligence shop during Desert Storm, and who provided intelligence support to UNSCOM as part of the Operations Planning Cell from 1995 to 1997. Bill would work in New York as my deputy for intelligence. UNSCOM finally had a concealment investigation infrastructure that was up to the task at hand.

Introducing that team into Iraq was a less straightforward matter. We had to avoid ruffling feathers, not only with the Iraqis but with the other UNSCOM staff. Getting the Concealment Investigation team to work in a complementary fashion with normal inspections would require a delicate diplomatic balancing act, but I was confident that Chris Cobb-Smith, the leader of the Concealment Investigation team, could pull it off.

I flew to Tel Aviv, where I joined up with Spike, the Australian photographic interpreter who had taken over from my friend and veteran colleague, Gerard Martell. Spike was busy trying to finalize the imagery support for the upcoming inspection, selecting U-2 images of locations that might be of interest based upon Israeli intelligence. By this time, the Israeli reputation regarding their ability to find locations in Iraq had become legendary. I was confident that if the Israelis said something, I could rely on it.

While in Tel Aviv, I went downtown to meet with Moshe Ponkovsky and Roni Ortel, the technical intelligence specialist, in the Kirya, the Israeli

Defense Headquarters facility. The Israelis had acquired some sensitive intelligence detailing an emerging relationship between the Karama Factory, an Iraqi establishment that dealt with ballistic missile research and development, and a Romanian aerospace company, Aerofina.

The cooperation between Karama and Aerofina appeared to be 'ongoing', involving a contract between the two entities that had been signed and was in the process of being implemented. According to the Israelis, four shipments had been made, involving specialized machine tools, jigs and fixtures that could be used in manufacturing components of guidance and control units and liquid fuel engines in ballistic missiles.

However, the Israelis had detected a glitch in the proceedings. The Iraqis were looking for additional quality-assurance documents for the items already received, as well as operational manuals for the equipment in question. The Karama Factory, working through a Jordanian intermediary export-import company, Rouge Establishment, wanted to bring to Iraq a delegation of Romanian engineers from Aerofina to guide their Iraqi counterparts at Karama through the operation of the equipment in question, making sure the Iraqis could manufacture the required parts for their missiles to the appropriate specifications. The Rouge company was arranging for a visit to Romania by an Iraqi delegation, headed by the deputy director of the Karama Factory, Dr. Hamid al-Azawi, to close the deal. 'We were impressed with your ability to act on the Gharbieh information,' Ponkovsky said, referring to the November 1995 intercept in Jordan. 'We wondered if you might be able to do something similar with this?'

When in London, I had been meeting on and off with a man I will call 'the Don', an active agent in the British Secret Intelligence Service (better known as MI6). The Don was a tall, intense man who looked like an Oxford professor (hence the nickname), whom I first met in the spring of 1996, when Sarah Parsons introduced us. It was clear that he was working a network of human sources who were familiar with Baghdad and the Iraqi security organizations (it turned out that these sources were from Iyad Alawi's Iraqi National Accord, who in the spring of 1996, as we have seen, were working closely with the CIA to launch a coup to topple Saddam Hussein). I had provided the Don with U-2 prints, and he returned the prints freshly annotated with a detailed breakdown of what facilities were depicted. Since then I had met with the Don on a regular basis. I felt that the information Ponkovsky had given me might be best handled by the

Don, and mentioned this to Ponkovsky. 'You have our permission to share this information,' he said.

I flew to London, where I took a cab to the new, green-glass covered MI6 Headquarters Building at 6 Vauxhall, resting on the banks of the River Thames. My passport was taken by the security guard, and I was ushered into a waiting room, furnished with plush couches and armchairs, where I sat, awaiting my escort. Within minutes the Don appeared, and walked me through additional security barriers and into the heart of the building. We took an elevator up to the fifth floor, and then walked down a corridor with offices to my left and right, their doors shut and locked, each one marked with letters and number that indicated to the initiated who occupied the room, and what they did, but for someone like myself, meant nothing. Soon I found myself at a side conference room with a fantastic view of London and the Thames. Sandwiches and drinks were laid out on the table, and there were several MI6 officers, all neatly attired in dark suits and conventional ties, standing about the table. It was a warm, friendly meeting, and based on the questions being asked, and comments being offered, it was clear that MI6 had been following my efforts in Iraq for some time.

The Don brought the meeting to order, and made it clear that MI6 was ready to help UNSCOM in any way possible, and were always open to new ideas. I briefed the MI6 officers on the Israeli information on Aerofina, and the Don sent for a particular specialist, who joined us in the conference room and took copious notes. 'We promise to get back to you,' the Don said.[3]

The Don gave me the name and contact information of the MI6 station chief in New York, whom I'll call 'the Flyfisher' (he turned out to be an avid sportsman who frequented the trout streams of Upstate New York). 'Since we are expanding our cooperation,' the Don said, 'we need to improve our ability to communicate. The Flyfisher will be able to assist in this matter. You should schedule an introductory meeting when you return to New York.'

Finally, after almost a month's delay, the UNSCOM 201/207 inspection was ready to begin.

I flew to Baghdad on 19 September, with a team of three other inspectors – Charles Harper, a British diplomat, Patrick Hamzideh, a French Arabic-speaking inspector, and a US Army intelligence specialist who also spoke Arabic.

That evening I met with Hossam Amin and other Iraqi officials at their headquarters building near Baghdad University. I introduced the team and its mission, and laid out the schedule of work. 'We have for some time now been requesting interviews with specific Iraqi officials we believe relevant to our disarmament work in Iraq,' I said by way of introduction. 'For too long now the Iraqi side has prevented these interviews from occurring. In keeping with the demands of the Security Council, including those put forth in their resolution 1115 [just passed in June, promising new sanctions should UNSCOM report any aspect of Iraqi non-compliance], I am requesting that the following list of persons be provided to the team for the conduct of the required interviews.' I handed Hossam Amin a paper that listed the names of several Special Republican Guard officers, including the former commander himself, Kamal Mustafa.

This was a big event. I later found out that the day before the interviews took place, the head of the counter-UNSCOM section of the Mukhabarat provided a special briefing based on the past questions and areas of inquiry I had been pursuing when it came to the concealment mechanism, trying to identify my main points of concern. A brief was provided which outlined everything the Iraqis thought I knew about the Special Security Organization and Special Republican Guard. 'Assume he knows the basics about your organization,' the Special Republican Guard officers were told by the Mukhabarat agent. 'Don't give away anything, but don't lie. He [Ritter] is good at picking out the lie.' The Special Republican Guard officers were instructed by the director of the Special Security Organization to be fully cooperative, but to provide no information that would allow UNSCOM to further its investigation into presidential security. 'We must end this now,' the director was quoted as saying.[4]

So on 22 September we finally came together, UNSCOM and the assembled officers of the Special Republican Guard, led by General Kamal Mustafa. Kamal Mustafa ran the meeting, with no one daring to answer without looking in his direction first. For a man who possessed so much power, Kamal Mustafa looked surprisingly average. He was short and pudgy, with a soft, round face and double chin. He dressed well, wearing an expensive gray silk suit, and crisp white shirt. But his looks were deceiving. He controlled the other Special Republican Guard officers in the meeting through his sheer presence. When he spoke, he did so without hesitation. Unlike the others, he had to only look to himself for guidance on what to say.

In the end, in a shocking development that contradicted everything they had previously told UNSCOM about the role of the Special Republican Guard in past concealment activities, the Iraqis admitted the Guard's direct involvement. The only catch was the issue of who exercised the ultimate command and control over the Special Republican Guard concealment operation. 'There were no orders from anyone other than Hussein Kamal,' Kamal Mustafa said, and everyone agreed. 'We did this thing on a personal level, responding to Hussein Kamal as individuals, not as part of an organization.' So once more they were blaming everything on their 'treacherous' scapegoat, now conveniently dead.

I asked about the existence of a document concerning the movement of nuclear material, which was copied to 'the Commander of the Special Guards'. 'That is what people know me as,' Kamal Mustafa said. 'But because I was involved as an individual does not mean the Special Republican Guard was involved as an organization.'

The interviews were over. I thanked all of the Iraqis for their cooperation, and told General Amer Rashid, who was observing the proceedings, that I appreciated his cooperation. 'I hope this matter is settled,' he said.

'I wish it was,' I replied honestly. 'Hopefully soon.'[5]

This was a major breakthrough. With the Iraqi admission of the involvement of the Special Republican Guard in concealment activities, we were now in a new phase. Prior to this we had been investigating intelligence leads about the Special Republican Guard, trying to find out information. Now we were in the much easier position of having to verify what the Iraqis were saying.

After a brief trip to Bahrain to check on Chris Cobb-Smith and the Concealment Investigation team's preparations for the upcoming inspection, we returned to Baghdad on 27 September. We met with Hossam Amin that night, per our usual procedures, and introduced the team and its mission. Hossam Amin was not happy. He thought he had seen the last of me for a while after the UNSCOM 201 mission. 'We hope you are here to do serious work, Mr. Scott,' he said. 'We hope you are not here to provoke a crisis.' I assured him I was not.

Unfortunately, our inspection hit a snag on the first day, when we were trying to gain access to the barracks of the 5th Company, 2nd Battalion. This was the unit I believed had provided the personnel and vehicles used to move biological agent in the summer of 1995, if the Israeli intelligence report we had was accurate. Our primary route took us to the end of the road leading to the 2nd Battalion Headquarters, and instead of turning right and returning back to the Airport Road, we tried to turn left, on a road which would lead us directly to the 5th Company. However, the Iraqis stopped us, stating that we were trying to enter a 'Presidential Area'.

Tariq Aziz was contacted, and he demanded to know the exact location where the team wanted to go. I refused to provide this, referring to the agreement he had made with Rolf Ekéus, but said that I was not going to inspect any presidential facilities, only military barracks. The Iraqis insisted that there were no military barracks in the direction I wanted to go, only 'presidential villas'. I consulted my map and overhead photographs, and reconfirmed what I knew to be the case: I was right, and the Iraqis either didn't know the area in question, or were lying. When the Battalion Commander of the 2nd Battalion chimed in, saying he knew the area and there were no military units or barracks where I was heading, I knew they were lying.

I called Richard Butler and reported the situation. I noted that we had been denied access to a facility that the Iraqis now knew we had an interest in, and as such the integrity of the inspection had been compromised. Butler concurred, and ordered the inspection effort at this site to be terminated under protest.

Up until now, the UNSCOM 207 team had performed flawlessly. Chris Cobb-Smith had the Concealment Investigation element fine tuned to accomplish their myriad of complicated tasks smoothly and discreetly. For a 'shake out' inspection, things were going very well. We still had some issues to resolve concerning access to sites, but I believed that we would be leaving Iraq with the Concealment Investigation team firmly in place and ready to begin a months-long inspection campaign that would bring the issue of concealment to a close once and for all.

UNSCOM 207 was never intended as an inspection that was going to find proscribed material (although we would have been happy if that had occurred). It was an inspection to facilitate the entry of the Concealment Investigation team into the world of UNSCOM inspections, both in terms of its ability to work well with the other UN inspection teams, and in implementing the sensitive site inspection modalities with the Iraqis.

However, things on the ground in Iraq were starting to get complicated. On my return to the Baghdad Monitoring and Verification Center I was approached by the chief inspector of the Biological Monitoring Team, Dianne Seaman. These teams carried out the day-to-day task of monitoring

Iraqi factories and related facilities for compliance. There were also the aerial inspection team, and now the new Concealment Investigation team. While UNSCOM 207 was still in Bahrain, on 25 September, Dianne Seaman had conducted a no-notice inspection of the Iraqi National Standards Laboratory, where she ran into two Special Security Organization officers carrying a briefcase trying to sneak out the back of the building. Dianne Seaman, displaying remarkable calm and focus, seized the briefcase and had it sent to the BMVC for further analysis. Inside the briefcase she discovered a document showing a variety of biological test results, and reagent test kits for botulinum toxin and clostridium perfringens, two agents that were both naturally occurring as food poison, but which had been weaponized by the Iraqis in the late 1980s. The document wasn't conclusive evidence of a weapons program, but she believed that it could show a covert effort by Iraq to isolate and concentrate the toxins from these two bacteria, something prohibited under Security Council resolution. Furthermore, the Special Security Organization agency identified in the documents was an entity called the 'Special Biological Activity', a title which in and of itself was curious. She wanted to send the document out for a more detailed and accurate translation, but had brought the matter to my attention because she knew I was focused on the Special Security Organization as a possible conduit for ongoing concealment activity.

I recommended to Richard Butler that we seek to interview the two Special Security Organization officers involved in the incident, and seek clarification as to what the document represented. We should, I said, also seek to inspect the offices of these two men to confirm their story. If the Iraqis did not fully cooperate, then we should immediately seek to inspect the headquarters building of the Special Security Organization, which had been identified by numerous sources as being located in the Al Hyatt building next to the Republican Palace. Butler needed time to think the matter over. As it was, we had two more days of inspections planned, so while Richard Butler pondered our proposal, UNSCOM 207 got back to work.

On 1 October, the last day of the inspection, we headed towards the Republican Palace. Our target was the Archives of the Special Security Organization and Special Republican Guard, where we hoped we could find incriminating documents about past concealment activity. If such documents were discovered, then we were to proceed directly to the headquarters of the Special Security Organization in an effort to force the issue of past concealment once and for all. However, the site turned out to be a bust – instead of the Archives, we found that the building had recently been turned over to the presidential *diwan* (office) of Saddam Hussein. We were granted access, and upon determining that we were in the wrong place, I called the inspection off. It was a disappointing way to end the inspection.

When I got back to the BMVC, however, the situation had changed dramatically. Richard Butler had approved holding a meeting with the Iraqis about the Special Security Organization documents. If Dianne Seaman and I did not feel that we were being given adequate answers, we were authorized to carry out a night inspection of the Special Security Organization headquarters. I immediately put Chris Cobb-Smith on notice to prepare for a night inspection, while Dianne Seaman and I proceeded to the National Monitoring headquarters, where Hossam Amin was waiting with the two involved Special Security Organization officers. We both pressed the Special Security Organization officers for answers about the documents they had been carrying, and the unit they worked for. Neither were forthcoming.

I challenged Hossam Amin, saying that we could do this the easy way, which would be to have the two officers cooperate, or the hard way, which would be for UNSCOM to carry out a night inspection to resolve the issues. We continued to be stonewalled. I declared the meeting over, and notified Hossam Amin that we would be conducting a night inspection. He genuinely looked confused. 'But you said your inspection was finished,' he complained.

I pointed at the two Special Security Organization officers. 'They just restarted it.' Hossam jumped to his feet, and cursed me. He accused me of deliberately provoking a crisis where none existed. He refused any cooperation with me or my team. I restated my intention to inspect, and Hossam had no choice but to calm down.

Just before midnight on 1 October, I led a fourteen-vehicle convoy across the Tigris river, towards the Republican Palace. As we approached a series of checkpoints near the palace, our convoy was split up at a traffic light and confronted by armed Special Republican Guard soldiers, who were clearly shaken up by our presence. One of the senior Iraqi minders, Colonel Bassim, had to interpose himself directly in between myself and an Special Republican Guard soldier who was preparing to shoot me with his AK-47 automatic rifle. Another Special Security Organization officer had leveled his pistol at my head. Down the street, Chris Cobb-Smith's vehicle, which had pulled ahead, found itself surrounded by machine-gun-wielding Special Republican Guard soldiers. It took a few minutes for the Iraqis to calm the situation down, but eventually we were able to regroup and gather the inspection team in one location, just short of the intersection with the traffic light. Within minutes Amer Rashid arrived, and approached me. 'Where is it you wish to go, Mr. Scott?' he asked. I pointed down the road, towards the presidential palace. 'My dear,' he said, 'that is a palace, and this is impossible.' We had a standoff.[6]

Over the course of the next hour, Amer Rashid and I wrangled over the details of where I wanted to go, while Tariq Aziz and Richard Butler did the same over the phone. After Richard justified my actions based upon the document seized by Dianne Seaman, Tariq Aziz lambasted Butler for allowing an inspection based upon such flimsy evidence. 'This is a test for food poisoning of the food used for Saddam Hussein, nothing more,' Tariq Aziz said. 'It has nothing to do with any weapons of mass destruction.' Butler disagreed, and demanded the team be allowed to go forward.

To help move matters forward, I finally told Amer Rashid exactly where we wanted to go – the Al Hyatt building. 'Why?' he asked.

'It is the headquarters of the Special Security Organization,' I said, and Amer left for consultations. He returned shortly.

'My dear,' he said, 'You are wrong. This building is empty, and is not what you are looking for. I cannot let you inspect, however, because this is a presidential palace, and as such off limits to you. But you are making a mistake if you continue to insist on an inspection.'

I relayed this information to the chairman, who again talked with Tariq Aziz. The Iraqi deputy prime minister mocked Butler, saying if he insisted on pressing this matter, not only would the team be denied entry, but he, Tariq Aziz, would personally lead a delegation of journalists into the Al Hyatt building to show the world that it was 'as empty as the false accusations made by your inspectors'. Faced with this intransigence on the part of the Iraqis, Richard ordered the team withdrawn, and the next morning UNSCOM 207 left for Bahrain.

Chapter 20

False Starts
October–December 1997

At the time, I viewed the Special Security Organization Headquarters standoff as just another denial of access. A little bit more adventurous than the others, perhaps, but nothing earth-shattering. We had been down this route before with the Iraqis – many times. Each previous time we had found a way to navigate through the conflict. I was confident that this crisis would prove the same.

One of the reasons for my optimism was the fact that, despite the confrontation, we had extracted an amazing confession during my interview with the former Special Republican Guard Commander, Kamal Mustafa – the Special Republican Guard *had* played, as I had contended and the facts demonstrated, a major role in past concealment activity. I had been pursuing this issue for over two years now. I remembered Amer Rashid and Amer al-Sa'adi's pointed denials – there had been 'no involvement of the Special Republican Guard whatsoever in the events of summer 1991', they had told me, repeatedly. It was these denials, and the overwhelming body of evidence to the contrary, that made the notion of a retained Iraqi weapons of mass destruction capability credible. Now, for the first time, the Iraqis were admitting a role by the Special Republican Guard. This was an amazing breakthrough that I believed gave UNSCOM a solid foundation for bringing the concealment investigation to a close. With the Iraqi confession about the Special Republican Guard came the ability to accurately detail the events of the summer of 1991 – the period of unilateral destruction. Once we mapped out those events accurately, we would have a clear picture of what had been destroyed, how it had been destroyed, and who had destroyed it.

This was the weak link in all of UNSCOM's analysis regarding a retained Iraqi capability. If the Iraqi claims regarding unilateral destruction held, and were factored into the overall issue of a 'material balance' in accounting for Iraq's past weapons capabilities, then we were on the verge of finding Iraq to be free of its proscribed weapons and programs. Iraq would be disarmed.

If, on the other hand, we found that the true events of the summer of 1991 showed a continued pattern of concealment and deception, of incomplete destruction and efforts to retain not only weapons of mass destruction capability, but also the concealment mechanism used to hide this capability from the inspectors, then we would know that the Iraqi claims of complete destruction were false. This certainty of knowledge would enable UNSCOM to reject with confidence the Iraqi claims, and aggressively demand that Iraq submit new, accurate declarations, and support them with verifiable documentation.

Right now, UNSCOM was stuck in the middle of the two positions: we were demanding a new, accurate declaration supported by verifiable documentation, while being unable to prove the Iraqi claims regarding the summer of 1991 false. I believed that the concealment mechanism investigation was on the verge of reconciling these two positions once and for all. The only problem was, I didn't yet know on which side the final conclusion would fall – compliance or non-compliance. But I did know that, thanks to the series of inspections we had just completed, UNSCOM was closer than it had ever been to making such a conclusion. For the first time I could see a light at the end of the tunnel.

Politics, however, have a way of skewing things, and the situation between UNSCOM, Iraq and the Security Council was heavy with politics. Unlike last June, when Iraqi obstruction of the UNSCOM 194 inspection prompted an immediate and strong response by the Security Council in the form of resolution 1115, the events of the night of 1–2 October drew silence. This was strange, because according to resolution 1115, any report of Iraqi non-compliance by UNSCOM was supposed to result in the immediate application of travel sanctions against the leadership of Iraq. The report of Iraqi soldiers aiming loaded weapons at UNSCOM inspectors was greeted with a total lack of action.

This was partly because Butler had promised to abandon the 'forensic' inspection approach during his visit to Baghdad in July 1997, and because some members of the Security Council had sympathy for the Iraqis' response to aggressive inspections of their most sensitive security organizations. More importantly, the ambiguity surrounding Iraq's weapons status suited the USA's regime change agenda very well, and they were not about to argue other Security Council members into supporting aggressive inspections which might clear up the WMD picture, and hence get sanctions lifted. I gradually realized that in this political environment I was not going to get the kind of backup I needed to investigate the Special Security Organization and close the case on concealment.

This entire process was complicated by the fact, as relayed to me by Burt, that my concealment paper had just been adapted as an official intelligence report for use inside the CIA's intelligence analysis system. What had been prepared as a guideline for investigative operations, postulating the hypothetical existence of various proscribed weapons, had instead become a foundation of 'fact' for intelligence analysts and government policymakers. Burt told me that the most popular reading of my paper was the annexes on hidden weapons and documents. What had always been speculation had now become an 'official UNSCOM position'. This had serious political ramifications in the face of ongoing Iraqi obstruction: now that UNSCOM and the CIA were quantifying actual weapons stockpiles, the Iraqi threat took on a reality that before had been lacking. The drafting of the concealment paper, which had been intended as a legitimate endeavor in support of disarmament, had just corrupted the entire process by empowering those who supported continued sanctions and regime change vis-à-vis Iraq with a powerful, yet artificial, weapon.

Having done their best to meet the legitimate requirements of the UNSCOM investigation into the concealment mechanism, by October 1997 the senior Iraqi leadership realized that there could be no satisfying UNSCOM's search for truth without compromising the security of Saddam Hussein to an unacceptable level. After the withdrawal of UNSCOM 207, the Iraqi government made a decision to stop cooperating with UN weapons inspectors until what they deemed the compositional bias (i.e. too many American and British inspectors) was addressed. The Iraqis did not want to be seen as acting precipitately, however. They simply waited for the right time to strike.

On 6 October Richard Butler issued his biannual report on UNSCOM's work in Iraq. This report was devastating in its criticism of Iraq, accusing it of delaying the submission of full declarations and of obstructing the work of the inspectors, the most recent example of which was the Al Hyatt incident of 1–2 October. Butler did not reveal that in fact the documents Dianne Seaman had found were claimed by Tariq Aziz to be samples of Saddam Hussein's food tests. On 12 October the Iraqi deputy prime minister wrote a scathing letter to the president of the Security Council, criticizing the Butler report, condemning the policies of the USA and the UK, and attacking one inspector in particular as the manifestation of all that was wrong with UNSCOM – Scott Ritter.

'The latest problems cited by the executive chairman,' Tariq Aziz wrote, 'in his latest report, happened to the inspection team headed by the American officer Scott Ritter. Scott Ritter himself was the chief inspector of the inspection team which created the problems last June that led to the adoption of the Security Council resolution 1115,' Tariq Aziz noted.[1]

Tariq Aziz's letter sent shockwaves through the Security Council, especially among members, led by Russia, France and China, who were critical of America's Iraq policy, and the perceived US domination of UNSCOM. The USA countered this by focusing on the credibility of the Security Council. They emphasized process over substance. If Iraq was permitted to dictate the terms of its disarmament in the face of numerous Council resolutions, then the Council would lose relevance. This debate went back and forth in the corridors of the United Nations, and between national capitols. In the end, the USA won out – on 23 October the Security Council passed resolution 1134, which condemned Iraq's failure to fully cooperate with inspectors.

Four days later, Richard Butler wrote to Tariq Aziz, proposing that the two sides meet to try and work out a way forward. On 29 October, Butler got his response: the Iraqis stated that they would no longer work with any US inspectors assigned to UNSCOM. This proved to be a huge blunder on their part. That same day, the Security Council issued a statement condemning Iraq's decision. The secretary-general, Kofi Annan, dispatched a high-level delegation to Iraq to try and find a solution to the crisis, but the delegation returned empty-handed. On 12 November, the Security Council passed resolution 1137, which not only condemned Iraq's actions, but also now imposed the travel sanctions called for by resolution 1115. The next day, the Iraqi government ordered all UNSCOM inspectors out of Iraq within twenty-four hours, prompting yet another statement of condemnation by the president of the Security Council. The situation was rapidly spinning out of control.

While this drama was unfolding, work at UNSCOM had not stopped. The Israeli intelligence concerning Iraq's interest in the Romanian company, Aerofina, had caught the attention of MI6. In late October 1997, I received a call from the Flyfisher, the MI6 station chief in New York, who informed me that MI6 had not only agreed to approach Romania about the issue, but also wanted to take our cooperation one step further, suggesting that I should travel to Bucharest to make the case myself on behalf of the UN.

I was losing patience with the diplomatic game around me, and I was anxious to get on with some proper evidence-based disarmament work. I left New York on 3 November, traveling to Bucharest via Frankfurt. I was met at the immigration checkpoint by 'Miss Moneypenny', the MI6 station clerk in Romania. She drove me to the residence of the MI6 station chief, (referred to here as 'the Salesman'), who was operating in Romania under diplomatic cover.

At their home, I had a meal with the Salesman and his wife (a former MI6 operative herself until sidelined by the birth of their baby boy). The Salesman was a tall, slim man in his mid-thirties, with dark hair. His wife was likewise very tall, and quite striking. With their newborn son, and modest apartment, they looked more like your average middle-class family getting by in a solid, yet unspectacular, fashion. This image was soon altered, however, by the reality that I was dealing with an MI6 operative implementing his country's national security policy, not a commercial representative pushing some product line.

After the meal, the Salesman took me to my hotel, the Intercontinental Bucharest, where I checked in. From there, he drove me to a facility out past the Bucharest Airport, an unmarked dacha tucked away into a grove of mixed pine and deciduous trees. This was a safe house of the Foreign Counterintelligence Office of the Foreign Intelligence Service (SIE).

The Salesman and I were met by two senior Romanian intelligence officers, who led us into the dacha, to a wood-paneled conference room, complete with one-way windows and facilities for recording conversations. There was a black-topped table, surrounded by four chairs. The room was otherwise sparsely furnished. A bottle of mineral water, along with some glasses, was placed in the middle of the table. Not so long before, this building had been under the control of Nicolai Ceaucescu,

The Romanians fingered a piece of paper, a report from MI6 headquarters in London detailing my mission and what was desired. 'We have read your message,' the counterintelligence director said. 'We are ready to cooperate on every level with the Special Commission and the United Kingdom.' He looked over at his female colleague. 'Romania wants very much to become an integral member of NATO, and as such we understand we need to operate in accordance with the standards of conduct and international law which such membership entails.'

The Salesman provided the Romanians with a briefing which underscored the current situation between Iraq and the Security Council. This situation, he said, dictated a rapid operation to intercept Iraqi missiles, an action which could be used as leverage by UNSCOM and its allies to gain maximum advantage within the Security Council. The Salesman further noted that, while Romania had already cooperated in interdicting material and equipment intended for Iraq (a cooperation I was unaware of), the Special Commission desired additional support so that the associated Iraqi procurement network could be identified and terminated. Again, the Salesman pointed out, this action was required in rapid order, given the developing crisis situation between the United Nations and Iraq.

The MI6 station chief noted that the best approach would be for a trilateral covert operation designed to acquire information relating to this Iraqi procurement effort in Romania. The Special Commission, armed with this information, could then expose this Iraqi covert procurement activity, which was proscribed by Security Council resolution. This exposure would need to be orchestrated, the Salesman said, in a manner that achieved the best operational and political results for all parties involved. The specific mechanism for exposing any information gained through such an operation could be worked out at a later date. The current problem was to get access to information pertaining to the Romanian company, Aerofina, that had been identified as being involved with Iraq. In this, the Salesman said, the Romanian government was believed to be the only available channel.

The Salesman was working off a memorized script which not only laid out the objectives for any cooperation between the UK, Romania and the Special Commission, but offered a glimpse into what was driving the British decision to assist UNSCOM in this effort. I was focused on the disarmament aspect of this operation. The British seemed focused on the political aspects. If this cooperation succeeded, the British were hoping to use the results to trump whatever momentum the Iraqis were picking up at the United Nations. The British seemed to be throwing NATO membership in as a sweetener, but I just wanted the missile parts.

The Romanians agreed with the MI6 agent that this was a project worth supporting. They said that they would begin immediate covert surveillance of Aerofina. However, they lacked any specific intelligence about the personalities believed to be involved. The Romanians were happy to conduct a crash recruitment of an involved individual (i.e., to use blackmail) for the purpose of obtaining documentation and other background information, but they needed a starting point, a name. It was my job to come up with one. The British, for their part, agreed to provide technical assistance to the Romanians which would enable the SIE to isolate, record and assess communications of Aerofina and the Iraqis, as well as other assistance in covertly monitoring the Iraqi delegation while it was in Romania.

The next day, I flew on to Tel Aviv, where I had arranged a meeting with Moshe Ponkovsky on 6 November. At the meeting, I pressed the Israelis for the final nugget of information the Romanians needed to go forward. At first Moshe Ponkovsky hesitated, because to give more than they already had could potentially compromise Israel's own delicate sources of intelligence. My request went up to the director of intelligence, Major General Ayalon, who cleared my request with the prime minister, and within hours I got the answer I needed: the Romanian contact for the Karama deal was the commercial manager of Aerofina, a certain Dumitru Tudorica.[2]

I flew back to London, and on 8 November reported my 'find' to the Don and the other MI6 officers in a meeting held at MI6 Headquarters. And thus was born Operation Air Bag, perhaps the most unique and intricate intelligence operation undertaken by the UN weapons inspectors. Working back from Mr. Tudorica, the Romanians, with assistance from MI6, were able to find someone close to the Iraqi deal who, with the appropriate pressure brought to bear, agreed to cooperate. My understanding was that this individual had been engaged in some shady business practices involving the theft of government property and, when given the choice between cooperating or going to jail for a long time, chose cooperation. The British, working their Jordanian sources, were able to penetrate the Amman offices of 'Rouge Establishment', the procurement front company that had been identified by the Israelis as being involved with the Romanian deal. Again, a Jordanian businessman who valued money more than loyalty had been identified and given the right offer. We now had all the elements of the operation in place. All we needed was for the Iraqi delegation to travel to Romania.

While I was pressing forward on the Romanian front, the situation regarding UNSCOM and Iraq was getting worse. By 20 November, the crisis between the Security Council and Iraq had come to a head, with the USA dispatching six B-52 heavy bombers to the Indian Ocean island base of Diego Garcia, within striking distance of Iraq. The Russian government attempted to broker a solution. With the full support of the US Secretary of State, Madeleine Albright, the Russians got the Iraqis to back down, and on 20 November announced that Iraq would once again cooperate with all of UNSCOM's inspectors – including Americans.

In exchange for this concession, the Security Council ordered that an emergency session of the Special Commission meet to discuss the status of UNSCOM's work, with an eye on perhaps altering the mandate and methodology of the inspectors. The French, Russian and Chinese delegations were working together to attack the American dominance of UNSCOM, which they increasingly saw as an arm of US foreign policy. UNSCOM's mandate eventually emerged intact from this battle, but only just.

I was eager to get the Concealment Investigation team back to work so we could move decisively forward. But the team had been dormant since September. I needed help in getting it back on track. My relations with Charles Duelfer had, during this time, undergone a strange metamorphosis. Whereas in the past I was pretty much operating on my own, with limited supervision, the current situation, with its heavy political character, dictated my going to Duelfer for help. The animosity of the previous spring, in the aftermath of my confronting him about the CIA's covert communications station operating in Baghdad under UNSCOM cover, had given way to first a truce, as I built the Concealment Investigation team and deployed it to Iraq, and then to an alliance, in the aftermath of the 1 October crisis outside the Special Security Organization Headquarters when Duelfer and I found ourselves on the receiving end of anti-American attacks.

I had, by a strange twist of fate, become 'American' again in the eyes of Washington. The official embrace of my 'concealment paper' by the CIA made my denigration a thing of the past. The CIA had, for the moment, accepted what they believed to be my conclusions about Iraqi WMD, without accepting the context in which these conclusions were made, and what the original intent was when deriving these findings.

Suddenly, in this time of crisis, I was again politically useful to the USA. I was a high-profile American at the center of a crisis with Iraq who could be legitimately portrayed as working not for the unilateral interests of the United States of America, but of the United Nations. The USA needed to co-opt my legitimacy without compromising their policy. My work with UNSCOM would be supported because not to support it would be seen as giving in to the Iraqis. But this was 'skin deep' support, of the process only. The substance of my work – confrontation-based inspections designed to crack the concealment mechanism, were not to be embraced. These, after all, were what had gotten the world to where it was at the time in relation to Iraq.

I tried my best to divorce myself from these political machinations. My job was to inspect, and I turned my attention to getting Chris Cobb-Smith and the Concealment Investigation element back to work as soon as possible. 'Back to work' meant carrying out inspections of sensitive sites designed to trigger the kind of activity we wanted to exploit with the Special Collection Element communications intercept operation. I knew that this was a politically sensitive time for UNSCOM, but I also knew that the clock was ticking on the entire issue of concealment mechanism inspections. On 20 November, immediately after the Russians announced their brokered deal with Iraq, I drafted a memorandum for the executive chairman.[3]

I recommended a three-day series of inspections, starting on 22 November, targeted against known Special Republican Guard camps in the Baghdad area. Richard Butler concurred, the only stipulation being that the inspections wouldn't start until 25 November, to give the chairman time to coordinate with the USA about the political ramifications of such inspections. For better or worse, UNSCOM and the Americans had found common cause against Iraq.

Chris Cobb-Smith and the team were ready to get to work by 24 November. He had assembled missile, chemical and biological experts from the BMVC monitoring staff in addition to the core Concealment Investigation team, and had everyone on standby, waiting for the 'go' order from New York. I knew very well how it felt to sit in Baghdad, watching the hours tick away on the clock, as New York dithered.

Three hours and several conversations with Cobb-Smith later, Richard

Butler still hadn't shown up. It was past midnight in Baghdad. Finally, I got a call from Butler's secretary. 'The chairman would like to see you,' she said. The news wasn't good. 'The Secretary of State [Madeleine Albright] has asked me not to do the inspection of the Special Republican Guard sites you have proposed,' he said. 'She views such inspections as too provocative at this juncture, especially given her undertaking with Yevgeny Primakov.' Secretary Albright had given her word to Primakov, the Russian Foreign Minister at the time, that UNSCOM would do nothing to deliberately sabotage his diplomatic achievement in securing the Russian-brokered agreement with Iraq – even if this meant impeding the legitimate work of UNSCOM.

I stood there, stunned. 'Mr. Chairman, the whole purpose of the Concealment Investigation team being in Baghdad is to be provocative so that we might best detect evidence of concealment. The concept does not work if the team is static, or reduced to assisting in monitoring inspections. You have taken a big gamble in deploying this team; let them do their job.'

Butler held firm. 'The United States will not back our carrying out such inspections at this time, Scott. I know how important it is for your team to be active, but they will have to wait until a less politically sensitive moment.'

Cobb-Smith and his team were growing increasingly frustrated, chomping at the bit to do their job, and yet being held back over and over again. For the team, their presence in Iraq was a colossal waste of time and effort. I agreed, but was unwilling to give up without a fight. If I let the Concealment Investigation team return now, then I was condemning the Concealment Investigation concept to death, and with it the entire concealment mechanism investigation. I knew in my heart that we were close to bringing this matter to closure. A concerted effort, given the proper support, would either prove that the Iraqis had disarmed as they said, or were retaining proscribed material and weaponry.

As aggressive as I wanted to be, however, Richard Butler remained paralyzed until the Security Council had made up its mind what it wanted to do about Iraq. Butler met with the Council throughout the day on 6 December, and in private with the British and American representatives. He finally got his marching orders: to go to Baghdad, and to press the Iraqis hard for a resolution of issues pertaining to inspector access to sensitive sites.

Charles Duelfer was ecstatic about Butler's upcoming visit. 'We can finally scrap these damn sensitive site modalities,' he told me during a break in the meetings. Duelfer, like the rest of the US government, was contemptuous of the Ekéus-brokered deal. The modalities for the inspection of sensitive sites (see Chapter Thirteen) were seen as an impediment to American policy objectives. These modalities allowed the inspection process to be controlled, both by the Iraqis, and by the inspectors. As difficult a time UNSCOM had had with Iraq since June 1996 regarding inspections, none of the achievements in advancing the issue of concealment could have been made without the inspection modalities. UNSCOM would never have been permitted to access the sites and organizations it had if it had tried to gain access with a team of fifty, versus the four permitted under the modalities. The success of these inspections in pushing Iraq closer to disarmament threatened the US and UK policy of perpetual sanctions. 'The Brits and Americans are leaning real hard on Butler to throw out the entire agreement and stick with the original concept of 'anytime, anyplace' inspections,' Duelfer said.

Butler confirmed this. At the end of the day on 6 December, Butler summoned me to his office. 'I need an inspection ready to go to Iraq in a week. It needs to be tough, hard-hitting, legitimate. It needs to stand up to the scrutiny of Iraq's friends on the Council, and yet still have enough teeth to pressure Iraq on sensitive and presidential sites.'

I said I could do it, and that I would have a plan put together by noon the next day. I decided that one of the key sites to be inspected was the headquarters of the Special Security Organization. We had received fresh intelligence from a US-controlled defector about underground tunnels and passageways associated with the Special Security Organization Headquarters facility that were alleged to be used for storing prohibited weapons. I wasn't overly impressed with this information, but felt that since the aborted inspection of this facility back on 1 October had initiated this entire crisis, it was only fair that we should now include this site as part of any inspection effort designed to assert the very right of access we were defending.

The real heart of the inspection, from a disarmament point of view, rested with two other targets: the Jabal Makhul presidential palace, and the presidential *diwan* in downtown Baghdad. Since our inspection of the Tikrit area in June, during UNSCOM 194, we had been receiving intelligence reports from the US about the Tikrit Special Security Office undertaking a quick-reaction operation in response to that inspection, one which involved moving material into the perimeter of the Jabal Makhul presidential palace complex for safety.

We had tried, and failed, to gain access to Jabal Makhul in September, during UNSCOM 207. Now, with the Security Council backing us, I thought this would be the perfect site to test whether or not the Iraqis would allow us access to presidential areas. And, this time, there was a twist. The Defense Intelligence Agency, through its Human Intelligence Service, had become aware of an Iraqi defector under the control of German intelligence.

According to this defector, an engineer, there was a network of underground pipes installed inside the perimeter of Jabal Makhul, and these pipes, which could be accessed by large manhole-type coverings, were used by the Iraqis to store boxes of documents in order to keep them away from the UN weapons inspectors. Making the defector's tale even more credible were CIA satellite photographs of a mobile crane operating near where one of the manhole entrances was said to be located. In theory, this intelligence was as good as it gets: human intelligence detailing the activity, and imagery suggestive of such activity taking place.

We greeted the information with the usual mixture of excitement and skepticism which accompanied human intelligence, or HUMINT revelations. Ever since information from 'Defector Source 385' had led the UNSCOM 16 inspection to the hidden archive of nuclear weapons-related documents back in September 1991, HUMINT had come to play an important role in shaping the work of the inspectors. In the immediate aftermath of Desert Storm in 1991 there was a surge of Iraqi defectors who claimed to be involved in Iraqi weapons of mass destruction programs. Some of these defectors, like DS-385, were the real deal. Others proved to be less than credible. However, by 1992 the stream of defectors had slowed to a trickle, and by 1993 had stopped altogether.

Then, in 1994, there was a spike in the number of defections from Iraq by people alleging to be part of the Iraqi weapons programs. However, the CIA treated these new defectors with great suspicion, believing many of them to be double agents 'dangled' by the Iraqi intelligence service in an effort to learn more about how UNSCOM received the information that went into the planning of inspection activities. The end result was that by the summer of 1995, HUMINT as a source of information useful to weapons inspectors had all but dried up.

This situation changed dramatically in August 1995, with the defection of Hussein Kamal, Saddam Hussein's son-in-law. Hussein Kamal himself, through his debriefing by Rolf Ekéus and others, proved to be an intriguing HUMINT source, claiming both that Iraq had destroyed its weapons of mass destructions in 1991 and that Iraq was actively engaged in concealing WMD, depending on the audience. Hussein Kamal's tenure as a HUMINT source was short-lived, perishing with him in a hail of gunfire shortly after his return to Iraq in early 1996. But Hussein Kamal brought with him another defector, Izzadin al-Majid, a former officer in Saddam's Special Republican Guard who had played a central role in concealing weapons of mass destruction-related material from UNSCOM in the summer of 1991. Given the fact that the Iraqi government had denied any such involvement in concealment activity by the Special Republican Guard, Izzadin was a potentially invaluable source of information. I personally led the UNSCOM effort to exploit Izzadin, meeting him in Jordan in May 1996, and later at a CIA safe house in Washington during September 1996. Izzadin's information was invaluable in helping UNSCOM compel the Iraqi government to finally admit the role played by the Special Republican Guard in concealing WMD from the inspectors in the summer of 1991, something Kamal Mustafa, the former Special Republican Guard Commander, confessed to me in an interview in September 1997.

Izzadin wasn't the only HUMINT source UNSCOM was working post-1995. In 1996, the Israeli government shared with me the existence of its own network of agents operating in Baghdad, and allowed me to forward questions to them via their Israeli handlers. The Dutch Secret Security Service (BVD) and I developed a relationship that allowed me access to their own pool of Iraqi defectors. One of these defectors in particular, codenamed 'Fulcrum', proved very useful. The BVD made Fulcrum available to UNSCOM after trying to pass his information to UNSCOM through the CIA. When the CIA failed to deliver the information in its complete form, the BVD took matters into their own hands, and I became the chief conduit for this new HUMINT relationship. A byproduct of the cooperation with the Dutch was the recruitment of an Iraqi ballistic missile engineer, known as 'Source A', who I originally debriefed in Amman, Jordan, in August 1996. When he later appeared as a refugee in Europe, I approached the BVD about his potential value as an intelligence source, and the BVD took him in under their wings. Source A provided a large amount of valuable data about ongoing Iraqi efforts in the field of ballistic missiles, some of which was directly relevant to the ongoing Operation Air Bag involving Iraqi efforts in Romania. Even MI6 got in on the game, providing me with a shopping list of its Iraqi agents, part of Iyad Alawi's Iraqi National Accord network, each identified by a code name and basic biographical data ('former Mukhabarat agent with some overseas experience', etc.), and allowed me to submit questions for each source to answer.

Since 1993 the CIA had been working with Ahmed Chalabi and the Iraqi National Congress (INC) in the processing and evaluation of defectors who made their way out of Iraq and into the CIA-controlled enclave in Kurdistan. Some of these sources on the surface looked appealing, but upon closer examination were determined by the CIA to either be outright frauds or double-agent 'dangles' controlled by the Iraqi Mukhabarat. Ahmed Chalabi furthered the environment of doubt and mistrust in the CIA about Iraqi defectors by fabricating his own 'sources' and inserting them into the stream of defectors being processed by the CIA. Chalabi had been carefully following what the CIA was looking for in a defector, and would prepare his 'defectors' carefully, giving them cover stories and information that would make them look both attractive and credible to the CIA. But the CIA was quickly alerted to Chalabi's games, and the Iraqi opposition leader quickly fell out of grace.

Chalabi and the INC continued to lurk in the background, trying to peddle his misinformation to any sympathetic source. His anti-Saddam message caught the attention of conservative politicians in the USA, who used Chalabi's 'intelligence' to bolster their case that the Clinton administration was being ineffective in containing Saddam Hussein's WMD ambitions. Through this conservative link, Chalabi was introduced to Judith Miller, a journalist with the *New York Times*, and to Charles Duelfer, the UNSCOM deputy executive chairman. Duelfer, a long-time 'background' source for Judith Miller (they would have long lunches where Duelfer would provide her with off-the-record 'inside information' about what was happening behind the scenes in UNSCOM and Iraq), was convinced that Chalabi was a goldmine of useful data that UNSCOM desperately needed to get its hands on. In October 1997, Duelfer summoned me to his office, and informed me about his desire to establish contacts with Chalabi. I was told to take the lead on this effort.

Shortly after this meeting, I was informed of the defector who allegedly knew about Jabal Makhul, and duly dispatched Bill, the former Delta

Force intelligence analyst, to Germany to meet and debrief him. Although I remained skeptical about the CIA's human intelligence sources, I was willing to try anything that might move inspections beyond their current stalemate. In the end, the defector provided some leads that we thought might be useful for the 218 inspection.

On 7 December, I presented the inspection plan to Richard Butler for his approval. He signed off on all of the proposed sites, with one caveat: he would hold off on signing the actual NIS documentation, the 'search warrants' which authorized inspectors to inspect, pending the results of his scheduled meetings with Tariq Aziz in Baghdad. I was to deploy the team to Bahrain, assemble the team, begin training, and wait.

Butler seemed pleased with my preparations. 'I told you,' he said, 'that we would strike when the time was right. The time is now. Your inspection will be a critical test of Iraq's willingness to abide by its undertakings. Good luck.' I called Chris Cobb-Smith, and told him we were back in business. The new inspection, to be called UNSCOM 218, had just become a reality.

As planned, Richard Butler and his delegation flew to Baghdad. Butler was armed with the Security Council presidential statement of 3 December, which had been carefully crafted by the British and Americans to be exceptionally tough over the issue of inspection team access. He was to go to Baghdad and emphasize the Council's position to the Iraqis – let UNSCOM inspect, or else. Waiting in the wings to test the results of Richard's visit was my team, UNSCOM 218.

The critical meeting took place on the morning of 15 December, in a large hall in the Ministry of Foreign Affairs building. Richard Butler wasted no time in getting to the crux of the matter, the issue of access to sensitive sites. 'From the standpoint of the Commission,' Butler said, 'these modalities have not worked satisfactorily… they were done with the good reason of wishing to show respect to Iraq's national security concerns. I am not sure how well they have done that job. But I am sure they have not done our job well. They have been applied in a way that has reduced the credibility of our inspections and that has prevented us from being able to give satisfactory reports.'

Tariq Aziz held his fire, waiting for Butler to finish. 'With respect to the same document,' Butler continued, 'what has emerged since it was offered to you by Chairman Ekéus is that there have been an increasing number of sites that we have needed to go to where it hasn't been a question of this document not working but in which Iraq has said it has no application, that those sites are outside of the scope of the modalities document.'

Tariq Aziz, in responding, let it be known that while Iraq was willing to show some flexibility with regard to inspections of national security sites, when it came to presidential and sovereign sites, the Iraqi position was clear: no inspections.

Richard Butler pressed the point for clarification. Was Tariq Aziz saying that presidential sites were off limits to inspectors? Tariq Aziz was unequivocal. 'Yes.' Iraq was taking a hard line.

But then Butler did something quite extraordinary – he folded. As Charles Duelfer listened in horror, the UNSCOM chairman agreed to keep the modalities for sensitive site inspections intact, the only modifications being the chief inspector's ability to negotiate a larger number of inspectors on the access team if the situation warranted. Tariq Aziz nodded his agreement. 'Yes.'[4]

Butler was to all intent and purposes finished. He had accomplished his mission, receiving from Tariq Aziz a firm understanding of the Iraqi position vis-à-vis sensitive sites. But Tariq Aziz was not yet quite finished. 'I would like you just to put on the record that since the beginning of 1996 until 29 October 1997 the number of sensitive sites which were inspected by your teams is 103… If you don't want to answer this question, fine, but I want to put it on the table and I hope you would refer to it in your report to the Council – in how many of those inspections did your inspection team find concealed weapons or materials which belonged to the prohibited weapons? My knowledge is that there were none… nothing was found that was prohibited. I am not challenging the right of UNSCOM to continue inspections. Please understand me well, but I think after this experience of two years it is also fair to draw some conclusions about the inspections and the results of those inspections. As you know,' he continued, 'the right of inspection is not an objective by itself. It is a means to reach the truth, it is a means to be certain that by monitoring means Iraq is not reproducing prohibited weapons.'

Richard Butler was planning to leave Baghdad on 16 December. He had arranged to brief the Security Council on 18 December. I still had vital documents that needed to be signed by Butler if the UNSCOM 218 inspection was going to be conducted. Charles Duelfer agreed to press Butler for a meeting before he left for New York. I waited in the Baghdad Monitoring and Verification Center. I got a call from Duelfer within the hour. 'Butler has agreed to have dinner with you tonight. Bring your documents, and be prepared to sell him again on the concept. He's going soft.'

To a casual observer, this would have looked like your typical business dinner, if a little on the relaxed side. Butler, the CEO, regaling his bored deputy and two attentive junior executives (I had brought Chris Cobb-Smith along), with tales of his latest corporate conquest. The difference was that instead of spread sheets, the bag at my side contained operational documents which, if executed, could very well trigger a regional war. But these documents seemed to be the furthest thing from Butler's mind as he told war stories about how crass and crude Tariq Aziz was.

The clock was ticking, and Butler's hour of departure was fast approaching, and still he exhibited no interest in moving on to the inspection. He was retelling his conversation about presidential sites, and Tariq Aziz's blunt refusal to consider inspections of these locations, when Duelfer, much to his credit, broke in. 'It would appear that Tariq Aziz built his own trap,' he said.

'Why would you say that?' Butler asked.

'Well, the Council seems intent on hanging tough on the issue of access,' Duelfer noted, 'and Tariq Aziz's statement is an outright challenge to the will of the Council. If we call Tariq Aziz's bluff by sending an inspection team in to take on the issue of access, including presidential sites, the Council would have no choice but to back us up.'

Butler scowled. 'Would it?' he said. 'It seems to me that the Council could very well seek to avoid a confrontation over the issue of access, and leave us in a very difficult situation.'

I was surprised by what I was seeing. Far from the cocky Richard Butler who strutted the hallways in New York proclaiming the modalities 'dead on arrival', the man before me was pensive, cautious, uncertain of himself. I started briefing him on the planned inspection, but while he appeared to be listening, he wasn't responding. His mind was obviously on how he was going to explain to the USA that he had failed to kill the sensitive-site modalities. We sat around the table, four men, waiting for something to happen to break the silence.

As if on cue, Duelfer's cell phone rang, and he took the call, leaving the table for privacy. A few moments later, he returned, a big smile on his face. 'That was Bruce Reidel, over at the National Security Council.' Reidel was a former Pentagon official who ran the Iraqi desk at the NSC. He and

Duelfer were long-time friends and colleagues. 'He said Sandy Berger had reviewed the target list, and the US was giving us the green light to go with the inspection.'

At this, Butler seemed to perk up. 'Did he really?' he asked.

All of a sudden our table was a bustle of activity. Target folders were extracted from my bag, and I walked Butler through the specifics of each operation. As we progressed, he seemed to regain some of his lost spirit. I passed the target folders over to him, and he signed each page where indicated. Our first day of inspection would be 18 December, the day of Butler's briefing to the Security Council. Given the eight-hour time difference, New York would have wind of any fallout from the inspection prior to that meeting.

Dinner was over. I had my signatures, and Butler had a plane to catch. He wished Cobb-Smith and me good luck before excusing himself. Duelfer hung back. 'Well, we're still moving forward,' he noted. 'I'll do my best to keep his resolve up.'

I shook Duelfer's hand. 'Let us do this inspection,' I said. 'You won't be upset with the results.'

Cobb-Smith and I headed to the bar for a few beers before we, too, headed for bed. He was excited, but also sobered by what he had seen. 'Well, I guess I can tell everyone now how we started a war,' he said. 'I didn't realize Butler took orders from the Americans, though.'

I had to laugh at that one. 'I don't know where he is coming from, Chris. One minute he's hot, the next he's cold. One minute [US Secretary of State] Albright's telling him to hold back, the next [US National Security Advisor] Berger's saying to charge forward. Who knows?' I took a sip of my beer. 'But at least now you have some insight into why the past few months have been so screwed up. In defense of Richard, it's really gotten quite political.'

Two days into the UNSCOM 218 inspection, disaster struck, in the form of a phone call from Richard Butler. 'There is much concern here that UNSCOM not be seen as deliberately provoking a crisis,' he told me. 'It seems the Americans are concerned that your inspection will be played as a US effort to trigger a war.' I knew what was coming next. 'The Secretary of State herself has asked me to hold off on any inspections of presidential areas for the time being.'

I protested this decision. Butler was apologetic, but firm. 'It simply isn't good timing, Scott,' he said. 'Madeline needs time to test her agreement with

Primakov, and doesn't want it to appear as if UNSCOM was deliberately sabotaging the effort. The Secretary of State has told me that the United States simply isn't prepared to support a major confrontation with Iraq at this time,' Butler said. 'She says that after the New Year the Americans will be in a stronger position militarily and politically to back UNSCOM up as much as required.' Butler's voice softened. 'I promise you,' he said. 'You will be able to carry out your inspection, with all of the sites included, in early January once the US is better prepared to support us.'

A few moments later, I took a call from Charles Duelfer, who told me pretty much the same thing. 'What about Berger and the NSC approving our mission?' I asked. Duelfer was bitter. 'Who the hell knows who is talking to who around here anymore. You're screwed, Scott. Make the best of it.' The UNSCOM 218 inspection was, to all intents and purposes, over. It had never really had a chance.

Before I left Iraq, the Serb again requested a 'walk' together. 'Where are you going with all of this, Mr. Scott?' he asked. 'All of Iraq wonders. We mobilized for your arrival. Minister Council's were convened to discuss your mission. We opened ourselves to you in September, letting you meet Kamal Mustafa and the Special Guard officers. We think you have all the information you need to solve your problem. Why are you not advancing your case? Why this inspection?'

I knew the time was past for a recitation of my concerns over concealment; I had made them many times before, and the Serb could recite them from heart. 'We live in a political world,' I said. 'Things aren't as easy to do as you might think.'

The Serb nodded his head. 'If the sun is setting on the logic of your investigation, and politics has become the key element driving this adventure, then I am afraid that this will not end well.'

Unfortunately, I shared that dark assessment.

Chapter 21
The Death of Inspections
January–August 1998

By the end of 1997, the Mukhabarat's counter-UNSCOM unit had, by their own account, successfully penetrated almost every aspect of the UNSCOM operation in New York and Baghdad. They were able to monitor an inspection's development from inception to implementation. With French technical assistance, provided via the French economic liaison in Baghdad, they were able to listen in on all 'secure' phone calls made between Iraq and New York, as well as any made between Iraq and the capitals of nations providing the inspectors. Charles Duelfer, in particular, provided excellent intelligence every time he placed a call from the Baghdad Monitoring and Verification Center's 'secure' phone. The Iraqis had tape after tape of Duelfer speaking to US government officials and, according to the reports of these conversations, Charles's real mission was to facilitate US policy, not to pursue the mandate of the Council.[1]

I strongly suspected this to be the case, and was determined to do something about it. I had approached Burt and the CIA to open a safe house in New York so that the Concealment Investigations Unit could have some place secure to work, plan inspections, and store sensitive data. Burt continued to promise to support the idea, but kept coming back to me with questions such as, 'What is it you and your people plan to do with such a facility?' Incredulous, all I could do was say, 'Our job.'

Doing 'our job' was foremost in my mind. Richard Butler supported the resumption of inspections and by 11 January 1998 I was back in Iraq, leading the UNSCOM 227 inspection. I had been able to convince both the USA and the UK that the counter-concealment plan still needed to be fully tested, and all personnel and capabilities had been reassembled under the capable leadership of Chris Cobb-Smith. In addition to the normal slate of 'concealment' targets, I had planned, in great secrecy, a preemptive inspection of a facility next to the UNSCOM Baghdad Headquarters in the Canal Hotel, which we believed was housing a communications intercept station run by the Mukhabarat. This inspection was carried out, only to find an abandoned 'language training lab' formerly operated by the Ministry of Tourism (the Canal Hotel had been a training facility for that ministry before being turned over to the United Nations). At the time we assumed we had hit a dry hole, but this was not the case. Three days before that inspection, based upon intelligence received from their agent in New York, the Mukhabarat evacuated its intercept station next to the Canal Hotel – which turned out to be the very 'language training lab' we ended up inspecting. I knew how closely protected our plans for that particular inspection were, which meant that if UNSCOM had been penetrated in New York, it had been done at a very senior level.[2]

The next phase of the inspection was built on US intelligence claims that Iraq had used live human subjects for biological weapons testing in 1995. The subjects in question were apparently taken from the notorious Abu Ghraib prison. I decided to inspect three separate prisons, including Abu Ghraib, looking for any documents that might indicate such experiments had in fact occurred. The inspections provided no evidence that Iraq had done what the USA claimed. They did uncover the horrific reality of the prison system of Saddam Hussein's Iraq, where everything from execution chambers to children's prisons were discovered. Our job, however, was not to judge the human rights record of Iraq, but rather to implement disarmament, and the sites inspected had nothing to do with WMD. We finished the first inspection with a visit to the *Amn al-Amm* Headquarters, where I grilled the leadership of Saddam's secret police on their potential involvement in transporting WMD.

The Iraqi government did not react well to what they viewed as an unprecedented intrusion into their internal affairs, and that night ordered that all cooperation with my inspection be stopped. We spent three more days waiting for Iraq to change its mind.

But the inspection was over. Charles Duelfer called me, and instructed me not to make a big deal out the situation. 'Come back home, and everything will be explained,' he said. I made a brief appearance before the press, where I announced the withdrawal of the team and told the assembled journalists, 'I'll be back.'

Once again, Madeleine Albright and Sandy Berger had got cold feet about confronting the Iraqis over the issue of inspector access. Maintaining Security Council unity over economic sanctions trumped supporting disarmament, at least as far as the USA's Iraq policy was concerned.

But the news got worse. The CIA, working closely with Charles Duelfer, finally issued a formal memorandum detailing the procedures to be used when taking U-2 film to Israel – the film had to be under the control of an American photographic interpreter assigned to UNSCOM, had to be stored at the US Embassy, and no prints could be made. We were already storing the film at the US Embassy, and the issue of prints, although limiting, could be overcome by good note taking and the USA agreeing to provide prints after the fact. However, the requirement of an American CIA agent being present, while not objectionable, meant that we were now prisoner to the CIA, who never provided anybody to fill this position. The U-2 cooperation with Israel, one of the most productive intelligence activities UNSCOM had ever engaged in, was finished.

The issue of Ahmed Chalabi and the INC reemerged during this time. Charles Duelfer had provided me with some contact information on how to reach Chalabi, who was by this time maintaining dual residencies in London's prosperous Mayfair district, and Washington's equally affluent Georgetown. Between my inspection activity and Chalabi's transatlantic travels, finding a date convenient for both of us was proving difficult, but finally we agreed upon a meeting in London, on 24 January 1998.

I flew to London, accompanied by Gary, the Special Collection Element team leader, and met with Ahmed Chalabi and his intelligence chief. Chalabi was courteous, and seemed anxious to help out UNSCOM with its mission. Upon greeting me, he asked me how I liked the intelligence on the Jabal Makhul palace from the defector we had debriefed in Germany in November 1997. I was taken aback, because up until that moment I had always assumed the Iraqi defector was an American asset operating under German protection. Chalabi corrected my assumption. 'He is controlled by me. He is one of my spies.' Chalabi was clearly trying to impress me with his bona fides. 'I have a large network of spies inside Iraq, including inside the Iraqi government itself,' Chalabi told me. 'I can get you any information you need. Just tell me what you want.'

This should have sent alarm bells sounding in my head. In the intelligence world, one never gives away the complete picture of what you know and what you don't know; this too easily allows you to be manipulated by sources which miraculously 'confirm' data you already have while filling in the gaps in the intelligence picture. However, I was under pressure from Charles Duelfer to make this new relationship work, and I proceeded to brief Chalabi on UNSCOM's understanding about what Iraq might be hiding. This included speculation about the possible existence of mobile biological laboratories and agent production facilities. Chalabi took all of this information in. 'I will get back to you soon,' he said. We exchanged secure e-mail addresses, complete with cryptographic keys that enabled us to communicate without others reading what we were sending.

Within three days of our meeting, Chalabi started streaming information to UNSCOM via this e-mail link. Some of this data reinforced information we already had. Other data was new. But I was taken aback by the fact that the vast majority of the new 'intelligence' provided by Chalabi was directly contradicted by what we knew from being on the ground in Iraq. His descriptions of facilities and organizations simply didn't match reality. And when we did use his intelligence to direct an inspection team, we ran into the same result – none of the information was even close to reality. Read at a distance, by someone with no firsthand experience in Iraq, Chalabi's data appeared spectacular. But once subjected to the harsh light of reality, it was quickly exposed as fraudulent. We continued to receive e-mail data packages from Chalabi throughout 1998, but after a while we no longer treated this data as anything more than a curiosity. Chalabi had lost all credibility with everyone in UNSCOM save Charles Duelfer, who continued to press me to make use of Chalabi's material.

When, several years after leaving UNSCOM, I was to read through the intelligence provided by Chalabi's 'source' ('Curveball'), which formed the centerpiece of the Bush administration's case for war, I was struck by just how similar this data was to some of the speculative 'intelligence gaps' I had provided to Ahmed Chalabi back in 1998. This was just before inspectors left Iraq for good, meaning that none of the claims made by his 'sources' could be tested.

I didn't get too much time to dwell on Chalabi's flakiness at the time. Larger issues were brewing. Over recent months, many in the Clinton administration had started to view Iraqi actions towards the weapons inspectors as a legitimate cause for military action, and the Pentagon had begun to deploy military units into the Persian Gulf region for this purpose. However, the Clinton administration had completely bungled the presentation of their arguments in the media, culminating in the public humiliation of Madeleine Albright, Sandy Berger and Secretary of Defense William Cohen at a nationally-televised 'roundtable discussion' on the Iraq issue.

As a result, there was no domestic support for military action. The Clinton administration needed a diplomatic 'out' to help them backtrack, and turned to Kofi Annan and the United Nations for help. Madeleine Albright informed Kofi Annan that the USA would support any agreement that got the inspectors back to work in Iraq. Thus empowered, the secretary-general flew to Baghdad, and on 23 February 1998 concluded an agreement known as 'Memorandum of Understanding' which established specific rules for the conduct of inspections of sites deemed 'sensitive' by the Iraqi government, including a special protocol for what were considered 'visits' by inspectors to presidential palaces.

Kofi Annan got his diplomatic victory, but the Memorandum of Understanding had a huge political fallout in Washington. In the aftermath of the failed Butler visit to Baghdad in January 1998, the Clinton administration had embarked on a bipartisan effort to gain Congressional support for a military strike against Iraq, arguing that the Iraqis were committed to deceiving the inspectors. Now they were having to claim that the Memorandum of Understanding would solve the Iraq problem. Having reached out to the Republicans in the House of Representatives and the US Senate, their own hawkish sentiments were being turned back on them. Albright's solution was to design a 'test' for the new agreement which the Iraqis would be bound to fail, thus providing the administration with fresh public justification for military action.

Richard Butler needed to come up with a 'test' inspection quickly, and for that he turned to me, since I had had more experience at 'testing' the Iraqis over the years than anyone else. I had been closely following the diplomatic intervention of Kofi Annan and, by the time he returned from Baghdad, I had already thought of ways to robustly test the Iraqi commitments contained in the Memorandum of Understanding. I briefed my proposal to Charles Duelfer, who in turn relayed its main components to the National Security Council staff.

To see whether the Iraqis really intended to cooperate, I had prepared a list of sites which were legitimate from an arms control perspective (meaning UNSCOM had credible information that linked these locations to proscribed activity), but which were known to be sensitive from the Iraqi perspective. It was important that the sites chosen were justified by reasonable arms control concerns, otherwise my 'test' would make the weapons inspectors seem like an arm of the US government. I proposed a two-phased approach to the inspection, the first phase of which would include going to sites previously attempted to be inspected by UNSCOM, and the second to entirely new sites, including several which I believed fell under the category of 'presidential palaces' but which had not been declared by the Iraqis as such.

I was building a trap from which I believed the Iraqis could not extricate themselves. Once the Iraqis had agreed to allowing unfettered inspections of the known sites of interest (which Charles Duelfer and I believed would be fully evacuated of anything of interest prior to the arrival of the inspection team in Iraq), we would then proceed on with inspection of all the new and highly sensitive sights. Included in my 'shopping list' were three 'presidential palaces', which the Iraqis had failed to declare out of bounds. Duelfer and I were convinced that the Iraqis would seek to re-designate these sites as 'presidential' upon the arrival of the inspection team, allowing UNSCOM and the USA to declare the entire Kofi Annan Memorandum of Understanding, including the presidential site visit 'protocol', as null and void, all the while retaining the integrity of the inspection process.

The Clinton administration fell in love with the concept of a robust 'test' of the Kofi Annan agreement. However, my proposal was deemed too 'elegant'. 'Too many legalities,' Charles Duelfer told me. 'We need to simplify it.' What Charles Duelfer wanted to do was add a new site to my initial list of inspections – the Iraqi Ministry of Defense. Bruce Reidel, a senior Middle East expert on the National Security Council, had proposed this addition, and told Duelfer that it had the support of the entire Clinton administration. 'But we have no WMD-related reason to inspect,' I protested to Duelfer. 'Tariq Aziz gave us the reason when he told Butler that to try and inspect the Ministry of Defense meant war,' Duelfer replied. 'We cannot allow the Iraqis to pick and choose which sites we can or cannot inspect. This is about process, not substance.' And so the Ministry of Defense was added onto the list of inspection sites, and my non-declared presidential palaces removed, together with all other locations not yet attempted for inspection. The decisive 'test' desired by the Clinton administration would hinge on one site – the Ministry of Defense.

Two days after Kofi Annan's return to New York, Richard Butler, Charles Duelfer and I flew down to Washington for consultations with the US government. Butler went to the State Department, where he met one-on-one with Madeleine Albright. Charles Duelfer and I headed for the White House, where I was to brief the National Security Council on the inspection plan in the White House Situation Room. I recalled wryly the acrimony that had filled the room last time I was there, in the aftermath of the UNSCOM 182 fiasco. This time the atmosphere was quite different. The briefing went well, with everyone excited about the plan until I raised the issue of timing. 'In order to prevent the Iraqis from raising any objections,' I noted, 'we will need to approach other nations besides the United States and Great Britain to contribute the bulk of the team's inspectors. This will take time.' 'How much time will this take?' asked the deputy national security advisor, Jim Steinberg, who was chairing the meeting. 'About two weeks,' I responded, much to the disappointment of the attendees. 'Actually, we need the inspection to reach its decisive moment by March 8th,' Steinberg responded. Charles Duelfer spoke up, cutting me off. 'We can do that,' he said. Steinberg then asked who would lead the inspection team. I always viewed this issue as the exclusive prerogative of the executive chairman, but again Charles Duelfer jumped in: 'We believe the best candidate for this position is Scott Ritter.'

Shortly after my return from the White House briefing, I was formally notified that I would, in fact, be the chief inspector for the upcoming inspection, and was summoned to the office of Bill Richardson, the US Ambassador to the UN. I sat in the plush leather upholstered arm chair, looking around at my surroundings. Richardson's office was outfitted with various mementos reflecting his former status as a Democratic Congressman from the State of New Mexico, including a large yellow and red state flag adorning the far wall. We all sat around a small coffee table. Richard Butler sat next to Richardson, an easel with a mounted erasable whiteboard between them.

Butler had called me in to impress on me the urgency of the situation. 'We need an accelerated inspection timetable, Scott,' he explained. He made it clear that this came straight from Clinton's national security advisor, Sandy Berger. Using a marker on the easel, Butler drew a chart on the whiteboard listing two timelines. One he labeled 'Inspection', the other 'Military Action'. Down the side of the board he wrote out the dates in March from the first to the fifteenth. Butler circled the number 8. 'We need to have a crisis with Iraq by this date,' he said, tapping the board with his pen, 'so that the US can complete its bombing campaign by this date,' his pen moving to circle the number 15. 'I have been told that the US has a bombing campaign prepared which needs to be completed in time for the Muslim religious holiday that begins on 15 March.'

I sat there, stunned. What I was observing was nothing less than total collusion between a United Nations official, Richard Butler, and the USA, over military action that had not been sanctioned by the Security Council. 'What if the Iraqis cooperate?' I asked.

'Tariq Aziz has pronounced the Ministry of Defense as a red line,' Butler responded. 'He can't afford to back down without losing face.'

Under most circumstances, Butler's statement would have compelled me either to speak up, or to resign. However, I was in the middle of a gigantic struggle over my viability as an UNSCOM inspector. While Sandy Berger and Secretary of State Madeleine Albright were keen on this inspection going forward (in their view, it would pave the way for decisive military action that might enable the US government to declare inspections dead in the face of Iraqi obstruction), they were not happy with me leading it. In this, they were joined by the secretary-general, Kofi Annan, who had implored Richard Butler to select a chief inspector with a 'softer touch'.

The fact was, however, that for this inspection there simply was no other option. No one had been so deeply involved in the complexities of the concealment issue, or knew so well the data on the sites and materials being looked for. If I bowed out, there was simply no one who could fill my shoes on such short notice. I didn't like it, but felt at the time that I had no choice but to execute the mission as best I could.

Bill Richardson, who didn't get on with Madeleine Albright and disagreed with many of her policy decisions, also realized that no one else could do the job. He helped convince Richard Butler to keep me on as chief inspector, despite Albright's instructions to the contrary. Once the team arrived in Bahrain, however, Albright exploded, and ordered Richard Butler to remove me as the chief inspector. 'He can train the team in Bahrain,' she told Richard, 'and advise them once they are in Iraq. But he cannot go in.'[3] However, when the UNSCOM 227 team was informed of this, they protested en masse, sending Richard Butler a letter informing him that if I was not the chief inspector, there would be no inspection.[4] None of my deputies was willing to step in as my replacement under these circumstances. Faced with this rebellion, Butler again reversed himself and, against the wishes of the Secretary of State, authorized me to lead the team into Iraq.

The easy part went smoothly enough. In terms of it being a test of inspection modalities, my mission was proceeding fine. Finally, we had but one last challenge before us. On 8 March, as ordered, I led my team to the Iraqi Ministry of Defense, where we were immediately stopped by Iraqi soldiers. I radioed back to our communications center that access had been denied. As well as notifying the UNSCOM chairman, the center placed another phone call, this one to a secret CIA team in Manama, Bahrain. The Iraqis' intransigence was reported, which was in turn passed on by the CIA team to the headquarters of the US 5th Fleet, also in Manama. Admiral Thomas Fargo, the commander of the 5th Fleet, was standing by with his battle staff, waiting for this communication. On his order, dozens of naval vessels, destroyers and submarines plying the waters of the Persian Gulf, were placed on high alerts. Each vessel contained numerous highly lethal, and extremely accurate, cruise missiles.

Also cruising in the warm waters of the Gulf were American aircraft carriers, giant floating cities, which were capable of launching dozens of modern aircraft, each armed with laser-guided munitions capable of precise destruction of designated targets. Admiral Fargo's order prompted the aircraft carriers to begin loading bombs and missiles onto fueled aircraft, while onboard pilots and aircrew were issued their initial briefings on strike locations. Similar briefings were taking place at US Air Force facilities in Bahrain, Saudi Arabia, Kuwait and Qatar, where dozens of fighter-bombers and other combat support aircraft were deployed, awaiting instructions.

In Kuwait, Admiral Fargo's orders sent elite commando forces into motion, including the dispatch of special helicopter-borne teams into the deserts of Iraq, where they would await orders either to rescue any aircrew that might be shot down by Iraqi air defenses, or the rescue of any UN inspectors that might be taken hostage by the Iraqis.

On my team outside the Defense Ministry was an American commando from Delta Force, the covert US Army hostage rescue unit, who had secret communications devices and homing beacons secreted on his person that would assist in any potential rescue operation. We also had a pair of elite Australian Special Air Service commandos, part of a larger deployment of the Australian SAS into Kuwait, where they assisted Delta Force and other US commandos in preparing for special operations inside Iraq.

The Special Collection Element, led by Gary, was also hard at work. The same frequencies monitored by the British intercept operators on behalf of the UN inspectors were also used by the senior Iraqi leadership and their security detachments, enabling anyone listening in to determine the precise location and activity of those being listened to. In addition to notifying my inspection team of suspicious concealment-related activity, the British operators also fed the CIA team at Gateway information about the location of senior Iraqi officials, including those closest to the Iraqi president. Thus, in addition to listening to Tariq Aziz, the Iraqi deputy prime minister, discuss the effort by my team to inspect the Iraqi Defense Ministry with Abid Hamid Mahmoud, the secretary and closest bodyguard to Saddam Hussein, the CIA team was able to pinpoint their respective locations, sending these coordinates to Admiral Fargo's staff, who in turn had them programmed into the guidance computers of the cruise missiles being prepared for launch.

It seemed that Madeleine Albright and Sandy Berger would have their war, after all. And if war came, the CIA was bound and determined to take out as many of the senior Iraqi leadership, up to and including Saddam Hussein, as possible, thereby accomplishing at long last its presidential directive for regime change in Iraq.

It was while all this military and diplomatic activity was going on that I, sitting in the Ministry of Defense car park, had begun to seriously question what I and my team were doing at the center of it all. I'd been waiting in my Nissan for a while, when Amer Rashid, now the oil minister and a senior spokesperson on WMD issues, arrived on scene, driven in an immaculate black Mercedes Benz Sedan. 'What are you doing here, Mr. Ritter?' he asked, as he exited from his vehicle. 'What is it you want to accomplish?'

I pointed over to the Ministry of Defense building. 'I have designated this site for inspection, and in accordance with the terms agreed upon in the Memorandum of Understanding between Iraq and the secretary-general, I am demanding immediate, unrestricted access.'

Amer Rashid's eyes narrowed to slits. 'This is impossible,' he said. 'You know very well that this site touches upon the most sensitive aspects of

Iraq's national security. Iraq will never allow this site to be inspected, even if the consequences are war.'

It was like a script being played out before my very eyes. We arrive at the site, we declare our intent to inspect, the Iraqis refuse, and the war begins. It seemed as if events were on automatic pilot. I didn't argue the point, only telling Amer Rashid that I would be reporting back to the executive chairman that 'the Memorandum of Understanding was dead.' Those words, as if by magic, changed everything. Amer Rashid went to his Sedan, and placed a phone call from a mobile secure phone, using one of the radio frequencies the SCE was monitoring back at the Baghdad Monitoring and Verification Center. According to the transcripts of the ensuing conversation, Tariq Aziz was taken back by my sudden pronouncement. 'What does Mr. Ritter mean by "dead",' he asked Amer Rashid to find out. Soon the entire secure phone network was abuzz with my pronouncement of the 'death' of the Memorandum of Understanding. Abid Hamid Mahmoud, the presidential secretary to Saddam Hussein, asked Tariq Aziz about what was happening. Apparently I wasn't playing the game the Iraqis had envisioned.

Amer Rashid came back to me. 'Look, we do not want a crisis. This is a very sensitive matter, and we need to work things out.' I was ready to depart from the site, having ordered all inspectors back to their vehicles. I gestured towards the Ministry of Defense building. 'My instructions are to inspect that building. Every second my team remains locked outside these gates is time in which I cannot guarantee the integrity of the site. If you are willing to allow my inspectors to secure the perimeter of the Ministry of Defense facility, in order to prevent anything or anybody from entering or exiting the site, I will report this back to the executive chairman as a positive step, and see how he responds. If not,' I concluded, 'I will have no choice but to depart the site, thereby condemning the Memorandum of Understanding to death.'

Amer Rashid didn't even blink. He turned to the soldiers manning the gate, and barked out an order in Arabic. The soldiers immediately lowered the 'dragon's teeth' barrier, and swung the gate open. Amer Rashid turned to me. 'Please, enter the facility, and secure your perimeter. I promise nothing will be removed from this site without your permission.' Amer Rashid looked me in the eye. 'And please, Mr. Scott,' he said. 'No more talk of killing the Memorandum of Understanding.'

I ordered my inspectors inside the Ministry of Defense compound, where we immediately established a 360-degree perimeter around the building, securing all exits. I established a communications center of my own in the ministry parking lot, setting up a satellite phone link where I could speak to New York and Bahrain via a secure line. Madeleine Albright, Kofi Annan, Richard Butler and Admiral Fargo were all waiting for the order to go to war, but they weren't going to get it just yet.

Amer Rashid and I talked through the procedures that had been agreed on between Richard Butler and Tariq Aziz in December 1997. We eventually reached an understanding, and the crisis was defused. We entered with eighteen inspectors, two more than the sixteen-inspector ceiling that Tariq Aziz had told Amer Rashid was as high as the Iraqi side was prepared to go. The team scoured the Ministry of Defense building from top to bottom, staying until 4 a.m. the next morning. Any issue which touched on the national security of Iraq, such as inspecting the Minister of Defense's office, or the National Military Operations Center, was put in my hands, and Amer Rashid and I would do the inspection together.

Amer Rashid and the deputy minister of defense, who oversaw our work, broke for dinner, and invited Chris Cobb-Smith and me to join them. While we ate rice and kebab, Amer Rashid grilled me about the inspection, and my work overall. It was familiar territory which the two of us had been going over for years. 'How can you trust those who provide you information?' he asked. 'How do you protect yourself from their agendas?'

I pondered that for a moment, and then responded: 'After doing this for so long, I think UNSCOM is in a position to be able to filter out the bad information from the good. We are very aware of what the policies are of the nations which support us, and we take this into consideration before acting.'

Amer Rashid was concerned about the inspection of the Ministry of Defense. 'We know America would lick your feet if you could only start a war,' he said. 'We are grateful that you are here as an inspector, not as a representative of your government.' He then raised an issue that took me by surprise. 'And how do you find the Israeli intelligence you are getting? Has it been helpful?'

I had established a relationship with the Iraqis, over the years, based on trust. My policy was never to lie to the Iraqis about what I was doing when it came to my official UN work. 'Yes,' I said, 'the Israelis have been very helpful, so much so that it will be difficult for them to say that Iraq has weapons of mass destruction, since UNSCOM has investigated every lead and found no such weapons. The last hurdle is concealment.'

Amer translated my words to the deputy minister of defense, who raised his eyebrows, smiled and nodded. Amer Rashid turned back to face me. 'You are an honest man, Mr. Scott. Iraq appreciates this, even though your own government does not.'

In the end, nothing proscribed was found at the Ministry of Defense. Madeleine Albright, in France, was furious when the French told her that according to their sources, Iraq and UNSCOM were getting along famously, and the inspectors were actually finished with the inspection.

The American military had been placed on high alert, and everyone in the US chain of command was confident that there would at last be a window for military action against Iraq. Our inspection diplomacy with Amer Rashid, put an end to these plans. I was no longer viewed in Washington as an asset that needed to be managed, but rather as a problem that needed to be removed.

So it was Charles Duelfer who led the next team into Iraq, this time to test the new modalities for conducting presidential site 'visits'. While I was involved in training the team in Bahrain on inspection methodology and tactics, the CIA had taken responsibility for the actual inspection planning. The CIA had also inserted several structural engineers onto the team, who evaluated each one of Saddam's palaces from the standpoint of a potential aerial attack. Charles Duelfer supported all these activities. While Duelfer later complained that the inspections were 'a sham', saying the Iraqis had too much time to prepare (and, hence, the inspectors found nothing), it was in fact Duelfer perpetrating a sham, turning UNSCOM into little more than an espionage tool to be used by the CIA to spy on Saddam Hussein.

Another charade was acted out on my return to New York. Richard Butler, who had almost caved in to the pressure placed on him by Albright to remove me as chief inspector, introduced me to Kofi Annan, who had earlier called me a 'cowboy' and who had felt my presence in Iraq would be controversial. I was now being asked to brief the secretary-general about the mission. Kofi Annan praised the work of my team, and (this I could barely believe I was hearing) my diplomatic skills.

But I had bigger issues to deal with than Richard Butler's and Kofi Annan's political games. After shutting down the U-2 cooperation with Israel, the next step for Steve Richter was to shut down the Concealment

Investigations Unit's SIGINT operation. Through Gary, my British communications intercept specialist, I found out that the reason the CIA had agreed to support the enhanced SCE operation in March and April was to fine tune a national collection resource, a Vortex spy satellite, that was scheduled to be launched sometime in late summer 1998. The National Security Agency, however, was not happy about such an effective intelligence resource as the Special Collection Element being controlled by UNSCOM. They leaned heavily on the British to withdraw their support for the program, which effectively killed it as an UNSCOM resource.

I made a last-ditch effort to save the SCE, flying to Israel in April with the DAT tapes collected by the SCE during the presidential site visits. Moshe Ponkovsky had left his position in External Affairs, and my new point of contact was an Army Lieutenant Colonel, Jacov Katz (pseudonym). I had requested that Katz arrange a meeting with the new director of research for the *Aman*, Brigadier General Amos Gilad, who had taken over from General Ami-Dror.

I asked General Gilad if the Israelis would agree to provide the actual transcripts of the SCE intercepts, so that I might make a bid to save the SCE operation. 'Without the transcripts, I cannot justify continuing to provide Israel with these tapes,' I said. I told General Gilad that I was working with the Australians to find replacements for the British as SCE operators, and if the Israelis would agree to process the information collected by the SCE, and provide actual transcripts to UNSCOM, then I might be able to convince Richard Butler to keep the program alive, regardless of the American actions. General Gilad promised to do his best.

With inspections pretty much put on hold following the presidential site visits, UNSCOM found itself stagnant for most of the month of April. Operation 'Air Bag, as the joint British-UNSCOM-Romanian effort to stymie the Iraqi procurement effort in Romania was known in MI6, proceeded slowly.

We knew that Dr. Hamid al-Azawi, an Iraqi missile specialist, was due to travel out of Iraq to meet a representative of the arms manufacturers Aerofina. But we didn't know when or where. Suddenly, in early May, we got a breakthrough. An MI6-controlled spy working inside Saddam's presidential palace, who went by the codename 'Sprint', made contact with his MI6 handler in Jordan. That day, the handler sent a top-secret cable back to MI6 headquarters in London saying that Dr. Hamid had left Iraq with an operating budget of $900,000, and had been personally authorized by the Presidential Economic Office to 'close the deal' with Aerofina.[5]

In Romania, surveillance teams were placed on high alert, awaiting the arrival of the Iraq delegation. On 15 May, as predicted by Sprint, Dr. Hamid and his team finally made their appearance in Bucharest. Romanian intelligence agents planted in customs saw his baggage as it went through the security conveyer belts, and noted some interesting-looking documents. The Romanian agents tracked the Iraqis back to their hotel, and made sure listening devices were planted in their rooms. Through listening in on the Iraqis' phone calls, Romanian intelligence found out where they were due to meet Aerofina the next day, and planted video cameras there. As the Iraqis slept that night, an MI6 agent, known only as Q4G4, crept into their rooms and took digital photographs of the documents identified by Romanian intelligence in customs.

The next day, when the Iraqis met the 'Aerofina' representative (in reality an intelligence agent), they bragged about their ability to circumvent international sanctions, and negotiated terms for the delivery of ballistic missile components from Aerofina.

The trap was set. Now all we needed to do was to figure out how we would take advantage of these developments. Despite all of the setbacks involving my work with UNSCOM, by early June I believed I had a plan that might allow me to get back on track regarding the concealment investigation. Thanks to Operation Air Bag, UNSCOM could now expose the covert efforts of the Iraqi government to acquire ballistic missile technology in direct violation of Security Council resolutions.

I felt we needed to capitalize on any momentum generated by the Romanian affair to focus the Security Council on the issue of concealment and the need for Iraq to come clean with the documents and information required for UNSCOM to verify their disarmament declarations. Without this new information, UNSCOM was deadlocked.

On 8 June, I met with Richard Butler and Charles Duelfer in the UN cafeteria, the most secure place we could come up with to discuss my proposals. We grabbed a corner table, away from prying ears, and I began my presentation. The Romanian option was an easy sell. It was still in the exploratory stage, and Butler readily signed off on my travel authorization to go to London and Tel Aviv to coordinate with the British and Israeli authorities on how best to proceed.

I also raised the issue of the communications intercept program. The

SCE team, which Gary and his British operators had run effectively for over two years, had been shut down by the CIA. Now the CIA wanted to replace the SCE team with its own capability, which would be run outside of UNSCOM's control. I told Butler and Duelfer that this was tantamount to spying, and that I wanted nothing to do with it.

For the first time, the two men seemed uncomfortable with what I had to say. I knew they had both been in contact with senior officials from the US government about the SCE, and that they were under strict orders not to discuss this matter with me. They mulled over my words. Duelfer spoke first. 'This is a very sensitive matter, Scott. We're trying to work things out. The issue centers around control of the intelligence collected from this effort. It's clear that as the head of the concealment team, you are the only one who can provide the operational and logistic support to any collection effort in Baghdad.'

Butler nodded in agreement. 'This is just a temporary measure. The goal is to go to a fully automated system by September which is independent of UNSCOM. We just need to hold down the fort until then, and we can't do it without you.'

'I still don't like the idea of UNSCOM being part of something it doesn't fully control. Such control has been the foundation of this project since its inception. I think this is a bad idea. However,' I said, 'it is your decision to make. As your specialist, however, I'm saying this is not the right thing to do. But if you instruct me to support this new idea, I will. Just don't expect me to endorse it. I think we should be looking for an alternative that we have more control over.'

'What do you want to do, Scott?' Butler asked.

'I'd like to keep at least some of the old SCE capability in place so that we can keep the Israeli initiative alive. With your permission, I'd like to raise this with the Israelis during my upcoming visit.'

Butler looked over at Duelfer, who shrugged. 'OK, raise it. When you get back, we'll make a final decision. We should keep all options open.'[6]

I flew to London, and met with MI6 about Operation Air Bag at their Vauxhall headquarters. After we finished, the Don and I headed off to lunch at a posh restaurant in London, where we met with two other MI6 officers overseeing a psychological warfare effort, known as Operation Mass Appeal. Mass Appeal served as a focal point for passing MI6 intelligence on Iraq to the media, both in the UK and around the world. The goal was to help shape public opinion about Iraq and the threat posed by WMD. The focus of the Mass Appeal officers was on how we could exploit the Romanian operation in the media.

I brought them up to date on the Air Bag effort. 'If this goes as planned, then UNSCOM should be able to get some good press for a change.' The Don agreed.

The MI6 black propaganda specialists spoke up. 'We have some outlets in foreign newspapers – some editors and writers who work with us from time to time – where we can spread some material. We just need to be kept informed on what you are doing and when, so we can time the press releases accordingly.'

I looked over to the Don. 'I'll keep working this through the Flyfisher, then?' I asked. All agreed that was the best route.

I then proceeded to an MI6 safe house off of St. James's Park. The safe house was an old home that had been taken over by MI6 during the Second World War. It had the feel of old England, with plush carpets, oriental rugs, leather upholstered furniture, and large curtains and window dressings. I was ushered through security, and led upstairs, where I found Sarah Parsons, from Rockingham, and three of the Falconer's people sitting around a wooden table, examining documents. A four-person American delegation was also present, including Burt.

'The Fullback', one of the Falconer's agents, passed out folders stamped 'Top Secret', and a series of codewords identifying the material as extremely sensitive. Inside were photographs of drawings, documents and missile parts, the handiwork of the MI6 agent who had broken into the hotel room of Dr. Hamid and his fellow Iraqis in Bucharest. After allowing enough time for everyone to study the contents of the folder, the Fullback opened the discussion. 'Unfortunately, our analysis of the missile parts and drawings show that these are standard surface-to-air missile components, not SCUD as we had originally hoped for.'

Sarah Parsons spoke up. 'The question is, therefore, where do we go from here?'

One of the CIA officers spoke up. 'Clearly, this isn't what we had hoped for. If these were SCUD related, we'd have a clear-cut case for going to the Security Council. But now it is very ambiguous.'

'There is nothing ambiguous about this at all,' I said. 'We have here a clear case of Iraqi violation of Security Council resolutions. It doesn't matter that this isn't proscribed under 687. This is a violation of export-import controls and declaration requirements under 715. What the Iraqis are doing here is illegal. It's black and white. We've been waiting for something as clear cut as this to come up, and now it has. I don't see how we have any choice but to move forward.'

'Move forward how?' one of the American CIA officials asked.

'We stick with the plan. The British continue to press the Romanians for release of the audio and videotapes for use in the Council. I will try to get the Dutch to agree for the travel of the defector to New York to testify before the Council. And UNSCOM will work on preparing an inspection which capitalizes on this.'

'Your plan,' Sarah Parsons said, 'seems too complicated. Technically, you are correct. This appears to be a violation. But it is not the dramatic violation that we needed to sway the Council.'

'This may be the only violation we get,' I responded. 'The Iraqis have clearly stated that they are not cheating. We can prove otherwise.'

'The fear is that we will expend great resources in bringing this case to the Council, and in the end it won't impress,' she said. 'People may say "Is this all you've got?" We can't afford that kind of debate at the moment.'

'Here we have a clear example of cheating, a dramatic case of covert procurement run out of the presidential office in Baghdad,' I said. 'This case justifies everything UNSCOM has been doing over the past few years. It would silence the critics of our concealment investigations. It would legitimize our insistence on full access to all sites, including presidential. It could help galvanize support for UNSCOM in the Council like we haven't seen for years. And you don't want to go with it?'

Again Sarah Parsons responded. 'The fear is that the Council may not react the way you think they might. We can't afford that.'

I now knew the effort was lost. Air Bag was, to all intents and purposes, dead as a viable operation. And I was quickly losing my own viability as an inspector.

The meeting was over. The Fullback collected the documents, and the Americans made their way back to the US Embassy to report on what had transpired. Sarah Parsons wished me well, and left for her office. I was dejected. Air Bag was the last real operation I had going. More than that, it was the last cooperative effort between British intelligence and UNSCOM. By shutting down, the Brits were not only killing the operation, but acquiescing in the total US domination of UNSCOM.

From London I flew to Israel. Jacov Katz was at the airport in Tel Aviv to meet me. He drove me to the Israeli Military Intelligence headquarters, where I met with him and Roni Ortel, the Israeli technical intelligence specialist, on the second floor of the External Affairs building.

I brought Jacov and Roni up to speed on the developments in London. 'Maybe the best thing to do would be to simply stop the Aerofina deal,' Roni said. 'This would represent a victory of sorts.' I knew Roni was probably right.

Roni left for his office, and was replaced by Sharon, the communications intercept specialist from Unit 8200 who was now running the SCE cooperation instead of Dani. She had with her a sheaf of papers, which she handed to me. I looked down at the document, a verbatim transcript of Iraqi conversations intercepted by the SCE team during the presidential site inspections in April 1998.

Sharon and the analysts walked me through the document. They had some questions over some of the personalities who were being heard, and based upon my firsthand experience, I was able to clarify the picture. There was no doubt that we had penetrated the inner sanctum of Iraqi decision making. Tariq Aziz, Amer Rashid, Abid Hamid Mahmoud – we were eavesdropping on them all. The entire presidential security establishment was now an open book for us. All relevant Special Security Organization directorates – Security, Transportation, Communications – came to life on these pages as they responded to the activities of the inspectors. There were no 'smoking guns' in this transcript, given the nature of the inspection (no one expected to find anything related to WMD during the presidential site inspections; it had been strictly a political show).[7]

The Israeli transcript proved that the SCE had tapped into the decision-making cycle of the Iraqi leadership. If UNSCOM was going to carry out the kind of concealment-oriented inspection that I had outlined to the executive chairman for this July, then we would need this capability.

'This is fantastic,' I said, looking up from the document. I discussed my inspection plans for the future, including restarting the SCE so that UNSCOM could feed the Israelis more tapes, and thus produce more transcripts like the one I now held in my hands. The mood of the Israeli team suddenly turned dour.

Jacov spoke up. 'Your chairman is not the only one who has been subjected to pressure from the Americans. We, too, have been told that it isn't in our best interests to keep helping UNSCOM in this fashion.'

I had come to Israel to try and keep the SCE effort alive. The USA had just killed it. As one of the young Israeli analysts explained, 'We've been assured by the Americans that we will get the intelligence information from whatever arrangement the US puts together. We just can't share it with you or UNSCOM.'

Jacov was truly upset. He had been a deputy to Moshe Ponkovsky back in 1994, when I first came to Israel, and had witnessed our cooperation grow into something real and meaningful. He knew that what was transpiring now represented the end to it all.

I never felt more defeated. I spent that night visiting my old haunts. The Indian restaurant in Old Town Jaffa. Drinking a pint of Gold Star beer in the beach side pub of the Holiday Inn. Standing on the balcony of my hotel room, watching the waves crash into the sand of the Tel Aviv beachfront. In the morning I flew back to New York. It was to be my last trip to Israel.

I met with Richard Butler and Charles Duelfer upon my return from Israel to deliver the bad news. 'The Israelis have pulled out of the intelligence cooperation, citing US pressure,' I said, getting straight to the point once the room had emptied of the other inspectors.

I had brought with me the Israeli transcript of the April SCE mission. 'Look,' I started, passing the copy across the table, 'we finally got what we were looking for all along – complete access to the intelligence. It is every bit as good as we were hoping for,' I continued, 'and now, thanks to the Americans, even this is going to be denied to us.'

'That isn't any of our business,' Duelfer said.

'Of course it is,' I answered back. 'This was our project, designed to gain access to exactly the kind of information that the Israelis just provided. And now we're just going to roll over and let the Americans stop the whole show?'

'The Americans have a right to protect their own interests, Scott,' Duelfer noted.

'And we have an obligation to protect ours,' I snapped back. 'Or have you stopped wearing a "Blue Hat" altogether?' referring to our status as UN representatives. Duelfer and I eyed each other warily.

Sensing the tension, Butler intervened. 'I think we should realize that we're all on the same side here, Scott. This represents a very difficult issue. Charles and I have paid a visit to the NSA, and we've been assured that we will be given full access to the information we require to do our job, in accordance with our security clearances and need to know. We have also been assured that you will be provided with reports, too, that will assist you in doing your job. You just won't be given the same reports as us, because of your lack of security clearance.'

I fingered the Israeli transcript. 'Do you realize what you're saying? What I'm holding here is the raw data that would enable UNSCOM to finally get its hands around the issue of concealment, and you're giving it away, with no way of knowing that what you'll be getting from the Americans is the entire picture or not.' I turned to Duelfer. 'Remember when, at the beginning, the US said that there was nothing of value in this project? Over 900 hours of tape, and they couldn't find anything of value? What makes you so confident at this point in time that their analytical capabilities have improved to such an extent that you can jettison me and my team, when we're the ones who stuck with it and finally got the project to produce a result?'

Butler replied for Duelfer. 'It's politics, Scott. Sometimes we have to settle for the less than perfect scenario. In any case, we've been assured that we will get the information we need, and that nothing will be held back. You need to start looking at the big picture, and keep in mind that while this may represent a personal setback for you, it is actually the best means possible for moving the process forward.'

It seemed that I had just about overstayed my welcome as an inspector. The only thing that kept me 'viable', and as such prevented my resignation, was my continued working relationship with MI6. On 28 June, I was asked by the Flyfisher to come over to his office for a meeting. In the high-security area of the UK Mission's twentieth-floor office, the British spy passed me a file containing top-secret documents which detailed reporting from a human source inside Baghdad who claimed Iraq was hiding ballistic missile components in a Ba'ath Party headquarters in downtown Baghdad.

I was carefully briefed by the Flyfisher that the intelligence contained in this file was considered 'extremely sensitive', and that I should avoid mentioning any names or organizational affiliation when preparing inspection planning documents so as to protect the source providing the intelligence. I was also told that the intelligence was considered 'perishable', and that if UNSCOM did not act on it within a period of a few weeks, it should no longer be considered 'actionable'.

Acting under these guidelines, I prepared inspection planning documents that described the Aadamiyah District Ba'ath Party as an 'evacuation site for Military Industrial Commission material and activities proscribed by Security Council resolution', noting that the site was 'believed to be an evacuation site for ballistic missile components'. However, while the documents played down the significance placed on this information, the verbal presentations made by myself to Richard Butler highlighted the controversial nature of the inspection target, and the intelligence backing its nomination.

Although Butler approved the inspection to go forward sometime in mid-July, a last-minute intervention by the Americans resulted in this effort being postponed. I had heard it all before: 'It's not a good time politically for the United States,' Butler told me, explaining Albright's latest intervention.

Richard Butler was busy trying to prepare a document charting the 'way forward' with Iraq. In a series of meetings with his staff, he asked for our input. He went around the room, getting discussion topics from each of his experts. He passed me by, and settled down to start writing. 'Excuse me,' I interjected. He ignored me, and kept writing. 'What about concealment?' There was no response. Everyone in the room, including Charles Duelfer, looked at me, and then at Butler, who just kept on writing. After an uncomfortable pause, I asked again, 'Mr. Chairman, what about the issue of concealment? It has been a central part of every presentation made to the Iraqis in the past, and you can't simply ignore it.'

Butler scribbled a bit more, put down his pen, and looked at me. 'And what should I say, Scott? What are they concealing, exactly?'

I was stunned. 'You've approved my inspections based on this notion of concealment. We've almost gone to war based on this notion of concealment. And now you ask me to justify it to you, as if this is the first time you're hearing it?'

Butler didn't even flinch. 'We are looking for a new way forward, Scott. We need to develop new approaches. So unless you can tell me what it is we're looking for, and why, I see no reason why we should raise the matter with the Iraqis.'

Up until now, my 'concealment paper' was unknown to most UNSCOM staff members. So was almost every aspect of the work I did with UNSCOM. 'Concealment' to them was a theory, not a reality. With few exceptions, no one else in the room knew what Butler and I were talking about. 'You've read the same reports I have, Mr. Chairman. You know what we are looking for.'

Butler looked around the room. 'We can't talk about that here,' he said.

I slammed my palm down on the table, making everyone, including Butler, jump. 'But that does not mean that the issues raised don't exist! They are real, and you know it. And now you're just walking away, as if it all doesn't matter?'

Butler sat in silence, looking at me. He then picked up his pen, and resumed writing, as if the incident that had just occurred never happened. I had simply ceased to exist.

So that was it. Richard Butler had given up trying to provide an authoritative assessment of Iraq's unaccounted for weapons, which would – one way or another – end the sanctions regime that had been in place since 1991. He had decided to play the USA's game, where UNSCOM would carry out limited inspections to try and prove the negative, which would be doomed to fail. Even if these inspections found nothing, Iraq would not be pronounced as having been disarmed because the USA would carry on claiming that Iraq had weapons. It was the Iraqis' word against the Americans'. An investigation into concealment was the only way to break this deadlock, and Butler had just consigned it to the waste-bin of history.

On 3 August, Richard Butler, on the instructions of the Security Council, traveled to Iraq as the head of a large UNSCOM delegation, in an effort to try and get UNSCOM's work in Iraq back on track. Our run-in over the strategic direction on UNSCOM momentarily forgotten, he instructed me to have an inspection team on standby in Bahrain to execute a large concealment-type inspection if the Iraqis did not fully cooperate. By this time though, the UNSCOM operation in New York was so fully compromised to the Mukhabarat that every detail of our plan was known to the Iraqis. Tariq Aziz had no intention of walking into Butler's trap.

Within twenty-four hours, the Iraqis had declared that they would no longer cooperate with Richard Butler as the head of UNSCOM. I made a desperate bid to deploy the inspection team regardless, noting that it would be best to get the Council to focus on Iraqi obstruction of an inspection team, especially one armed with high-quality intelligence such as that provided by MI6 about the Aadamiyah Ba'ath Party headquarters, rather than what some might interpret as a personal squabble between Butler and Tariq Aziz.

Butler agreed but, after consulting with Madeleine Albright from a US Embassy phone in Bahrain, changed his mind. Under orders from Sandy Berger, I was confined to the UN headquarters in Baghdad, prohibited from engaging in any inspection activity, until I was ultimately withdrawn from Iraq on 8 August.

Back in New York, I decided to give Richard Butler and the USA two weeks to convince me that there was serious support for the resumption of inspections. Butler virtually ignored me, and all the Americans could do was have the Counselor call me over to his office at the US Mission, where I was put on a secure phone line. On the other end, an official from the National Security Counsel implored me to stay on.

'Will you support continued inspections?' I asked.

'We cannot at this time,' came the reply.

'Then we have nothing to talk about.'

After hanging up the phone, I asked the Counselor what his impression was of what was going on with regards to US support for inspections. 'After your inspection of the Iraqi Ministry of Defense in March,' he told me, 'the White House got fed up with UNSCOM and inspections. They were not interested in real disarmament, just the illusion of disarmament. UNSCOM's job was to do only that which was necessary to produce two reports to the Security Council a year which legitimize the continuation of economic sanctions. This is the unstated policy. The president may talk about giving UNSCOM all the support it needs, but the reality is that Madeleine Albright and Sandy Berger have already convened a special meeting of the National Security Council, and the decision was made to stop UNSCOM from carrying out any inspections that might result in a confrontation with Iraq. The US simply will not threaten Security Council unity on sanctions over the issue of intrusive weapons inspections.'

'How do they expect us to accomplish our mission?' I asked, incredulously.

The Counselor shrugged. 'They don't.'

It was 26 August 1998. I had served as a weapons inspector for nearly seven years. I returned to my office, drafted my letter of resignation, and submitted it to Richard Butler. My time as an inspector was over.

All those Lies

Looking back on the events that have transpired since UNSCOM left Iraq, I am sometimes struck by the irony of it all. For seven years, I and hundreds of other dedicated arms-control professionals struggled to achieve an objective that people said couldn't be accomplished: disarming Iraq when Iraq didn't want to be disarmed. And then, more than six years after my resignation, I turn on the television and see my former boss, Charles Duelfer, issuing a report which concluded that Iraq had in fact disarmed by the summer of 1991. Inspections had worked, after all. Why then did the USA and its allies apparently feel so threatened by Iraq's weapons of mass destruction that they invaded the country in March 2003?

The establishment line is that decision-makers acted in good faith on the basis of intelligence, which turned out to be faulty. The US Senate Select Intelligence Committee issued a report in July 2004 which placed the blame not on the politicians who made the call, but rather on the CIA. The Senators' report was followed by a special commission appointed by the US president himself, which also found the CIA's pre-war assertions about WMD in Iraq to be 'dead wrong'. Similar reports from investigative bodies in the UK, such as the Butler Commission, have reached the same conclusion – the reason Iraq's weapons capabilities were so grossly exaggerated was that the intelligence services didn't get the right information.

The notion of the war in Iraq resulting from an intelligence failure is very convenient for all parties involved. The intelligence community can simply say that intelligence is a tricky business, and sometimes you get it wrong. This, of course, provides a convenient excuse for the politicians, and compliant media, to contend that they were simply acting in the public interest based upon the information they were given.

Certainly the Iraqis themselves didn't help matters by being less than straightforward with the international community. But the real reason that the inspections regime which began in 1991 failed to certify Iraq's weapons status was that the United States of America never intended for it to succeed. Although at the United Nations the USA paid lip service to the idea that Iraq would get sanctions lifted if it complied with the inspectors, time and time again as an inspector I came up against the fact that whenever we were close to a breakthrough on Iraq's final status, the USA would withdraw its support. The conclusion is inescapable: they did not want us to offer a definitive assessment of Iraq's weapons status.

Not only was the US government willing to prevent the dissemination of accurate assessments, they were willing to promote what even their own intelligence services classed as highly dubious assessments, such as those produced by Iraqi National Congress leader Ahmed Chalabi. Indeed some of the information produced by Chalabi dovetailed suspiciously well with areas that UNSCOM were known not to know about, and which therefore could not be disproved. This nexus of deception and opportunism is embodied in the person of Curveball, the alleged Iraqi defector whose claims served as the basis for much of the US case for war against Iraq.

In the end, to accept the concept of Iraq as an intelligence failure, one must first accept the premise that the USA was implementing, as its primary objective for Iraq, the Security Council's resolutions on disarmament. This argument is simply not sustainable. The behavior of the United States government and its intelligence agencies during my time as an inspector was not that of a government that was serious about disarmament. Support for UNSCOM's mission was, at best, tailored to the political imperatives at any given time. There was a total willingness to compromise the integrity of UNSCOM (and with it the whole notion of multilateral disarmament) for short-term tactical advantages in the battle between the US and Iraqi regimes. Towards the end of the inspections era, elements of the US government actively sought to make UNSCOM's job more difficult by cutting it off from intelligence sources. Disarmament was simply not the USA's principal policy objective in Iraq after 1991. Regime change was.

The CIA was designated as the principal implementer of this policy. Therefore, when one looks at the March 2003 invasion of Iraq and the subsequent removal from power of the government of Saddam Hussein, the only conclusion that can be reached is that the CIA accomplished its mission. Iraq was, in fact, a great intelligence victory, insofar as the CIA, through its manipulation of the work of the UN weapons inspectors and the distortion of fact about Iraq's WMD programs, maintained the public perception of an armed and defiant Iraq in the face of plausible and plentiful evidence to the contrary. We now know that both the US and UK intelligence services had, by July 2002, agreed to 'fix the intelligence around policy'. But the fact remains that, at least as far as the CIA is concerned, the issue of 'fixing intelligence around policy' predates July 2002, reaching as far back as 1992 when the decision was made to doctor the intelligence about Iraqi SCUD missile accounting, asserting the existence of missiles in the face of UNSCOM inspection results which demonstrated that there were none.

As an American, I find it very disturbing that the intelligence services of my country would resort to lies and deceit when addressing an issue of such fundamental importance to the security of the USA. Intelligence, to me, has always been about the facts. When intelligence is skewed to fit policy, then the entire system of trust that is fundamental in a free and democratic society is put at risk. Iraq, and the role of the CIA in selling the war with Iraq, is a manifestation of such a breach of trust.

I have made it my responsibility to speak the truth about Iraq, based on what I know – my firsthand experience and observations. Today, with the CIA redrafting its pre-war intelligence to make it appear consistent with the fact that Iraq had disarmed by 1991, and that there were in fact no weapons of mass destruction, or programs involved in the manufacture of weapons of mass destruction, we are in danger of history likewise being rewritten. There is wide acceptance of the fact that the CIA is a profoundly damaged institution, and there are many programs and initiatives underway to try and remedy this. This makes it all the more important to fully understand what happened in the past. We cannot ignore or run away from difficult and inconvenient history. In writing this book, I have gone on record about my personal experiences as a weapons inspector in Iraq. I hope that in the process I have made some contribution to a better understanding of the delicate relationship between politics, diplomacy and intelligence.

Intelligence is always at the service of a country's national interest. But when intelligence is misused in support of politicians' agendas, that national interest is undermined, if for no other reason than that intelligence loses its credibility. Many errors of judgment were made by many people over Iraq. The only way to move forward is to look at the past honestly, and learn from its mistakes.

Notes

Prologue: In the Eye of the Storm

1. Speech by President George H. W. Bush, 28 October 1990.
2. Testimony to the US Congress by Secretary of State James Baker, 23 May 1991.

Chapter One: A Delicate Balancing Act

1. The U-2, a high-altitude photographic surveillance aircraft developed for the CIA in the 1950s by the famous 'Skunk Works' of Lockheed Aircraft, gained notoriety in 1960 when one of the U-2s, piloted by Gary Powers, was shot down near the Soviet city of Sverdlovsk while carrying out a covert photographic mission over the Soviet Union. Since that time the U-2 had gained a near-mythical reputation as a spy plane of great capability. It was a U-2 that photographed the Soviet missile deployments in Cuba in 1961, leading to the Cuban Missile Crisis, and U-2 aircraft had been involved in nearly every American military crisis since that time. By 1991, all U-2 aircraft were flown by the US Air Force and, despite their advanced age, were considered among the most effective surveillance aircraft in the American inventory.
2. Inspections in Iraq were carried out by teams from both UNSCOM and the IAEA. Of the two organizations, UNSCOM was the only one authorized to designate sites in Iraq for inspection. As such, all inspections, whether UNSCOM or IAEA, were numbered in chronological sequence (i.e., UNSCOM 1, UNSCOM 2, etc.). Each inspection was also referred to by its specialty, such as Ballistic Missile (BM) 1, or IAEA 2, etc. For example, UNSCOM 3 was BM 1, and UNSCOM 16 was IAEA 6. For clarity, all inspections will be referenced by their UNSCOM number only.

293

3. All information pertaining to source DS-385 and CIA involvement in early UNSCOM inspection target selection is derived from personal notes made of conversations with involved personnel as well as review of pertinent documents.

4. Within the Operations Directorate, the task was given to the International Activity Division (IAD). Resident in IAD was the paramilitary arm of the CIA, known as the Special Activities Staff (SAS). The SAS was composed of several operational branches – such as Air Branch, Ground Branch and Sea Branch – reflecting specific operational skills, as well as functional groups. One of these functional groups was the Foreign Training Group (FTG). The FTG had the task of forming the Operations Planning Cell (OPC), the entity responsible for providing operational intelligence and inspection operations planning support to UNSCOM. The OPC also had to carefully coordinate its activities with the Directorate of Operations Near East Division (NE), which was responsible for all CIA activities in Iraq and its environs. All information is derived from the author's personal interaction and communications with involved personnel.

5. 'SCUD' is a North Atlantic Treaty Organization (NATO) codename for the missile system known in NATO as the SS-1B, or in the former Soviet Union as the R-17. The SCUD system used by Iraq is more accurately referred to (using NATO designations) as the SCUD-B. However, the SCUD which UNSCOM inspectors were most concerned with was an indigenous modification known as the *Al Hussein*, which had a longer range than the SCUD due to the Iraqis lengthening the oxidizer and fuel tanks, and reducing warhead size. The *Al Hussein* is sometimes referred to as the *Al Hijara* or *Al Abbas*, Iraqi designations for variants of the *Al Hussain* missile with greater range. Unless otherwise specified, the use of 'SCUD' in this text will be referring to the *Al Hussein* missile.

6. See IAEA 'Preliminary Report of the Sixth IAEA Inspection in Iraq', 3 October 1991.

7. UNSCOM Note for the Record, 'Meeting with Ambassador Pickering, 1720, 27 September 1991'.

8. The US government has been reluctant to discuss the operation of Gateway. However, the nature of this operation was highlighted in revealing fashion in an early State Department communication, where it was noted that 'the US is supplying by far the largest number of technical and administrative experts now assisting UNSCOM in New York and substantial briefing/debriefing services to UNSCOM in New York, Vienna and Manama. We have more than doubled the size of the

US Embassy Manama to make these services available to UNSCOM.'
US State Department Message, 'UNSC Res 687: SPECOM Requests for
Transport and Team Support', 10 June 1991, page 4, paragraph 12.

9. Aspects of this animosity spilled over into the public arena when, in
the fall of 1991, a French weapons inspector gave an interview to the
newspaper *Libération*. According to this interview, the French inspector
was surprised by 'the behavior of some of his American colleagues,
apparently American CIA agents who were working more on behalf
of the CIA than on behalf of the United Nations. Their task was to
obtain information, as well as to provoke the Baghdad authorities, in
order to justify a new intervention by American aircraft with the aim
of "returning to finish the job".' This interview prompted an official
complaint from the Iraqi government to the United Nations. See Security
Council document S/23197, 5 November 1991, 'Letter Dated 31 October
1991 From the Permanent Representative of Iraq to the United Nations
Addressed to the Secretary-General'.

10. UNSCOM Memorandum, 'An Assessment of Iraqi Compliance with
Security Council Resolution 687 (1991) Regarding the SCUD Missile
System', 22 October 1991.

11. The *Al-Nida* launcher was an emergency expedient developed by the
Iraqis after the invasion of Kuwait. Recognizing the Iraqi Army's need
for additional mobile missile launchers, Iraqi engineers took heavy fifty-
ton flatbed trailers and mounted fixed-arm launchers on top. This was
an unwieldy, yet functional, arrangement. Space limitations dictated that
the launch control electronics and starter fuel mechanisms be mounted
on a separate vehicle, which would drive up to the *Al-Nida* prior to
launch. The *Al-Nida* was deployed and used during the Gulf War.

Chapter Two: The Bumpy Road to Independence

1. UNSCOM 24 Training Handout, 'General Principles of Operation:
Room Checklist', December 1991, and 'UNSCOM 24 Document Search
Standard Operating Procedures', 17 December 1991. The origin of the
authors of the latter document could be discerned when, in comparing
an inspection to a raid, the author noted that 'The inspection, like the
raid, is a surprise and violent action. Once you gain the momentum,
your adversary is off balance. Do not lose this advantage.' Op. cit.,
paragraph 6.e.

2. Extracted from Personal Notes, 'Inspection of the Al Karama Police
Barracks', 10 December 1991.

3. See 'Report of Ballistic Missile Inspection Number 7 (UNSCOM 24) in Iraq, 7–13 December 1991', dated 5 January 1992, for a full account of the UNSCOM 24 inspection.
4. UNSCOM Note for the File, 'Meeting with the Deputy Prime Minister: 22 February 1992, 1200–1400 Hours'.
5. For outstanding insights into the thinking of Rolf Ekéus during this period, see Tim Trevan, *Saddam's Secrets: The Hunt for Iraq's Hidden Weapons* (New York: HarperCollins, 1999), pp. 154–62. Tim Trevan served as a special advisor to Ekéus during this time period.
6. The entire meeting is extracted from UNSCOM Note for the File, 'Meeting with the Deputy Prime Minister: 22 February 1992, 1200–1400 Hours'.
7. Letter from Iraqi Foreign Minister Ahmed Hussein to the Secretary-General, dated 24 February 1992.
8. UNSCOM Note for the File, 'Meeting with the Secretary-General, 2 March 1992'.

Chapter Three: Showdown in Baghdad

1. Tariq Aziz acknowledged that Ekéus had told him about the existence of these photographs in a conversation with the author in September 2000. Tim Trevan, who was close to Ekéus at the time, also asserts this took place. See Trevan, op. cit., p. 162.
2. Personal conversations between the author and involved Iraqis, including Tariq Aziz, Amer Rashid, Amer al-Sa'adi, and others, in September 2000 and September 2002.
3. UNSCOM 31 supporting document, 'Transcript of Meeting with Iraqi Officials on the Destruction of Missiles, Daura, Iraq, 20 March 1992'.
4. See UNSCOM Inspection Report, 'UNSCOM 31/Ballistic Missile Inspection 9, 21–30 March 1992', for a full account of the UNSCOM 31 inspection.
5. See 'Executive Summary of UNSCOM 40/Ballistic Missile Inspection 12, 11–29 July 1992', for a full discussion of the UNSCOM 39/40 inspection activities.

Chapter Four: Counterattack

1. Iraqi Intelligence officials later admitted that they had snuck the most sensitive documents out of the building hidden in the clothes of female employees on the first day of the standoff in front of the Ministry of Agriculture, after deliberately creating a confrontation with inspectors

by sending out a female who had nothing hidden, but was frisked by inspectors anyway. When the inspectors backed down, the Iraqi intelligence service promptly hid documents on the female staff, and the archive literally walked out past the unsuspecting eyes of the inspectors. Personal conversation, author with involved Iraqi officials, December 2004.

2. UNSCOM Memorandum, 'Meeting with General Amer Rashid, 17 August 1992', 18 August 1992.
3. Letter from Robert Gallucci, Assistant Secretary of State for Political Military Affairs, to Ambassador Rolf Ekéus, dated 30 September 1992.
4. UNSCOM Note for the File, 'Meeting with the Secretary-General, 14 October 1992'.

Chapter Five: Assassinating the Truth
1. See 'Report of UNSCOM 45 (Fourteenth Ballistic Missile Inspection), 16–30 October 1992', inclusive of Annexes A–Z, AA–DD, concerning the activities and findings of the UNSCOM 45 inspection.

Chapter Six: Shifting the Goalposts
1. 'Mission Concept of Operations, OPERATION CABBAGE PATCH', dated 24 June 1993.
2. 'GPR Mission Report', 8 November 1993.

Chapter Seven: New Friends
1. No criminal charges were ever filed against this individual. In fact, no proof of wrongdoing has ever been uncovered. For this reason, the individual will remain unnamed. However, when confronted with the charges, the individual refused to cooperate with investigators, increasing the suspicion among those who were aware of the matter that the individual was, in fact, cooperating with the government of Iraq.
2. The story of the role played by the Iraqi Mukhabarat was told to the author by the chief of the Mukhabarat's UNSCOM unit in December 2004. Given the difficult security situation in Iraq today, this individual's identity cannot be revealed, even though he has cooperated with the CIA and other US government agencies about Iraq's WMD programs.

Chapter Eight: A Fresh Start
1. See UNSCOM Note for the File, 'Modalities for Sharing U-2 Product with Supporting Nation', 10 July 1995.

Chapter Nine: Adventures in Amman

1. The passage concerning the Iraqi decision regarding the documents is taken from several discussions between the author and high-level Iraqi officials, including Tariq Aziz, Amer Rashid, Amer al-Sa'adi, and others, held in September 2000, September 2002 and December 2004.
2. The author has spoken with CIA personnel present at this debriefing, as well as British MI6 personnel and Jordanian intelligence personnel, about this event.
3. Note for The File, 'Conversations with Lieutenant General Hussein Kamal Hasan al-Majid, 22 August 1995'.
4. See UNSCOM Memorandum for the Record, 'Meeting Between United Nations Special Commission Representative and the Chief Intelligence Officer of the Royal Court of Jordan, 10–11 November 1995'.

Chapter Ten: A Breach of Trust

1. All details are from author's notes based on a discussion of the events with Charles Duelfer.
2. UNSCOM Information Background Paper, 'United Nations Special Commission Concept of Operations for Special Inspection Activities', 6 December 1995.
3. See 'How Some Special Prohibited Materials were Received from the Gharbieh Establishment Without Notification of the National Monitoring Directorate nor Notifying the Special Commission in the Wake of the Flight of the Traitor Hussein Kamal', Official Iraqi Investigation Report, 12 December 1995.

Chapter Eleven: The Listening Post

1. His true identity will be protected, since he may still be on classified assignment with the US government.

Chapter Twelve: The Managers

1. See 'Note for the File. Executive Chairman's meeting with Mr. Tariq Aziz, Deputy Prime Minister of Iraq, Foreign Ministry, Baghdad, 24 April 1996'.
2. The information concerning Steve Richter's response to the UNSCOM 143 inspection is based on the personal observation of the author, as well as conversations between the author and personnel who worked in the CIA during this time period and who were directly involved in the events described.
3. Conversation between the author and the chief of the Mukhabarat's

counter-UNSCOM team, December 2004.

4. All information concerning the Iraqi response to the UNSCOM 143 inspection is based on conversations between the author and the chief of the Mukhabarat's counter-UNSCOM team, and the author and the 'Serb' (both individuals' identities need to be protected, given the dangerous political situation inside Iraq), held in September 2000, September 2002, and December 2004.

5. Letter from Rolf Ekéus to Amer Rashid, dated 26 April 1996.

6. 'UNSCOM ASS-1 Special Mission Situation Report 1', 8 May 1996.

7. 'UNSCOM ASS-1 Special Mission Situation Report 4', 11 May 1996.

8. 'UNSCOM ASS-1 Special Mission Situation Report 5', 12 May 1996.

Chapter Thirteen: Blowback

1. The author has spoken with several CIA and MI6 officials who have confirmed most aspects of this account. For a good recounting of the machinations of the June 1996 coup against Saddam Hussein, see Andrew and Patrick Cockburn, *Out of the Ashes: The Resurrection of Saddam Hussein* (HarperCollins, 1999).

2. Uday's conversations were picked up by Gary and the SCE. I was later told of the content of these conversations by a CIA official who had read the transcripts. Also, additional details of this confrontation were provided by a senior Iraqi official who was familiar with the Iraqi investigation into the shooting incident.

3. Conversations between the author and Tariq Aziz, September 2000 and September 2002, and between the author and the chief of the Mukhabarat's Counter-UNSCOM cell, September 2002 and December 2004.

4. UNSCOM Note for the File, 'Executive Chairman's meeting with Mr. Tariq Aziz, Deputy Prime Minister of Iraq, Foreign Ministry, Baghdad, 7.20–10.20 p.m., 19 June 1996'.

5. Ibid. p. 2.

6. 'Modalities for Inspections of Sensitive Sites', 22 June 1996, paragraph 4.

Chapter Fourteen: The Poison Pill

1. SCE Intercept Logbook, 11 June 1996.

2. UNSCOM 155 Situation Report 1, 16 June 1996.

3. The CIA had copies of a videotape alleged to have been made by a Shi'a resistance movement, the Da'wa, which showed a convoy allegedly carrying Saddam Hussein being ambushed by a rocket-propelled grenade. The vehicles involved were silver Mercedes Sedans.

4. UNSCOM 155 Situation Report 5, 21 June 1996.
5. UNSCOM Note for the File, 'White House Meeting, 20 August 1996'.

Chapter Fifteen: The Con Game

1. 'Statement of His Excellency Mr. Tariq Aziz, Deputy Prime Minister of Iraq, Baghdad, 26 August 1996'. For instance, Tariq Aziz quoted from the 5 June 1996 report, which stated 'The Commission... has a good overall picture of the extent of Iraq's past chemical capabilities and that the essential elements of it have been destroyed.'
2. UNSCOM Paper, 'Support for Enhanced UNSCOM Inspection Operations', 6 September 1996.
3. UNSCOM 158 Situation Report 2, 27 November 1996.
4. UNSCOM Memorandum, 'Status of UNSCOM Requests for Inspection Support from the US', 10 December 1996.
5. 'Inspection Concept of Operations', 24 December 1996.

Chapter Sixteen: White House Blues

1. 'Inspection Concept of Operations Against Proscribed Iraqi Operational Missile Force', 7 January 1997.
2. These details about the White House meeting have been extracted from the briefing slides used in the presentation, as well as the author's notes made during the post-briefing discussion.
3. Author's notes from the meeting. The conversations were reconstructed afterwards by discussing the meeting with Roger Hill and Chris Cobb-Smith.

Chapter Seventeen: The Truth Emerges

1. 'Concept Paper for Ongoing, Continuous Investigations of the Iraqi Concealment Mechanism', 22 May 1997.
2. Author conversations with involved CIA personnel.
3. 'Notes on Camera Monitoring Activities', 26 May 1997.

Chapter Eighteen: Unraveling Concealment

1. Note for File, 'Talking Points for the Executive Chairman', 16 June 1996.
2. 'Meeting with General Amer Rashid at the Oil Ministry', 8 June 1997.
3. Author's discussions with Tariq Aziz, September 2000, September 2002, and with the Mukhabarat's chief of the counter-UNSCOM unit, September 2002 and December 2004.

Chapter Nineteen: New Directions

1. UNSCOM Minute for the Record, 'Establishment of a Special Investigations Unit and Capable Sites/Concealment Investigations Team Within UNSCOM', 4 August 1997.

2. Since UNSCOM 150, the Australians had provided UNSCOM with the services of outstanding patrol medics from their elite Special Air Service Regiment. The commandos were not only skilled medical professionals (two actually performed emergency field surgery on sick Iraqis who might have died otherwise), but also unsurpassed operators who adapted to the new landscape of intrusive on-site inspection without any problems. These SAS medics had been an integral part of every team I took into Iraq. Tragically, Corporal Andy Russell was killed in action in Afghanistan in 2002, after his SAS long-range reconnaissance vehicle ran over a landmine. Andy left behind a young wife and newborn baby.

3. UNSCOM Memorandum, 'Operation Tea Cup V Concept and Background Paper', 18 September 1997.

4. Author's interview with the chief of the Mukhabarat's Counter-UNSCOM Unit, December 2004.

5. UNSCOM 201 Situation Report 4, 22 September 1997.

6. UNSCOM 207 Situation Report 6, 1 October 1997.

Chapter Twenty: False Starts

1. Letter from Tariq Aziz to the President of the Security Council, 12 October 1997, p. 1.

2. 'Operation Tea Cup V Update', 9 November 1997.

3. UNSCOM Memorandum, 'Resumption of Sensitive Site Inspections', 20 November 1997.

4. See 'Minutes of Meeting between the Special Commission Executive Chairman and the Deputy Prime Minister of Iraq, His Excellency Tariq Aziz', 15 December 1997.

Chapter Twenty-One: The Death of Inspections

1. Author's interview with the Mukhabarat Chief of the Counter-UNSCOM Team, December 2004.

2. Author's interview with the Mukhabarat Chief of the Counter-UNSCOM team, December 2004.

3. Personal conversation with Richard Butler, 3 March 1998.

4. Memorandum for the Executive Chairman From the Remaining Leadership of UNSCOM 227, 4 March 1998.

5. Author's notes from MI6 documents.

6.   Talking Points for Meeting with Executive Chairman on Romania, SCE and Israel, 8 June 1998.
7.   Transcript of Senior Iraqi Conversations, 26–27 March 1998.

Index